D0876432

PUBLICATIONS OF THE FOUNDATION FOR RESEARCH IN
LEGAL HISTORY, COLUMBIA UNIVERSITY SCHOOL OF LAW

Early American Land Companies

THEIR INFLUENCE ON CORPORATE DEVELOPMENT

Early American Land Companies

THEIR INFLUENCE ON CORPORATE DEVELOPMENT

BY SHAW LIVERMORE

1968
OCTAGON BOOKS, INC.
New York

Reprinted 1968

by special arrangement with Harvard University Press

OCTAGON BOOKS, INC.
175 FIFTH AVENUE
NEW YORK, N. Y. 10010

Library of Congress Catalog Card Number: 68-16511

Printed in U.S.A. by
NOBLE OFFSET PRINTERS, INC.
NEW YORK 3, N. Y.

EDITOR'S INTRODUCTION

THE objectives of most legal historical inquiries are practical and for this reason are usually fixed by what is presently important. This concentration upon contemporary law frequently has the unfortunate effect of predetermining the range of inquiry and of permitting current opinion to creep back into times where it does not belong. It is easy to forget the tricks which the process of evolution may play upon the eventual progeny if one peers too hopefully for the lineaments of the infant in the features of the ancestor. In dealing with history of the corporate idea it has been very tempting to consider only what is properly pedigreed and to be impervious to the lapse of time. For one thing, on the side of dogma, there has been so little disturbance in fundamental premises over the course of three centuries. Then, too, there has been the regular occurrence of identical enthusiasms and identical prejudices respecting the corporate device. The student is still taught in substance that "a corporation aggregate of many is invisible, immortal and rests only in intendment and consideration of the law."[1] Mr. Pollexfen in 1683 inveighed against the size and power of the East India Company[2] in terms no more and no less bitter than are today directed at the behemoths of America.

There are other reasons why the corporate device maintains a sovereign position in the literature, laying upon even the most detached inquirer an irresistible spell. During the early decades of the nineteenth century it rose to predominance over other types of association both in the variety and in the number of uses to which it was put. This numerical preeminence has lent it an overshadowing significance. Moreover, this rapid rise in favor necessitated some stirring in the long-stagnant body of judicial thought respecting corporations, so that by the middle of the

[1] *Case of Sutton's Hospital,* 10 Coke, 23, 32b.
[2] *East India Company* v. *Sandys,* 10 State Trials, 371 (1683).

nineteenth century there had come into being a corpus of distinctively American jurisprudence, grounded, indeed, upon the English common law, but in point of detail an original contribution. Throughout this period problems of associations were debated chiefly in courts or in legislative bodies. As there was no store of economic theory at hand the idiom of discussion was taken from the law, and where it ran beyond purely technical matter it was conducted with reference to political rather than economic considerations. What was therefore thought and spoken of corporations in the America of the early nineteenth century was essentially in the older legalistic tradition, and when the economists busied themselves with this device they literally had their work cut out for them.

The compactness of corporate doctrine does not rest alone on the apparent self-sufficiency of the sources. The attribution of legal personality to the corporation marked it from the beginning as a thing apart, and facilitated the growth of opinion that it was no mere species of association, but a particular genus. This notion was of great utility to American courts after the Revolution, enabling them to force the growth of legal doctrine in step with the hothouse florescence of corporate enterprise. At the same time it prevented any mature consideration of the problem of associations in general, for the judges did not see the existing groups as manifestations of the associative impulse, brought out by experience and needs. The judges were not realistic but moved in the old metaphysical tradition, and so persisted in thinking of the person instead of the group which underlay it. To be sure, one could hardly have expected a judge, obliged to rule on a demurrer to a plea of *nul tiel* corporation where a group was imperfectly organized under a registration statute, to have pondered the vagaries of the associative impulse. On the other hand, this is precisely what one ought to expect of the historical scholars whose concern must be with the doings of men as well as with the rules by which they were supposed to abide.

In suggesting that a proper historical approach to the corporation in America is to regard it as but one manifestation of the associative spirit, we seek a means of reconciling the two sharply contrasting epochs of its development here—the early period of restriction and the subsequent period of legislative indulgence. It is only by choosing this approach that the later developments fall into correct perspective and, instead of overmastering the inquirer, can be made the subject of critical appraisal.

Until American legislatures first undertook, in the youth of the Republic, to simplify and make easy the acquisition of corporate status, the situation here was essentially a replica of the English scene of a much earlier time. It was exceptional for any group to have a corporate charter, and it was usual for groups without this privilege to conduct themselves as if they possessed it. This meant in effect that the traditions of the homeland were carried on in the colonies without change, a phenomenon that requires some explanation.

When English lawyers first became familiar with the corporate concept they associated it with the bodies which had received charters from the Crown.[3] Since the charter was a privilege, the acquisition of corporate status remained for centuries somewhat difficult to obtain and always costly. The doctrine of lawyers and judges was, of course, no check upon the associative impulse. The formation of groups organized for various purposes continued, and, as it became presently apparent that the corporation was a favored child of the law, such unchartered groups tended to imitate the internal constitution of chartered bodies and were not above exercising rights which could only be derived from the Crown but which the passage of time might render colorable. Both for fiscal and for political reasons there was always considerable pressure exerted by the Crown against such impertinence. This policy had its roots in the *quo war-*

[3] This is discussed in Goebel, *Cases and Materials on the Development of Legal Institutions* (1937), 551 *et seq.*

ranto proceedings of the thirteenth century, and was subsequently variously expressed in mortmain statutes, the prohibitions against unlawful assemblages, the acts in support of the established religion, and finally in the Bubble Act of 1720. But none of these measures was more than transiently effective.

At the close of the middle ages the rule was judicially settled that only the king could make a corporation, but even the repetition of this rule did not effectively eradicate the popular notion, strong because it was very old, that substantially the same result could be obtained by free association, *viz.,* the formation of a community possessing perpetuity. Under the early Tudors there were practical obstacles in the way of possible administrative attempts to suppress the unincorporated groups or at least to embark on a policy of *Gleichschaltung.*[4] Consequently, right into the reign of Elizabeth the popular conception remained a more real and a more active factor in the lives of the subjects than did the doctrine of the courts.

Until the problem of large-scale overseas enterprise gave to the corporate device and the royal prerogative respecting it a new economic significance, the question of how a group was organized was preeminently a political matter; the economic issues were largely fiscal. Political considerations remained important well into the seventeenth century and had much to do with the role which the corporate idea played in the thinking of those who opposed the existing order. It is from this direction and not from official quarters that current discussion of associations first becomes of consequence for America. And it is specifically in the hotly contested realm of religion and religious organization that the debate begins.

That interest in questions of organization focused upon religious and not commercial bodies was due to the peculiar prob-

---

[4] These aspects of Tudor policy will be considered in a forthcoming investigation of the Foundation for Research in Legal History on business control under the early Tudors.

lems of the dissident groups that settled here. They were not only deeply perplexed respecting their status *vis à vis* the English government, but they were still more concerned over how a church was properly constituted and over reconciling their peculiar beliefs with the practical necessities of daily life. In New England the solution to all these several problems stemmed from the early speculations of the Brownists and from the first experiments of the so-called Separatists. The Brownist theories have been related to the teachings of the Anabaptists of the Continent,[5] although it seems not unlikely that they likewise owed something to deep-rooted English beliefs in a right of free association.

The most characteristic tenet of the Brownists was the notion of the covenant[6]—in form a solemn covenant with God (a promise by the body of believers to do His will) and a second and sometimes written covenant made with one another, promising to work for the Lord, to avoid evil, to do good, and to stand together. The covenant idea was taken from the biblical accounts of God's covenant with the Israelites, and its immediate function was the creation of a church. What gave the conception its peculiar appeal to Englishmen, and hence relates it to the never-dormant English notions of forming a commonalty, was the lavish use of analogies from the picture of contemporary corporate organization.[7] This was true not only of John Robinson, the lead-

[5] Burrage, *The Church Covenant Idea* (1904), 43.

[6] The best discussion of the covenant idea is in Burrage, *op. cit.,* and his *Early English Dissenters* (1912), 2 vols., *passim.* The earliest use of the covenant during the Reformation as a device for organizing a church occurred in 1523.

[7] The analogy is already apparent in Browne's definition of a church as "companie or number of Christians," etc. (Dexter, *Congregationalism of the Last Three Hundred Years* [1880], 105) and Barrowe and Greenwood's definition, "a companie of Faithfull people . . . joyned together as members of one bodie" (*ibid.,* 222–223). Barrowe was a lawyer and hence one might properly expect an emphasis upon the corporate character of the church. *Cf.* further, Browne, *A Booke which Sheweth the Life and Manners of all True Christians* (1582), 74: "For civil Magistrates there must be an agreement of the people or commonwealth." The Confes-

ing figure and most articulate writer among the early seven-
teenth-century Separatists,[8] but also of the Independent Puritan,
Henry Jacob.[9] The works of both these men are replete with references to English corporate practice. Both describe the church as
a "spiritual body politic," and Jacob, indeed, goes so far as to char-
acterize the Separatist mode of constituting a church by mutual
consent as being the same as that used in the creation of civil
corporations. There is much in these writings to suggest familiarity with contemporary discussion of the social compact, but the
images are all from English life.[10]

sion of the Separatist Church at Amsterdam of 1596, §38, states, ". . .
Congregations bee thus distinct and severall bodyes every one as a compact
Citie in it self. . . ." Printed in Walker, *Creeds and Platforms of Congre-
gationalism* (1893), 71.

[8] Robinson, 2 *Works* (1851), 135, *A Justification of Separation* (pub.
1610): "as a sheriff is appointed in a shire, a mayor in a city, a constable in
a parish, a steward in a family do necessarily presuppose the shire, city,
parish, family wherein they are appointed. And indeed, where should the
Lord set his stewards but in his family. *Is any society capable of the Lord's
officers but his corporation?*" Cf. *ibid.*, 440, 449; cf. also Robinson, *A Just
and Necessary Apology* (Latin ed. 1619, English ed. 1625) in 3 *Works* at
p. 64, where he refers to the church as a "spiritual politic body"; the Cate-
chism, posthumously printed in 1642 (*ibid.*, 431), "The church being a
most free corporation spiritual under Christ . . ."; *A Just and Necessary
Apology,* at p. 17, where the independence of municipal corporations is
again used as an illustration.

[9] Burrage, 2 *Early English Dissenters*, 157: "A true Visible or Ministeriall Church of Christ is a particular congregation, being a spirituall
perfect corporation of believers. . . ." "By a free and mutual consent of believers joyning and covenanting to live as members of a holy Society together in all religious and vertuous duties as Christ bee apostles did insti-
tute and practise in the Gospell, By such a free mutual consent also all
Civill perfect Corporations did first beginne." A further definition, p. 161:
"A true Visible or Ministeriall Church of Christ is a constant and com-
ple[te] societie of Christians or spirituall Body politike. . . ." Jacob spent
some time in Leyden in 1610 and fell under Robinson's influence. Dexter,
Congregationalism, 635. In that year (1610), Jacob published at Leyden the
work *The Divine Beginning and Institution of Christ's True Visible or
Ministerial Church,* in which he defines a church to be "A true Visible &
Ministeriall Church of Christ is a nomber of faithfull people joyned by
their willing consent in a spirituall outward society or body politike. . . ."
Burrage, *The Church Covenant Idea,* 60.

[10] There is direct proof that Robinson was acquainted with Grotius'

The frequent employment of the corporate analogy was more than a mere expository flourish. Across the Channel, the trend among Calvinist sects was toward independency and these reformed churches were organized as distinct corporate units.[11] This was recognized by the English dissenters as a source of strength, and the parallel with their own objectives was not overlooked.[12] Furthermore, the English sects were minority groups desperately intent upon acquiring status and freedom from episcopal control. They could hardly fail to be aware of the galling spectacle of foreign congregations worshipping as they pleased by virtue of royal patents of incorporation or royal license.[13] Dogma and expediency thus made of corporacy a vital point.

writings (*e.g.*, 1 *Works*, 156, 192), but none of the identifiable passages used by Robinson relate to compact discussion.

[11] Contemporary continental rules respecting corporations are discussed in Gierke, 3 *Das Deutsche Genossenschaftsrecht* (1881), 724 *et seq. Cf.* also Apeldoorn, 2 *De Kerkelijke Goederen in Friesland* (1915), 27, note 3; Hoffmann, *Das Kirchenverfassungsrecht der Niederlandischen Reformierten* (1902), 70, 76, 86. Sohm, 1 *Kirchenrecht* (1923), 645, discusses the origin of the reformed churches' conception of the congregation. The Calvinistic theories are discussed by Troeltsch, *Die Soziallehren der Christlichen Kirchen und Gruppen* (1912), 625 *et seq.* He treats the trend toward independency as a phase of neo-Calvinism at 733 *et seq.*

[12] Robinson, *Of Religious Communion* (1614), in 3 *Works*, at 128: "And where they allege that the Dutch and French Churches which we acknowledge for true churches were not established by such a separation as we make, they accuse them unjustly to excuse themselves.

"They were, at the first established of a sanctified people by voluntary profession, separating themselves into particular churches . . . and do still continue a separated people. . . ."

Cf. also the letter of Robinson and Brewster to Sir John Worstenholme, January 26, 1617, O.S., in Bradford, *History of Plimoth Plantation* (1899), 44.

[13] The most complete account of these foreign churches is in Burn, *History of the French Walloon Dutch and Other Protestant Refugees Settled in England* (1846). There were churches in London, Norwich, Colchester, Southampton, Canterbury, Sandwich, Glastonbury, Rye, Winchelsea, Yarmouth, Maidstone, and Dover. The earliest and most important of the foreign groups was John a Lasco's church in London. This had received a charter of incorporation from Edward VI (Burn, *op. cit.*, 265). The ordinance of John a Lasco was drawn on the theory that the visible church was a corporation (text in Richter, 2 *Die Evangelischen Kirchenordnungen des*

Before ever settlement was made in America, the practical implications of discussion are apparent. There is, first, an attempt by the Separatists to secure a license from the Crown.[14] In the project to settle in Virginia, the unitary nature of the group is stressed.[15] And, finally, as the Pilgrims ship for America, they make a fresh covenant[16] and are told by Robinson their pastor, "you are now become a body politic using among yourselves civil government."[17]

When the Separatists established their colony at Plymouth, the necessity of perfecting some form of civil order that would embrace those not of their church led to a further realization of their corporate theories.[18] Their state was theocratic, and although they maintained two sets of officers, one for civil and one for spiritual purposes, the records indicate that the body was one although the functions were separate.[19] In their laws the Plymouth men describe themselves as a "society" in 1632.[20] But in 1636 they have arrogated the title of a "colony and corporation."[21] They must have realized that in the eyes of English law they were no body corporate, but even as early as 1625 friends in England had counseled Bradford "to make your corporation as formal as you can under the name of the Society of Plymouth in New England."[22] For all the boldness of their faith in the right-

16ten Jahrhunderts [1846], 99). Hoffmann (supra, note 11) thinks the ordinances of this group had a great deal to do with the theories of continental churches.

[14] In 1617. Bradford, History of Plimoth Plantation, 38.

[15] Cf. the letter of Brewster and Robinson to Sir Edwin Sandys, ibid., 42; also p. 37.

[16] Ibid., 53.   [17] Ibid., 81.

[18] Bradford indicates that the Mayflower Compact was intended to keep in order persons not members of the church. Ibid., 109.

[19] Cf. the discussion in Goebel, "King's Law and Local Custom," 31 Columbia Law Review, 416 et seq. My views respecting the significance of the idea of free association have changed since that article was written.

[20] The Compact with Charter and Laws of the Colony of New Plymouth (Brigham ed., 1836), 30.

[21] Ibid., 35.

[22] In 3 Massachusetts Historical Society Collection (1st series), 33.

ness and creative magic of mere association, there is a certain pathos in this attempt to ape the formalities to which only a parchment under the Great Seal could entitle them.

The power of the Separatists' notion that a corporation could be formed by free association was by no means spent when its full implications were realized in the establishment of Plymouth. It was the juristic basis of congregationalism throughout New England for nearly two hundred years thereafter,[23] and was consequently marked for as great a destiny in its original ecclesiastical sphere as on the civil side. This came about through the circumstance that, when the churches in the more powerful and populous colony of Massachusetts Bay came to be established, the Separatists' practice of covenant was adopted.[24]

The colony of Massachusetts Bay enjoyed, as against Plymouth, the prestige of a royal charter and organized corporate government but this charter gave the company no power of granting charters to corporations within the confines of its colony.[25] The divergence from Anglicanism and the adoption of

[23] Generally on this see Dexter, *Congregationalism*, 413 *et seq.*; Felt, 1 *Ecclesiastical History of New England* (1855), 113 *et seq.*; Walker, *Creeds and Platforms of Congregationalism*, 116 *et seq.*; Burrage, *The Church Covenant Idea*, 88 *et seq.* In his later work, *Early English Dissenters* (vol. I, p. 357 *et seq.*), Burrage minimizes the influence of the Plymouth church. He is trying to show that the Massachusetts men were not Separatists of the Browne-Barrowe-Robinson lineage, and he assumes the professed allegiance of these men to the Anglican church to be a candid statement of their true position, whereas in fact it was pure camouflage. *Cf.* Osgood, 1 *American Colonies in the Seventeenth Century,* 203–204.

[24] Bradford, *History,* 317, 331–332.

[25] This was a well established rule of common law at the time, 49 Ass. pl. 8, Y.B. 49 Edw. III, 3, 4; Brooke, *Abridgement,* tit. *Corpor.,* 15, 45; *Case of Sutton's Hospital,* 10 Coke, 33b. Nevertheless, the Massachusetts Bay Company seems to have undertaken the erection of a few corporate bodies. There is a brief account of this by A. M. Davis, in *Corporations in the Days of the Colony* (1 *Publications of the Colonial Society of Massachusetts,* 1895), 183, which is closely followed by J. S. Davis, *Essays in the Earlier History of American Corporations* (1917), 49 *et seq.* It should be noted that prior to 1691 when Massachusetts became definitively a royal province, although at least two "private" corporations, Harvard College and a water company, had been created, the general court had hesitated to

the Separatists' practice of constituting churches necessitated the acceptance of the corollary that the duly constituted congregation was at once a "visible church" and a corporation. How completely this view was accepted is brought out in the literary controversy that developed with Presbyterians during the Revolution in England.[26] Thomas Hooker, the celebrated New England divine, elaborated the ideas of Jacob and Robinson anent the corporate character of the church, his claims for the civil corporate capacity of the church far exceeding anything hitherto advanced.[27]

In the Massachusetts legislation of this period,[28] the only stric-

create "public" corporations, as witness its failure to grant a charter to the town of Boston.

[26] *Cf.* Walker, *op. cit.,* 134 *et seq.*

[27] Hooker, *Survey of the Sum of Church Discipline* (1648). This book was written in 1645 as a refutation of Rutherford's *Due Right of Presbyteries.* Starting from the premise that the church is both a "body mysticall and a body politicall," Hooker throughout uses the analogy of civil corporations. It is the fact of voluntary association which makes the church, for "the corporation is a true body when it hath no major or other officer" (p. 11). For a church to come into existence "there must of necessity be a mutuall ingagement each of the other by their full consent before by any rule of God they have any right or power or can exercise either each toward the other." And now follows immediately an interesting acceptance of the social compact theory: "This appears in all covenants betwixt Prince and People, Husband and Wife, Master and Servant and most palpable in the expression of this in all confederations and corporations" (p. 69). "People must by mutual consent grow up into ingagement one with another into a corporation, before they should do the duties of a corporation" (p. 70). *Cf.* also page 73 as to the formation of the church: "An agreement of persons one to and with another to combine and consecrate in the waies and worship of Christ. 2. The doing of these duties. 3. The swearing they will do them. The first of these is the form [*i.e.,* forming] of a corporation. The other two may be done *when* they are incorporated." *Cf.* also pp. 92 and 221.

On the internal administration of the church the civil corporate analogy is freely used to describe the powers of election and expulsion. Indeed it ceases to be analogy and becomes precedent. *Cf.* pp. 221, 241, 247, and Part II, pp. 2, 45.

[28] *Colonial Laws of Massachusetts* (Whitmore ed., 1889), sec. 95 *et seq.,* Body of Liberties: "1. All the people of God within this jurisdiction who are not in a church way and be orthodox in judgment and not scandalous in life shall have full libertie to gather themselves into a church estaite. Pro-

tures put upon the formation of churches were that they conform with the orthodox views and that the magistrates and elders of neighboring churches should determine this. Neither of these provisions questioned the corporate quality of the church or the acquisition of this character by free association, but on the contrary recognized that only in this wise could a church be formed. The law was intended solely to assure uniformity of belief, for the Massachusetts Puritans were as intolerant champions of uniformity in America as they had been enemies of the principle in England. The effect of the statutes was thus merely to require conformity with the religious preferences of the Colony, and the approval exacted was not intended to operate in lieu of royal charter of incorporation. In other words, the statutes were merely restrictive and not constitutive.

Not only in Massachusetts did this conception of the corporate character of the church and the creative power of association become the accepted doctrine; it spread to other colonies in Connecticut and in Rhode Island where that violent Separatist, Roger Williams, sought to carry out on the basis of the same corporate principles the ideas of toleration which he believed to be implicit in the congregational theory.[29]

vided they do it in a Christian way with due observation of the rules of Christ revealed in his word." Secs. 3, 4, and 8 are recognitions of the powers of the church corporation to elect officers, admit and expel members, and conduct the business of the church.

Before this enactment, in 1636, the general court had declared that no churches would be approved unless the magistrates and elders of the majority of churches had previously been informed and approved thereof. Osgood, 1 *American Colonies in the Seventeenth Century,* 213. *Cf.* the provision "Eclesiasticals" in the *Laws* of 1660 (Whitmore ed., p. 147) where the approval of the elders of *neighbor* churches is required.

[29] Williams, *Bloudy Tenet of Persecution* (4 *Hanserd Knollys Society*), 46: "The church or company of worshippers . . . is like unto a body or college of physicians in a city—like unto a corporation, society or company of East India or Turkey merchants. . . ." And again, p. 247: "their civil New England state framed out of their churches. . . ." *Cf.* the compacts in Rhode Island, in 1 *Rhode Island Colonial Records,* pp. 14, 52, 70, 87, and the account of the New Haven compact in *Records of the Colony and Plantation of New Haven* (1857), 12, 15.

No clearer evidence of the admitted corporate capacity of the
Congregational churches is to be found than in relation to landholding.[30] Grants were made to the church, property was devised

[30] This particular problem is involved because of the close relation
which subsisted in Massachusetts Bay between civil and ecclesiastical affairs. This was inevitable as long as church membership was a condition
precedent to political capacity. Consequently we find that the erection of
the meeting house (used also for town purposes) was a duty of the civil authority and the revenues of the church were a part of the general taxation.
On this relationship, cf. MacLear, *Early New England Towns* (1908), 60
et seq. Nevertheless there were gifts and devises to the "church"; cf. *Records of the Church of Christ at Cambridge* (1906), 35 and 176; *Early Records of the Town of Dedham 1635-59* (1892), 92, and the statement in
Baker v. *Fales,* 16 Mass. 488.

The development of the precincts or parishes in Massachusetts greatly
complicated the situation (cf. here Reed, *Church and State in Massachusetts* [1914], 54, n. 7). The legal voters in a parish, contributing as they did
to church membership, were recognized to have a voice in the selection of
the minister irrespective of their church membership. By statute the church
was given the power to choose the minister but the choice had to be ratified by church-going inhabitants, whether members or not. The difficulties
resulting from this scheme led to the creation of powers of interference in
the general court. Cf. Osgood, 3 *American Colonies in the Eighteenth
Century* (1924), 126. A system similar to that in Massachusetts was introduced in Connecticut. In the latter state, too, it was not unusual for the
minister to be chosen by the parish before a church was organized. The
parish or society and the church thus existed side by side with joint control.
The question of the corporate character of the church itself was, however,
directly involved as a result, although the issue did not become acute until
the nineteenth century. In Massachusetts, any doubt as to which body was
to take property was resolved by a statute of 28 *George II* (1755), 3 *Massachusetts Provincial Acts,* 778, whereby the deacons, church wardens, and
other governing bodies of Protestant churches should be deemed corporate
bodies for purpose of taking by grant or devise and for purposes of suit.
Cf., e.g., also as to Rehobeth, 4 *Massachusetts Provincial Acts,* 463, 518, 542;
as to Connecticut, 5 *Public Records of the Colony of Connecticut,* 552;
6 *ibid.,* 33, 380, 427; 7 *ibid.,* 74, 211.

Notwithstanding the Massachusetts statute, the opinion at the opening
of the nineteenth century was that churches had always been bodies corporate; *The Rights of Protestant Churches in the Town of Boston,* in 3
Monthly Anthology (1806), 632. *Cf.* also *Brown* v. *Langdon,* Smith (N.H.,
1807), 178, for New Hampshire, and *Buckingham* v. *Northrop,* 1 Root
(Conn., 1773), 53, for Connecticut. In the latter case, a note was given to
deacons before the ecclesiastical society was legally constituted; it held that
the deacons of a church were a legal corporation.

It is needless to add that there has been no satisfactory legal historical

to it, and for over a hundred years no question appears to have been raised as to its capacity to deal with its property as a juristic entity. The absence of acts incorporating churches necessarily drives us to the conclusion that as far as ecclesiastical bodies were concerned, the Separatist doctrine that association alone was sufficient to make a corporation became for at least a century the accepted legal doctrine in the New England colonies not questioned judicially until the courts of later generations invented a theory which placated their outraged common law consciences.[31]

It is impossible to trace here the further burgeoning of the notion that by free association corporateness could be created. We have dealt with its initial manifestations in New England, but the idea was not confined to the particular breeds of dissenters which flourished there; it was active the length of the Atlantic seaboard. The truth is that among practically all the different sectarian types that had broken with the established church, the organization of particular churches rested upon the basic idea of the voluntary union of the believers, and of their vigor as societies deriving therefrom.[32] The fact that this idea was at work

study of these questions. There is material in Walker, *A History of the Congregational Churches in the United States* (1894), 220 *et seq.*

[31] Most of the difficulties of the courts were precipitated by the fact that the parish or "society" and the church exercised joint control over the church property. The most extreme position was taken by Parker, C. J., in *Baker* v. *Fales,* 16 Mass. 488, when he stated that the church had no legal existence save in connection with some regularly constituted society. The powers exercised by the parish or town and the statutes that constituted deacons, etc., a corporation had completely denaturized the original congregational conception so that the courts came to look upon the church more from the angle of its spiritual function than from that of its civil capacity. *Burr* v. *Sandwich,* 9 Mass. 276; *Avery* v. *Tyringham,* 3 Mass. 159. The result was naturally a great confusion of ideas and a complete disregard of earlier history.

[32] The formation of sects depended upon a conviction of the right of free association, since there usually was some established church from which these groups withdrew or to which they were in opposition. Their ideas respecting association were variously expressed as, *e.g.,* fellowship, fraternity, *collegium. Cf.* for the Quakers, Barclay, *Inner Life of the Religious Societies of the Commonwealth* (1876), 360 *et seq.,* and the docu-

so universally in relation to the matter of most vital individual concern gave it a power which can hardly be estimated.

The question how far the associative ideas which we have described reached over into secular matters is one which has never been investigated. The connection has been perceived in relation to the New England towns,[33] but it has to our knowledge not been considered in relation to settlements in other colonies. It is a problem of singular complexity, and discussion has been greatly obscured by the attempt to explain colonial developments in terms of the tests and classifications of the common law courts.[34] This is an impossible standard of interpretation since popular associative ideas had been in competition with the jurists' corporate concepts from the time these were first announced. In America these popular notions had been put into effect, and since there was in the seventeenth century no effective opposition from the common law side they had gathered considerable momen-

ment in the appendix to chap. xv; for the Baptists, *ibid.*, 595; on the Pietists generally, Heppe, *Geschichte des Pietismus und der Mystik* (Leiden, 1879), 9, 11, 293, 306; Troeltsch, *op. cit.*, 866; for those in Pennsylvania, Sachse, *The German Pietists in Provincial Pennsylvania* (1895). For the German Baptists *cf.* especially the document in Brumbaugh, *A History of the Brethren in Europe and America* (1899), 479 *et seq.;* for the North Carolina Moravians, *cf.* the document (1772) in Fries, 3 *Records of the Moravians in North Carolina* (North Carolina Historical Society), 996 *et seq.* With the exception of the Baptists there is no pressing of the English corporate image but as Troeltsch (*op. cit.*, 707) points out the association idea of the neo-Calvinistic groups is carried out in all sorts of human relationships.

[33] Eaton, "The Right to Local Self-Government," 13 *Harvard Law Review*, 441, 570, 638. Eaton has not, however, an adequate grasp of the significant religious doctrine.

[34] *Cf.* Davis, 1 *Essays in the Earlier History of American Corporations* (1917). The inadequacy of his adherence to common law tests is illustrated by his comment, p. 60: "We may pass over quickly the 'bodies politic' which were created by solemn compact by the early settlers of Plymouth and several towns of Rhode Island and New Hampshire. Whatever may have been the verbal usage or the expectations of the founders, such towns are clearly not to be classed as corporations in the accepted sense: for according to the law of the period, no corporation could come into existence without 'lawful authority of incorporation'; and no mere voluntary agreement, however solemn, could suffice to make a 'lawful incorporation.'"

tum. This was a social phenomenon of the first magnitude and it would be absurd to suppose that it was abruptly ended when the device of formal incorporation by governor's charter or by act of assembly came into wider use during the eighteenth century.

The transplantation to America of the practice and doctrine of the king's law respecting bodies corporate is significant chiefly in that a principle competitive to free association was now active. In the early eighteenth century, however, it does not appear that any concerted effort was made by ecclesiastical or municipal groups to procure charters. On the contrary, the aversion to even the mild form of control, to say nothing of the political permission implicit in such grants, was sufficient to have restrained them.[35] The reaction to Lord Cornbury's attempt to license non-Anglican churches in New York indicates somewhat the temper of these groups.[36] As for commercial enterprise, economic con-

[35] The attitude toward formal incorporation deserves comprehensive investigation for even in a single colony it is not consistent; some groups are disposed more favorably than others, and an unpalatable project is enough to cause a shift in viewpoint. Furthermore, the matter is closely bound up with the perennial terror of monopoly. The opposition to the Harvard charter in 1696 is based upon dislike of "corporations" (Osgood, 1 *American Colonies in the Eighteenth Century* [1924], 320). The Massachusetts assembly, even after it has effected clear-cut incorporations, persists in using forms in acts for the so-called incorporation of towns that contained none of the traditional expressions and often enough fails to use even the word "incorporate," as a perusal of the *Provincial Acts* discloses. This suggests that no necessity for formal corporate status was believed to exist.

It seems not improbable that the desire for charters was not keen once the implications of common law doctrine respecting the corporation were understood; *viz.* the power of visitation of eleemosynary corporations, the control over by-laws, and the final sanction of *quo warranto*. J. S. Davis has suggested that the matter of "style and title" was involved but he thinks this exaggerated. It accords more with the prevailing disposition of the settlers to believe that where charters were sought the "liberties and privileges" were closer to their hearts. In any event it is dangerous to generalize until the matter is more clearly examined, because events often caused a rapid change in opinion. *Cf. infra,* note 36.

[36] 3 *Ecclesiastical Records of the State of New York* (1902), 1487, 1615–1638. Cornbury's attempt to license ran counter to a fundamental rule of election by the congregation, although the opinion of counsel avers the act

ditions were not as yet sufficiently advanced to have led to an
extended employment of incorporation by fiat. In consequence,
usage, the factor most essential to assure the comfortable domi-
ciliation of common law practice, was slow in the making. Beyond this, the somewhat erratic policy of the home authorities
respecting the right of either colonial governor or assembly to
create bodies corporate itself operated as a check upon the
process.[37]

As the eighteenth century advanced, the aggregate number of
formal incorporations increased, the privilege being distributed
rather generally among various group types. The commercial
enterprise cannot be said to have preponderated, even at the end
of the colonial period. The reasons for this are several. In the
first place, a royal charter or parliamentary incorporation was
costly, and the legal status of a colonial charter or act was by no
means certain.[38] Furthermore, the extension of the Bubble Act
to the Colonies (1741), although it does not appear to have stimulated a policy of repressing colonial companies, remained at least
as a warning on the statute books. In the second place, limited
liability was not, at least as to business companies, a settled inci-

was contrary to Magna Carta and "the law for the Abolition of the Star
Chamber" (*ibid.*, 1629). It is possible that these events had something to
do with later attempts of reformed churches to secure corporate status as a
means of security; *e.g.*, 3 *Documentary History of the State of New York*,
549 (1720). And note in this connection the opposition of the Anglicans
to the grant of a charter (*ibid.*, 281).

[37] Russell, *Review of American Colonial Legislation by the King in
Council* (1915), 178.

[38] An episode in North Carolina politics illustrates this. In 1754 Governor Dobbs had been instructed to confirm, by charters of incorporation,
rights and privileges of towns and counties because the acts establishing
these had been disallowed. This instruction had been revoked in 1755 at
the instance of the assembly but the Governor, who was charging £10 a
charter, continued to issue such documents, and had made the right of
representation contingent upon corporate status. The Board of Trade in
1760 addressed a rebuke to Dobbs indicating that it did not regard the
charters as doing more than restoring a *status quo* disturbed by the dis-
allowance of the acts. 4 *North Carolina Colonial Records*, 43; 6 *ibid.*, 226–
229, 288.

dent of corporations, and hence the motive which later proved
so compulsive was absent. Finally, even the increase in formally
incorporated companies had not caused any substantial abate-
ment in the popular ideas respecting the effects of free association as respects the exercise of rights or privileges connected with
corporateness as the common law understood it.[39]

It has seemed necessary to sketch the outlines of colonial experience respecting associations, because in this new country there
was no other problem which loomed so large and which so constantly engaged the settlers' attention. Whether a schism was
brewing, a project being launched to convert Indians, a grant of
lands to be exploited, or a frame of government to be drawn, a
spate of discussion on the matter of organization was sure to
ensue. Not all the significant things said and written here were
in the grand style of political theory—of social compacts or the
indefeasible rights of men. The exchanges over petty issues of
social anatomy, because they were so usual and so widespread,
had an effect in developing the political consciousness of the
common man that will some day have to be assessed. Moreover,
these endless debates tended to keep both ideas and practice in a
state of flux. Thus the imitative process, inevitable in a colonial
society, was not confined to any single type of association moth-
ered in England. So far as its ambit was attenuated, this arose
from the rivalry of native experiment.

Although we have stressed the value of approaching the origin
of American corporate doctrine in terms of general ideas of association, the concrete manifestations of these ideas are best studied
in relation to a particular species of enterprise. It was invariably
the difficulties of coping with a practical problem that stimulated

[39] In this connection it should be noted that the New London Company
for Trade, after being incorporated by the Connecticut assembly, was
summoned by an informal *quo warranto* before this body. The company
denied jurisdiction and claimed "that they were a fraternity and not dis-
solvable." A. M. Davis, 2 *Currency and Banking in the Province of Massachusetts Bay* (1901), 108 n.

the ingenuity of the colonists, and only through observing their actions in respect to churches, towns, lands, banks, and the like does much meaning attach to their theories.

For various reasons the land problem was focal. It was the great commodity, bait for the greenhorns abroad, a spur to the restless at home, for its possession was the criterion of political rights, the assurance of social status. Inevitably, it was the first of the great American roads to affluence or ruin. In certain colonies the management and husbanding of the land resources had led to associative activity,[40] but it is not until close upon the middle of the eighteenth century that economic conditions were generally favorable to the launching of promotions on a large scale. The surge toward the West comes at a moment when the fortunes of the natives are such as to permit undertakings in the London manner. As Mr. Livermore shows, the range of choice was great, and so we shall find not merely the company formed after the image of those that had his majesty's letters patent, but copies of the colonial proprietorship and, in time, significantly enough, the joint stock association.[41]

Both before the Revolution and for some decades thereafter, the formation of companies for the merchandising of land was a dominant factor in the American business picture. Initially the repressive policy of the British government toward the development of colonial manufactures was to some extent responsible for the gravitation of surplus capital to the exploitation of the territorial domain and the impetus which this sort of enterprise thus received persisted. There were other factors at work, not the least of which was a feeling that the common good was being advanced in the development of physical resources and in the extension of the borders of civilization. From the first these enterprises possessed a marked political color, and they attracted persons who were prominent in public life.

The structure of the companies was affected in varying de-

[40] *Infra*, page 19.   [41] *Infra*, page 135.

grees by these several factors. But since the present volume is concerned primarily with the contribution of the land companies to the growth of American corporate doctrine, it will not be possible to pursue in detail these considerations of motive. It must be emphasized, however, that the objectives sought were most readily advanced by the employment of a non-participating form of undertaking with a continuity of structure, and that devices of this nature would appeal to personages whose energies were only partly engaged by such enterprises. These reasons also serve to explain why the land companies were so prominent among the forces which were driving toward a final break with the stiff traditions of common law rules of incorporation. This was not a result that was contemplated initially. The development before the Revolution proceeded subject to conditions and legal restrictions similar to and in cases even identical with those which prevailed in England, and was consequently influenced by the solutions which English business men were attempting. The practices thus induced persisted after the Revolution, for they seemed workable, and the vagaries of the legislatures which had captured the prerogative of incorporation had done little to make the acquisition of corporate status a definite benefit.

Despite the fact that the Revolution had completed the shift in the seat of the charter-granting authority, the prevailing legal theories respecting bodies corporate were not thereby shaken, nor was it feasible to use these theories to check the spread of the notion that corporate advantages could be had without formal incorporation. The common law conception of corporate capacity as a privilege was essentially incompatible with popular notions respecting associations, and particularly with the existing republican ideology. The transfer of the prerogative of creation to the legislature alone was a first step in the disintegration of medieval doctrine. What remained to be done was to effect the basic change that corporateness was a right and not a privilege. In this process it is obvious that the abandonment of the conception of the grant *ex mero motu* in favor of the contract theory played a very considerable part. For the new view not only extended the protection of the federal constitution to the state act of incorporation, but by treating it as of no greater significance than any bargain this view helped in the extinguishment of the privilege concept. Beyond this change in judicial theory we incline to the opinion that the easy assumption of incidents of corporate status by groups which had no vestige of formal authority to do so opened the way to a final reorientation of ideas. Apart from the special claims of any single association, it is obvious from the evidence that Mr. Livermore has assembled that the whole power of prescription was on the side of the companies. In the face of such a situation, it would have been futile to brandish even a fistful of *quo warrantos*. If large-scale enterprises were to be brought under the special procedural controls designed for the corporation, it was essential that the way be made easy into the fold that the law had designed for them. The answer was found in the general incorporation statutes, and with these began a new epoch.

JULIUS GOEBEL, JR.

AUTHOR'S FOREWORD

THIS study was originally undertaken as an inquiry into the internal characteristics and legal status of land companies in the Revolutionary period. It quickly became apparent that there existed no complete historical survey of these projects as a group, and no integration of the numerous excellent monographs and scattered secondary material concerning them. Consequently, the discussion of individual land company operations in the pre- and post-Revolutionary generations which is presented in Chapters IV and V of this book will, it is hoped, prove helpful to the historian.

The student of legal history and forms will find herein a theory of the origin of the modern business corporation and an analysis of the influence of unchartered bodies such as the land companies in shaping it. The law has regarded the unincorporated association as a modified or complex partnership. The surviving joint stock association of American law is still so regarded in textbook classifications. But the eighteenth century association was, in terms of business realities, a corporate body. Professor Goebel points out in his Introduction how deep-rooted this conception was in the Colonies. An effort is made to show that the rise of these true corporate entities, stubbornly dubbed partnerships by the courts until well into the nineteenth century, helped materially to force the enactment of general incorporation laws in the United States and the registration acts in England. They assumed the mantle of the legal corporation, and are thus the real forebears of today's business corporation. The older semi-political (a more precise phrase than the hackneyed *quasi-public*) chartered bodies belong to another branch of the family tree. It will be necessary to stress frequently in the course of the discussion this unorthodox explanation of the origin of the modern private business corporation.

Fusion of the forces of social science to reach common objectives is a popular rallying cry of scholars of today. As a professing economist, the author has had, in carrying to completion a study in legal history, a practical lesson in the value of this principle. He has benefited by its vitality in the scholarly world, through the enthusiastic willingness of members of the staff of Columbia University to sponsor and give aid to the undertaking. Dean Roswell C. McCrea encouraged it from the beginning, while Professor A. H. Stockder of the School of Business and President Dixon Ryan Fox of Union College and formerly of the Department of History at Columbia University gave specific help and advice, as did Professor Carl H. Bridenbaugh of the Department of History of Brown University. Professor Julius Goebel, Jr., of the School of Law of Columbia University suggested the original inquiry and supervised it as one of the studies sponsored by the Foundation which he directs. But he has done far more; his specific and cogent criticisms have affected the whole presentation and brought improvement at innumerable points.

From the resources and staffs of libraries and historical societies, to which acknowledgment is made in footnotes, much valuable assistance has been received. Many other individuals have given help by correspondence, or by reading portions of the text. I am particularly grateful to Mr. Armand DuBois for material copied in the British Museum and the Public Record Office, London.

My sincere thanks are due to the Legal Research Committee of the Commonwealth Fund for their interest in the undertaking and for their support. Mr. George Welwood Murray, Chairman of the Committee, was kind enough to read the entire manuscript critically. The breadth of interest of the Committee is indicated by their support of a project which wanders bravely but perhaps not too far beyond the strict boundaries of legal research.

S. L.

September 1938

TABLE OF CONTENTS

I

THE PROBLEM

THE corporation is a central fact in our complex economic
organization. In it we see a particular device which has
served with extraordinary efficacy the capitalistic *Anschauung*.
Not only is it the indispensable mode of existence for giant enterprises, but it is equally valued by the small, vigorous concerns
whose continued healthy existence in the most advanced capitalistic country presents a constant challenge to the Marxian
prognosis. Furtherance of our knowledge of the underlying
forces determining corporate development must be esteemed a
prime objective of both the economic and the legal historian.
To this end, it is not sufficient merely to assemble an imposing
array of pre-seventeenth century forms of business organization,
and to declare that the corporation of today rests upon one or
another of the models so herded together. Nor is it any sounder
approach to treat corporate evolution as linked closely with successive attempts by the political state to restrain or encourage
the economic activity of citizens. The attempt will be made
herein to show that the collective desire of the business community for effective organization of enterprise and the *will* to
use the form which at the time is needed despite legal or political
obstacles have been the real influences molding the corporation
of today. To illustrate the thesis in some detail, a critical period
in American economic development will be used.

It is perfectly true that men draw upon the experience of the
past, necessarily and constantly. But to concede this does not pre-
clude stressing even more the truth that practical men reject
much of what has been received and use only that which is immediately applicable.[1] Active business leaders in whose hands

---

[1] The framers of the Constitution of 1787, of whom a majority were
business men or of the class closely associated with them, drew upon the

determinative economic power rests are less typically students of the past than legislators and courts. In any business community a ferment of progress is at work which is quite unrelated to any specific precedents of a past era, and it is a familiar truism that legal mechanism does not maintain realistic contact with such economic change.

The first business organisms possessing the true character[2] of a corporation as we now know it appeared in the German and

past for numerous specific ideas, but the instrument they produced nevertheless was unique. If originality characterized American political thought in the last quarter of the eighteenth century, we would expect it to be even more evident in economic affairs.

[2] Truly corporate bodies, as distinct from partnerships, arise when men devise effective means of participating in an enterprise as a "side-issue," apart from other activity to which they devote their principal business time and effort. The test is a practical one; it is not concerned with the philosophical inquiry into the potential creation of a new entity or "personality." The word *effective* connotes that business leaders must find the device attractive to outsiders, who need only be promised the opportunity for profit. Perpetuity, concentration of managerial powers in the right hands, and free transferability of interest are the essential means to that end.

As and where these are first properly offered, the real roots of the modern corporation may be sought. The partnership concept presumes a full devotion of the participants' time, energy, and capital, equality in managerial power, freedom to terminate the undertaking on notice or for cause, and liability *in solido* for all debts incurred. From the opposed presumption of only a part-time interest and relatively modest investment of capital in an enterprise come the familiar fundamentals of the modern corporation. Max Weber stressed this turning-point in his *General Economic History* (Knight translation, New York, 1927), 185, 225–228. These basic differentiations, appearing only sporadically before the seventeenth century, are the foundations of the corporation. Beside them, sovereign sanction—a charter—as the mark of corporateness, has come to be a superficial characteristic.

The *temporary* undertaking is less important than the *permanent* association that offers to business men the right of "side-issue" participation. For this reason, mining organization, as German scholars have correctly understood, is far more important than ocean commerce in illustrating post-Roman emergence of the corporate idea. The creation of long-continuing enterprises in which shares may be held by men whose chief business activities and interest lie elsewhere becomes of major importance in ushering in modern methods.

Austrian mining districts in the fifteenth century.[3] Faced in that nascent industry with the practical problem of conducting enterprises which in economic nature strongly suggested modern capitalistic industry, men turned to the conceptions of share capital, continuity of existence, transferability of interest, and delegated powers of management. In the same period of economic expansion, collective effort became necessary in another direction. Overseas trade in the sixteenth century underwent as great an expansion in Western European countries as had occurred four centuries before in Italy.[4] Where absolutism reigned, as in Portugal, government kept a close restraint upon the exploitation of the new trade routes; but ambitious men, particularly in England, saw that by proper organization they might secure for themselves some of the fruits of East Indian intercourse.

It is historically clear that in both these fields government had felt that its interest must be protected. Control over mining and a share in its product had almost from the dawn of history been a prerogative of sovereignty. Foreign trade similarly had been regarded by English monarchs for centuries to be so bound up with political maneuvers as to be necessarily under royal control at all times. Where central sovereignty was weak, as in much of the decaying Holy Roman Empire, rulers exercised only partial or intermittent control so that many voluntary unchartered bodies sprang up in Germany and Austria to carry on mining. They were strikingly suggestive of our modern corporate bodies. But the Tudor monarchy, as we should expect, met the challenge of the ambitious new enterprises by insisting that they be carried

---

[3] For a brief summary of this development and of the extensive study of it by German scholars, see Jacob Strieder, "Origin of Early European Capitalism," 2 *Journal of Economic and Business History*, 1 (1930).

[4] Mediterranean commerce produced the *commenda* and the sea loan—significant advances in the art of business organization. *Cf.* Byrne, *Genoese Shipping* (Cambridge, 1930), *passim.*

on under royal charter.[5] The English chartered corporation as
the strong Tudors and the Stuart monarchs created it—and it
must be remembered that charter-granting was not really a Parliamentary function until 1689—thus rested on a peculiar foundation. It was a political creation, as truly as the Durham palatinate
or the Liberty of the Five Ports had been.

Tracing the pattern of historical development for these crown-
chartered bodies has been attractive to historical scholarship.[6]
But as an explanation of the character of the modern corporation, such inquiry is far from adequate. Incorporation open to
all upon compliance with simple, uniform requirements laid
down in advance is vastly different from incorporation bestowed
only when and where a monopoly privilege of some sort is present. It does not explain so important a transformation to suggest
merely that the state's position in charter-granting became more
and more unimportant, or that the element of sovereign sanction
gradually disappeared.[7] The change was radical in the truest
sense, going to the very roots of the institution.

Business men came to challenge the state's original attitude
because, during the course of the eighteenth century in England,
they encountered a pressing need for the unique values of the

[5] Elizabeth was willing enough to stimulate the natural greed of her
subjects by permitting their entry into every form of endeavor—from mast-
cutting to piracy—which might coincidentally further the economic power
of her kingdom. But they must operate under her watchful eye. When
Daniel Hochstetter came to England from Germany to develop non-ferrous
mining, he obtained a charter (1564) for the Mines Royal that was primarily a grant of exclusive privileges in conducting his enterprises. Scott,
2 *English, Scottish and Irish Joint Stock Companies to 1720*, 385. Significant is the space devoted by Lipson to the chartered companies of the
Tudors and Stuarts in 2 *Economic History of England*, 269–370. The East
India Company and the long subsequent series of chartered trading and
colonizing enterprises resulted from the same political attitude—jealous
control coupled with deliberate stimuli to self-interest in the form of monopoly grants.

[6] Scott's three-volume work, just referred to, is the outstanding example.

[7] As A. A. Berle and G. C. Means state, 4 *Encyclopedia of the Social
Sciences*, 412, in the article on "Corporation."

corporate mechanism. It was a need felt generally in the business community, not sporadically as in preceding centuries. Unfolding of opportunities for the employment of capital in wholly new fields was characteristic of the entire century. Just at the end of the seventeenth century, the substantial group of Dutch business men and stock traders who followed William of Orange to London brought with them a degree of familiarity with corporate shares as vehicles for speculation hitherto unknown in the English business community. In the succeeding boom years this new knowledge bore astonishing fruit, and in the years 1693 to 1696 there was witnessed in London a stock market "boom" which displayed a thoroughly modern aspect, a transplantation of Dutch business methods and attitudes. It has become a familiar episode in English history through Macaulay's graphic description. Despite the reassertion of governmental supervision in the Bubble Act, the knock at the door again became insistent as economic change accelerated its pace during the century. In the American Colonies, obviously, this shift in the economic foundations of the corporation was delayed by their later development. It was compressed into the seventy-five years beginning in 1750 and extending to 1825; and because of the peculiar subordinate sovereignty of the colonial governments, it may be said to have really taken place after 1785. The end-result in both countries was a triumph for the principle that incorporation, with all its legal as well as its economic advantages, should be open to all upon easy equal terms.

Yet the state and the courts were stubborn. Too long had the corporation been an agency of political policy to be quickly and facilely reshaped into an everyday tool of business organization. Lawyers could not realize that what had happened by 1825 was just such a commonplace adoption of the corporate device, entirely beyond the pale of legal sanction. As will be seen herein, the courts, when faced with evidence of the existence of corporate mechanisms possessing everything but charters, persisted in denying that they could be anything but partnerships. They clung to their illogical position in the face of the impending recognition by legislators of the right of business men to form such *de facto* corporations by the passage of general incorporation laws. Neither legislatures nor courts were really alert to assist and facilitate economic growth by making available to all comers the corporate privilege. Grudgingly and reluctantly they permitted the change under pressure from the business community.

What was the general nature of this period, so important in the evolution of corporations? Historians have supplied rich and discursive answers to that query. It will be presumed here that the main currents of American development from 1750 to 1830 are familiar to the reader. Particularly in the description of specific enterprises, the factors conditioning westward expansion will not be described anew, lest one more jejune survey of the influence of the frontier be added to those now on the historical shelves. The year 1750 is more than a convenient reference date to mark the beginning of the change in attitude among business men already described; there is abundant historical evidence that the decade centering thereon marked the real beginning of economic expansion in the Colonies. Enterprise began to reach out beyond a purely local scale and to imitate the wider scope of overseas trade. The generation rising to power in that decade, or just subsequently, included such men as George Croghan, Sir William Johnson, Richard Henderson, George Morgan, Samuel Wharton, Ethan Allen, the Gratzes, and scores of others who conceived of business and trade on the grander scale. Historians have recognized the controlling influence exerted by these men on the political as well as the economic future of the country.[8] Speculation appeared, to an extent which has

---

[8] To name Frederick J. Turner suffices, for in his earlier studies of the moving frontier he showed keen appreciation of the leadership of the land merchandisers. Others have simply followed him, most noticeably

tricked some historical writers[9] into a warped conception of its determinative effect upon colonial political affairs. Others, with more balanced hindsight, see in this generation simply the first evidence of the "Big Business" outlook in economic affairs.[10] That modern phrase comes close to expressing, succinctly, what is stressed here: that men were coming to conceive of all business operations on a new plane, one that inherently required a new framework within which to accomplish changed objectives.

The conflict between a legal attitude toward business organization resting on a sixteenth century foundation and the realistic need for a new form was intensified after 1785. To illustrate what resulted from this collision of economic and legal forces, we shall utilize here a form of enterprise overwhelmingly important as an example of the new plane of business operations. This was land merchandising, so typically American and so absorptive of the energies of restless leaders in the last quarter of the eighteenth century. Successfully to pre-empt huge areas of virgin territory and control its distribution required combinations of capital and unified control. Individual small-scale methods could not cope with the problem. No other country had such an asset or

Alvord. Both men displayed a far more tempered and balanced attitude toward land speculation than some more recent writers who are apparently walking in the footsteps of Beard.

[9] For example, a recent work by T. P. Abernethy, *From Frontier to Plantation in Tennessee* (New York, 1932); at page 45 the author makes this statement: "Speculation in lands was the most absorbing American enterprise during the later Colonial, the Revolutionary, and the early Republican periods—in those days, the country was run largely by speculators in real estate." Later, in speaking of William Blount, he says: "The entire Southwest was his hunting ground and he stuffed his pockets with the profits of his speculations in land." This attitude contrasts with that of Alvord, typified by such a statement as the following: "Bold speculation was one of the characteristics of the eighteenth century" (1 *Mississippi Valley in British Politics* [Cleveland, 1917], 86). Volwiler, in his *George Croghan and the Westward Movement* (Cleveland, 1926), is also temperate.

[10] Particularly J. T. Adams, in his *Revolutionary New England* (Boston, 1923). Journalistically, rather than historically, Sakolski stresses the point in his *Great American Land Bubble* (New York, 1932).

the hope of attracting a population which could utilize it. The
organizations created to meet the unique situation were completely the result of the planning and of the decisions of business
leaders who accepted the challenge of opportunity.

The land companies must therefore be described here with
some care, because they were an indigenous response of American business men to a problem entirely our own; moreover, they
have not elsewhere been critically examined as a group. An attempt will be made to make a reasonably complete survey of all
land projects in the period 1750–1800 and to indicate in appended
notes the principal sources of detailed information about each of
them.

In form and operation these companies were surprisingly prophetic of the nineteenth century corporation; yet no one of them
ever secured a charter. It will be important to observe how rapidly
during the fifty-year period they progressed away from the partnership concept toward the practical form of a corporation. As a
group they present the best American counterpart of the English
joint stock company or association,[11] which was evolving in the
mother country during the same half-century. Mere factual description will not suffice. The origins of the apparent attitude of
leaders that they could proceed to create such bodies in the face
of legal antagonism and restraint must be searched out. It will
be necessary also to trace the struggle with legislators and courts
which delayed ultimate fulfilment of the promise first held forth
by these bodies to business men: that a free right to organize as a
corporate unit belongs to all on equal terms.

[11] The characteristics and business importance of unincorporated companies in England during this period are described by A. B. DuBois in *The
English Business Company after the Bubble Act, 1720–1800* (New York,
1938).

II

PRECEDENT FORMS OF ASSOCIATION

IF THE voluntary association of business men is to be put forward as the real progenitor of the twentieth century corporation, it becomes necessary to examine possible sources or models upon which men in the eighteenth century could have drawn for their conception of its character. In particular, it is essential to discover if possible the deeper roots of the idea that a unitary business organism, possessing all the traits of a corporation minus its legal sanction and privileges, could be created at will by any group of men. This is the idea, inherent in the voluntary association, which distinguishes the corporation of today from its crown-chartered predecessor—an idea which legislature and courts came ultimately to accept.[1]

It will be seen in due course that the creators and guardians of law did not make this concession without a struggle. In the seventeenth and eighteenth centuries the corporation was viewed strictly as a quasi-public body, created legitimately only to advance the public or national welfare and not primarily for private profit. In consequence, it usually possessed some public adminis-

---

[1] The year 1850 in both England and America conveniently marks the date of this fundamental shift in legal thinking. The English Companies Acts and our own general incorporation laws in substance have said to the business community: "Since you believe that a true entity for business purposes can be created by voluntary agreement, we prefer to have you bring such organizations under our supervision; such small and routine requirements will be laid upon you that you will be encouraged to secure the specific legal advantages which a charter offers, to be added to those fundamental business advantages which you have long possessed." Legislatures did not consciously change their attitude on charter-granting in order to bring about a better ordered world. They accepted a situation which business had created: the free and general use of the association principle, resulting in large numbers of business entities operating, in all except the technical legal sense, as corporations. Maitland calls the 1862 Companies Act one of "capitulation" (3 *Collected Papers,* 389). See also Chapter VIII, *infra.*

trative powers and monopoly privileges which only the state could grant and enforce. Any wholesale creation of legal personalities—the modern result of our general laws—was repugnant to this conception of the nature of a chartered body. Especially in a nation where a central sovereignty was supreme, maintenance of this attitude was essential. The state could not brook potentially powerful rivals which it had not created and licensed; at times it even feared the power of its legitimated offspring. Consequently, it logically was forced to restrict the number, size, and privileges of chartered bodies; it also took care to bar the door to similar groups lacking the sanction of a charter. Men should be rigidly restricted to the use of the time-honored partnership[2] if they were unable to secure the charter so jealously guarded.[3] This would perhaps be the situation today, both in England and the United States, if no economic pressure for change had made itself felt.

Because there was such a sharp and definite conflict between the legal attitude[4] and the economic necessities of the situation, it is necessary to do more than describe the immediate circum-

[2] Witness Lord Eldon as late as 1824 in *Natusch* v. *Irving,* 2 Cooper 358: "The principles which a court would act upon in the case of a partnership of six must, as far as the nature of things will admit, be applied to a partnership of six hundred."

[3] The Continent, because it inherited from Roman Law the conception of societies outside the state's purview, and because central sovereignty was typically weaker than in England after 1700, came much earlier to approve the principle of free assumption of corporate privileges by any group so choosing. Added to these causes, if we are to accept Gierke's *Genossenschaftstheorie,* was the Germanic temperament or tradition, so implacably on the side of freedom of association in all respects.

[4] Best known perhaps is Maitland's work in interpreting the opposed legal theories and bringing before English readers the accomplishments of German scholars in this field. Compressed into the 45 pages of Maitland's introduction to his own translation of that small part of Gierke's work entitled *Political Theories of the Middle Age* (Cambridge, 1900) is an excellent summary of the theoretical conflict. He has elsewhere developed further the same point of view; *e.g.,* 3 *Collected Papers,* "Trust and Corporation"; also *Township and Borough* (Cambridge, 1898), 14–23. Though he reached far back into medieval thinking, Maitland was quick to perceive

stances surrounding the growth and activity of one highly important group of voluntary associations, American land companies. What evidence had there been previously that, faced coincidentally with a need for unified economic action and a legal prohibition, men would move counter to legal rule and

how the rise of the joint stock company in the nineteenth century focused the conflict on a new *locus*. A brief summary of Maitland's chief points (summarized from the work of Gierke in turn) will help to clarify the issue referred to in the text. References will be made to pages in his introduction.

The sixteenth century reception of Roman Law in Germany was not thorough, for there were many concessions made to Germanic customs or tradition. Moreover, Roman Law then stood as interpreted by commentators; particularly, in the field of corporation theory, Pope Innocent IV (before his elevation he was Sinibald Fieschi) seems to have been the real father of the fiction theory, about 1243. But in modified Roman Law as it was received, the corporation was regarded strictly as a fictitious, juristic person. It was incapable of will or intention, and therefore innocent of potential crime or tort. It could be created only by the sovereign power and endowed with specific, limited attributes, among which were the power to acquire property and enter into contracts. It could be continued in existence after the death of all its human members or "guardians," a conception well suited to ecclesiastical corporations (Maitland, xx).

English lawyers were as unprepared as those of medieval Germany with any well-rounded theory to oppose to this polished Italian doctrine. It spread as university teaching developed. In the eighteenth century and after, judges could assert—though not unanimously—that it was a common law crime to "presume to act as a corporation" without permission of the state. As for the daughter country, "nowhere has the Concession Theory been proclaimed more loudly, more frequently, more absolutely, than in America; nowhere has more lip-service been done to Fieschi," says Maitland (xxxi). The legal mind thought the framers of the Mayflower Compact thoroughly "ignorant" (*ibid.*). But a later age has come to feel that the ostrich-like attitude expressed in the lawyers' unwillingness to recognize true personality in unincorporated groups is an "offense against jurisprudence" (xxxii)—a "fatal blunder . . . from which some of the less pedantic kinsmen in the Colonies kept themselves free when they suffered the New England Town to develop its inherent corporateness" (xxxv).

Professor Barker's recent English translation of additional portions of Gierke's work, *Natural Law and the Theory of Society* (Cambridge University Press, 1934), complements Maitland's contribution. Included are particularly illuminating surveys of seventeenth and eighteenth century German thought on the fundamental character of corporations (especially 173–195 of Volume I). Gierke's own comments constantly oscillate be-

tradition? Certainly Americans did so with respect to the land enterprises of 1750–1800. Some tradition, some experience within the horizon of the ordinary citizen, must have swayed them.

Too little attention has been paid by legal historians to the vigorous prevalence among Anglo-Saxon peoples of the conception that a group of individuals may by voluntary agreement create functioning business or social organisms which truly possess a separate "personality." This belief runs in an unbroken thread through many phases of English history—the boroughs and towns, the gilds and religious bodies,[5] and finally the unincorporated joint stock association.[6] With reasonable consist-

tween emphasis on the nature of the political state and on the nature of private associations (corporations) and so are much less valuable to the student of the problem at hand than such a survey as Maitland's.

Sir Frederick Pollock has uttered a word of warning concerning the acceptance of Roman Law in England ("Has Common Law Received the Fiction Theory?" 27 *L.Q.R.* 219 [1911]; especially the final footnote, in which Gierke's approval of his argument is referred to). There is little or no evidence of conscious acceptance, by either judges or legal writers. Coke, in his famous Sutton's Hospital summary (10 *Coke* 32) used words "wholly repugnant to the first and most important consequence of the Fiction Theory, namely that a corporation has only that capacity which is expressly conferred on it." But Pollock hardly answers successfully the well-supported claim that the doctrine of *ultra vires* rests necessarily on the theory. Nor does he stress the point that the whole process of strengthening central sovereignty in English legal history laid the foundation for a strict treatment of the corporate privilege long before there was knowledge of Roman Law. Incorporation by prescription (further evidence against the theory) belonged largely to pre-Tudor times. The idea of limits on corporateness has thus been more firmly imbedded in English law than it would have been as an importation from Italy. But the acceptance of Pollock's point does not alter the fact that phraseology at least was borrowed from Roman Law writers (witness 1 Blackstone's *Commentaries,* 472, and Marshall's definition in *Trustees of Dartmouth College* v. *Woodward,* 4 Wheaton 518).

An acute recent summary of this whole problem is by Max Radin, "Endless Problem of Corporate Personality," 32 *C.L.R.* 643. In summarizing, he says (at 658), "Psychologically and socially, the unincorporated body usually has the same amount of personality, *the same right to be an entity* [italics added], as the incorporated one."

[5] *Cf.* Editor's Introduction, *supra.*

[6] Professor Warren has said in his *Corporate Advantages without In-*

ency, English law for centuries opposed this popular attitude by insisting that no body of men could be treated as a *legal* unit without the express consent of the sovereign power.[7]

The clear expression of the former attitude among the settlers of New England has, as a special case, become of prime interest to American historians. The settlers at Plymouth,[8] in Rhode Island, in the Connecticut Valley, and on the eastern end of Long Island thought of themselves as practical corporate entities, operating as they knew incorporated towns or trading companies could operate. Throughout English history similar bodies had tried to establish themselves without permission, and for centuries they had been periodically persecuted or interfered with by the Crown.[9] The three Connecticut towns in the *Fundamental Articles* of 1639 certainly had no burning desire to create a democratic form of government.[10] On the contrary, the government

corporation (Chicago, 1929), at 7: "if the conception of many individuals as merged into a composite unit is a fiction, such fiction is certainly not of legal origin. Such a conception is a familiar popular mode of thought. We find evidence . . . in all literatures, even the rudest. And our own language has a great number of words which connote such a conception—tribe, nation, army, regiment, guild, labor union, church, club, society, school, college, etc."

[7] As Warren points out (*ibid.* at 8), there were exceptions: church wardens were allowed to function as an entity without a charter; in early times, the Court of Exchequer permitted unincorporated bodies to be sued as though incorporated. *Cf.,* also, Madox, *Firma Burgi* (London, 1726), 85. But Warren fails to mention other more important instances where the courts yielded ground—the gilds in England, and the proprietorship in the New England Colonies. Both will be discussed below.

[8] Professor Goebel points out that the attitude of the Plymouth colonists in regarding themselves as a corporate body was without warrant, viewed in the light of strict common law rules; Editor's Introduction, *supra,* xiv.

[9] As early as 1179, Henry II amerced several gilds which had no charters; Madox, *op. cit.,* 26. The inquiry into gild charters of 1389 was an effort to force all such bodies to secure charters, and thus be a source of revenue. Charles II's attacks on the City of London can be traced to this centuries-old conflict between the Crown and the courts, on the one hand, and the popular will to create independent organizations, on the other.

[10] As J. T. Adams pointedly demonstrates in his *Founding of New England* (Boston, 1921), 192–195.

thereby established was oligarchical. But what did lie behind the articles was the deeply rooted belief that, by such a formal agreement, a governmental or social body could be rightfully created. The settlers thought of themselves as a *community* in the true sense, best expressed in the older word *commonalty* so often used by the old gilds to describe their collective membership.

Nor was this belief confined to the fanatical English leaders of the New England settlements.[11] A demonstration of all these outcroppings in the political, social, and business activities of the English people is a separate task in itself, as yet undone. What can be accomplished here is a brief survey of specific instances wherein this idea was prominent or uppermost in the minds of Colonial Americans. At least one Colonial institution where an opposite ideal was controlling must also be briefly examined: the proprietary grant. Some of these examples may be assumed to have been within the knowledge of late eighteenth century American business men. Assumptions as to what men knew or did not know at some date in the past are always hazardous, but the men who organized associations for land settlement or for speculation were in a surprising number of cases demonstrably drawing for inspiration upon one or another of the sources to be examined cursorily here.

THE GILDS AND BOROUGHS

It is usually not understood that, during almost the entire history of craft gild organization in England, unincorporated gilds functioned alongside those which had been able to secure or to

[11] H. L. Osgood, 1 *American Colonies in the Seventeenth Century* (New York, 1904), *passim,* gives detailed attention to the New England Colonies. Adams, *op. cit.,* brings out their true character succinctly. For the lesser known circumstances in Rhode Island, *cf.* "Records of the Narragansett Proprietors," Volume I of *Rhode Island Colonial Gleanings* (Providence, 1894). For the case of Southampton, New York, in 1640, *cf.* 1 *Southampton Records,* edited by W. S. Pelletreau (3 vols., Sag Harbor, N.Y., 1874–1878), 1–5, where the covenant for that town is reprinted.

afford the expense of a Crown charter. Unwin,[12] in his careful study of the hundreds of London bodies in existence at one time or another through ten centuries, points out that this condition recurred and was not confined to any one century or decade. Clearly, Englishmen steadily believed that they could attain the practical status of a corporation without sovereign authority, despite periodic efforts by the law or the Crown to enforce the requirement of a charter as a prerequisite to any operation as a legal entity. He summarizes the situation clearly: "It would be a great mistake to regard the legal formalities of incorporation as in any way essential to the corporate spirit. That spirit had become universal among all classes . . . before the end of the fifteenth century."[13]

The Crown attacked this attitude because potential revenue was being lost so long as unchartered bodies flourished. They could be forced to pay a price for the right to regulate the activities of their members and otherwise invade the field of public law. The most successful foray of the Crown against the unincorporated bodies was in the last decade of the fourteenth century. After the Parliamentary inquiry of 1389, which in turn resulted from the struggles of the Lord Mayors Brembre and Northampton to impose political control on the London gilds, many new charters were granted. By 1450 "incorporation became the established rule."[14] The charters were formal: that of the Tailors in 1408 constituted them a "sound perpetual and corporate fraternity," gave them the right to have a common seal, to plead and be impleaded, to have and to hold lands.[15] Specific provisions permitting the holding of lands in mortmain, up to a certain

---

[12] Unwin, *Guilds and Companies of London* (London, 1909). For our purposes, his discussion is more satisfactory than Charles Gross' *Gild Merchant* (Oxford, 1890), since the latter does not discuss the detailed structure of craft groups. This is true also of many other studies of an historical character in this field.

[13] *Ibid.*, 172. [14] *Ibid.*, 161.

[15] *Ibid.*, 159.

limit, were frequent in this quarter-century period when most of the major gilds were chartered. But Unwin, surveying the whole sweep of development, stresses the fact that the internal organization and powers of compulsion over the membership so essential in gilds had all been previously developed when they were merely fraternities under the technical sanction of the Church.[16] Most of them had been created as such superficially religious bodies in the reigns of Edward III and Richard II. The charters around 1400 merely gave legal instead of ecclesiastical sanction to a functioning organism devised and developed by business men.[17]

But the culprit would not remain quiescent. Nor did the Crown remain as watchful. Unwin[18] points out that "of the sixty crafts . . . at the Guildhall in 1531 not more than half were incorporated, but at least a dozen of the remainder were organized in the same fashion. Legal incorporation was needed to consolidate the new type of association whilst it was in process of formation, but . . . its features might easily be copied by companies that were not incorporated." Clearly, men felt free to go ahead, achieve organization, function as a body, without the permission of the Sovereign.

Why then were charters sought by bodies on their own initiative when, during the sixteenth and seventeenth centuries, they had been generally unmolested except by city governments? It was because the charters of the older and stronger gilds obviously gave them certain powers conducive to a stronger monopoly control than could safely or effectively be exercised without one. The Pewterers accumulated money for over fifteen years in order to buy a charter; its principal benefit, of which they made immediate use, was its grant of the right to send out "searchers" into the small towns, who seized bad metal, levied fines on the unsuspecting independents who belonged to no gild,

---

[16] Merchant gild organization was also formal as early as 1200. *Cf.* Gross, *op. cit.,* ch. 2.

[17] Unwin, *op. cit.,* 169–171.   [18] *Ibid.,* 169.

and forced workers in those towns to join the gild with a substantial entrance fee![19] This was in the sixteenth century. Yet the
attitude of such a group toward a charter foreshadows exactly
the attitude of the seventeenth and eighteenth century business
communities: a charter was to be sought in specific cases because
it permitted monopoly rights or privileges. But if such privileges
were not needed, effective operation as a business unit was perfectly possible without a charter. Trustees typically held the legal
title to land and a gildhall on behalf of such unincorporated
groups, and their internal affairs were conducted without appre-
ciable differences.

The craft gilds, in their heyday during the sixteenth century,
were an all-important form of business organization. They were
a senile institution by the eighteenth century, and hence it would
be folly to point to them as a direct source of practices or methods
for the business men of that day. The fact, however, that some
operated without charters amid those with charters may well
have been known.[20] But most suggestive is the clear demonstration in gild history of the *will* of business groups to go ahead
with their basic form of organization irrespective of their possession or lack of a charter.

Just as emigrants from England had had acquaintance with
gild organization, so also had they been in direct contact with independent boroughs. Participation in borough affairs afforded
experience with the internal functioning of a collective body of
men highly conscious of its *corporate* character. The borough
very frequently was the manager of lands[21] and as such directed

---

[19] *Ibid.,* 164–166.

[20] The Carmen's Company had the longest continuous existence of any
London company; yet it was not incorporated, deriving its rights from
municipal licenses. The members sold their "stalls or stands" to successors
as freehold possessions, just as shares would be transferred in a trucking
company today. Unwin devotes considerable space to this extremely interesting body, *ibid.,* 356 *ff.*

[21] *Cf.* Sydney and Beatrice Webb, 2 *English Local Government* (London, 1922), 276.

in a very real sense the economic life of its freemen and inhabitants as well. It taught men brought up in towns the conception of a corporate body functioning as continuously and uninterruptedly as the gilds.[22] There were, furthermore, the same conflicting attitudes concerning the need for specific charter grants as we have noted in the gilds. English law, up to the days of reform in the nineteenth century, always admitted that a corporate character could be acquired by prescription.[23] Boroughs which claimed such a venerable origin for their corporate rights were probably not slow to boast of it or to reiterate their claims on all occasions. Finally, the attacks of the last decade of the Stuart dynasty upon borough charters is profoundly important here for its effect upon men's thinking about the true nature of a corporate body. The Webbs, in their careful study, found that most of the English boroughs were forced in 1683–1689 to surrender their charters or have them declared forfeit.[24] The boroughs nevertheless continued to function and to exercise all their powers of government. As a result, during the eighteenth century many of the townsmen came to regard a charter as of little controlling importance. There were "innumerable instances . . . of radical changes in the constitution of particular Municipal Corporations,"[25] simply by the adoption of new by-laws. The concept of corporate independence and self-sufficiency received undeniable impetus from this period of resistance to Stuart assaults. Revocation, forfeit, and re-grant of charters all over the kingdom destroyed what sanctity the idea of a Crown charter may have acquired under the Tudors. The rights and powers of self-government by political entities remained unscathed.

The gild and the borough, as everyday institutions, almost certainly had some direct influence upon an exclusively Colonial

---

[22] Maitland says of Cambridge: "The town is a person, and may be a landowner among landowners, lessor, hirer, creditor, debtor. It will soon begin to speculate in land." *Township and Borough*, 85–86.

[23] *Ibid.*, 19.   [24] *Op. cit.*, 267–272.

[25] *Ibid.*, 272.

device which in turn became a model for the eighteenth century
bodies with which we are concerned. That was the town proprietorship, and a careful examination of its structure from the
economic standpoint is essential.

THE NEW ENGLAND PROPRIETORSHIP

The residents of Massachusetts, Connecticut, and New Hampshire were in close contact with group management and disposition of land during the eighteenth century.[26] The town proprietorships in these corporate colonies afforded a training-
ground for the natural leaders who later participated in more
speculative land enterprises in Ohio and elsewhere. The training
was unique, because there were then few chartered business corporations in the Colonies; shipping, foreign trading ventures, or
crude public utilities were the only areas of activity where experience in business enterprise could have been secured, and these
did not appear in any numbers until after 1760. Historians have
regarded the town proprietorship as an institution of especial interest, but the studies made have not presented much intensive
analysis of the actual mode of operation after 1700.[27]

[26] Land disposition in eighteenth century Rhode Island tended more to
resemble that of the South. *Cf.* Edward Channing, *Narragansett Planters,*
Johns Hopkins Studies, 4th Series, No. 3 (Baltimore, 1886).

[27] Melville Egleston, *Land System of the New England Colonies* (Johns
Hopkins Studies, 4th Series, 1908), seems to be the standard reference on
the topic. It is incomplete in important respects. R. H. Akagi, *Town Proprietors of the New England Colonies* (Philadelphia, 1929), is much more
detailed and satisfactory. H. L. Osgood's discussion in 1 *American Colonies
in the Seventeenth Century,* 424 ff., is an excellent brief analysis. MacLear,
Early New England Towns (New York, 1908), deals with only five towns.
N. P. Mead, "The Connecticut Land System," 16 *Political Science Quarterly,* 59 (1906), has been used as a source of information by some; this
author (at page 72) makes the startling misstatement that the New England town proprietors were "reproductions on a smaller scale" of Maryland and Pennsylvania. Actual town or proprietorship records have formed
the most valuable source here, since historical students in using such source
material neglect the very aspects of organization of most importance to
the central theme of this study.

Charles Francis Adams, in 7 *Proceedings of the Massachusetts Histori-*

The ideal of group control, or the conception of a "compact," runs through the whole early history of New England.[28] It is especially important here to trace this feeling of a group entity, or quasi-corporate existence, through the history of the town proprietorship, because such bodies were essentially business projects, albeit with important social influence. They clearly represent one of many outcroppings of that fundamental idea or social "drive" which has already been stressed, *viz.,* that by voluntary agreement and association there could be created business units possessing the powers, characteristics, and rights of corporations. Osgood recognized the validity of this view; he declared that the proprietorship group as a functioning organization "formed a *de facto* land company, as truly as did the companies which received the grants of the New England colonies."[29] J. T. Adams stresses the same point and says that "the semi-independent communities were entirely without legal authority."[30]

The New England colonies possessed the explicit right to make regrants of lands within their jurisdiction; this power was strikingly reaffirmed in the 1662 charter of Connecticut.[31] Hence a group receiving a grant of territory from the General Court in Massachusetts or Connecticut felt independent of any relationship to the Crown or to any authority which could interfere with the later disposition of their lands. This feeling was to some degree rooted in the fact that at the very start in Massachu-

---

cal Society, 2nd Series (1892), 172 and 441, presents a view on the origin of the New England town opposed to that of most modern historians who stress the Church's influence. He regards the town as strictly a commercial organization, just as the Massachusetts Bay charter of 1629 was commercial. "The plantation or town was a commercial company, the partners in which by degrees were developed into a political community" (p. 186).

[28] J. T. Adams, *Founding of New England* (Boston, 1921), 98 *ff.*

[29] I *American Colonies in the Seventeenth Century,* 461.

[30] *Op. cit.,* 209.

[31] The third specific power granted to the "body politic and corporate" of Connecticut was the right to possess and sell real estate and chattels. The charter is reprinted in G. H. Hollister, *History of Connecticut* (New Haven, 1855), Appendix B, 476, and in many other places.

setts Bay and in Connecticut the individual settled without formal grant. Moreover, the importance attached to purchase from the Indians was likewise involved. Thus, in early Rhode Island the acquisition of the Indian title was thought to be paramount,[32] and merely perfunctory approval of the purchase was made by the legislature.

The attitude of the Massachusetts General Court toward grantees after 1640, and toward the degree of authority given them, is of direct interest here. In the case of Worcester, in 1667, a committee was named to have charge of the settlement; the assembly simply approved perfunctorily a petition from the group proposing the new settlement. This was nearly the typical method of making grants which prevailed during the following century.[33] Formality in the grants was lacking, and not until well into the eighteenth century is there evidence that the legislatures thought they were creating corporate bodies of the public type.

In June, 1669, this four-man committee for the Worcester settlement proceeded to draw up an agreement: "Records of the Orders and Agreements of the Committee appointed and authorized by the General Court, for managing and ordering a new plantation, now called Worcester, which are laid as foundation principles and rules concerning the affairs of that place; con-

[32] This belief that a direct purchase from Indians by private individuals could give valid title persisted throughout the eighteenth century and recurred periodically in legal controversies over title. Roger Williams in 1634 first expounded this view during his attacks on the authority of the Puritan oligarchy. *Cf.* Staples, *Annals of Providence* (Providence, 1843), 26–27, and James E. Ernst, *Roger Williams, New England Firebrand* (New York, 1925), 100 *ff.* Judicially, it was finally disposed of only in 1823, by Chief Justice Marshall in the case of *Johnson's Lessee* v. *McIntosh,* 8 Wheaton 543. The Camden-Yorke opinion was the best-known defense of the doctrine; Marshall realized that it referred only to India. Below in Chapter IV, especially note 69, will be discussed the important influence of this opinion of England's law officers on pre-Revolutionary land plans.

[33] *Records of the Proprietors of Worcester, Massachusetts,* edited by F. P. Rice (Worcester Society of Antiquity, 1881), 12. An almost exactly similar procedure is seen in the case of Waterbury, Connecticut, in 1673–1685. *Proprietors' Records* (Mattatuck Historical Society, 1911), 1.

cluded at a meeting of the Committee in Cambridge, July 6, 1669."

There were seventeen clauses in this formal agreement.[34] Lots were to be granted according to "the quality, estate, usefulness of the members and other considerations, in the discretion of the committee"—evidence of a centralization of management! There was provision for laying out highways, for clearings, for a common wood-lot, for a church. In clause 11 was this striking evidence of group consciousness: "It is ordered and concluded that all common charges that shall or may arise . . . such as purchase of the Indians, surveying of the towns and drawing a plat of it, laying out lots . . . or any other matter . . . conducing to the public welfare or good of the place, shall all be paid and provided for by a common stock raised upon the inhabitants in proportion according to their respective grants."[35] Late comers or purchasers were to pay their proportion of what had been spent prior to their settlement.[36]

[34] Worcester *Records*, 14 *ff*.   [35] *Ibid.*, 18.

[36] At the end of the articles, where settlers were all obliged to sign, was the following clause: "we do hereby engage and oblige ourselves, heirs, executors and assigns severally unto the said Committee and the honorable General Court and also each unto the other as we are and shall be inhabitants . . . and do declare that we have taken our respective house lots . . . according to the articles, agreement, orders and conditions before expressed and recorded in this book . . . and we do further engage and bind ourselves, our heirs, executors and assigns to perform and observe and keep our respective duties and covenants . . . in witness whereof we have set our hands, etc." Thus, the articles constituted a three-sided contract, (*a*) between the state, through its committee, and the settlers, (*b*) the settlers among themselves, and (*c*) less certainly between the corporate body and the settlers, especially the *later* settlers. This is the nature of the modern corporate charter, at least in the opinion of some. *Cf.* Berle, *Cases on Corporation Finance* (St. Paul, 1930), 3. The formal act of signing is strikingly suggestive of "signing the articles" in the large English unincorporated joint stock companies, upon becoming a member.

In the case of Waterbury, where bonus lots were offered to settlers, it was "always provided that such persons as shall be excepted [*sic*] to be free of the said allotment shall subscribe to the Articles formerly made." *Records,* 10. The use of a term common in English borough and gild practice—"to be free of"—is notable.

During this early period, the famed Hadley covenant[37] was created *prior* to confirmation of the grant by the general court. It had the same general character. It provided for the payment of costs incurred in acquiring the Indian title, required each signer to cultivate properly his share of land, and provided for the drawing of lots in the assignment of land. In case of failure to pay a share of the expenses or actually to settle in the town, the share involved would be forfeited. By the fifth clause of this agreement, no one could sell any land until he had actually lived in the town three years, and then to no one except "as the town shall approve on."

Legal informality was also the rule in making the allotment of land.[38] One phrase was "granted and laid out to so-and-so."[39] "By virtue of a grant" or "by order of" were also used. In a modern New York case[40] involving the validity of such informal grants, Chief Judge Cardozo upheld vigorously the practice, as had the courts of the New England states a century before: "Forms of alienation established by tradition must be given a significance consistent with the beliefs and expectations of those who brought them into being." But it was almost universal, at least prior to 1750, to require settlement on or cultivation of the land in order to validate the grant.[41] This attitude has been hailed as evidence

---

[37] 3 *Massachusetts Colonial Records,* section 1, 328.

[38] *Cf.* the statement in *Coburn* v. *Ellenwood,* 4 N.H. 99, *infra,* footnote 50.

[39] Worcester *Records,* 31.   [40] *Beers* v. *Hotchkiss,* 256 N.Y. 41.

[41] True in Worcester, Waterbury, Cambridge, Salem, Providence, Portsmouth, R. I., *inter alia.* There were, of course, varying requirements as to improvements and the time limit, which was often extended by vote if there had been an Indian uprising or some other untoward event. For record of an actual forfeit in 1680, *cf.* Waterbury's *Records,* 13.

Chief Judge Cardozo, in the case referred to in the preceding footnote, seems to be wrong in his estimate of this requirement. In the case at issue, he discarded proof of actual possession as immaterial to the validity of a disputed title to land on Long Island, originally land divided by a proprietorship among its members at the time of the Revolution. "There was no thought, we may be fairly sure, in the minds of the people of those days, in the minds of members of an unsettled and primitive community, that

of the "communistic" origin of the New England town. Less fancifully, it is to be regarded as a business principle, adopted to insure success for the whole settlement. Certainly it affected the practice of the eighteenth century land projects which were headed by New England men, and still later found embodiment in the national land policy.

The origin of the distinction between the body of proprietors and the body of the voters having political privileges has been of deep interest to historians.[42] The necessity for any distinction arose only in scattering instances before 1700. New immigration simply went to new locations, so that the original church-member proprietors and their descendants were the only inhabitants to become freemen. In scattered cases this was not true,[43] and there were resulting manifestations of exclusiveness on the part of the body of proprietors. Thus as early as 1635 Watertown passed its order that no "forreiner" coming into town should

immediate possession would be necessary to validate a title, except perhaps, the symbolical possession that comes from livery of seisin." As a generalization about the New England proprietorships, or even about Long Island proprietorships, this statement is hardly correct. Nor is it probably true that livery of seisin bothered the clerks, moderators, or "prudential committees" in confirming grants after 1700. James Sullivan, in *History of Land Titles* (Boston, 1801), 88, points out that "when the country was first settled, ceremony of livery of seisin was in use," but "the Law of 1642, in the Colony of Massachusetts, rendered it useless." In Maine it survived until 1692. But compare the stress laid upon "seisin and possession . . . and all acts of ownership" by the Lord Chancellor in 1750; *Penn* v. *Lord Baltimore,* 1 Vesey 444, at 451 and 453.

[42] *Cf.* Osgood, *op. cit.,* 467. The sharp cleavage between burgesses or freemen and ordinary inhabitants of English boroughs in the seventeenth century is well known. *Cf.* S. and B. Webb, 2 *English Local Government,* 292–302. The influence of Church membership upon the right to vote in the Puritan colonies must also be noted. J. T. Adams, *Founding of New England,* 162.

[43] In Salem there was a long controversy, ended in 1702 by the grant of freemen's privileges to a group who were technically "squatters" but who had been able to retain land enough to deserve the status of freemen. Disposition of remaining common land was by a majority vote in town meeting, however, so that the new group could not benefit by their voting status in securing more land. MacLear, *Early New England Towns,* 101 *ff.*

benefit by the commonage.[44] Ipswich in 1660 made a distinction between newcomers and proprietors. But as certain towns grew in importance because of their location or the rise of trades, the conflict became more serious. Until the conflict did arise, town meetings and proprietors' meetings were held at the same time and place, and the records were not differentiated.[45] But, curiously, some common land was owned by the town distinct from the undivided land belonging to proprietors. This seems to have resulted from forfeits or from later grants that the general court made to the town itself.[46]

By 1690, in many towns individuals questioned the right of the proprietors to grant a valid title to land. In both the Massachusetts and Connecticut legislatures this question came up for frequent discussion in the succeeding generation. Had the original grants been made to a body of petitioners in trust for all later inhabitants, or had it been made to these petitioners solely in their individual capacities? As early as 1692 Massachusetts confirmed the right of the body of proprietors to make grants, and after 1698 it was universal to find the proprietorship organized separately from the town. Finally, in 1713, a law was passed prescribing detailed rules for the calling of meetings of "proprietors lying in common." Five proprietors could apply to a Justice of Peace for authority and then call a meeting by issuing a notice fourteen days in advance. At the meeting a clerk was to be elected who would keep official records; future meetings would be called by whatever method the majority decided upon. The effect of this act is noticeable in various records after 1714.[47] They became

---

[44] "Except that they buy a man's right wholly in the town." 1 Watertown *Records*, 2 (Watertown, Mass., Historical Society, 1894).

[45] In some town records, notes on the margin or at the end of the minutes indicated the actions taken by the proprietors present, acting as such. Akagi, *op. cit.,* 160.

[46] *Cf.* MacLear, *op. cit.,* 93, 104–105.

[47] For example in Watertown, where the proprietors' book had nothing in it prior to that date, except a bare record of land allotments. 1 *Records,* 22.

more accurate, and in many cases a basic list of proprietors alive and in possession of their land was made a part of the 1714 minutes.[48] The later act of 1753[49] in Massachusetts repeated the formality of the earlier statute, except that it required that forty days' notice be published in Boston papers to care for the needs of the new Berkshire towns. Legislative recognition of a quasi-corporate status was then virtually complete. The courts in the early nineteenth century recognized that the proprietorship possessed such a status.[50] This course of events is clearly suggestive

[48] Akagi, *op. cit.*, 66, cites cases where everyone in possession of land at this time was accepted as a proprietor without further proof, because of the lack of adequate records.

[49] Many writers have thought this act to be the initial recognition by Massachusetts of the quasi-corporate status of the proprietorship.

[50] In *Proprietors of Monumoi Great Beach* v. *Rogers,* 1 Mass. 159 (1804), Judge Strong said: "This is a species of corporation different from corporations in general; this is intended to die; those to live forever. I make these observations to show that common law rules . . . do not apply in all instances to this kind of corporation. The Statutes [of 1713 and 1753] take away no rights . . . which, as tenants in common, they had before . . . but on the contrary give them new powers." He permitted validation of a land claim without written records of the proprietorship's existence.

An especially full statement was given by Chief Justice Richardson of New Hampshire in *Coburn* v. *Ellenwood,* 4 N.H. 99 (1827), as follows: "The original proprietors of our townships very early exercised certain corporate powers with respect to the management and disposal of their lands; and their successors have continued to exercise the same powers." He then referred to statutes providing for dues, for the sale at auction of delinquent shares, and for officers, regular meetings, etc.

"No statute is however to be found, in which they are expressly declared to be corporations.

"It is not now to be doubted that the proprietors of common and undivided lands are corporations; or that they can by vote authorize agents to make conveyances in their names; or that deeds properly executed by such agents may be valid to pass the estate."

In this case, interestingly enough, the court laid so much stress upon the informality of land allotment that it threw out a claim based upon an allotment where a deed had been expressly required in the vote of the meeting, which deed in proper form the clerk had failed to execute.

Connecticut had a similar controversy in 1703–1723. The result was an act of 1723 ordering town proprietors to organize separately, choose a clerk who would keep records, and by a majority vote dispose of their lands. An amendment provided for the same method of calling a first

of the gradual elevation of voluntary business associations to a formal corporate status by the general laws of the mid-nineteenth century.

A student who has examined a great many of the New England proprietorship records points out that after 1715 there was an "amazing degree of regularity" in their procedure and records.[51] The clerk often held office during his life-time and acted with a standing committee of three or five members which was instructed to "manage the prudential affairs of the proprietors." Frequently, also, there was a surveying committee. It is easy to conclude that these groups provided training in business procedure throughout New England.

Several other interesting characteristics of the proprietorship give evidence of its corporate character and may well have influenced current ideas of business organization. (a) In 1694 Massachusetts gave them the power to bring suits as a corporate body. (b) In 1727 the same state permitted them to levy fines and to pass by-laws. In her 1753 act, Massachusetts gave, in addition, specific authority to levy assessments on the membership for expenses. Prior to that time expenses had been met from the proceeds of land sales. (c) Restriction on sale of land by the members had an interesting history. Prior to 1659 Connecticut forbade sales to outsiders unless the town gave permission. By 1700, however, this reflection of religious exclusiveness seems to have disappeared.[52] As this prohibition waned, holdings of land became freely alienable, as shares of stock are today. (d) Absentee owners were frowned upon in many towns as late as 1725, but when Massachusetts began to dispose of her Berkshire lands, proprietorship rights were bought and sold speculatively in Boston and Hartford. Throughout the period 1750–1770 there is frequent record of such speculative transactions, apparently quite profit-

meeting as Massachusetts had prescribed. An act similar to these two was passed in 1718 in New Hampshire.

[51] Akagi, op. cit., 190. [52] Ibid., 78.

able.[53] In several instances agents were sent to New York to sell rights in newly created townships. Such absentee owners often became delinquent in contributing their share of initial expenses. In 1738 and 1739 Massachusetts passed two laws giving proprietorship groups the right to sell such shares at auction, pay the amount due out of the proceeds, and divide the "overplus" half to the town and half to the delinquent.[54] (e) Finally, there was clear delegation of authority in the group as it became stabilized. Sometimes this power was in the hands of the clerk, acting with the advice of committees. In other cases it was given directly to a small committee, especially where the proprietors were absentees.[55] Two moderators, elected in 1720 in Waterbury, were "to act jointly and severally as moderators to lead in the affairs of proprietary concerns in common lands." In 1754 the same proprietors appointed two legal agents, empowered to "commence any action or suit against any town or person, in behalf of the

[53] J. T. Adams develops this point carefully in his *Revolutionary New England* (Boston, 1923), 259–264.

More recently F. M. Woodard has presented detailed evidence of the speculative character of the Windsor proprietorship in Vermont in *Town Proprietors in Vermont* (New York, 1936). The project was "promoted" by Colonel Josiah Willard in 1760–1761, and 500 acres in the new town were reserved for Governor Benning Wentworth of New Hampshire as a willing coadjutor in making the grants for towns along the Connecticut River Valley. The charter was printed in blank, with spaces for later entry of names, number of shares, date of first meeting, officers, and exact boundaries (p. 50). Settlers were required to farm only 10 per cent of their holdings, and meetings of proprietors were always to be held separately from town meetings. For the first four years, proprietors' meetings were held elsewhere than Windsor, and only three of the original 59 proprietors ever settled there (p. 61). There were records of sales at five shillings per share, and of the 23 people who finally came to own the land within the town, only three were original petitioners (p. 64).

The same author, in tracing the history of Hyde Park, shows that of 38 proprietors, five were well-known New York speculators, and that by 1812 one man had come to own a large majority of the shares by purchase of those forfeited for non-payment of taxes (pp. 131–146). Governor Chittenden of Vermont is known to have been a participant in forty-two town grants in 1779–1781 (p. 130).

[54] Akagi, *op. cit.*, 216.   [55] 1 *Rhode Island Colonial Gleanings*, 32.

proprietors, that shall be thought necessary." Such agents had, several years previously, been authorized to represent the proprietors in suits against them. There was no legislative sanction for this action, so important in its implication of a corporate attitude on the part of the members.[56]

It was suggested above that there are some apparent links between the organization of the craft gild in England and the proprietorship as it functioned in the seventeenth and eighteenth centuries in New England. To advance such a statement is to enter upon the uncertain ground of historical speculation. Yet because discovery of the real roots of our present-day corporate structure is a goal of this study, some suggestive similarities ought to be summarized.

The annual meetings of the proprietorships were often no more than an annual feast, paid for out of the common treasury or by assessment on the members. Many proprietorship records in later years contain principally the record of expense of these annual affairs.[57] The analogy to the well-known practice of the craft gilds is obvious.

Attendance was compulsory in the early proprietorships, and fines were levied for non-attendance.[58] Of course this was the practice also in the seventeenth century chartered corporations, and its adoption there has been traced to the gild.[59] Interestingly enough, this attitude disappeared slowly among the towns, and after 1700 is seldom met with in proprietorship records.

The most curious link with English prototypes is the use of the term "bachelors' rights" in Connecticut towns,[60] where very small lots were sold or given to new settlers. This is the term which was applied originally to indentured servants of English gild members; they remained unmarried for a term of years. Later it came to mean simply a younger group, possessing the

---

[56] Waterbury *Records*, 97, 185.   [57] Akagi, *op. cit.*, 205.
[58] For the case of Salem before 1680, *cf.* MacLear, *op. cit.*, 91.
[59] 8 Holdsworth, *H.E.L.*, 194.   [60] *E.g.*, Waterbury.

"freedom of the gild" but with other rights less than those of full members. Often they were young sons of members, being groomed for later membership in the ruling oligarchy, a sort of Junior Chamber of Commerce.[61] They married freely, but the term "bachelor" remained in common usage to connote "junior member." Quite clearly it was used in this same sense in New England towns.

Especially in the thirty years just prior to the Revolution, the proprietorship functioned as a business unit for the profitable distribution of a land grant, and not solely as a social instrument to aid settlement. Members who actually took up residence on the grant were also interested in the profit motive, because there were always large areas left undivided when a new town was laid out. Much more so were the absentee owners, who either joined a petitioning group or purchased an interest solely to resell their shares at an advance. The town proprietorship presents the primary example of organization with which the average citizen throughout New England had contact. It was in reality a corporation. It possessed "corporateness" long before legislatures or courts conceded the point. Upon what stronger ground could Revolutionary business leaders, in the New England area at least, rest a contention that a charter was unnecessary, except for a monopoly or a special privilege?

THE PROPRIETARY COLONIES

For a few land projects prior to the Revolution, the organization of the proprietary Colonies both for conducting the business of selling land and for carrying on effective government was also a model upon which to pattern. In particular, it is clear that the Henderson schemes and the Vandalia scheme, to be discussed below,[62] were both based almost entirely upon proprietary principles. This is not surprising, because in the Carolinas and Pennsylvania the lawyers and the governing class were naturally

[61] *Cf.* Unwin, *op. cit.,* 25.   [62] Pp. 90–97, 119–122.

familiar with their own form of government—because of the numerous political quarrels that occurred, if for no other reason.

The peculiarities of this form of Colonial government derive from the institution of medieval palatines.[63] Why the Stuart kings resorted to it for the government of the middle colonies has never been fully explained. It is, of course, well known that in the charters of Maryland, New York, and Carolina there was specific mention of the old rights of the Bishop of Durham. The charter granted to William Penn did not mention Durham specifically, but its wording was practically the same as the others. The original grant of these powers was believed in Stuart times to have been forced by the exigencies of the defense in the north.[64] It has been suggested that these Colonial charters were granted at the time when the Stuart kings were anxious to exalt the Crown.[65] They cast about to discover a form of grant which would embody the medieval ideas of feudal authority, as contrasted with the ideas of self-government flaunted by the New England corporate colonies, and would assure the proprietor vice-regal powers. Furthermore, they were dealing (in New York) with conquered territory and elsewhere with territory where there might be danger of French, Spanish, or Indian aggression. The county palatine was the form of grant ideally suited to both these conditions. It was analogous to the modern "buffer state," since the palatinate powers were far more extensive than in any other feudal fiefs created by the English Crown. In Durham the Bishop was a feudal sovereign:[66] all land was held

[63] The best comparative study of the proprietaries, free from tedious detail, is that in Osgood, 2 *American Colonies in the Seventeenth Century*.

[64] Lapsley, in his *County Palatine* (New York, 1900), denies this, and states that the powers of the bishopric originated in Anglo-Saxon times and were simply confirmed by the Conqueror; but in the seventeenth century the accepted explanation of its origin was that given above.

[65] Goebel, *Some Legal and Political Aspects of the Manors in New York* (Baltimore, 1928), 4–5.

[66] The process by which the Bishop's tenure was declared to be feudal rather than ecclesiastical in nature, as early as 1088, is described in Chap-

directly from him; he possessed full seignorial rights; land was escheated to him rather than to the King upon convictions for treason.[67] In addition he possessed the usual royal claims over forests, mines, shipwrecks, and discoveries of treasure. The various officials were similar to those of the King, and there was an entirely separate judicial system. Separate chancery courts, for example, existed in Durham as early as the fourteenth century. The Bishop could coin money, issue writs and commissions, grant charters of incorporation, and grant full pardons. Councils called by him were empowered to levy and collect taxes.[68] Henry VIII, as part of his program of centralization, took over the judicial systems of Chester and Durham,[69] and invited both these palatines to send representatives to the English Parliament; Chester did so, but the Bishop of Durham sent none until 1675. Despite this Tudor effort to trim away judicial power from Durham, in the charter given to Lord Baltimore (which became the model for later charters) we find him possessed of full power to appoint a judiciary.

The revival of the palatinate in its original form could not help but arouse the ambitions of courtiers of Charles I, and create the desire to secure similar grants in the Colonies. Just so would a man of Richard Henderson's type[70] in 1765 enviously look back to the charters of the seventeenth century[71] as the model for his own ambitious Kentucky scheme.

ter II of G. B. Adams, *Council and Courts in Anglo-Norman England* (New York, 1912).

[67] Lapsley, *op. cit.*, 41, 54, 55.

[68] For descriptive reference to all these palatinate powers, in the order set forth above, *cf.* Lapsley, *op cit.*, 58, 162, 187–189, 35, 70, 151–152.

[69] *Ibid.*, 196–198.   [70] *Cf. infra*, p. 90.

[71] From the point of view taken here, the Carolina charter is of especial interest. In that case the grant of powers to govern, as well as to possess and sell the land, was made to eight separate individuals. 1 *North Carolina Colonial Records*, 20 *ff.* This was an extremely important change from the idea of granting governmental powers to one individual, such as the Bishop of Durham or Lord Baltimore. It is important, furthermore, because the eight individuals were not incorporated in any way. There was

The charter granted to the Duke of York in 1662 was in form similar to those given earlier. The grant to William Penn, as the last of the four principal proprietary domains, included some revisions giving more power to the home government; it thus reflects the changing situation under Charles II after 1675. Notable in the Pennsylvania charter are the expressly reserved rights of Parliament to collect taxes from the new colony,[72] and the reserved right to review all colonial acts and approve or reject them within five years.[73]

The grants made to the various proprietors were personal in nature, so that all holdings of land were derived from the proprietors,[74] not from a so-called popular assembly such as the Massachusetts general court. Furthermore, all political rights existed by virtue of the permission of the proprietor rather than by any free determination within the group. It is quite obvious how important the projectors of speculative colonies after 1750 would feel this difference to be. They desired to retain not only the rights of possession but also the right to control political expression within their domain.

But during the years of active experience with proprietary government in the middle colonies, substantial changes were occurring. The familiar English process of encroachment by the legislature on the rights and powers of the executive had been actively under way. The long and tedious process of bickering in the various legislatures occupies a constant place in the politi-

no limitation upon the right of these eight men to sell or bargain away their power to govern, any more than there was doubt cast upon their power to sell land. Throughout the charter "assigns" was inserted after the names of the group, as well as "heirs and executors." How important this free right of alienation of the governing power became is well illustrated in the familiar history of East and West Jersey. 1 *New Jersey Archives*, 332, 375 *ff.*

[72] 2 Osgood, *op. cit.*, 12.   [73] *Ibid.*, 11.

[74] "The granting of land and the regulation of its settlement were primarily functions not of township, county, or the general assembly . . . but were entirely those of the Lord Proprietor." Mereness, *Maryland As a Proprietary Province* (New York, 1901), 50.

cal history of these colonies. Consequently, when the imitators of the proprietaries came to work out their own schemes they were found willing to grant initially large power to the popularly elected legislative bodies. They were more interested, for the most part, in retaining full control over the sale of land than in permanently retaining any governmental power. The business aspect of a Crown grant had become the more important.[75]

Certain specific characteristics of the proprietary colonies require some comment. Making the grant to individuals opened the way for resales at will. The practice of selling part of the grant, much as shares of stock could be sold, did not appear in the case of Maryland or Pennsylvania, but, as has already been indicated, it was an outstanding characteristic of the Carolina and Jersey holdings.[76] Knowledge of this possibility of subdivision made the proprietary idea much more attractive to later land speculators. In the case of East Jersey, for example, the number of proprietors was almost immediately increased to twenty-four by sales of shares.[77] It seems quite certain that the eight proprietors of Carolina might have divided up their holdings by sales; as Osgood says, "The undivided shares might at any time have become divided shares."[78]

[75] Cf. Bond, *Quit Rent System in the American Colonies* (New Haven, 1919), *passim;* and also Mereness, *op. cit.,* ch. 2. It is interesting to note the optimism with which individuals in the colonies began their efforts to secure proprietary grants from the Crown. They seemed to rely on the fact that new colonies so created would play a part in the defense of English territory from French aggression. This was stressed especially by the projectors of the 1748 Ohio Company and later by Richard Henderson. Defense had been the primary reason for the creation of palatinates on the borders of England. But the projectors seemed to forget that all the American grants had been made only to individuals or groups who were either close to a Stuart king or to whom he was obligated. Furthermore, the possible business value of a new proprietary grant in these cases was far greater than any defensive value which they might possess.

[76] 2 Osgood, *op. cit.,* 17–18.

[77] The deed from Elizabeth Carteret and the trustees for Sir George's estate to twelve proprietors, in 1681, is found in 5 *New Jersey Archives,* 366. These twelve took in twelve others in full partnership.

[78] 2 Osgood, *op. cit.,* 19.

Especially in the case of Pennsylvania, many varied sorts of land offers to settlers were made by the proprietors.[79] This flexibility in the handling of the granted territory probably appealed strongly to the later groups. In Maryland several so-called manors were erected, some of which were reserved for the proprietor himself. There was thus apparent a literal interpretation of the full power of the proprietor to create holdings in the feudal manner if he so desired.[80]

Finally, it is important to note that proprietary government, by its character, tended to favor grants to individuals rather than any grants to groups of settlers. This was in diametric opposition to the influence exerted by the New England corporate colonies. The use of the proprietary model was therefore adapted to a system of direct sales to incoming settlers, in such a region as Richard Henderson acquired in Kentucky. Inherent in the nature of the proprietary grant, of course, was the conception of a special privilege. The late Tudor and early Stuart practice has already been described as a political control over the grant of corporate charters, a subordination of economic considerations to the aims of state policy. The great chartered trading and colonizing corporations, and the patents to Lord Baltimore and other proprietors, were thus twin survivals of Elizabethan or Stuart methods, existing side by side. Both lent re-enforcement to the idea that for *special* business privileges a governmental grant was essential, in sharp contrast to an opposed stream of popular thought—that any group of business men could associate freely

[79] Shepherd, *Proprietary Government in Pennsylvania* (New York, 1896), 47, note 1, and 75.

[80] In Carolina, in the original plan of settlement of 1665, there were to be "seignories" of 72,000 acres, "landgraves" of 48,000 acres, and "caciques" of 24,000 acres. There was elaborate designation of powers and privileges belonging to these feudal units. Better testimony could hardly be found to demonstrate the power of the idea of a palatinate to survive through several centuries of governmental centralization and abolition of feudal prerogatives. *Cf.* Smith, *South Carolina as a Royal Province* (New York, 1903), 35.

and, just as freely, could participate in any lawful business anywhere. Practical realization of this doctrine was one phase of the
triumph of *laissez faire*. But men of the nineteenth century who
actually succeeded in securing the privilege of free incorporation as a matter of right could look back to an early manifestation of the same spirit—the creation of town proprietorships in
New England with virtually no legislative interference or supervision. The New England example taught the lesson of freedom
in economic organization, just as the proprietary grants taught
the opposed and to-be-discarded lesson that charter grants were
to be reserved for the few.

III

COLONIAL BUSINESS ORGANIZATION

APART from forms of organization known to them in political or social relationships, projectors of land companies could turn to the ordinary framework of commercial activity in the colonies. It is true, of course, that such a man as Richard Henderson[1] would probably have had only indirect contact with merchants, belonging rather to the lawyer-officeholder group in the Carolinas. It is even more certain that the leaders of the later Ohio Company or of the Connecticut Land Company were primarily drawn from the agricultural population. But a majority of the companies with which we are concerned were molded and directed by men from the merchant class in the larger cities or the trading group in the smaller towns. What direct experience did these men possess out of which they could fashion, independent of any charter grants, effective companies functioning as corporate bodies?

The sharp advance in relative importance of the individual merchant and of ordinary partnerships in trade from the beginning to the end of the eighteenth century can hardly be overstressed. The chartered corporation, in England and America, was in eclipse. This was due fundamentally to the rise of free trade, symbolized best by the overthrow of the Merchant Adventurers at the end of the seventeenth century.[2] A secondary influence was the Bubble Act. More will be said at a later point in this chapter of this decline of the corporation in England which was reflected in the Colonies. Partnership was even more markedly the dominant form of enterprise in the last half of the eighteenth century in the Colonies, where the importance of import and export trading naturally favored it, than it was in

---

[1] For his background and training, see *infra,* p. 90.
[2] Lipson, 2 *Economic History of England,* 265–266.

England. But, even in England, for one East India Company there were scores of individuals trading in areas or in goods formerly controlled by regulated companies;[3] for one body of Hostmen in the Newcastle coal trade there was a score of independent coal mine owners scattered over the kingdom. For one Mines Royal and Mineral and Battery Works,[4] there were scores of independent ferrous and non-ferrous metal mining establishments under the direction of individual entrepreneurs or partnerships.

The business classes of Boston, New York, Philadelphia, Charleston, and smaller cities were merchants or combined merchant-manufacturers operating on a small scale. Since the disappearance of the joint stock enterprises, so popular for colonizing purposes, the circumstances of Colonial economic growth had overwhelmingly favored them. The simultaneous decline in popularity in England of all regulated companies and of monopolies possessed by joint stock companies very nearly freed Colonial enterprise from the heavy hand of chartered monopolies in trade, so long a handicap to the more able entrepreneurs in England. There thus grew up a class of men who for selfish reasons were ready to oppose monopoly grants to corporations or small groups—until of course they could participate in or benefit by such grants as a result of their influence in the legislatures of newly-independent states.[5] But until 1790 the business classes

[3] Thus not only the Merchant Adventurers before 1700, but the Eastland Company (1673), the African Company (1698), the French and Spanish Companies (before 1675), and the Russia Company (1699), all lost exclusive privileges in trade and the right to exclude "interlopers," or independent merchants, before the beginning of the eighteenth century. They were all regulated companies, not joint stock enterprises. *Ibid.*, 315–366.

[4] These pioneer chartered corporations, dating from the middle of Elizabeth's reign, combined in 1663; they lost their monopoly of copper mining in 1689. *Ibid.*, 176.

[5] Descriptions of the American business community in the last thirty years of the eighteenth century abound with references to partnerships existent not only in commerce but in the small manufacturing undertakings associated with sea trade or basic commodities. Thus, according to Free-

certainly favored small-scale, individualistic enterprise; and on this ground supported the cause of independence, though on a purely political basis. They could be opposed to violent revolution or to the relaxation of English authority over the Colonies.[6]

The dominant partnership form was closely associated in Colonial business with two variations which must be briefly noticed. One was joint ownership of property, occurrent without concomitant partnership obligations or relationships. This was frequently seen in the ownership of ships,[7] but appeared occasionally in the control of other property. It represented no progress toward the corporate conception of unitary control over capital contributed by many, since questions of policy beyond the original agreement were almost non-existent. Closely analogous to these joint ownerships was the typical method of joint subscription in insurance underwriting.[8]

man Hunt, *Lives of American Merchants* (New York, 1858), many individuals spent their early business careers in such enterprises; in nearly every case their connection with corporations, as late as 1825, was incidental and entirely subordinate to other activities. *Cf.* 1 *ibid.,* at 139: "Merchants . . . of moderate fortunes engaged in branches of business which it was thought in Europe could only be safely carried on by great chartered companies, under the protection of government monopolies."

Similarly, in Ritter, *Philadelphia and Her Merchants* (Philadelphia, 1860), and Barrett (pseud.), *The Old Merchants of New York City* (5 vols., New York, 1862), there is confirmatory evidence. *Cf.* in the latter work, especially vol. 1, 85, 255, 331; vol. 3, 131, 154; vol. 5, 69.

[6] The influence of this factor in rallying many of the merchant class in the seaboard cities to the Revolutionary cause has been stressed by most historians. J. T. Adams, in his chapter on "Big Business" in *Revolutionary New England* (Boston, 1923), stretches the existing evidence to portray the emergence of nineteenth century modes of thought and action in the business classes after 1760. A. M. Schlesinger analyzes this whole situation in his *Colonial Merchants and the Revolution* (New York, 1918).

[7] An excellent description of this method of financing ship construction is found in Lucy S. Sutherland, *A London Merchant, 1695–1774* (London, 1933), *passim.* The joint owners typically leased the completed vessel to trading merchants or to the East India Company. The law was willing to treat such organizations as tenancies in common of real property.

[8] Quaint phrasing describes insurance as it was conducted in England in 1601 (cited by Lipson, *op. cit.,* vol. 2, 195): "It hath been time out of mind an usage amongst merchants both of this realm and of foreign na-

The concept of a joint adventure was a very early shift of emphasis in partnership relations, and this is the important point to be considered here. The joint adventure as patterned on the *commenda* model of the later Middle Ages is commonly accepted as a forerunner of joint stock companies both in England and on the Continent.[9] The *commenda* arose in the shipping trade of the Mediterranean, where risks were great and where there was need for concentration of managerial power, both in the initiation of the enterprise and in its later conduct by the captain during the voyage;[10] the supercargo became in later centuries the agent pos-

tions, when they make any great adventure (specially into remote parts) to give some consideration of money to other persons (which commonly are in no small number) to have from them assurance made of their goods, merchandises, ships, and things adventured, or some part thereof, at such rates and in such sort as the parties assurers and the parties assured can agree, which course of dealing is commonly termed a policy of assurance." Sixteenth century underwriting in England, according to the historians of Lloyd's, "was not a specialized business." Merchants took shares in policies through brokers who were often the same men who acted as agents in the disposition of cargoes. Candelen's patent for a monopoly of registration of policies as a means of reducing fraud was granted in 1574 and was partially effective for a century, with the aid of the Court of Assurances. Neither the registration system nor the Court was popular, and both disappeared in 1688–1689 following a century of public or registered policies. By 1700 the writing of policies was as private and individualistic as it had been in 1550, and Lloyd's finally appeared to fill the need of some mode of organization. Private underwriting was strengthened by the terms of the act incorporating the Royal Exchange and the London Assurance Companies, which never in the first decades of their existence did more than 10 per cent of the business. *Cf.* Wright and Fayle, *History of Lloyd's* (London, 1928), 35–42, 63–65.

In Boston in 1789, insurance was "an affair of individual adventure, in which in the then existing paucity of investments, private underwriters engaged." Hunt, 1 *American Merchants,* 140.

[9] For the orthodox statement of this "blood relationship," *cf.* Max Weber, *General Economic History,* 223–229.

[10] Richard C. McKay, in his breezy maritime history of New York, *South Street* (New York, 1934), speaking of the frequent gatherings of merchants at taverns to mix pleasure with business, says (p. 22): "The master or other officer of the ship . . . would be included in the gathering, because at that time shipmasters and supercargoes often owned a share in the vessel and were also the business managers: they not only paid the

sessing full power when a return cargo had to be secured on the spot. The joint adventure persisted in the shipping trade for centuries,[11] and was a typical feature of colonial trade prior to and after the Revolution.[12] Participants had no more control over their "share" than a modern stockholder. But commercial voyages were always temporary and specific in character unless they were coupled with a monopoly of trade in a certain area such as were in later days possessed by the great chartered companies. Shipping alone could never become a really fertile field for continuously functioning bodies of a corporate character. On the Continent and in England, coal and metal mining were the earliest stimuli to the development of true joint enterprise along the lines of the modern corporation; on the Continent this source-relationship is of especial interest here because many such enterprises were established, and operated for many years, without charters.[13] They exhibited those qualities of continuity, delega-

running expenses of the ship, but bought and sold the cargoes. . . . The profit of the owner depended to a considerable degree on the shrewdness and honesty of these men. . . ."

[11] Early judicial familiarity with the joint adventure principle is clearly demonstrated in an English case of 1704 dealing with salvaging expeditions on the joint account of four men. The executors of the Duke of Albermarle alleged that a third trip had been entered into (and had resulted in losses) without his consent. The court held him bound—"in all sea-adventures the act of the majority of the part-owners concludes the rest" —despite any incidental covenants to the contrary. Recovery from the Duke's executors for his share of the loss was ordered. *Falkland* v. *Cheney*, 5 Brown's Cases in Parliament 476.

[12] Thus Hunt, *op. cit.*, at 146, speaks of "the practice, at that time very general on the part of persons not engaged in trade, of sending what were called adventures. This was done . . . by all classes of the community— by professional men, by females, and by minors. . . ."

[13] Jacob Strieder, foremost student of mining enterprise as the cradle of modern capitalism, says: "The mediaeval ancestors of our nineteenth and twentieth century captain of industry are not really to be found among the Italian entrepreneurs. They are to be sought rather in the Germany of the late fifteenth and early sixteenth centuries, whose capitalists controlled the flourishing mining industry. . . ." "Origin of Early European Capitalism," 2 *Journal of Economic and Business History*, 16 (1930).

tion of authority, and "side-issue" relationship of the furnishers of capital which have previously been described[14] as the earmarks of the true corporate body in the business sense.

Where in the American Colonies are such associations to be found? Land companies, the subject of inquiry here, are the prime examples. But before turning to a description of them, a small number of early undertakings may be described, for to a greater or less extent they exhibited the essential qualities which mark the break away from partnership. Examples of this sort, occurring before 1750, are of particular value in contrasting the true association on the one hand with the prevalent commercial partnership of the seventeenth and eighteenth centuries, and on the other hand with the chartered corporation. The attempts of men to secure the business benefits of a close-knit association *sans* charter can be observed in these instances. The characteristics which were later to mark the association as a distinctive form of business organization are present in varying degrees. Intentionally, the undertakings selected for discussion are widely diverse in nature; collectively, the evidence is thus more convincing. The paucity of preserved descriptive material narrows the range of choice.

THE LYNN IRON WORKS

The Lynn Iron Works of 1645[15] preceded by more than one hundred years the date chosen here as marking the beginning of intensive business expansion in the Colonies. In this case, there hardly can be said to have been any real development of a corpo-

---

[14] Chapter I, *supra,* note 2.

[15] It must not be inferred from the selection of this enterprise that it was the *earliest* business undertaking with group characteristics. Aside from the chartered companies, two earlier instances (at least) of unincorporated bodies actively engaged in business projects are historically familiar. (1) In 1616–1617, members of the Virginia Company participated in the "Society of Particular Adventures for Traffique with them of Virginia in a joint stock"; this was familiarly known as the "Magazine." It had no separate charter, but was organized with a director and five committees, with pen-

rate body. Yet the project illustrates the Colonial attitude in the first half of the seventeenth century toward development schemes, much more suggestive of the monopoly-grant concept than of the voluntary association of the next century.

A group of London merchants, organized by John Winthrop, Jr.,[16] and Captain Robert Bridges of the Bay Colony, secured from the Massachusetts general court on October 15, 1645, a twenty-one-year monopoly of iron making and of the management of all iron mines then known or thereafter to be discovered.[17] They did not secure a charter from the Crown at any time, although there was probably an effort made in this direction. Obviously the disturbed civil conditions in England stood in the way of success.

There were two interesting provisions attached to the monopoly grant. One was that there must be actual production of

alties for those delinquent in subscriptions. 1 *Records of the Virginia Company*, 238, 244, and vol. 2, 305; also Scott, 2 *Joint Stock Companies*, 256–258. The "Undertakers for the Plantation of the Somers Island" (Bermuda) was a similar sub-venture, from 1612 to 1615; a second Bermuda adventure was begun in 1617 after the division of land. 2 Scott, 260–264. (2) When the Massachusetts Bay Company decided to move to the colony, three trustees took over the trading rights and certain property, to be managed for the benefit of the members in England who had contributed. Apparently Winthrop, who was to act as one of the managing trustees, neglected the enterprise after he reached Boston; although some concessions were granted, no accounting was ever rendered to the supposed beneficiaries in England. Osgood, 1 *American Colonies*, 147–150.

[16] In *Massachusetts Historical Society Collections*, 5th Series, vol. 8, at 36, is reprinted a petition of Winthrop to Parliament in 1643 for £1,000 compensation for the loss of a ship which had started for Boston loaded with supplies and men for the undertaking. Not until the next year did he commence negotiations with the general court. Evidently the group backing him had already been organized at this time. The whole project is sketchily described by N. M. Hawkes, "The First Iron Works in America," 22 *Magazine of American History*, 404 ff. Much original material relating to the project as it was continued after 1650 is preserved in the Business Historical Society Library, Harvard University.

[17] Hawkes, *op. cit.*, 407. The "answers" of the court to Winthrop's petitions, and the rules governing the undertaking, are in 2 *Massachusetts Colonial Records*, at 61, 81, 125, and 185.

iron within three years, the other was that freemen of Massachusetts must be allowed to become "Adventurers with the Undertakers" by purchasing shares in units of not less than fifty
pounds. One thousand pounds was named in the act as the original capital contributed by the "Undertakers."[18] Most of the other
provisions in the act sound strangely like privileges given to public utilities at the end of the eighteenth century. There was first a
grant of land made in six different places in the Colony, to be
selected by the adventurers as areas most likely to contain iron.[19]
Three square miles was the maximum allotted in each of these
areas.

From free or waste land in the Colonies wood or other material
to build dams could be taken at will. The right of eminent domain was granted if the land needed had already been pre-
empted by settlers. Its valuation was to be determined by three
"indifferent men,"[20] one selected by the general court, one by the
land owner, and one by the adventurers. The stock of goods for
merchants was to be free from all "taxation, assessments, contributions, and other public charges."[21]

For a period of twenty-one years the members were to be free
from militia duty and were to be given equal rights with the freemen of the Colony. Most interesting was the added clause that
the adventurers and the employees should be treated on an equality with freemen by the laws of the church congregations in the
Colony![22] Perhaps in return for these privileges, the owners were
required to provide a means whereby the iron workers and their
families could be instructed in the knowledge of God, if any
mines were located at a remote place. A final clause in the act

[18] Quite certainly this represented the loss in 1643 for the redress of
which Winthrop had unsuccessfully petitioned Parliament.

[19] Marsh or bog land was then the typical source of iron.

[20] 2 *Massachusetts Colonial Records*, 61.   [21] *Ibid.*

[22] One more bit of evidence for the historians of the "Religious State"
in Massachusetts!

permitted iron to be shipped abroad, with no export duty; no shipments were to be made to hostile countries.

A diary of John Winthrop for the winter of 1644–1645 describes his travels through the Colony seeking potential ore sources.[23] His uncertainty obviously led to the request for power to select sites at will at a later time in the general court's grant. It is known only that actual production was undertaken in Saugus, on a part of the famous Hawkes farm. A pile of "tailings" is still distinguishable at a point on the Saugus River a short distance from Lynn (whence the project derives its name).[24] Some ore was also taken from a district within the present town of Nahant.

Two letters from the "undertakers" in England to Winthrop,[25] written in 1645 and 1647, are in each case signed by all of the nine men concerned. But in the later letter four new partners appear, indicating a turnover of 45 per cent in the membership in less than two years. Several of these men were later prominent in the Colony, notably Richard Child. The first letter introduced one Richard Leader as the manager of the whole project, to whom Winthrop was to give an "accompt" of his expenditures and work up to that time, and from whom he would receive a receipt discharging him in full from responsibility. The second letter expressed concern over their fortunes, and with the poor quality of the workers who were willing to emigrate. It was devoutly hoped that the unruly group then being shipped over would be "cured of their distempers" after a period of residence in New England. A year later, 1648, a letter from Leader to his friend Winthrop intimated that he was about to quit his post.[26] Operations were suspended by the original group in 1649 or 1650. The later his-

---

[23] Reprinted, partly in Latin, in 8 *Proceedings of the Massachusetts Historical Society,* Series 2, 4 ff.

[24] 22 *Magazine of American History,* 411.

[25] Printed in 8 *Proceedings of the Massachusetts Historical Society,* Series 2, 15–16.

[26] 3 *ibid.,* 192.

tory of mining in the same location is interesting, but not of direct importance here.

THE FREE SOCIETY OF TRADERS[27]

This society was sponsored by William Penn in the first flush of idealism at the start of his colonization efforts, in 1682. It corresponded in general purpose to the many independent trading projects which the members of the Virginia Company sponsored in the first few years of that effort,[28] but it was to be open to ordinary settlers in the Colony, whereas in Virginia only members of the parent company could participate. It was intended as a stimulus to land settlement as well as to trade in necessary commodities. At a meeting of the "governor and freemen" of the Colony in England in May, 1682, the articles were "ratified," and the initial organization was established.[29] It was not a monopolistic body, but possession of a technical charter from Penn (though this was never confirmed) made it closely resemble a corporation.

The articles as Penn announced them provided in the preamble for this initial meeting of May 29, 1682, and for subsequent annual meetings in November. Members of the society could vote by mail if unable to be present. After the proposed removal to the Colony, stockholders who were residents of England could have only one vote irrespective of their total interest. If, however, they owned at least one thousand acres in the Colonies, they could vote in proportion to their investment up to a maximum of three votes for an investment of £300. It was intended to have the meetings in Philadelphia as soon as the Colony got

---

[27] The articles of agreement and a brief description of this organization are to be found in 5 *Pennsylvania Magazine of History and Biography,* 41 *ff.* It is referred to in most of the histories of Penn's colony. *Cf.* Scharf and Westcott, *History of Philadelphia* (Philadelphia, 1884). Davis, in 1 *Essays in the Earlier History of American Corporations* (Cambridge, 1917), 41–45, gives a careful summary of its activities.

[28] Scott, 2 *Joint Stock Companies,* 256–257.

[29] 1 *Pennsylvania Colonial Records,* 40.

under way. The minimum subscription was to be £25; this could be split into five parts, but one person only would be accepted as the voting holder of the share. Five per cent was to be paid in on the subscriptions. Clearly, popular subscription was to be encouraged.

Management of the project was to be in the hands of twelve men and the president, who would thus have a deciding vote. The appointed treasurer as well as the president were required to own either 5,000 acres of Pennsylvania land or at least £100 of the society's stock. They were to serve for seven years, but could be dismissed at any annual meeting for good cause. Declaration of dividends or the undertaking of any projects had to be approved by a meeting of the "court" of stockholders. The books were to be closed every seven years, at which time there was to be a re-subscription for a similar term of years.[30] No mining could be undertaken without the approval of the Pennsylvania assembly. Finally it was provided that, upon failure of a member to pay his later installments, his share could be transferred to a new buyer, apparently with no provision for refund of his original 5 per cent payment.

Independently of the charter, Penn donated to the society 100 acres in Philadelphia and 20,000 acres in the country, the latter carrying with it the early manor privileges.[31] Mining, the fur trade, and encouragement of emigration were immediately established as objectives. In 1683 and 1684 a number of cargoes of commodities were shipped over at a profit, and some small mills were erected. Total capital subscribed had been £5,400, of which 5 per cent was presumably paid in during the summer of 1682.

[30] Obviously an imitation of the early practice in the East India Company.

[31] *Cf.* Scharf and Westcott, *op. cit.,* 89. These privileges included three members of the council (which had a total membership of 72), power to levy taxes in its own area, privilege of court-baron and court-leet, view of frankpledge, two justices' courts a year, a three-fifths claim over all ordinary minerals discovered, and the right to establish fairs and markets.

Trouble began in 1683 with the failure of the Colonial assembly to confirm Penn's charter. In later years suits were brought against the officers rather than against the company, and its land was held by trustees;[32] thus both its enemies and its officers seemed to agree that it had no corporate existence, and was merely carrying on as a private association. For five years after 1684, its history was a story of bickering among the officers, with the assembly, and with Penn at home. The capital was quickly exhausted, suits were instituted to collect accounts, and gradually all activity was suspended. In 1721, thirty-five years later, the assembly passed an act authorizing dissolution and directing the distribution of the assets.[33] Governor Keith appointed trustees who carried this out.

THE FRANKFORT COMPANY[34]

This was a land settlement project in Penn's colony at about the same period as the Free Society of Traders. It is of unusual interest because it included features derived from German and Austrian practice; it also affords comparison with the structure of later eighteenth century companies, to be examined below. The articles of agreement were signed by twelve men as a private contract, but a copy was filed in the public records of Frankfort in accordance with the continental legal rules governing such voluntary associations;[35] twelve copies were made for the signers.

The descriptive terminology used in the articles was derived from the older German and Austrian mining ventures first known to have existed in the late fifteenth century.[36] There were

[32] Davis, op. cit., 44.

[33] 3 Pennsylvania Colonial Records, 138.

[34] Described by Pennypacker in his Settlement of Germantown (Philadelphia, 1899), 21–52, and much less satisfactorily in "Articles of Agreement of the Frankfort Company," 15 Pennsylvania Magazine of History and Biography, 205 ff.

[35] Infra, p. 70.

[36] Cf. Strieder, Zur Geschichte Kapitalistischer Organisationsformen (Munich, 1925), 13–52; for a discussion of mining shares and organiza-

to be five "main-stem" divisions of 5,000 acres, each of which could in turn be broken up into small parts by later sales. Each of these "stems" had an elected head officer known as the "stem-head." In their hands rested the full power of management. The term "stems" had been general in Germany in the preceding century in mining enterprises.

The idea of a purchase of land from Penn originated with a religious group in Frankfort associated with Spener's College of Pietists. In 1683 Pastorius, then in London, purchased for the group 15,000 acres of land from Penn, later increased to 25,000.[37] The original group of twelve, largely teachers or ministers, decided not to emigrate, and instead decided to attempt small sales of the land to associates or members of the same group in Frankfort. The agreement constituting the Frankfort Company was signed in November, 1686; their interests varied from 833 acres up to 4,000 acres apiece.[38]

Clause 1 declared that all property, including chattels, "shall now and hereafter be and remain common in Equal Right according to everyone's above specified share." Expenses and profits were to be similarly divided, according to the next following clauses. The fourth clause placed the powers of management in the hands of the "stem-heads," five in number, one for each five hundred acres. An agent and attorney, and a substitute for him, were to be appointed to reside in Pennsylvania and report annually in two duplicate copies, to be sent on separate boats. In Frankfort, there were to be two paid clerks to care for correspondence, who might or might not be members of the company as well. Under direction of the "stem-heads" they were to keep records, but all matters of importance had to be approved in a

tion in the Middle Ages, cf. the article "Kux" in Adrian Beier, *Allgemeines Handlungs-Kunst-Berg und Handwerks Lexicon* (Jena, 1722).

[37] Pennypacker, *op. cit.*, 23.

[38] The agreement is reprinted by Pennypacker in translation, *op. cit.*, 32, 34. A copy of the original is in the library of the Historical Society of Pennsylvania.

meeting. A subscriber desiring to emigrate could secure sixty city acres for each one-hundred-acre share owned. He could secure sixty more on favorable terms, and was to be given preference in using the company's common property (if any).

A seal was to be designed and used and a duplicate of it sent to America; this seal apparently was of the same importance for transactions as would have been the case with a chartered corporation in England at this time, despite the absence of any direct governmental sanction for the organization. Another extremely interesting provision was one that made the shares of any member dying intestate revert to the society, according to the familiar rule of joint tenancy. Again, no resale of allotted land could be made unless the "stem-heads" consented to the sale and declined to purchase themselves. Even after a sale had been made, the company could repurchase at 10 per cent under the sale price within a year. There was, finally, a provision for arbitration in case of disputes—evidence of the influence of the continental law merchant. By this clause (the twelfth), members agreed in advance to abide by the award of the arbitrators, nor would they regard as altering such an award any later decision by the proper judges or courts. If any member disregarded this provision, he would automatically forfeit his share and in addition be liable to a fine.[39]

Pastorius remained the resident agent of the group until 1700, when a new group of three men were constituted joint agents, apparently to stimulate more sales of the property; several heirs of the original group had come into possession of shares and wished to realize on them.[40] Of the three, one (Falkner) turned out to be dishonest; with the help of forged powers of attorney and the notorious adventurer Sprogell he succeeded in alienating to accomplices most of the land. Ejectment suits were unsuccessful in 1708–1709, apparently because of bribery of lawyers and

[39] How a fine levied in such manner could be collected was not discussed!

[40] The power of attorney to these agents is in Pennypacker, *op. cit.,* 39.

judges.[41] The surviving heirs in 1720 offered to deed any remaining equitable interest they might have in the original purchase to the Society for Propagating the Gospel, but no acceptance was ever recorded; acquisition of a mere right to bring suit against unlawful possessors was perhaps not an attractive gift in the eyes of the society.[42]

THE CONNECTICUT COPPER MINES[43]

Copper deposits in the vicinity of Simsbury and Wallingford were discovered soon after 1700. After a period of wrangling over the proper method of conducting the crude mines, the Connecticut general court in 1709 passed an act to establish a mode of control. The difficulty had been that land owners upon whose property the ore had been discovered were unable to adjust their conflicting claims, or to decide upon a plan for actually mining the metal. A managing committee was named, with power to execute leases and contracts for smelting. Several German miners were brought over, and the location of the first smelter became known as "Hanover."

This early set of rules for the organization of the Simsbury

[41] This was asserted by Jawert, one of the other trustees. *Ibid.,* at 47. Pennypacker has been unable to discover that any redress for these fraudulent sales was ever secured.

[42] *Ibid.,* at 50.

[43] This Connecticut undertaking is described in Benjamin Trumbull, *History of Connecticut* (New Haven, 1818), at 40, and in N. A. Phelps, *History of the Copper Mines and Newgate Prison* (Hartford, 1845). In "The Newgate of Connecticut," 15 *Magazine of American History,* at 321, N. H. Egleston claimed that, prior to the act of the legislature mentioned above, "a working company was formally organized under a charter, said to have been the first granted for mining purposes in our country." He gives no authority, and Davis, who was particularly interested in the priority of Colonial corporations, seems to reject the claim but with no evidence of a careful checkup; 1 *Essays,* 93.

The special legislative treatment for the mines is suggestive of the relations of the Prince of Wales, and in later years of Parliament, to the stannaries of Devon and Cornwall; *cf.* G. R. Lewis, *The Stannaries* (Cambridge, 1908), especially 86 *ff.*

group was duplicated in similar legislation for the Wallingford area in 1719. Of the two laws, the latter is more carefully worded and contains more interesting detail.[44] The 1709 law merely ordered the organization of proprietors and an annual meeting to choose a managing committee. The powers of the committee, and the duties of the appointed arbitration commissioners, were the same as in the later law.

This later act provided that any three interested proprietors might, in March of 1720, issue a call for a meeting of all proprietors in April. A majority of those owning land in the two areas would be a quorum. A clerk was to be chosen to keep records and to call any necessary special meetings. In general the proprietors when so meeting were empowered to direct the operation of the mines, to determine the "proportion of money to be levied" and all other matters of importance, as had been the case in the 1709 law. Obviously, the legislature had in both cases drawn upon the analogy of town proprietorships and was creating partial political supervision over the bodies as thus established.

Some details in the act specifying the powers of the proprietorships are of particular interest here. The groups were to have power to make their own by-laws and to levy fines for infraction of such rules, not to exceed forty shillings for each offense. No by-laws were to be contrary to the laws of the Colony. At annual meetings the members could "appoint a committee, or committees, trustees or agents, for the doing or managing of any matter or thing in behalf of the said proprietors."[45] This standing committee was given the particular duty of dealing with refractory members who refused to contribute their share of time and labor to getting out the ore. If such refusal was persistent, the committee was directed to agree with one of the other proprietors, or even with a stranger, to come in and work the delinquent's share

---

[44] Cf. 5 *Connecticut Colonial Records*, at 104, and vol. 6 at 154 and 339.
[45] Trumbull, *op. cit.*, at 46; 6 *Connecticut Colonial Records*, 157.

for one year. Such an agreement could be continued until all expenses incurred on behalf of the stubborn member had been covered four times over. In these clauses there was a close similarity to the act of 1709.

The legislature backed up these plans by creating another commission of three men to hear controversies and suits arising within the body of proprietors. This commission was to rank equally with the county courts, would receive similar fees, and would be served by the sheriff. From a decision of the commission, appeal could be taken only to the general assembly. Members of the commission were to be endowed with proper powers under the great seal of the Colony, and were given much more carefully defined powers than the group appointed for Simsbury.

In 1712, between the passage of these two quasi-charters, the general court expressly approved leases which had been negotiated by the Simsbury group as well as by more informal groups in Wallingford and Farmington. These operating leases were given to Jonathan Belcher (later to be the noted native governor of Massachusetts) "and partners."

The mines were worked intermittently until the decade following 1750; other discoveries were made along the same range of hills, running from Holyoke to New Haven. In 1773 the abandoned shafts were acquired by the Colony for a penitentiary; the purpose was to make an underground dungeon of the shafts and drifts. Escapes were ridiculously easy, however, and after 1780 buildings and walls were erected, to become Connecticut's famous Newgate. Actual mining was resumed on parts of the property by private owners in the nineteenth century, until Lake Superior ore was discovered.

THE PRINCIPIO COMPANY

The thesis that mining, even more than shipping, first evoked capitalistic forms of organization is further illustrated by a number of other projects which appeared in the Colonies. Other than the above copper mining venture, the most interesting of the group is the Principio Company. Its history has been sketched by Henry Whitely,[46] based upon correspondence of Thomas Russell, one of the prime movers. Russell and Stephen Onion came to Maryland in 1722 to establish an iron mining company; associated with them were a "party of English merchants and capitalists." As pioneers, they chose the name Principio. Whitely, in the manner common to historical observers, erroneously states: "which name they afterwards assumed when they *incorporated* themselves as the Principio Company." No charter was ever secured, and obviously the company was an association, closely akin to the land companies of a half-century later.

During the next fifty years ore was mined in at least six locations, and the iron acquired a high reputation for quality in England after 1730. Acquisition of one site brought Augustine Washington into the company; he owned a one-twelfth interest, and

[46] In three articles entitled "The Principio Company," in 11 *Pennsylvania Magazine of History and Biography,* 63, 190, 288. A collection of letters in the British Museum (*Additional MS.* 29,600, especially f. 9 and 16) relates to affairs of the company from as early as 1726 to as late as 1769.

As a contrast to the status of the Principio Company, it is particularly interesting to note that an obscure enterprise for exploiting the copper deposits of the Upper Michigan Peninsula actually received a charter which was never used. The project was sponsored by one Alexander Henry, whose record of travels in the western country written just prior to the Revolution is a well-known historical source book: *Travels and Adventures of Alexander Henry* (New York, 1809; new edition 1897). It resulted from Henry's discovery that the Indians were making use of surface outcroppings of copper in the now famous area (pp. 220–229). The members of the group were the Duke of Gloucester, Sir William Townsend, the Russian Consul at London, and four prominent London merchants. Sir William Johnson was also asked to join.

The charter was engrossed in 1772, and is to be found in the *P. R. O. Register,* P. C. II, 116. The company's title was "The Governor and Company for Adventures in Working Mines in and about Lake Superior." Monopoly rights (clearly from the precedent petition the prime reason for seeking the charter) were granted over a strip of land extending sixty miles back from the shore line. The company was prohibited from entering the fur trade or building forts. There were twenty-eight shares. The charter was easily secured, perhaps because of the presence of two prominent Whig "insiders" among the incorporators. But the charter was never taken

left it to Lawrence Washington upon his death. When Maryland confiscated Tory property in 1780, the Principio mine sites were included, excepting Russell's share, who had become a resident and a patriot. The assembly used the phrase "property of the persons commonly called by the name of the Principio Company, except the part, share, and interest of Thomas Russell," clearly denying the existence of a corporation. Russell then owned one-eighth of eleven-twelfths of the property, indicating that eleven shares other than Washington's had dwindled to eight by the deaths intestate of members or the reversion of their shares to the remainder. This characteristic classifies the body as nearer the ordinary business partnership than an association with free transferability of shares.

THE EQUIVALENT LAND COMPANY[47]

It will be pointed out in the next chapter that aside from the New England townships and the various chartered colonies themselves, there were no organized land companies before 1745. Occasionally the so-called Equivalent Company is referred to as an organized land project because historians have known of it through the voluminous diary left by Cadwallader Colden. It was not a company in the sense that that term is used herein, but it may be included in the group being described here because it did represent some degree of group consciousness. Some five or six thousand acres of land were involved, which had been ceded to New York in the settlement of a long-standing boundary dispute between Connecticut and New York. This land was located

out of the Seal office "owing to our ill-success," according to Henry (p. 228).

Still another pre-Revolutionary company organized for mining is mentioned briefly by Bruce, *Virginia Iron Manufacture* (New York, 1930), 22. It was the Albermarle Furnace Company, organized in Virginia in 1771 with a capital of £1,200.

[47] In 2 *Cadwallader Colden Papers* (New York Historical Society *Collections,* 7 vols., 1917–1923), 65, may be found the essential information about this rather unimportant organization.

in the area directly west of the present town of Ridgefield, Connecticut.

On May 18, 1732, the New Yorkers who had purchased the land from the state (by not altogether regular methods) made and signed an agreement for mutual protection. This agreement is what has been mistaken for articles of association, typical of the later speculative undertakings. The agreement provided that in case of the eviction of any of the holders a meeting would be called in a public house in New York City, to be chosen by the person molested. There was a provision requiring public notices of the meeting. On the basis of one vote for each one hundred acres, there were sixty-six votes in the group. At the meeting two-thirds of those present could vote a tax on all the other members to provide funds for the defense of the particular member attacked in the courts.

The same process would be followed in providing for the expense of an ejectment action against trespassers (obviously the Connecticut citizens who refused to abide by the boundary decision). If one of the subscribers were permanently ejected after proper legal efforts had been exhausted, he was to be compensated out of the group funds on the basis of £5 per hundred acres. Any new purchasers of land in the area were to be bound by the agreement, presumably by the insertion of the pertinent clauses in deeds of sale. Each subscriber was to furnish a penal bond of £200 to guarantee his proper contribution, and the bond was to be secured by his land as well.

It is very clear from the agreement and from Colden's correspondence for several years that there was no other purpose behind the agreement than the conduct of legal actions and the proper compensation of ejected members. Taxes or levies were not paid after about the third year,[48] and the whole agreement became ineffective.

[48] Colden mentions his own obligation on such levies, *op. cit.*, 72.

THE LAND AND SILVER BANKS IN MASSACHUSETTS[49]

The various efforts in the Colonies to secure the issue of paper money after 1700 are familiar episodes in Colonial history. Rapid growth of population produced a shortage of hard money in the trading centers, and merchants were typically supporters of plans to increase the amount in circulation. In 1686 Massachusetts had attempted to organize a bank of issue, and a special printing press was purchased before the scheme was abandoned in 1688. Immediately following the controversy over the charter, there were a few "Old Charter" bills issued, from 1690 until 1702. After 1702 the general court issued the first of the so-called Province Notes. Tax income for six years had been pledged, with the natural result that depreciation began.

In the face of this difficulty a proposal was made in 1714 to the Massachusetts general court to permit a private partnership to issue notes in conjunction with an agreement among merchants of the city to accept such notes in trade.[50] However, the legislators continued to favor issue by public authority, and £260,000 of province notes, secured by real estate, had been issued by 1728. They were receivable for taxes at 5 per cent discount. Yet by 1733 there was a renewed demand for more notes, and certain Boston merchants by a private agreement issued about £110,000 of notes secured by silver at the rate of nineteen shillings per ounce of silver. These rose to a premium in later years over the accepted

[49] This account is chiefly summarized from two articles by Andrew M. Davis in Volumes 3 and 4 of *Publications of the Colonial Society of Massachusetts*. In Volume 4, at pp. 126–200, are the lists of subscribing partners, and a *verbatim* reprint of the articles of each project.

[50] The New London Society United for Trade & Commerce, of 1732, was thus hardly the "prototype" for the Land Bank, as Adams calls it (*Revolutionary New England,* 155); the career of this group, which procured one of the earliest business charters from Connecticut on the false pretense that it was to be a trading society somewhat like Penn's Free Society, is sketched by Davis in 1 *Essays,* 22–25. Its attempt to issue paper money brought revocation of the charter.

currency in general circulation, in terms of which silver had appreciated. A precedent for private issue was thus established.

In 1737 and 1738 the province issued new public bills and made the older issues redeemable in silver at three different rates, so that the notes in circulation became known as "old," "middle," or "new" tenor according to the rates specified. This confused situation set the stage for the controversy in 1739–1740 over the proper future course of action for Massachusetts to follow. The bitter contest in the summer of 1740, between the proponents of a Land Bank to issue notes secured by mortgages and those who favored notes based only on silver, is of outstanding importance in Massachusetts Colonial history.[51] The opposition of the governor to the Land Bank scheme led him finally to remove from office many local officials who had participated in it, and his denunciation of the plan to the home government was the immediate cause for the extension of the Bubble Act, in 1741, to include all the Colonies. Under it all those connected with the Land Bank scheme were made liable to heavy penalties, and in a few instances these were enforced. Civil suits arising out of the prohibition of the plans dragged on for many years.

The articles of agreement of the two bank plans are available[52] and are probably the most valuable examples in existence of Colonial business organization prior to 1750, despite the fact that there was never any real operation in either case. They reflect the prevailing notions of what a large unincorporated association should be. Because of the wealth and position of the merchants who supported the Silver Bank it is probable that its articles were drawn up by a trained lawyer. The close similarity of the Land Bank articles to a formal partnership agreement leads to this same conclusion, despite the fact that its backers were in general from the country towns and far less wealthy or influential. The

[51] For the effect on the Massachusetts political situation, cf. Adams, *Revolutionary New England*, 156–160.
[52] 4 *Publications of the Colonial Society of Massachusetts*, 126 ff.

conflict between the two groups was suggestive of the future struggle between country and city, between agriculturalists and merchants.[53]

In the Land Bank agreement, the first five clauses were in the nature of a preamble, specifying (a) the total capital—£150,000; (b) the voting power—a maximum of four votes for any "undertaker," arranged on a scale from a £75 subscription, which secured one vote, up to four for the holder of the maximum of £2,000; (c) the requirement that, in return for the notes, each subscriber would give to the directors a mortgage on land worth one and one-half times the amount of notes received; and (e) the additional requirement of a personal bond, with two sureties, for this amount. In other words, notes were to be printed and issued to subscribers, secured by land mortgages and personal bonds and repayable serially in notes or acceptable commodities over twenty years. By securing colony-wide participation, it was expected that the issued notes would be generally accepted in trade and would circulate freely after being spent initially by the "partners" in the bank. The annual repayments would provide the bank with a growing fund which could be loaned to commercial borrowers; interest thus earned would be the source of dividends for the subscribers.

In the second part of the articles, the directors (who were named to hold office until displaced) undertook to make annual reports, to supervise the required repayments each year, to pay dividends out of interest earned on the accumulating repayments, and after twenty years to pay a final *pro rata* dividend.

In the third part, each subscriber bound himself to do certain things as a partner in the enterprise. He agreed to the repayment plan, and agreed to accept the bills in trade. He bound himself to pay a *pro rata* share of any and all losses which might be incurred, and to indemnify the directors. He agreed to furnish better mortgage security if requested, and to accept the valuation

[53] 3 *ibid.,* 53.

of the directors as well as their prices on the commodities presented as annual repayments.

Additional articles were very detailed. By simple majority votes of the directors and members, by-laws could be passed and amendments to the articles accepted. Directors could be removed "for fraud" by a majority vote. Suit could be brought against any subscriber for "neglect" of his annual 5 per cent payments. The date of the annual meeting was specified, with provision for calling special meetings by newspaper notices. The articles thus disclose a genuine similarity to later formal associations, while in outward form the two agreements followed the ordinary form of a partnership agreement.[54] This transitional character makes them of especial interest.

The Silver Bank articles were similar in general form; many clauses are directly repetitive of those of the Land Bank. But the annual repayments by subscribers were to be in silver bullion, the really important difference. Subscribers signed fifteen separate bonds to secure these payments, and gave adequate surety (but not land mortgages). To secure the governor's approval, it was agreed after the articles had been drawn up to maintain a free exchange of the bills at any time for Colony bills, but the members as well as the directors agreed to refuse bills of "neighbouring Governments."[55]

Voting power was to be in direct proportion to subscriptions (the "aristocratic" principle), with maximum holdings, however, limited to £8,000. Although A. M. Davis, the investigator of these projects, says that the Land Bank "was not a joint stock company, nor did it have transferable interests,"[56] the eighteenth article of the Silver Bank plan provided that at any annual meeting a new undertaker could be brought in for acceptance in place

[54] The terms used as well as the arrangement of the agreement show this.

[55] Evidence of the ever-present jealousy toward Rhode Island.

[56] 3 *ibid.*, 38.

of one retiring. Evidently the more experienced merchants backing the Silver Bank wanted transferability of the shares. Included among the signers were many of the "best names" in the city, later to become prominent Tories. Although the governor was personally friendly with the group, this scheme also languished when the Bubble Act was made to apply to Colonial companies.[57]

STATUS OF THE CORPORATION, 1750–1790

It must be categorically emphasized that in the last half of the eighteenth century, at least in the Colonies, the corporation was not a favored form of organization in the business community. It was decidedly in disfavor. To point out in detail all the reasons for this situation is beyond the scope of this inquiry.[58] Factual evidence of the operation of important land enterprises without in any instance the help of incorporation is the best testimony which can be brought forward; in succeeding pages this will be presented. To review briefly the legal position of corporations as determined by the Bubble Act, court decisions, and business sentiment seems essential to an understanding of the *milieu* in which unincorporated land companies appeared after 1750.

The fifty years prior to the Revolution were the period when the agitation surrounding the Bubble Act had real influence in England and, consequently, in the Colonies. The hectic periods

[57] Occurring somewhat later than the date suggested here as marking the era of active organized associations, an attempt to "restrain trade" among New England dealers in an essential commodity must be mentioned because it shows the use of the formal private agreement to make such a restraint effective. This was the "Spermaceti Combine," described in *Massachusetts Historical Society Collections,* 7th Series, vol. 9 (vol. 69 in revised classification), 88. J. T. Adams uses it as a prime example in his rather strained attempt to demonstrate the rise of "big business" in his *Revolutionary New England,* at 255.

[58] DuBois has examined the influences in England which placed chartered corporations in the background in his *The English Business Company after the Bubble Act, 1720–1800* (New York, 1938).

of expansion in corporate activity in 1688–1695 and in 1716–1720 have seemed to be, historically reviewed, simply interesting steps along the path of progress toward the present-day corporation. In reality, the events of 1719 and 1720 put far more than a passing damper on enthusiasm for charters and the corporate form. The course of development in business structure was definitely changed. By 1760, the era which had ended forty years before with the Bubble Act must have seemed to Colonial business men a closed chapter in past history, and its effects accepted.

The clumsy statute of 1720 known as the Bubble Act has been characterized in harsh terms by nearly all commentators.[59] Yet it had a remarkable practical effect. It drove underground the efforts of business men to secure effective unitary control in their enterprises. They thus gradually came to discover that the state need not be appealed to for permission and help in conducting business operations. Only in certain narrow areas of the business world need the particular advantages of a charter be sought. They proceeded to accomplish their purposes by adapting the old rigid principles of partnership to new exigencies. Occasionally they secured legal complaisance toward circumvention of the law as it had stood on the statute books for more than a century.[60] But most important, they came to rely more and more on the old, deeply-rooted doctrine which the Act professed to attack—that men may associate so as to operate effectively as a corporate body without the aid or sanction of the State.

In the light of later history, it is amazing to look back upon the specific purposes and prohibitions of the Bubble Act.[61] It

[59] Holdsworth states aptly the basic futility of the Act: "The House of Commons neglected the deeper causes of the panic . . .; and they concentrated their attention on one cause only—the extension of the joint stock system by the manner in which societies, which were not incorporated, usurped corporate form, and the consequent growth of the 'pernicious art of stock-jobbing.' What was needed was an Act which made it easy for joint stock societies to adopt a corporate form, and, at the same time, safeguarded both the share-holders . . . and the public." 8 *H.E.L.*, 219.

[60] DuBois, *op. cit.*, at 30 and 287.   [61] 6 *Geo. I*, ch. 18.

plunged into entirely new ground, creating statutory offenses unknown to the common law. "The extreme poverty of the ascertained rules of law applicable to commercial societies, whether corporate or unincorporate"[62] provided no foundation for the provisions of the Act.

In the first place, the vague phrase naming as a nuisance the "presuming to act as a corporate body" never received any support from English judges in the succeeding century. It stands as one of the most inept phrases ever used in an important statute.[63] The only use ever made of it was in connection with the other offenses named in the Act.

It was quite different with the second general offense, the creation of a transferable stock. This was something definite, and if joint stock associations had not successfully avoided indictments by Crown officers there would undoubtedly have been many convictions under this heading. In the first case which arose under the Act,[64] Lord Ellenborough succeeded in avoiding the provision only by pointing out that the Birmingham Flour and Bread Company, under indictment, permitted to its members only a limited right of transfer.[65]

[62] Holdsworth, 8 *H.E.L.*, 215.

[63] *Cf.* Lord Ellenborough's remarks in *Rex* v. *Webb*, 14 East 406, at 413 (1811).

[64] *Rex* v. *Webb*. There had been one indictment in 1725, but none in the intervening 86 years.

[65] That use of transferable shares ranked as a common law offense prior to the Act is of great importance for the later development of associations. In 1828, *after* the repeal of the Act, Chief Justice Best declared categorically that "there can be no transferable shares of any stock except the stock of a corporation"; *Duvergier* v. *Fellowes*, 5 Bingham 267. Lord Eldon, as pointed out in the argument of counsel (*ibid.*, at 261) also believed it to be a common law offense. This view was completely reversed within fifteen years, so that Justice Tindal could say in 1843, with just as much certainty as his learned predecessor of 1828: "The raising of transferable shares of the stock of a company can hardly be said to be of itself an offense at common law; no instance of an indictment at common law for such an offense can be shown." *Harrison* v. *Heathorn*, 6 Man. & G. 81, at 141; *cf.* also *Garrard* v. *Hardey*, 5 Man. & G. 471 (1843). After that time there was never any doubt in English law concerning the right of partnerships

At the time of the Act both business men and lawyers were extremely hazy as to the exact distinctions between corporations and unincorporated societies. The only thing they were sure of, as Scott has indicated,[66] was that a charter was necessary if some trading area monopoly or special privilege in the nature of a public utility were being sought. Many groups simply bought a patent which had been granted to a single individual, exploited it, and made no effort to secure a charter. Many went ahead in the boom days of 1692–1695 without either a charter or a patent. Furthermore, although men were quite clear as to the nature and operations of corporations in the field of local government, they were very uncertain of their exact status when engaged in business undertakings. During the seventeenth century, the existent chartered companies for foreign trade, colonization, and a few domestic undertakings, vacillated between the regulated company form and operation with a true joint stock.[67] They had not even developed any hard and fast rules governing their own internal administration. Thus the loss of corporate privileges was not a very certain loss, except as it became less easy to secure monopoly privileges.

Aside from the influence of the Bubble Act, there developed a strong prejudice against the granting of exclusive charters in the

or associations to make their shares transferable. B. C. Hunt summarizes this controversy, *Development of the Business Corporation in England, 1800–1867* (Cambridge, 1936), 41–44.

In American law, it was possible for Chief Justice Parker, in what seems to be the earliest case dealing directly with transferable shares (*Alvord* v. *Smith*, 5 Pickering 232 [1827]) to approve completely a clause in an agreement of an association formed in 1817, providing for free transfer of interests by simply lodging with the clerk a written certificate. He said that "This interest [of a shareholder] may be disposed of by contract of sale . . . without any further ceremony." To this statement the Chief Justice appended a footnote, pointing out that in the English law of partnership a stranger could not be brought in without consent of all the other partners; but he added that this was not at all the law in Massachusetts. He did not even honor the Bubble Act by mentioning its direct prohibition of transferable shares.

[66] 1 *Joint Stock Companies*, 329.   [67] *Ibid.*, 163 *ff.*

foreign trade field among members of Parliament and in the business community. The Crown, particularly after 1680, became increasingly jealous of such organizations as the East India Company and the New England corporate colonies. This political attitude was accentuated greatly after the overturn of 1688. Finally, there was steadily growing in England (also reinforced by the political events of 1688) the doctrine which was so forcibly reiterated in 1775 by Adam Smith[68]—that a free entry into trade by individuals or groups should be preserved, as against any system of granting charters. The wholesale increase of associations offering shares to the public as early as the boom days of the last decade of the seventeenth century was thus in part due to the increasing strength of the idea that incorporation was needed only for some monopoly privilege and that these grants were essentially political in character. The outburst of speculation came in that particular decade because of the Dutch influence, then so marked in English business affairs. The group of traders who followed William to London brought with them familiarity with transferable shares as a mode of speculation and provided the immediate impetus to the stock boom.

Under these stimuli, the development of the true joint stock associations with delegated power, transferable shares, succession of members, and ability to function as a unit, had already begun. Crown charters were valued only for special purposes. If no charter was held, none the worse: the group proceeded as an association so long as no monopoly privileges were needed. Chartered and unchartered groups might operate side by side, with no difference except that the former had sought and secured some particular privilege needed in its field. The Bubble Act made charters harder than ever to secure, and forced the association principle to become the main reliance of the business community.

The extension of the Bubble Act in 1741 to include the Colo-

[68] With none of the originality ascribed to him by economists.

nies might seem to have settled the question of the right of un-incorporated groups over here to "presume to act" as corpora-tions. But the occasion of the extension was a very special one;[69] it was sought because the Land Bank scheme in Massachusetts was thought harmful in a high degree to the public welfare. Colo-nial business men would naturally have concluded that the Act was aimed solely to stop wildcat bank schemes or projects which interfered in some other way with the prerogatives of the govern-ment.[70] This view was essentially the general interpretation put upon the Bubble Act by English judges after 1800[71]—that only where an enterprise menaced the public welfare could it be brought under the ban of the statute,[72] and that otherwise men

[69] *Cf. supra*, p. 58.

[70] Davis has examined carefully the attitude of the Colonial govern-ments toward their power to create corporations, in 1 *Essays*, 2–28. He concludes that the Colonial assemblies which undertook to create corpora-tions were forced to rely upon an implied power so to act; and the ques-tion whether this implication was justified remained somewhat unsettled throughout nearly the entire Colonial period. He points out that there was a wide difference of opinion among various royal governors after 1725 as expressed in their communications to the home government. Some felt that there was no power in either themselves or the Colonial assemblies to create corporations, while others believed that an act originated by an as-sembly and approved by themselves would be a valid charter. He believed that there was doubt concerning the power to create corporations in the proprietary colonies; he failed to realize that the full palatinate powers granted in the proprietary charters would necessarily include the power to create full-fledged corporations. *Cf.* Lapsley, *County Palatine*, at 36; and also Clause XIV of the Maryland Charter secured by Lord Baltimore, reprinted in Mereness, *Maryland as a Proprietary Province* (New York, 1901), at 515. But certainly there was no such power in the early *corporate* colonies to create what would in effect be "corporations within a corpora-tion." J. T. Adams, *Founding of New England* (Boston, 1921), 153. Not until 1772 was there any general approval given by the home government to the chartering of Colonial corporations.

[71] *Cf.* Lord Ellenborough in *Rex* v. *Webb*, 14 East 406.

[72] In a well-known modern case, *Phillips* v. *Blatchford*, 137 Mass. 510, at 513, Justice Holmes said: "We attach . . . little weight to the argument that the Bubble Act was made applicable to America in 1741 . . . it may be that some few English statutes, passed since the emigration, were adopted by our courts . . . but the fact that, as far back as the records of our judicial decisions extend, this Act has not been practiced on in the

should be free to enter into such private associations as they saw fit.

Among the general body of colonists there was, furthermore, more or less constant opposition to the presence of chartered corporations in the field of general business activity because the chartered company was associated with the idea of monopoly. The direct influence of the chartered colonizing units had long been forgotten, and the chartered trading companies had by 1750 come to be regarded purely as semi-political "vested interests" dating from a previous era in English history. This persistent sentiment was strongly reflected in many of the ratifying conventions of 1788. According to the Hancock-Adams resolution in the Massachusetts convention, an amendment to the new Constitution was needed to insure "that Congress erect no company of merchants with exclusive advantages of commerce."[73] Five states

courts, but has been ignored by them, is strong evidence that the Act was not among those that were kept in force after the Revolution." *Cf. supra,* note 65.

[73] *Cf. Elliot's Debates* (Washington, 1836), 135–136, 181; and S. B. Harding, *Federal Constitution in Massachusetts* (Cambridge, 1896), 88. The same amendment was discussed in the North Carolina convention; L. I. Trenholme, *Federal Constitution in North Carolina* (New York, 1932), 184.

The controversy over the power of the *old* Congress under the Articles of Confederation to grant charters reflects this same fear. Its act of December 31, 1781, incorporating the Bank of North America, was halfhearted, since it included a clause recommending joint incorporation by the states.

In a letter to Edward Pendleton, written January 8, 1782, Madison described the attitude in Congress upon the granting of the charter which had been vaguely promised. When the matter was brought up "the general opinion though with some exceptions was that the confederation gave no such power and that the excuse of it would not bear the test of a forensic disquisition." He added that many members felt a Pennsylvania charter "would have given them a sufficient legal existence in every state." He approved the final form of the charter, feeling that it was an admission of a lack of power to grant charters and an "antidote against the poisonous tendency of precedents of usurpation." The letter is reprinted in full in 6 *Letters of Members of the Continental Congress* (E. C. Burnett, Ed., Washington, 1929), 290.

At the time that Pennsylvania withdrew its charter to the bank, James

at the same time specifically recommended an amendment to the new instrument which would include such a prohibition on the power of Congress. That such an amendment was not included in the original ten submitted for ratification by the first Congress seems to have been due to the belief that Congress would never dare to assert such a power. This in general has been the result, with important exceptions, and in our early history many believed (as the 1790–1791 bank controversy demonstrated) that Congress could not charter any corporation whatsoever.

Chartered corporations to conduct public services—water works, aqueducts, canals, highways, and bridges—might have been regarded more tolerantly before 1790 had the need for their services been more pressing. At this time in England such organizations were being freely chartered. A very few such bodies were chartered before 1775 by Colonial assemblies, including some wharf and insurance companies which most nearly resembled actual business units. It was for this group also that most charters were granted by the various states from 1785 to 1800.[74] By 1800 the sharp prejudice against all corporations had been softened by the desire to encourage these public service enterprises. The rush to grant charters from 1797 to 1800 was mainly caused by this shift in sentiment. Not for nearly another decade, however, was there general willingness in any of the legislatures to charter ordinary business groups.

Even this cursory survey of the period 1750–1790 shows that,

Wilson was active as the bank's counsel. He believed that the power to govern the Northwest Territory (which was not seriously questioned) was the strongest analogy to the power of the old Congress to grant charters to corporations with nation-wide scope. His arguments (2 *Wilson MSS.*, 101 *ff.*, Library of the Historical Society of Pennsylvania) foreshadow the better-known statement of Hamilton in 1790.

[74] Davis found that, of 317 corporations chartered by the states before 1800, about 240 were of this public utility character; 62 more were for banks or insurance companies, where the corporate form was recognized as superior. Only 13 or 14 could be said to have been concerned with ordinary business activity, and some of these were only indirectly so involved. 2 *Essays,* 27.

as an everyday example of business organization that would be familiar to the more intelligent and active leaders in business, the formal chartered corporation was of negligible importance. Those interested in organizing land projects passed by the corporate form and proceeded to build associations possessing unique characteristics that clearly distinguished them from either partnerships or corporations.

FRENCH AND CONTINENTAL LAW

One final word must be said to complete an analysis of the background against which the land companies emerged. Because during and after the Revolution the contacts between American and Dutch or French business men increased markedly, it is logical to expect that continental practice influenced the ideas and conceptions of speculative leaders in the latter portion of the period under review here. There is much evidence in the lives of men such as Duer, Morris, Constable, Craigie, and Flint that they were in as close business contact with Paris as they were with London. With Holland, relations were similarly close, particularly after about 1785 when Dutch bankers began their campaign of purchasing American debt obligations for private speculation.

The late eighteenth century in both these countries was a period of experimentation in forms of business organization, finally terminated by the Code Napoleon in 1807.[75] The Ordinance of 1673, which grew out of the Colbertian efforts to assist business men in every possible way, had formally legalized the *commandite* or limited partnership. It first introduced the principle which has since so constantly affected Continental corporate law

[75] Professor Stanley E. Howard has written two thorough analyses of French law as it concerned business organization prior to the nineteenth century; "Business Partnerships in France before 1807," 7 *Accounting Review,* 242, and "The Société Anonyme," 8 *ibid.,* 11. His work draws heavily on secondary sources, particularly Raymond T. Troplong's *Du Contrat de Société Civile et Commerciale,* a detailed legal commentary on this period written in 1843 (Paris).

—the requirement of registration of such a partnership before a notary or other official, and the filing of the articles. A newly formed general partnership, *"société générale"*[76] in the old terminology, also was required to register any variation of powers within the partnership, for example, delegation of authority to some partners as against others. The purpose of publicity was mainly to protect creditors who were being defrauded by traders from the northern Italian cities.[77] After a generation this requirement was poorly enforced, but it was revived in the nineteenth century as one method of regulating business bodies.

In addition to these two vaguely defined forms of partnership and the scattering corporations created by Crown charter, there grew up in this century the *association en participation*,[78] which was not registered and varied widely in its purposes and in the degree of formality with which it was organized and conducted. It was used frequently in such ventures as the tax-farming syndicates, where the members often desired secrecy for political reasons; they did not desire to register names or any articles of agreement. Under such conditions there was a strong similarity to the modern joint adventure—that is, a risk-sharing enterprise formed for a single undertaking. Another example of such an *association* was that formed for speculation in commodities at the great fairs or markets. Finally, there was frequent utilization of this form in shipping ventures, and in the wholesale purchases of

[76] The word *société* is derived directly from the Roman *societas*, which means strictly the partnership without separate legal personality (as contrasted with *universitas*). That the civil law came to invest the *société* with a *corps moral* was a result of "Germanic" tendencies.

[77] As early as 1315 Louis X had tried to force publicity for Italian bankers' *commandite* partnerships for the same reason. In Italy in the thirteenth and fourteenth centuries, registration was required for *commenda* contracts under the law merchant. Later the rule was applied to partnerships, so that Colbert was merely adopting a familiar rule of the law merchant in Italy.

[78] Howard points out the clear similarity of groups which were given this title to the modern joint adventures and syndicates, a conclusion analogous to that reached in this study concerning speculative organizations of the late eighteenth century. 8 *Accounting Review*, 17–18.

imported cargoes—a clear analogy to the same form in use in England and the Colonies. Many records exist to indicate the frequency of the syndicate form in this field, usually created solely by informal letters assigning shares to a correspondent. In no case was any name adopted for the *association,* it being conducted directly by one of the participants. *Pro rata* responsibility for debts was in all cases recognized as a distinguishing feature. Undoubtedly the *association* form was well known to Americans and presented a model which could be used advantageously by Duer, Morris, and others.

Later commentators on French law stressed the significance of the 1673 ordinance in raising the *société en commandite* to the status of a corporate entity, a *société* possessing a *corps moral.*[79] Its use expanded rapidly after 1700, and transferable shares for the limited partners early became common. Thus, Law's "Bank General" of 1716 was a *commandite* partnership with transferable shares, a fact unnoticed by most of the historical commentators on Law's schemes. It became a typical form of business organization in France and Holland between 1720 and 1800, with many variations in form going unremarked by governmental authorities. In Holland the form was known as a "negotiation,"[80] and there was a similar confusion in legal terminology and in what the exact status of a given organization before the law might be.

Lacking any formal definition of a *société* in the law, and having no formal lines of demarcation between a large *commandite*

[79] Troplong, *op. cit.,* 157.

[80] The Dutch *negotie* was so translated by Professor Paul D. Evans in his *Holland Land Company* (Buffalo, 1924). *Cf. infra,* p. 207. Professor A. H. Stockder has pointed out to the present author that the term, derived originally from the Latin *negociator* as used to supplement *mercator,* had a broad general meaning in Dutch financial usage. It meant substantially the same as "a deal" in modern Wall Street slang; in other words, a transaction in stocks or bonds bought at wholesale and quickly resold. It did not mean any specific form or method of flotation. The word, and the plural form *negotien,* is so used in issues of *De Koopman* in 1768–1775.

partnership and a chartered corporation, on the one hand, and between such partnerships and the *association,* on the other, much uncertainty resulted. Business men, "lacking codified ordinances or statutes which provided adequate classification of form and rules of procedure, adopted forms and variations of their own."[81] The 1807 Code attempted primarily to end this vagueness and whimsical variation by strictly defining three forms of *société:* the ordinary partnership—*générale;* the limited partnership—*commandite;* and the joint stock association—*société anonyme,* the latter being a recognition of what many so-called *commandite* partnerships had in actual practice come to be.

In one American land enterprise, "Castorland," to be described below,[82] there was a *commandite* partnership organized in 1792, with several hundred potential limited partners possessing transferable shares. Its form shows only the most tenuous connection with what American law would designate as a limited partnership. But the shareholders were designated as "dormant partners," and a director and five commissaries were given all the powers of management such as unlimited partners might possess in modern times.[83] In all other respects, however, "Castorland" was to function practically as the large English joint stock associations were beginning to function at this time. There were to be a stock register, three general assemblies a year, voting provisions, and compulsory dissolution votes at the end of a certain number of years. American business men[84] of the 1790's undoubtedly knew of the operation of such groups, and could imitate everything except the distinction between limited and unlimited partners.

---

[81] Howard, 7 *Accounting Review,* 250, note 25.

[82] In Chapter V.

[83] In the Code of 1807, the limited partners in a *société en commandite* were positively forbidden to participate in management.

[84] William Constable, leader of the New York merchant class, conducted the negotiations with the "Castorland" promoters.

Surprisingly diverse sources guided American business leaders of 1750–1800 when they set about organizing and conducting the most important single business operation of that day—land merchandising, either on a profit or a non-profit basis. Because governmental prerogatives were sought in many of the undertakings before 1775, men turned their attention to the proprietary principle of the Middle Colonies; because actual settlement by division of the acquired land was often a prime motive throughout the half-century, the New England proprietorship served as a model; because, finally, the undertakings were for profit by a resale of the land, business organization as it then existed was used. Chartered corporations were not used, not only because charters were difficult to secure before 1775, but because no need was felt for the monopolistic privileges which were synonymous with a charter to all business men of the time. Men clearly believed that an effective corporate entity, merging the interests of all in one body, could be secured as a natural right of citizens.

The state of the law both in England and on the Continent in the late eighteenth century was such that wide variation in the forms which business groups adopted was the rule. Hence out of this period came many examples of what was only slowly recognized by the law as the joint stock association. Much later the law also came to recognize and define the joint adventure and the syndicate, also existent in New York and Philadelphia in the boom of 1789–1792. Certainly this was one of the highly important originating periods in business history with which the law typically catches up a generation later. To some of the actual enterprises where this business originality held sway, attention must now be directed.

IV

PRE-REVOLUTIONARY LAND COMPANIES

IN presenting here descriptions of a group of land enterprises, the primary object has not been to proffer a daybook account of their histories but rather to portray the attitude and objectives of their sponsors. For this a simple round-up of a score or more articles of agreement is not enough. Some critical description is necessary in order to assay correctly the business and the legal significance of the varying structures encountered. We have already remarked that what occurred, most markedly in land companies but elsewhere as well, was a steady progression away from partnerships of individuals toward *de facto* corporate bodies. It is believed that the selected examples here presented will support the conclusion that business associations at the end of the eighteenth century were not modified partnerships, but had become corporations in all but the technical legal sense. What was being fashioned by the business class was an instrument which a generation or two later came finally to be endowed by legislators with the necessary legal attributes of the corporation. Land merchandisers helped to construct for a later generation this invaluable tool. Courts and legislators merely acquiesced in adding the valuable blessing of legal privileges.

Material has been selected first because it throws light on the thinking or the attitude of leaders; did they regard their enterprise as possessing corporate character in the *real* as contrasted with the *legal* sense? It is necessary to show some direct evidence regarding the internal structure and mechanics of various enterprises. Our selection thus does not include some enterprises which for historians possess special significance, because available material does not serve that purpose. Some few of this sort are grouped together at the end of this chapter and the next following, since collectively these ill-described projects do add somewhat to our understanding of the point of view men had toward the bodies they were creating. Winnowing out facts or writings or actions which are of real help has been difficult because students of history, examining records and documents, have not been interested in selecting materials directly germane to our purpose. Fortunately, many original documents have been preserved, either in manuscript or as reprinted *verbatim* by historical bodies, and from them the best deductions can be drawn. These same documents are numerous enough to permit (in Chapter VI) an adequate synthesis of the details of internal structure. The unincorporated association, forerunner of the nineteenth century corporation, can be seen in this important type of enterprise assuming a definite and unmistakable character of its own.

As the reader has been warned, we must presume familiarity with the main currents of American economic and territorial growth. There will consequently be included only brief résumés of the broad background against which the various enterprises sprang up; they were scattered from Maine on the east to Illinois on the west and Spanish territory on the south, and owed their existence to diverse sectional factors. But enough description will be included to identify each project to historians and to clarify the attitudes of their sponsors.

THE 1748 OHIO COMPANY[1]

In Virginia from 1700 to 1740 there was still ample territory for expansion under the system of individual grants of land. There had been a fan-like growth of cultivated area back from the tidewater region. Furthermore, the period of peace between

---

[1] This body is, of course, to be distinguished from the later project by which Marietta was settled. It had such an important influence that it is mentioned in practically all histories of the colonial period. The efforts of the company to survey and establish claims to land on the upper reaches of the Ohio helped to precipitate the French War in 1754.

The papers of the Ohio Company were in the possession of a member

France and England after the Treaty of Utrecht prevented the injection of political considerations into the Colony's land policy. As a result, very few efforts were made in this period even to explore the area west of the first Appalachian ranges. The journey of Governor Spotswood to the Shenandoah was one of the few exceptions to this general lack of interest in the western territory.

After about 1740, however, both these conditions changed. By 1739 renewal of warfare between France and England was a certainty. Spain, under a Bourbon, was also included in England's enmity; an immediate result was the 1740–1742 attacks on Florida by Oglethorpe. French traders were especially active in extending the range of their intercourse with Indians, and in these years they built up the relationships with Indian tribes that were so difficult for the English to break up until after 1760.

The Indian Treaty at Lancaster in 1744 was the immediate stimulus to the Virginia landowners to plan for pre-emption of the lands west of the Shenandoah. Four large grants were made in 1745 to several groups of petitioners.[2] Thomas Lee, who be-

of the Mercer family residing in Alexandria when the town was occupied by Federal troops in 1861. The trunks of papers were broken open by soldiers and much of the material burned on campfires. Some of the soldiers, however, took home parts of the material, hoping to sell the letters to autograph dealers. Some of these were sold in Utica soon after the war for $50, but most of the letters were probably clipped for autographs and destroyed. A few of the papers came into the possession of the Historical Society of Pennsylvania, but the great bulk of what might have been a valuable historical source is lost.

Much of the best available information concerning the later fate of this company is in Kate Mason Rowland, *Life of George Mason* (2 vols., New York, 1892). Petitions of the organizers and official communications from the Lords of Trade relating to the company are reprinted in the Appendix of Fernow, *Ohio Valley in Colonial Days* (Albany, 1890) and in *Journals of Christopher Gist,* edited by W. M. Darlington (Pittsburgh, 1893).

[2] Four grants were made to groups of twelve, twenty, eleven, and eighteen persons, respectively. The last was known as the Greenbriar Company. Etting Collection, 1 *Ohio MSS.* 80, Library of the Historical Society of Pennsylvania, and Call, *Virginia Reports,* 21. For a 1749 grant of 800,000 acres to the Loyal Company, *cf. Revised Code of Virginia* (1819 edition), Appendix II, 343–347. The later career of this company, under the leader-

came the first president of the Ohio Company, was a Virginia delegate at the signing of the treaty. Actual plans for the project moved slowly, however, and it was not until May, 1748, that a group formed themselves into a "company."

This project, like so many other land projects that have attracted the attention of historians, has been variously called a corporation, a company, and a partnership.[3] It seems clearly to have been a trading partnership; the references to the company in the papers of George Mason and in English official records are the best extant proofs.

Probably to give the concern proper connections in London,

ship of Doctor Thomas Walker, was strikingly parallel to that of the Ohio Company. Walker's journal of an exploratory trip through the grant in what is now eastern Kentucky is reprinted in L. P. Summers, *Annals of Southwest Virginia* (Abingdon, Va., 1929). His career is outlined by Archibald Henderson in 41 *Proceedings of the American Antiquarian Society*, New Series, 77–178.

The political conditions in Virginia which led to these grants, as well as the formation of the Ohio Company, are described in T. P. Abernethy, *Western Lands and the American Revolution* (New York, 1937), ch. I. This comprehensive study of western land settlement (excluding activities in New York, Pennsylvania, and Vermont) has appeared since the present study was written. It is valuable for those making an intensive study of the political background of many enterprises examined here, but its title is misleading for primary emphasis is laid on Virginia's policy. The Loyal Company is treated at some length.

[3] H. T. Leyland, in an article, "The Ohio Company, A Colonial Corporation" (vol. 16, *Quarterly Publication of the Ohio Historical and Philosophical Society*, 5), decides that the weight of evidence favors the status of the company as a corporation. Davis, 1 *Essays*, 96, says that it has "frequently been called a corporation, with a Crown charter; but I have been unable to verify these statements." Leyland cites Darlington as his authority for deciding that it was a corporation, but a careful study of the references made to the company there clearly indicates it to be a large trading partnership. He states that the company "received its charter" on May 18, 1749. This, on the contrary, was the date when confirmation of the land grant was made in Virginia, and seems to be the source of the confusion among historians on the status of the company. The original petition of the group in 1748 is decisive; it stated that "we have entered into a partnership by the name of the Ohio Company." P.R.O., 5 *Colonial Office Papers*, 13/27, f. 55. The existence of this petition was apparently not known by the above writers.

John Hanbury, a leading Quaker merchant of the time, was included as one of the original members. He would be able to make contact with the "right people" in securing confirmation of a land grant. Trading with the Indians was also mentioned as an object in the various petitions to the Crown, but after the first few years this plan lapsed. There were never more than twenty members, although there were numerous transfers of interest during the twenty-five years in which the project was active. Thomas Lee was succeeded as president by Lawrence Washington, half-brother of George. Augustine Washington, Governor Dinwiddie, and Robert Carter were among the members; John Mercer was the original secretary, and his son, George, became the company's agent in London in the later period, so that the official papers of the company came into his possession. All these men were members of the ambitious landholding class in Virginia. The fact that they made no effort to expand the membership, and paid but little attention to the trading side of the original scheme, indicates that it should be, to some extent, compared with projects patterned upon the proprietary grants of the previous century.

A petition to grant land was under consideration by a committee of council in 1748–1749,[4] and was referred to the Lords of Trade. In March of 1749 an order was issued to Gooch, Lieutenant Governor of Virginia, directing him to make a "grant to them and such others as they shall admit as their associates"; that "it is our will and pleasure and you are hereby authorized and required to make a grant of two hundred thousand acres to the said persons in Partnership."[5] If a fort were built and garrisoned and one hundred families seated on the territory within seven years, an additional grant of 300,000 acres was to be made.

After desultory efforts at exploration of the territory in which

[4] January 11, 1748, P.R.O., *Privy Council Papers,* II, ff. 101, 145.
[5] The original petition and various reports on the project are reprinted in Fernow, *Ohio Valley,* Appendix D, 240 *ff.*

the grant was to be located, the company secured Christopher Gist from North Carolina to make a survey.[6] His journals of this trip in 1751, and of his two later journeys, have become a valuable source of historical knowledge. His tour, made in 1751, indicated that it would be difficult to locate a tract of the proper size in an area attractive to settlers, and it was decided in the general meeting of 1751 to petition for one large area bounded by rivers and mountains, that would be easy to locate and cheap to survey. This petition, changing the size and nature of the grant, was granted.[7] Because of help in putting the petition through, the company, after another general meeting, "advised Mr. Hanbury of the proceedings and desired him to offer the Duke of Bedford a share, if he chose to be concerned, upon the terms of the Association."[8]

Favorable action on these requests, secured with relative ease, came largely because the ministry desired to erect a buffer line of colonization against the encroachments of the French. The company was careful to stress this consideration at all times. The encouragement given to this and other land enterprises was characteristic of British policy in this period, in contrast to that of the French. When, after 1760, there was added the objective of a rapprochement with the Indians under the leadership of Sir William Johnson and George Croghan, England had begun to use the methods of France, conjointly with her policy of encouraging land greed and land settlement. Historians have come to see the crucial importance of these projects in determining the issue of the colonial contest in North America.

The second grant was never finally confirmed in Virginia, and the affairs of the company languished after the Proclamation of 1763. George Mason worked intermittently seeking the

---

[6] 1 *Life of George Mason*, 58-61.

[7] It is recorded in the P.R.O., *P. C. Papers*, II, f. 103, dated March 28, 1754.

[8] Fernow, *op. cit.*, Appendix D.

final definitive grants.[9] George Mercer went to London in 1767 or 1768 to push the claim, but did little or nothing until he became involved in the Vandalia project, to be discussed below. He accepted two Vandalia shares as a substitute for the original grant, out of the seventy-two parts or shares into which it was divided—a ridiculously inadequate substitution of claims. The agreement which he signed ran in part: "We the Committee of the Purchasers of a Tract of country for a new Province on the Ohio in America, do hereby admit the Ohio Company as a Company Purchaser with us, for two shares of the said Purchase."[10] In return, he agreed to cease activity toward a confirmation of the original grant. But he was apparently purposely lax in communicating this move to his brother members; when it finally became known that he had neglected the original project, his agreement with the Vandalia promoters was repudiated at a meeting in 1773.[11]

Finally, in 1778, the Virginia assembly was petitioned to give patents of land amounting to 200,000 acres to the then members of the company "each in his own name, for his due share or proportion of two hundred thousand acres." This formed the basis of the land that was actually received, at the same time that other pre-Revolutionary projects asking confirmation from Virginia were being considered, most of them unfavorably. Mason was at this time influential in the assembly, being one of the dominant half-dozen Revolutionary leaders of the state. Land thus received was divided among the remaining members.

Other references to the company's affairs in letters to or from Mason are of interest here. In 1761 he was one of a committee in the company writing to Governor Dinwiddie asking for a final grant. It was a "committee of the Company" also that employed

[9] One petition is recorded as of June 21, 1765. P.R.O., *P. C. Papers*, II, f. 244.

[10] Reproduced by Leyland, *op. cit.*, ch. 3, note 42, and in the *Journals of Christopher Gist, op. cit.*, at page 244.

[11] 1 *Life of George Mason*, 147.

Gist and supervised the explorations.[12] In 1768 its activities apparently corresponded with those of a board of directors.[13] Earlier, in 1753, the committee of the company, acting again as directors would, "agreed and ordered that each member of the Company pay . . . the sum of twenty pounds current money" to build a road and a fort. Since apparently there were never more than twenty members,[14] there was little real need for public advertisements; consequently it can be assumed that newspaper notices had been formally required by the original articles of association.

In 1776 Mason made himself responsible for the cost of a survey that was to be "clear of both Henderson's and the Vandalia Company's claim." A total of £650 was expended, and only £199 had been raised when he wrote Robert Carter asking him to give £50 as his "quota" (indicating that there were then thirteen members, and that expenses were assessed *pro rata* according to the number of individual members, rather than by any rigid number of shares). Carter replied unfavorably, and Mason answered that if he did not care to make any further advances "you should let us know it candidly, that your shares may be disposed of for the payment, or sunk in the Company."[15] He offered to purchase one or both of Carter's shares. Such inter-member purchases for the price of an assessment had apparently accounted for the decrease in membership during the lean years. This phrase would indicate that the value of a share at the time

[12] *Ibid.*, at 78.

[13] *Ibid.*, at 131. He wrote: "There is to be a meeting of the Company at Stafford Court House on Tuesday the 23rd of February. . . . I enclose an advertisement to give notice of it, which you will please have inserted in the Virginia Gazette." He had already sent one to Annapolis.

[14] In 1770, Mason wrote: "As to the Ohio Company's affairs here I could have given him no satisfaction or information. It is absolutely more difficult to procure a meeting of our members than it is to assemble a German Diet; notwithstanding appointments and advertisements without number, I really believe there has never been a meeting of the Company since he [George Mercer] went from Virginia." *Ibid.*, at 151.

[15] *Ibid.*, at 189.

was *less* than £50, reflecting the uncertainty over securing final confirmation of the grant. Carter himself wrote in 1781 that he had purchased the shares of Augustine Washington and Gawin Corbin, but did not mention the price.[16]

In his will, Mason included the following clause: "I give and bequeath unto my son George and his heirs forever, all my stock in the Ohio Company as a member thereof, together with my share and part of all the said Company's lands."[17] This is in striking confirmation of the fact that transfers of interest were made individually by the members, with rights in land mentioned separately. No approval or particular form of transfer on company records seems to have been required. Nor was there any provision for a prior offer to the other members before a sale to an outsider. It seems true, however, that all sales of a member's interest were made to some other individual partner in the group, rather than to outsiders.

The members of the company referred to themselves as "adventurers" or "members" in their records and petitions.[18] Gist on one of his trips was warned that, if he were successful in negotiating with the Indians for a confirmation of land titles, he should take the deed only in the names of the members. He was furnished with a list. By most of the accepted tests, therefore, the company closely resembled the ordinary partnership, and displayed only occasionally those qualities which later in this period belonged to the true association.

THE SUSQUEHANNAH COMPANY[19]

This historically famous company stemmed from an entirely different colonial source than the Ohio Company, although it was contemporaneous with it. It is without doubt the best ex-

[16] *Ibid.*, at 6.   [17] *Ibid.*, at 461.

[18] *Cf.* Fernow, *op. cit.*, Appendix D.

[19] A full compilation of original documents relating to this Connecticut enterprise has been made, entitled *Susquehannah Company Papers;* they were edited by Julian P. Boyd for the Wyoming Historical and Geological

ample of the evolution of the corporate colony proprietorship into a commercial enterprise formed to exploit a new colony. The non-commercial character of the original New England proprietorship has often been stressed.[20] The establishment of new towns was by a true group effort, and although in later years the original proprietors may have benefited in many cases by the rise of land values, this was hardly a direct incentive. It is in such an enterprise as the Susquehannah that the speculative motive is seen emerging.[21]

Historians have laid great stress on this effort as a first indication of widespread interest in westward expansion.[22] The fact that there was a typically democratic interest in this enterprise, as against the private nature of the Virginia and Pennsylvania plans in the same period, has made it seem especially important. A century of training in group land settlement made the Connecticut leaders think in terms of hundreds of members rather than in terms of ten or fifty chosen "insiders."

Connecticut's claim to western lands beyond its present western boundary arose from its charter of 1662, which it had hastily secured from Charles II after the Restoration as one step in bring-

Society (Wilkes-Barre, 1930). Four volumes have appeared, carrying the detailed story up to 1770. Additional volumes will appear in the future. A great part of the material relates to the political controversy with Pennsylvania rather than to the enterprise itself. A brief résumé of the company's career by the editor of the *Papers* may be found in "Connecticut's Experiment in Expansion: The Susquehannah Company, 1753–1803," 4 *Journal of Economic and Business History*, 38.

Photostatic copies of 227 documents relating to the company, selected in 1845 from the files of the Connecticut assembly, are in the Connecticut State Library, as Susquehannah Company Documents.

[20] *Cf.* the discussion by Osgood in 1 *American Colonies in the Eighteenth Century*, 52, on this point. *Cf.* also Chapter II, *supra*, especially note 27.

[21] See Chapter II, note 53, *supra*, for the prevalence of speculation in town "rights" after 1760.

[22] This is true of all "modern" historians who have emphasized the frontier's influence, but Frederick Turner, in his *Frontier in American History* (New York, 1920), failed to stress the significance of the Susquehannah project, and mentions it only in a footnote, at p. 77.

ing itself back into the good graces of that monarch. The charter was loosely drawn, and was particularly vague in its definition of Connecticut's boundaries. Nevertheless, Boyd[23] has been unable to find any public expression of belief in the validity of Connecticut's charter title to western lands extending "to the South Seas" before 1750. In May of that year, ten persons, chiefly natives of Simsbury, petitioned the assembly at Hartford requesting that a township ten miles square "west of the Hudson" be granted to themselves and associates up to a total of sixty, free on condition that sixty families be settled there in the coming three years, "to give your Honours the pleasure and satisfaction of seeing a howling wilderness turned into fruitful fields."[24] Obviously, the sixty intended, in the true form of proprietorship, to settle their own families on the area granted. The petition was refused in both houses.

This idea of asking for land "which is not included in any of the charters to any of the neighboring governments" spread rapidly, probably by gossip and discussion among members of the assembly. In 1752 a similar petition carried 424 names, including several individuals from the eastern half of the state who were later to be prominent in the company's affairs. Governor Wolcott, who had stated in writing only a short time before that the Colony was bounded on the west by what later became the state line, was converted.[25] As late as 1751 a committee of the assembly had denied Connecticut's jurisdiction over any western territory, but from then on such opinions became conspicuously absent. Connecticut's agreement to the settlement of the 1725 boundary dispute with New York was the most certain legal ground for asserting that such rights did not exist.

In May, 1753, a new petition was presented by a group that included many new names. This was laid over for action the next fall. During the summer, on July 18, 1753, the Susquehan-

[23] 1 *Papers,* lvii.   [24] *Ibid.,* 2.
[25] *Ibid.,* 50.

nah Company was formally organized, at Windham. The "articles of agreement made and settled between us ye subscribers inhabitants of his majesty's colony of Connecticut—being memo-
rialists to a General Assembly of said colony—for the title to a
certain tract of land"[26] included the following interesting features. The purposes were declared to be to enlarge the English
settlements, to spread Christianity, and to promote their own
temporal interests. All agreed to pay two Spanish dollars for the
expenses of a "visiting committee" of seven who were to proceed to the Susquehannah and examine the area. This committee
was empowered to purchase land and to receive deeds made out
to each subscriber, *pro rata*. If expenses and purchase money exceeded the fund raised, each member was to contribute equally;
if the committee had money left, it was to be refunded in the
same way. The territory purchased was not to be less in extent
than twenty miles by ten miles,[27] nor was the amount paid to
exceed £1,000 in lawful money. The signing was not to be evidence of claim on any land (in order to enforce future contributions, apparently); those who signed but did not pay would not
be considered members. The visiting committee was instructed
to start in September, and did so. Another committee, of three,
was appointed to receive the money, pay it to the visiting committee, examine their accounts, and furnish lists of subscribers
to them for any deeds, and to give copies to show to others "for
reasonable pay therefor." Although it was not mentioned, half-
shares were obviously permitted, that is, a subscription of one
dollar. This privilege was ratified at a September meeting. By
the list of names, it is obvious that many rights were sold by the
visiting committee on their trip in New York and New Jersey.[28]

In September the second meeting voted a merger with a group

---

[26] *Ibid.*, 28–39.

[27] The final purchase was much larger.

[28] Traveling agents selling township "rights" in western Connecticut
and Massachusetts towns were a common phenomenon in the following
decade.

from Colchester which had been formed for the same purpose. Curiously, it was voted at this meeting that "no minor shall have any benefit by signing or subscribing to the aforesaid articles."

At a meeting in January, 1754,[29] it was decided, after a committee had reported, to raise the "enrollment fee" to four Spanish dollars, but a few members were taken at the old rate. Upon all old members an assessment of one dollar was laid at this time, so that the net increase for new members was only one dollar. A limit of five hundred was set on membership, and the additional 210 places were allotted to various counties, including fifty open to the colony as a whole. The same executive committee was continued and was given the right "to warn meetings when they judge it necessary and further to manage and order the prudentials of said Company." Timothy Woodbridge was appointed agent to deal with the Indians, and it was voted that he "be incorporated into this Company and entitled to one whole share" as a free donation. Governor Wolcott was requested to give a written approval to Woodbridge for the project, which he might use in dealing with the Indian chiefs; this the Governor did a few weeks later.

The project had received wide publicity by the winter of 1753–1754. Correspondence between Penn, Richard Peters, Sir William Johnson, and others is full of discussion; the minutes of the Pennsylvania council include several suggestions for balking the company's plan. Wyoming, the territory that was to be bought, had previously been reserved as hunting ground for the Six Nations by treaty. Pennsylvania had never purchased it, and in consequence the Pennsylvania claim seemed very uncertain to the Susquehannah leaders. They undertook to be the first to negotiate an outright purchase; the Albany Congress of 1754 provided the opportunity of dealing with the Iroquois chiefs. With the help of John Henry Lydius and a supply of liquor, a deed was negotiated granting a tract between the forty-first and

[29] 1 *Papers,* 42–50.

forty-second parallels, about one hundred twenty miles wide. The consideration was to be £2,000 New York currency, of which two hundred were paid down. The deed purported to be dated in July, but not all the signatures of the Indian chiefs were secured until the following March, many under questionable circumstances.[30]

At the same time, the Pennsylvania delegates thought to steal a march by getting a similar sale of land. The Pennsylvania deed was more regularly executed, and apparently was secured honestly. It covered the same area, and was signed by many of the same chiefs. Penn and Peters did not learn of the Susquehannah deed until September or October, and immediately began efforts to have it nullified. The contest that was to last for over thirty years was thus launched.

There are some scattered records that give indication of the formation of two other purchasing groups, the first and second Delaware Companies,[31] though no details of their existence are available. The purchases for these two were made also under Lydius' direction, and under equally suspicious circumstances. Notices of meetings and some other records indicate that the same leaders were concerned in both the Susquehannah and Delaware projects. In 1762, for example, it was voted at a Susquehannah meeting to appoint a joint agent to seek royal confirmation of titles.[32]

There is a gap in the records of the company between 1755 and 1761. War prevented any settlement. A group had gone out in 1755, but soon gave up the effort at colonization. With the prospect of peace, the enterprise took on new vigor. In 1762 a new settlement was made in the region, and the concern of the Penns and their representatives increased. By the summer of 1763 Eliphalet Dyer was on his way to England to try for royal confirmation. He abandoned the attempt late in 1764, and the com-

[30] *Ibid.*, lxxiv. [31] *Ibid.*, 50–53.
[32] 2 *Papers*, xx.

pany's interests were poorly represented in London from that time on.[33] In this period occurred the first vote of the company authorizing the committee to assign shares to people who would prove of value to the settlement. This later developed, in the seventies, into a system of granting free land to men who would agree to undergo military service.

In 1768 there was a renewal of interest, because of the Fort Stanwix treaty, and a new group of settlers went out in 1769.[34] In 1770 the Board of Trade refused to intervene to help Pennsylvania, and by 1774 the proprietary government had given up efforts to oust the Connecticut settlers. In that same year the Connecticut legislature erected a giant town, as large as the whole colony, out of the fought-over territory. This effort to extend the state's jurisdiction precipitated a bitter political contest within Connecticut, and finally came to naught when the Trenton commission of 1782 awarded jurisdiction of the area to Pennsylvania. Most of the rest of the history of the company is concerned with the efforts of Susquehannah leaders to retain physical possession of the land[35] and with contests over actual land titles. Many of these cases, in the Pennsylvania and Connecticut courts, were in litigation long after 1800.

In the later years, the standing committee became simply one or two leaders, such as John Franklin in 1784–1786. Elections became more and more perfunctory as the proprietors actually took up their land and lost interest. The giving of free shares to a militia was another abuse of the original structure that has been mentioned. After 1770 the details of giving out land were delegated to a settlers' committee. The first one was appointed at a

[33] *Ibid.*, xli.

[34] 3 *Papers*, xx.

[35] The "Paxtang Boys" were brought in to help, much as gangsters of the twentieth century were imported for Chicago and New York beer wars; a similar offer was made after the Revolution to Ethan Allen to bring in his Green Mountain Boys as strong-arm men. The biographer of George Morgan calls them the "Paxton Gang"; Savelle, *George Morgan* (New York, 1932).

meeting in 1768 to supervise the formal settlement of forty families; it was made accountable to the standing committee. In the year 1773, prior to the assumption of short-lived governmental control by Connecticut, a town government was set up in the valley, but the settlers' committee continued to control all matters concerning land and the adjustment of disputes independently. The methods used by the committee were fully reminiscent of the accepted pattern of Connecticut proprietorships. Groups of fifty were used as the basis of new towns, with three additional shares reserved for the school, the church, and the minister. Three or four types of land were established in the area chosen, and each share received one parcel of each type—the home lot, pasture, tillage, and woodlot form of allocation so familiar in New England.

Some other incidents are of more interest here than is the great amount of petty controversy and political argument that made up most of the company's history for twenty-five years. In 1768 the company voted to pay out of its treasury the expenses of anyone prosecuted by the Pennsylvania authorities; in 1769 several specific grants of expense money to the court at Easton were paid. The method of dealing with delinquent subscribers seems to have varied sharply. In July, 1769, it was voted in such cases that "so much of the respective rights shall then be sold at vendue, to the highest bidder, as shall raise the sum or sums in which they are deficient."[36] It was also voted that public notice of such sales be given to each proprietor concerned. A month later another vote was passed simply providing for a forfeit of delinquent shares.[37] Still later a "penalty rate" for readmission was established. The only registration of members was by lists at the end of minutes of meetings, of those who had purchased since the previous meeting. One case at least occurred where a member claimed payment but had not had his name recorded. In these cases, formal votes were taken to reinstate.

[36] 3 Papers, 155–156. [37] Ibid., 175.

THE TRANSYLVANIA PROJECT[38]

The Transylvania project of Richard Henderson is probably the most romantic enterprise of all those which there is occasion to examine here. That Daniel Boone was sent on exploring trips to Kentucky by Henderson's company was a fact not known to most of his contemporaries, nor seemingly to many of our earlier romantic historians. To modern writers, who are perhaps over-impressed by the influence of business enterprise upon colonial expansion, this interesting connection has seemed a cynical confirmation of their controvertible thesis that speculation in land was the absorbing attraction of the frontier.[39]

Richard Henderson's father was one of the lawyer-officeholders against whom the Regulator movement[40] of North Carolina was directed. He was for a long period High Sheriff of Granville County; and it was the sheriffs who seemed the most guilty of unfair exactions. Henderson himself became a sheriff and later a judge. In 1771 his home was burned by Regulators.

The historical opinion of the Regulator movement has varied from condemnation to justification. It seems certain that the exactions of the officeholding clique, against which the Regulator movement was directed, were oppressive. At least in the

[38] The important manuscripts relating to Henderson and Transylvania are in the *Draper Collection* of the State Historical Society of Wisconsin. There is material relating to the project in the *North Carolina State Records*. Archibald Henderson has written frequently upon the enterprise itself and the surrounding history; his *Conquest of the Old Southwest* (New York, 1920) is a complete, though somewhat popular, discussion. His article, "Richard Henderson and the Occupation of Kentucky, 1775," 1 *Mississippi Historical Review*, 341, deals with the 1780 effort. Abernethy, *Western Lands*, ch. IX, discusses the political circumstances.

[39] This point of view is most strikingly presented by Abernethy in both his studies of the Virginia-Carolina frontier; cf. Chapter I, note 9. Such a standard biography as R. G. Thwaites, *Daniel Boone* (New York, 1902), fails to mention that Boone was subsidized by Henderson.

[40] An excellent analysis of the underlying causes of the Regulator movement is that by Julian P. Boyd, "Sheriff in Colonial North Carolina," 5 *North Carolina Historical Review*, 151.

case of Henderson and his associates membership in the clique seemed to result in the acquisition of that rare colonial possession—free capital—without any direct participation in trade. Over a period of more than ten years, Henderson was able to advance a very considerable sum to pay for trips of exploration, Indian gifts, and the costs of erecting defenses and buildings, with no prospect of immediate returns.

As early as 1764 young Henderson and a few associates had underwritten an exploring trip by Boone and two other frontiersmen. In this group were probably Henderson's uncle, John Williams, and the Hart brothers who later became his partners.[41] But not until 1769 was the famous trip of Boone and Findlay undertaken, again in the interest of the Henderson group. The delay was probably due to uncertainty about the effect of the 1763 proclamation and the great distance of the new territory from North Carolina settlements. Boone did not return from this expedition until the spring of 1771, meeting during the course of it many of the adventures that have made his name so famous in romantic history. He made, prosaically, a detailed report to his land-seeking backers, and in their private correspondence in 1771 and 1772 occur many quotations and discussions of this document.[42]

Lord Dunmore's War temporarily procured a state of peace with the Indians of the Kentucky region, who had attacked exploring parties and settlers during the two preceding years. This peace came at the end of 1774, and was a signal to land-seekers to move into that region. It was common belief at that time that Lord Dunmore himself was interested in acquiring western lands, and had derived his military ardor from his land ambitions.[43] During the summer of 1774, just preceding this peace, the first Henderson group of which there is formal record had

[41] Henderson, *op. cit.*, 107.   [42] *Ibid.*, at 158.

[43] *Cf.* the opinion of Patrick Henry on his land affairs, recorded by Thomas Wharton in a letter to Thomas Walpole, September 23, 1774,

its meeting; it was called the Louisa Company and there were six full shares.[44] In addition to Henderson and Williams, the two Harts, Luttrell, and Johnston, three new partners soon joined —David Hart (a son), Leonard Bullock, and James Hogg.

The changed prospect for settlement was undoubtedly the incentive for a reorganization of the Louisa group into the Transylvania Company, on January 6, 1775. The articles of agreement aim clearly at the establishment of a proprietary form of government, and are quite closely analogous to agreements which in modern law would be termed joint adventures.[45]

On March 17, 1775, a treaty was concluded with the Cherokees consummating the purchase of the Transylvania Company territory for the sum of £10,000. The tract consisted of about twenty million acres—nearly all of present Kentucky and a large part of northern Tennessee. The price was thus between two and three cents an acre. Supplementary transactions made at this historic Indian meeting were the purchase by the Transylvania Company of a gateway strip in northeastern Tennessee, a purchase by the Watauga Association in the Watauga and Holston Valleys (for £2,000), and two purchases by Jacob Brown in the Nolichucky Valley. Part of the land purchased as the gateway in Carter's Valley was retransferred to Messrs. Carter and Lucas, who later purchased two of the eight shares in the Transylvania Company (as part of the consideration, probably). It is claimed that this whole series of transactions, as embodied in a treaty, was the result of one of the fairest and best-conducted Indian

"Letters of Thomas Wharton," 33 *Pennsylvania Magazine of History and Biography*, 444–445.

[44] This agreement is in Appendix A.

[45] The articles of agreement, from the *Draper MSS.* in the Wisconsin State Historical Society, are the most picturesque of any which have survived from this half-century; they reflect the excessively legalistic style of the same era in England. They are reproduced in full in Appendix B. Land warrants were issued in the name of "Richard Henderson & Company, Proprietors of the Colony of Transylvania." *Ibid.*, 1 CC 20.

meetings in Colonial history.[46] No liquor was permitted on the treaty grounds during the four-day period.

Immediately following the treaty Henderson and his partners, still using Boone as their field leader, moved to establish a settlement and forts, and to open a land office. There was comparatively widespread knowledge of Henderson's undertaking; he had been aiming toward the creation of a new proprietary territory for several years. Lord Dunmore denounced the whole project, Washington was concerned over it, and George Rogers Clark, in the winter of 1775-1776, was involved in efforts to deny the validity of Henderson's purchase in favor of Virginia's superior claim. The whole group of Virginia speculators in lands was harassed by a new threat, to be added to the competition they were receiving from Croghan, Wharton, Morgan, and other Philadelphia traders. It is possible that backing for Clark's famed later expedition was forthcoming because, if it were successful, Virginia's claim to western lands would be strengthened.

The efforts of Henderson to establish a democratic form of government (with, however, the eight proprietors retaining a full veto power), to secure recognition from the Continental Congress as the fourteenth colony, and to ward off the competing claims of Clark and other Virginians as well as of settlers in the area who claimed rights by prior arrival, are of deep historical interest, although they are of little aid to our present inquiry. It is of interest to note, however, that a Transylvania legislature, elected from the several small settlements in central Kentucky,

[46] *Cf.* Henderson, *op. cit.*, 224-225, for descriptions by eye-witnesses. *Cf.* also 1 *Calendar of Virginia State Papers*, 303-311, 315.

Henderson based the validity of the purchase upon the Treaty of Lochaber of October, 1770, whereby were reconveyed to the Cherokees all claims of the Mohawk Tribes to the Tennessee-Kentucky area which had been presumably included in the grant to the Crown at the Treaty of Fort Stanwix. Kentucky historians have agreed that the Crown did thereby give up its rights to the Cherokee Territory, and that Henderson's purchase was thus not within the forbidden area described in the proclamation which

met in September, 1775,[47] to elect Henderson and Williams as delegates to Philadelphia. In the same month the eight proprietors had a separate meeting and passed twenty resolutions prescribing the actions of its agents in dealing with the land assets of the company.[48] Henderson was elected president, and Colonel Williams was appointed land agent and invested "with full power, by letter of attorney" to make land sales. His salary was to be £150 for a six-month stay at Boonesborough. Seven resolutions set out specific directions to him in making grants. He was to reserve one-half the product of all non-ferrous mines (including sulphur) for the proprietors, to make no grants near salt springs or known metal mines; 2,000 acres were to be granted to Boone; exact surveys were to be made; and copies of deeds were to be kept for the proprietors. James Hogg was then appointed delegate to the Continental Congress, and was authorized to sell land on his trip to secure recognition for Transylvania as one of the "United Colonies." A special area of 200,000 acres was to be selected and set aside by Henderson for the proprietors exclusively. Other resolutions were votes of thanks to individuals, detailed instructions for grants to a minister and in return for certain supplies, and details of business conduct. These resolutions resemble collectively the votes of a modern board of directors, rather than those of a stockholders' meeting or a meeting of ordinary partners in an enterprise.

The claim of the company to quit-rents and to a veto power

followed Fort Stanwix. Evidence is noted in the *Draper MSS.*, I CC 132. *Cf.* also R. S. Cotterill, *History of Pioneer Kentucky* (Cincinnati, 1917), 83–84, representing the view of Kentucky historians that Henderson was legally justified in making his purchase from the Cherokees, and opposing completely the later claims of Virginia.

[47] There had been a prior meeting in May, but not of elected representatives.

[48] The minutes of this meeting are reprinted in full in the Appendix to Volume II of Hall, *Sketches of History, Life and Manners in the West* (Philadelphia, 1835).

over legislative acts aroused resentment both at Philadelphia[49] and in the settlements themselves. The outbreak of war was the direct event that put the company into difficulties from which it never recovered. Its success in holding title and enforcing land sales, even during a period of peace, would seem to have been uncertain. When, for example, the company raised the price of land from twenty to fifty shillings per hundred acres, with extra surveying fees, there was a great outburst of protest. In January, 1776, the payment of quit-rents was deferred until 1780 and certain fees were abolished. Such a regime could hardly have lasted in the face of the antagonistic attitude of the settlers. Revival of the proprietary principle, which Henderson contemplated, was thoroughly hopeless under 1775 conditions.[50]

In June, 1779, the Virginia House of Delegates, following two years of petitions and hearings, declared the Transylvania purchase void in so far as it lay within the claimed charter limits of Virginia.[51] As compensation for the payments made to the Indians, and for the other expenditures of the Henderson group, a tract of 200,000 acres was granted to the individual partners. This area lies in the region of the present town of Henderson, Kentucky, and much of it was sold by the partners in small parcels in later years.

Soon after this rebuff, Henderson, acting for the same part-

---

[49] Hogg apparently was very active among the delegates, who seemed to have plenty of spare time to discuss land speculation. He wrote to his partners in January, 1776, that he had seen a copy of the Camden-Yorke opinion in the hands of a member of the Illinois-Wabash Company, and quoted from it. In November, Silas Deane wrote him a long letter giving advice on the project. Hall, *op. cit.*, 228–279. Many years later Hogg changed his name to Walter Alves. It was through his descendants that most papers relating to the enterprise were preserved. *Draper MSS.*, 2 CC 34.

[50] Hogg, writing to his partners after visiting Philadelphia, had stressed the universal advice given him there to set up a free democratic government, avoid quit-rents, and even to prohibit slavery. Hall, *op. cit.*, 252.

[51] 1 *Calendar of Virginia State Papers*, 303 ff., 320.

nership, employed James Robertson as an understudy in the
Boone role to open up that part of the great purchase that lay
south of the extended Virginia line. Here, in 1780, was re-
enacted the same story. Henderson arrived at the settlement on
the Cumberland in May, 1780, wrote the famed Cumberland
Compact[52] and headed the 256 signers. It was to be the foundation of a government, and was essentially a contract between the
Transylvania partners and the settlers. The agreement has attracted historical attention because it included a provision for
the recall of unsatisfactory judges by the voters of the projected
colony. But these "judges" were semi-legislators, one being selected at each of the twelve "stations" in the area. They were to
settle land disputes, and act as criminal justices as well. Henderson's land books were to be open to them at any time. Provision
was made for adjusting the set price of £26-13s.-4d. per hundred acres if the currency depreciated further. In later resolutions the agreement was called an "association, confederacy and
general Government."

   The ending here was the same. Although a land office was
set up, Henderson was never able to give clear titles. North
Carolina in 1783 followed Virginia's lead and declared the purchase void in so far as it lay within the claimed area of that state.
In compensation, a similar tract of 200,000 acres was given, in
the Powell's Valley region, where land was then being given as
soldiers' bounties.[53] The legislative act made over the tract to the
partners individually by name "to hold the aforesaid portions in
severalty as tenants in common and not as joint tenants." Lucas
and Carter, who had meanwhile bought the interests of Williams and Johnston,[54] participated in the partition deeds that

   [52] It is summarized in P. W. Putnam, *History of Middle Tennessee*
(Nashville, 1859), 94–102.
   [53] 16 *North Carolina State Records,* 151.
   [54] There is other evidence relating to the Transylvania project which
indicates that the shares were transferable.
   In a petition drawn up in 1792 by surviving members of the group—

were executed among the Transylvania partners, and these deeds have since been regarded as the foundation titles in the district.

Thus the two schemes, with a combined life of about two decades, brought to their participants clear title to 400,000 acres of frontier land as recompense; a return far less than the expenditure of money which had probably been incurred.

In January, 1795, Hart, Williams, Bullock, and Hogg, as the only survivors of the group, petitioned Congress for compensation, since they had been forced to deed over to the Cherokees part of the land which Virginia had granted. Williams in this petition was called "Chairman" and there were several references to the "Company." Other extant records show that remaining members of the group regarded themselves as a company as late as 1797.[55]

THE COMPANY OF MILITARY ADVENTURERS[56]

The army engaged in the Havana Campaign of 1762, undertaken as one phase of the ambitious English effort against Spain,

John Williams, Leonard Bullock, James Hogg, Thomas Hogg, John Umstead (who had married Luttrell's widow), and David Hart—it was stated that on August 29, 1779, it had been agreed to allow survivors and assigns of the original group to share in the compensatory grant of 200,000 acres, after 10,000 acres had been given to Carter and Lucas. It was stated as the belief of the petitioners that "sales and conveyances have been made in like manner by other of the said partners by reason whereof persons to your orators unknown at present may have some logical or equitable interests in the land." *Draper MSS.,* 1 CC 227. This allegation is substantiated by the records of a meeting of attorneys on December 3, 1779, to divide up about 24,000 acres that originally had been allotted to Thomas Hart out of the 200,000 acre grant. He had sold a one-fourth share to Robert Salter and one-fourth to William Ory, both of whom were deceased. Their shares had remained undivided—further evidence of the attitude that their shares as purchased were in the "Company," not in specific lots of land. The purpose of the meeting was to draw lots for various parcels in the 24,000 acres, to settle the two estates. *Draper MSS.,* 1 CC 222.

[55] Hall, 2 *Sketches,* 271. There is record that in August, 1787, land sales were being made in Tennessee by General Samuel Hopkins as agent for Richard Henderson and Company. *Draper MSS.,* 2 CC 11.

[56] An excellent account of this effort to secure bounty lands after the Seven Years' War has been prepared by Albert C. Bates, of the Connecti-

included 1,050 Connecticut men under Generals Phineas Lyman and Israel Putnam. There were also some companies recruited in other portions of New England. Disease was the major enemy, for the city capitulated with a minimum of fighting. Deaths from illness during the summer of 1762 claimed over four hundred of the Connecticut contingent.

On the trip home, there was ample time for discussion of the probable size of individual shares in the captured Spanish treasures. For privates, it seemed that actual cash received would be small and the delay in receiving it long, despite the rosy promises of English recruiting officers. On June 15, 1763, there was held the first meeting of a group determined to secure a land bounty for their services in addition to the uncertain cash bounty. It was held at Hartford, and although no record of it is extant, later accounts show that General Lyman was probably named president, Captain Herlihy clerk, and Hugh Ledlie treasurer. The officers were those of a typical town proprietorship.

At the first meeting it was decided that $2 (Spanish) "advance" would be paid in to the treasury by all those who cared to join the effort, principally to defray the expenses of Lyman's trip to London. There was a standing committee of five members named, and nine "receivers" who were to collect new subscriptions and future assessments in various towns of the colony. Lyman started for England before the proclamation of October, 1763, granting bounty lands to soldiers in the successful war, had reached the American side.

Another meeting was held the following summer, on August 22, 1764. Lyman reported nothing but "good progress." It was

cut Historical Society, as part of his introduction to the society's volume *The Two Putnams* (Hartford, 1931), which contains chiefly journals kept by Israel and Rufus Putnam. The following account is largely summarized therefrom, although the journals had been reprinted elsewhere as early as 1852, by Hildreth, *Memoirs of the Pioneer Settlers of Ohio* (Cincinnati, 1852).

decided to levy another $3 payment on members, and also to let in members from other colonies who might be eligible at the $3 rate. Apparently such new joiners were not required to pay the first $2. Receivers were named in Boston and New York, and the five members of the standing committee signed an announcement of the invitation.

There followed a period of eight years when all activity at home seems to have been in abeyance. Lyman vainly attempted to secure a grant of some sort.[57] In the years after 1769 Lord Hillsborough seemed to be his chief stumbling block; the same individual was the nemesis of the Vandalia scheme which was on foot at the same time. In 1770 Lyman did succeed in getting 20,000 acres in West Florida granted to himself,[58] and was involved in other efforts to secure large areas. In desperation, he finally addressed George III directly, in April, 1772. The reply seemed so encouraging that he returned home that summer and on November 18, 1772, the company was revived by holding a Hartford meeting, of which a full record has been kept. It lasted three days.

Lyman was chosen moderator, a new clerk was named, and six new men were added to the old standing committee. Nine others were named on a committee to explore the land contained in the grant—although no official confirmation of any kind had been received. The group seemed to have Yankee "push" in matters of expansion and self-government. The explorers were to receive eight shillings per day, but were to pay all their own expenses. However, a vessel was to be provided for them, with a navigator, and they were permitted to hire four "able and handy

[57] Under date of May 11, 1768, there is record of a petition by Lyman to the Privy Council, referred to the Committee on Plantations, P.R.O., *P. C. Papers*, II, f. 176. A similar petition in *Colonial Office Papers*, 5/67, f. 367, is reprinted in 11 *Illinois Historical Collections*, 260. *Cf.* also his long address to Lord Dartmouth, *ibid.*, 265.

[58] P.R.O., *P. C. Papers*, II, f. 386.

men" at forty shillings per month plus thirty shillings for expense of feeding them. Four of the group were to proceed by land and the Ohio River instead of by sea to Florida.

Other interesting steps to reorganize the company were taken at this prolonged meeting. The books were to be kept open until the following December in order to secure new members. Each member would be given a formal receipt and his name entered in the company's books as a proprietor. All former receivers were discharged and some forty-five new men were appointed to this task of soliciting membership. The standing committee was empowered to select others. From the book of membership the clerk was directed to make up an alphabetical list for the use of the treasurer. The three-man standing committee was empowered to draw orders on the treasurer, settle all accounts, and supervise the treasurer's office. This committee was to conduct the business of the company during the periods between regular meetings and to "warn meetings" whenever they felt it necessary. Finally, it was voted to publish a summary of proceedings in six newspapers published in Connecticut, Massachusetts, New York, and Pennsylvania, obviously as a method of advertising the project to veterans of the war. From these published notices historians have derived most of their information concerning the doings of the group.

Israel and Rufus Putnam with two others sailed for Florida in December of 1772 and returned about eight months later; at this same time the group sent by land made a separate exploring trip. It was upon their journey that the Putnams kept a journal describing in considerable detail the districts around the Yazoo's junction with the Mississippi.[59] The trips of both parties were limited mainly to the small creeks and rivers tributary to the two large streams. The governor of West Florida at Pensacola had

[59] Hildreth, *Pioneer Settlers*, 38–53, gives the most interesting account of this journey to West Florida; the region around Natchez and the Yazoo River where the grant was located was to become noted fifty years later as the richest cotton land in the South.

received nothing from London even mentioning the supposed grant, but after some discussion he invited the group to come to their chosen district at the mouth of the Yazoo River and settle on the same terms which he was offering to other settlers. The assumption was that the area occupied would be confirmed later by the Crown as bounty land. The terms he offered were 100 acres for each head of a family and 50 additional acres for each member of a family, all *gratis;* additional land could be purchased at the rate of five shillings for each 50 acres. After two years a quit-rent would be demanded. In each area laid out for a settlers' group, land must be reserved for a minister and half as much again for the support of schools.[60]

In October, 1773, two months after the Putnam party had returned, their experiences in West Florida were discussed at another meeting. Many of the subscribers had meanwhile come to doubt Lyman's word as to the imminence of a Crown grant, and there was also a belief that the admittance of many non-veterans would spoil the chances of the group as a whole in securing their grant of land. Despite the uncertainty of the whole affair, four groups of "undertakers" were formed to go out and settle the land which had been tentatively reserved, and in the years 1774 and 1775 an unknown number actually left Connecticut and settled near the mouth of the Yazoo. Many of them, including General Lyman, died there within a year or two.[61] Interest at home waned rapidly because of the lack of any actual Crown grant, and the onset of the Revolution ended interest completely.

Twenty-four years after the settlers had gone out, in 1798, a

[60] About 380,000 acres were granted in this tentative manner, but never confirmed. The only expense was to be five shillings per 1,000 acres, to cover the costs of the survey. The area was thus divided into nineteen townships. *Ibid.,* 52, and 1 *American State Papers, Public Lands,* 257.

[61] Hildreth, *op. cit.,* 53, records that in August, 1774, one Michael Martyn wrote to Putnam from his new home on the Amite River within the present area of Louisiana. He was already ill at the time. In 1781, 140 of the surviving settlers left and reached Georgia. A few remaining were given titles by Congress after 1800. 1 *Am. State Papers, Public Lands,* 257.

group of heirs or friends of some of the leaders, headed by Timothy Dwight and John Porter, wrote to Ambassador Rufus King in London asking him to discover the status of Lyman's supposed promise of a grant. King had an investigation made of the records both of the Board of Trade and the Privy Council but in neither was he able to discover any sort of official record. Thus this project, conducted in many ways as a new town proprietorship, seems to have foundered on the false pride of Lyman. He was unwilling to admit that he had failed in his purpose in London. The expenditure for exploration was a total loss, and so far as is known the several hundred members who contributed small amounts received no compensation whatever.

THE MISSISSIPPI COMPANY

The formation of this project was directly stimulated by the prospect of peace in 1763. It was attractive to the same group of Virginia leaders who for fifteen years or more had been interested in acquiring western lands. The general plan was the same as in several other projects of the period: to form an association, petition for a grant, secure an extinguishment of the Indian title, and proceed with sales of land to settlers. Its fate was linked closely with that of all the enterprises aiming to settle and exploit the trans-Ohio or Illinois country. A dozen years of uncertainty and vacillation in the British ministry spelled oblivion for all such projects, except in so far as they received compensation later from the Virginia legislature or from Congress after the Declaration of Independence. It is this period that Alvord has treated so thoroughly.[62] The lack of definitive results for colonization and settlement, as well as for adequate government of the area, illustrates the shortcomings of the "push and pull" type of cabinet government by factions, then so dominant in England.

The first meeting of the group was June 3, 1763, at which the

[62] *Mississippi Valley in British Politics.*

general nature of the project was discussed, and the general plan of action laid down. The idea of limiting membership to fifty was adopted, each to receive 50,000 acres in the expected grant of 2,500,000 acres. Thirty-eight Virginians were the original members, including five Lees and three Washingtons.[63] Actual articles of agreement were adopted on September 26, 1763, presumably at the next meeting. Although they are easily accessible,[64] a summary of the provisions is valuable because of certain striking differences that set this attempt apart from others found in this particular period.

The preamble to the articles includes the phrase "we whose names are underwritten do agree to form a body of Adventurers by the name of the Mississippi Company." The clauses in the "rules and regulations" were 1) that the company would consist of fifty members, each to contribute equally to the expenses of securing a grant from the Crown. The terms of the grant were specified: 50,000 acres per member and twelve years' freedom from quit-rents and protection from "the insults of the savages" by royal troops. 2) Activity for securing the grant should commence before the full quota of members was secured. 3) The grant was to be made specifically in fee simple to the individuals, not in joint tenancy. 4) A general meeting would be held annually, at which a majority of the members residing in Virginia or Maryland would be a quorum; votes to be passed by a majority of those in attendance. 5) A president was to be elected at each annual meeting, and all votes were to be kept in a record book. 6) The principal business of each meeting would be the determination of an assessment, to be paid to the treasurer; any

[63] The preliminary rules and regulations adopted at this meeting, in Washington's handwriting, are preserved in the Library of Congress among Washington's papers. Additional correspondence relating to the company, from the Chatham papers in the Public Record Office, appears in 16 *American Historical Review*, 311.

[64] They appear, together with the petition submitted to the Crown, in 10 *Illinois Historical Collections*, 19 ff.

member not making payment before the next annual meeting after the demand was made "shall forfeit all right, title and interest in the said Company." 7) The treasurer was to enter a bond and make oath of integrity; he would also act as secretary, and would receive 5 per cent of all assessment money passing through his hands. 8) A committee was to be appointed, consisting of ten members (of which five should be a quorum) to carry out the company's purposes; it was to have stated meetings twice a year, at which any ordinary member present could also vote, as could the treasurer. 9) There could be no sale of shares without notice being given at an annual meeting, and a prior offer to the company. 10) If a full share were sold to several purchasers jointly, the company retained the right of naming the voter among them; if an original member sold a part of his share, he would retain the full vote belonging thereto; if a member bought other shares, he could not thereby increase his vote beyond one.

The tenth clause is of interest here in showing how thoroughly speculative the aim was. Any measure of success would instantly place a high value upon a share, so that members would desire to sell. But votes were not to be transferred outside the original circle.

In the fall of 1763 a petition was drawn up; Thomas Cumming was established as the company's agent in London, and an assessment of £122 was voted. It was also voted that the committee would have power to summon special meetings by two advertisements in the Virginia and Maryland *Gazettes*. Full powers were granted to these special meetings.

At a meeting in November, 1765, the quorum required was reduced to twelve, of whom four should be committee members. At this meeting it was also voted to allow two shares to be held by "special" English members—obviously men whose influence was needed in furthering the grant. This total of forty members seems to be the maximum that was ever reached, as an assessment in 1767 of about thirteen and a half pounds was levied on this number. At the 1767 meetings[65] the principal business was the ousting of five members for not "having paid their quota according to the original Articles." One man was declared not to be a member because he had never signed the articles. Four other new men were admitted, including the famous Dr. Thomas Walker, who at one time or another was connected with almost every major Virginia land speculation. In December also it was "resolved that Mr. Charles Digges have full power and authority to sell or dispose of his share in this Company to Mr. Thomas Montgomery or any other person that the Company shall hereafter approve of." It was also decided to go out and solicit certain persons to become members, including Arthur Lee, apparently to fill up the intended membership of fifty. To raise the assessment mentioned above, a meeting was scheduled for the following March to vote on it, but if there were not a quorum (and it was apparently expected that there would not be) the committee was authorized to declare it effective, and to employ an agent. Arthur Lee was secured for this task[66] and he presented the petition[67] for a grant of 2,500,000 acres in December, 1768.

The company was a complete failure. It never made any real progress after the date of this petition[68] and in Washington's records his total payment on assessments of over £25 was written off as a complete loss. George Grenville had declared, upon receipt of the first petition as early as 1764, that he was entirely opposed to such exploitation of the newly won territory by private groups, especially in one Colony. After 1768 the rising prominence of the Vandalia project killed any chances that such an area might be granted to Virginians, whose influence with the Whig ministry was at a low ebb after 1765.

[65] The minutes are reprinted in 10 *Illinois Historical Collections*, 570–572, for the May meeting, and in 16 *ibid.*, 144, for the December meeting.

[66] *Cf.* 2 Alvord, *op. cit.*, 93.

[67] P. C., Unbound Papers, 1768 (2).

[68] For comment by Lee in a letter that the petition was hopeless, *cf.* 16 *Illinois Historical Collections*, 543.

THE ILLINOIS-WABASH COMPANIES

Two purchases from Illinois Indian tribes, which were later consolidated into this project, were directly stimulated by the famous opinion of two high English law officials, Lord Camden and Charles Yorke, that direct purchases from Indians would give a sound title to western land.[69]

[69] The extraordinary influence which circulation of a garbled version of this opinion had upon the plans of several land groups has been emphasized by Alvord in his various studies of this period. He fails to stress the fact that it *was* garbled and was really a commentary upon the rights of the East India Company, for the guidance of the Privy Council in replying to one of the Company's petitions. Its use, presumably to justify land purchases direct from the Indians in America, in defiance of the settled policy of the Council, was pure chicanery. Probably hatched up by Wharton as a way to aid the Vandalia scheme, perhaps only on the ground that there was an analogy between the situation in India and that in America, it degenerated into a purported general sanction for all such purchases. Abernethy, *Western Lands,* 116–117, summarizes the conjectures of historians as to the responsibility for altering the opinion and circulating it among the land "lobbyists" in London.

The following quotation from the opinion of Lord Camden and Yorke, somewhat fuller than that given in other places, was copied at the India Office (Records Department, Charters and Treaties, 7 *Charters,* 103–105) by Professor Wayne E. Stevens of Dartmouth College and kindly transmitted to the author. He points out that the circumstances surrounding it make it clear that it was a specific answer to a specific question raised by the East India Company.

"As to the latter part of the prayer of the petition relative to the holding or retaining Fortresses or Districts already-acquired or to be acquired by Treaty, Grant or Conquest, We beg leave to point out some distinctions upon it. In respect to such Places as have been or shall be acquired by treaty or Grant from the Mogul or any of the Indian Princes or Governments Your Majestys Letters Patent are not necessary, the property of the soil vesting in the Company by the Indian Grants subject only to your Majestys Right of Sovereignity [*sic*] over the Settlements as English Settlements & over the Inhabitants as English Subjects who carry with them your Majestys Laws wherever they form Colonies & receive your Majestys protection by virtue of your Royal Charters. In respect to such places as have lately been acquired or shall hereafter be acquired by Conquest the property as well as the Dominion vests in your Majesty by virtue of your known Prerogative & consequently the Company can only derive a right to them through your Majestys Grant."

In the extracts circulated among the various land agents, the words "Mogul" and "Princes" were skillfully omitted, and also the first sentence

The firm of Franks and Company was one of the group of Philadelphia merchant houses whose business expanded rapidly after 1740 with the incoming tide of immigration, of which the Baynton, Wharton, and Morgan firm was probably the most famous. The Franks firm was ably directed, around 1770, by Bernard and Michael Gratz.[70] Their representative in Illinois in 1773 was William Murray, under whose direction the later purchases of land were carried out; he was made a partner of the firm at this time, which also included the Gratz brothers, David Franks, James Rumsey, and Alexander Ross.[71] Early in 1773 Murray had visited George Croghan who told him of the legal opinion that had originally been given to Samuel Wharton. He promptly wrote back to his partners of this changed aspect of the situation and secured some additional subscribers for the projected purchase.

When Murray arrived at Kaskaskia in the summer of 1773 he discussed with the local English commanding officer the significance of the opinion. The officer, however, continued to express belief that the general order against permitting land purchases was still valid. Murray, however, completed a purchase of land in July from a large assemblage of Indians and registered the deed at Kaskaskia in the prescribed legal manner. Captain Lord, the English officer in charge, immediately wrote to General Gage of the transaction and asked for instructions. The deed has been preserved in full[72] and indicates that the sale was made

of the above quotation. Marshall, in his 1822 opinion in the case of *Johnson's Lessee* v. *McIntosh*, 8 Wheaton 543, averred his belief that the opinion related to India only, and he may have had before him a full version of it.

[70] *Cf.* W. V. Byars, editor, *Bernard and Michael Gratz, Merchants of Philadelphia, 1754–1798* (Jefferson City, 1916).

[71] 2 Alvord, *op. cit.*, 201, note 370.

[72] In the *Illinois-Wabash Land Company Manuscript*, edited by C. W. Alvord (privately printed by C. H. McCormick, Chicago, 1915); the copy in the Illinois State Historical Society was kindly made available to the author. The older spelling of Ouabache in place of Wabash is often used by historians.

in the names of the individual subscribers to the project, rather than to the Illinois Company. The name of any company or group was not separately mentioned at any place in the deed. The agreement which finally set up a formal organization for these purchases was not accomplished until after the merger of the Wabash purchase with this first purchase by Murray.[73]

As Alvord has pointed out,[74] the specious doctrine of the Camden-Yorke opinion, that direct purchases from Indians could be made, was not accepted by leaders in the English cabinet after 1771. Indeed, their attitude grew increasingly distrustful of the results if the colonists were permitted to purchase western lands from Indian tribes. In the spring of 1774 this distrust reached a peak, partly as the result of the Boston Tea Party, and brought about the passage of the Quebec Bill. In order to offset this quickly expressed attitude of opposition among British army representatives and the Colonial government, Murray and his backers proceeded to seek confirmation of their title from the Virginian government. His method of doing this was a familiar, if not particularly honorable, one. He organized, in early 1775, the Wabash Company, which was to make another purchase and include as its leading member Lord Dunmore, Governor of Virginia. The very simple strategy in view was to secure Dunmore's support in London for a confirmation of both purchases. The latter had been interested in some projects of his own and expected to make his fortune by land operations. This connection with Dunmore was logical, because Virginia had claimed jurisdiction over the whole Illinois territory in which the two purchases were located.

All efforts to secure confirmation of the two purchases were suspended as news of fighting in New England reached Phila-

[73] Extracts from the manuscript records of the company just referred to include the articles of agreement drawn up for the merger. They are reprinted in Appendix C.

[74] 2 Alvord, *op. cit.*, 212–215; but this is obvious in view of the true character of that opinion.

delphia and Virginia. However, within one year individuals interested were busy with plans to secure confirmation of their purchases from an independent Virginia, in lieu of confirmation by London. The expedition of George Rogers Clark to the Illinois country was, therefore, of great importance to the syndicate. One student[75] of this period, who is not at all favorable to Clark as a Revolutionary hero, insists that the expedition was inspired by his connection with various land purchases which were in conflict with the Illinois-Wabash claims and aimed at establishing Virginia's sovereignty for that reason. Historians do not seem certain of Clark's position in this respect, just as they are uncertain of Patrick Henry's exact connection with Revolutionary land schemes, albeit the latter's leadership of one of the Yazoo companies is well established.[76] The truth probably is that while Clark had shares in several projects, just as did several hundred other ambitious Virginians, his motives were fundamentally patriotic rather than commercial. The manuscript record does not show who was the moving spirit[77] in reorganizing the two groups as the "United Illinois and Ouabache" Companies, and in bringing about a merger and a united petition to the Virginia legislature in 1778. The peculiar provisions which mark it as the first clear advance, among all the companies of this period, toward the true business company or association will be commented upon at a later point (Chapter VI). It created a body further removed from the partnership form than any other so far encountered.

The petition of the new organization shared the fate of the Henderson petition and several others that were examined by the Virginia assembly in 1778–1779.[78] The leaders in the assembly, especially George Mason,[79] desired to make a complete denial of

[75] A. Henderson, *Conquest of the Old Southwest*, 113.
[76] But *cf.* 2 Alvord, *op. cit.*, 207 and note 387.
[77] It was probably the Gratz brothers.
[78] 1 *Calendar of Virginia State Papers*, 271, 314, 315, 320.
[79] *Cf. supra*, note 6, for his personal stake in the rival Ohio Company.

any pre-Revolutionary purchases (except those in which they were personally interested!), so that Virginia could start her future colonial policy with a clean slate. Virginia's opportunity to do this, however, was cut short by the proposal, in the Articles of Confederation, for the cession of all Western lands then claimed or possessed by the various Colonies. As soon as it became clear that Maryland and other small eastern states would force this cession, as a condition of joining the Confederation, the various land companies transferred their efforts to the members of the Congress.

As part of the strategy in securing Congressional approval, some new interests were added around 1780. Addition of political leaders of Maryland (Governor Johnson and Charles Carroll) as well as of Robert Morris and the French Minister[80] to the roster of shareholders partially confirms the charge that self-interest of her delegates dictated Maryland's position on the question of land control. Control by the Confederation would distinctly favor the claim of the United Companies, and would render impotent the hostility of Virginia. The division of bonus shares, referred to in the merger agreement,[81] was aimed toward securing a confirmation of title from the Continental Congress. Among others who were drawn into the scheme was James Wilson,[82] who became the president of the group in 1781 and had probably helped to dictate its policies during the preceding three years. During the next ten or fifteen years several petitions were presented, and even as late as 1811 Congress received a petition from the survivors of the original group asking for some sort of

[80] In 1781 Morris held one share, Johnson one and a half, Carroll one-half. 10 *Wilson MSS.,* Library of the Historical Society of Pennsylvania; also *cf.* 1 Alvord, *op. cit.,* 303.

[81] See Appendix C, eleventh article.

[82] In addition to his one and one-third shares, Wilson was at this time attorney and proxy for at least five more of the 46 shares then outstanding. 10 *Wilson MSS.*

compensation.[83] No compensation was ever made and the company, as a speculative project, must be set down as a failure.[84]

THE ILLINOIS COMPANY

George Croghan has been justifiably described as one of the outstanding leaders in the westward movement after 1750.[85] He was early a leader among the Pennsylvania Indian traders, and in later years an intimate and confidant of Sir William Johnson. By his activities in trade he became associated with the important Philadelphia trading group of Baynton, Wharton, and Mor-

[83] The first petition to the new Federal Congress was presented December 12, 1791, and was signed by James Wilson, William Smith, and John Shee; it asked that one-fourth of the original grant be confirmed in return for a release of all other claims by the companies, as a "reasonable compromise." This received favorable report from a House Committee, but was reported unfavorably in the Senate. In 1797, Wilson signed another petition as president, in which he referred to the Camden-Yorke opinion, and to opinions of Wedderburn and McGrey in the litigation over Mason's 1659 New Hampshire purchase that Indian purchase gave valid title. This petition was rejected in both Houses. In October, 1803, John Shee signed another petition as the "sole survivor of the Committee appointed and authorized to solicit, manage, and negotiate the affairs of the Company with Congress." This also was rejected. 1 *American State Papers, Public Lands,* 27, 72, 160, 188.

[84] The United Companies were for a short period quite active in promoting colonization and attempting to secure broader distribution of shares in the project. In 1778 a document called "Terms of Settlement" was executed which included detailed regulations for settling Revolutionary officers and soldiers on the purchase. William Murray was appointed agent in Illinois to carry out these much delayed plans. At the same time Murray and Silas Deane were appointed agents to sell the shares of stock which had been set aside in the original agreement. They had little or no success in disposing of shares; the high price of £400 a share seems to have been the chief reason for the failure to sell them. In September, 1780, Silas Deane wrote Shee from Europe: "I have a prospect of doing something with the shares of the Illinois and Wabash lands, but I fear your limits are rather higher than they will go." 4 *Deane Papers,* 220, *Collections of the New York Historical Society,* 1887–1890.

[85] Volwiler, *George Croghan and the Westward Movement* (Cleveland, 1926), is a rounded discussion of his career, built up from meager sources; it stresses throughout his importance as a land enterpriser.

gan.[86] In the winter of 1765–1766 he persuaded them to join with him in a project to secure a Crown grant in confirmation of lands to be purchased in the newly acquired Illinois country.

The articles of agreement,[87] dated March 29, 1766, are the closest to being a plain partnership agreement of all the agreements for land enterprise in this period. The participants are called "party of the first part," "party of the second part," phrasing not found elsewhere. The shares were in equal tenth parts; William Franklin, Sir William Johnson, and Croghan were members in addition to seven of the Philadelphia merchants. The petition was to be for 1,200,000 acres, so that each share would be 120,000 acres—"each and every one of them shall stand and be seized of one undivided equal tenth part thereof." The preamble was: "Now this indenture witnesseth that the said parties respectively have covenanted granted and agreed to and with each other and by these presents agree . . . that they will form and enter into . . . one joint company and partnership." There were separate clauses for the agreement of each partner. Definite provision was made to increase the shares to twelve,[88] and later this limit was increased to sixteen.

The proposals to the home government were as follows:[89] the Crown was to purchase from the Indians land between the Illinois and Ohio Rivers, and to undertake to establish a proper civil government in the area. In return for an outright grant of 100,000 acres, the company would undertake to supervise the

[86] The rivalry between the Whartons and the Gratz-Franks group for western trade, and the conditions surrounding the Illinois and Wabash purchases are described at length by Abernethy, *Western Lands,* 24–38, and 116–122.

[87] They are reprinted in 11 *Illinois Historical Collections,* 203. The manuscript is in the library of the Historical Society of Pennsylvania.

[88] At Sir William Johnson's suggestion, in order to include General Gage and Lord Adam Gordon. Sullivan and Flick, 5 *Papers of Sir William Johnson* (Albany, 1921–1933), 128.

[89] *Cf.* Savelle, *George Morgan,* 57–58.

colonization of the land, largely by soldiers who had served in the Seven Years' War. Allotments would be made in the accepted fashion, including reservations in each township for clergymen. William Franklin wrote a short pamphlet expounding the advantage of the plan, which Sir William Johnson forwarded to England.[90] It was endorsed heartily by Benjamin Franklin, who passed the material along to Lord Shelburne.[91]

The enthusiasm of the Philadelphians for this project was soon dimmed by the prospect of securing grants at the Fort Stanwix meeting with the Indians. The resulting Indiana project absorbed the attention in particular of Samuel Wharton, who, with William Trent, sailed to England soon thereafter. Croghan also became far more committed to this project and to its successor, Vandalia.

Some land was purchased through Governor Wilkins in 1768 and 1769, in the Illinois territory. He took a one-sixth share in any proceeds from resale. The deeds from the Indians to Wilkins, and his deed to the company, were never confirmed by General Gage. But shares in this small amount of land were included in the assets of the bankrupt Baynton, Wharton, and Morgan firm after 1771 when its affairs were in the hands of creditors.

THE INDIANA COMPANY[92]

This group was simply an organization of merchants, largely operating out of Philadelphia, Lancaster, or Carlisle, who had lost goods in the Indian outbreaks of 1754 and 1763. The "Sufferers of 1754" had petitioned for redress either in money or land

---

[90] 5 *Johnson Papers*, 320 *ff*.

[91] 11 *Illinois Historical Collections*, 375.

[92] The best general account of this company is in Savelle, *George Morgan*, ch. 5, which is derived in large measure from original documents. Of the latter, the pamphlet entitled *View of the Title to Indiana* (printed in Philadelphia, 1776) in the John Carter Brown Library, has been consulted here also; it contains the executed deeds and minutes of meetings.

from both the Colonial and parent governments. These joined
with the "Sufferers of 1763" in the latter year; the same individuals were involved in several instances. Baynton, Wharton,
and Morgan of Philadelphia became the leaders; George Croghan was a member personally, and was in other ways associated
with this firm. Sir William Johnson became interested, probably
through Croghan, and at an Indian conference at Johnson Hall
in 1765 secured a promise of land cession from Indian leaders.

This promise was carried out at the Treaty of Fort Stanwix in
1768, as one of the agreements made before the Treaty itself was
signed. The land ceded consisted of 1,800,000 acres situated on
the Little Kanawha and Ohio Rivers, along the southern boundary of Pennsylvania at its western end. Gifts to the Indians as a
consideration for the cession were valued at £10,460. Since the
traders' losses involved had been computed at £85,916, the cession was divided into that many "shares," so that in later records
and petitions, the members of the group are listed as having anywhere from one hundred to several thousand shares. William
Trent and Samuel Wharton immediately set out for London to
secure royal confirmation for this Iroquois grant.[93] Two difficulties barred their path from the start. First, although Thomas

[93] This deed is reprinted in full in the pamphlet just referred to. The
cession was by the sachems to William Trent as "The lawful attorney and
agent" of the group of traders, although in legal form it was made to King
George "but to and for the only use, benefit and behoof of the said William
Trent, in his own right and as attorney aforesaid, his heirs and assigns
forever."

To dispose of opponents' later claim that the Iroquois sachems could
not rightfully cede this area in the Cherokee country, the pamphlet contained an opinion of Henry Dagge of Lincoln's Inn, dated March 20, 1775,
to the effect that the Iroquois were sovereign and transferred an absolute
title "subject only to the King's sovereignty over the settlements . . . and
over the inhabitants as English subjects." A supporting opinion by John
Glynn of Serjeant's Inn, reaching the same conclusion, was also included.
Both were endorsed with approval by Benjamin Franklin and Patrick
Henry, under date of July 12 and July 29, respectively, 1775 (during the
meetings of the Continental Congress).

Walker had signed the whole treaty in behalf of Virginia, the area assigned to the sufferers was clearly within Virginia territory, according to the oft-repeated assertions of that Colony. Second, it was part of the territory which the Iroquois claimed solely by reason of their conquests of the Cherokees. Just what land the Cherokees could rightfully claim and in future could deed to possible Virginia buyers or to Richard Henderson was a difficult problem to settle.

It is probable that there was no formal organization of the group at this time. The expenses of Trent and Wharton to London were "underwritten" by a small inner group: Croghan was to put up three-tenths, William Franklin (who had attended the treaty meeting) two-tenths, Baynton two-tenths, Morgan. two-tenths, Callender (another Philadelphia merchant) one-tenth.[94] Wharton reached London and at first was active in preparing a petition and securing influential friends. But early in 1769 he was attracted by more grandiose plans and was easily persuaded to merge this claim in the larger Vandalia project. It was understood that the new colony, when and if erected, would expressly confirm the Indiana grant.[95]

The subsequent delays involving Vandalia stiffened Virginia's opposition to all claims within her asserted limits. By 1774, when hope for Vandalia finally waned, George Morgan had quarreled with Wharton, and the affairs of Baynton, Wharton, and Morgan were in the hands of creditors. Morgan[96] directed a reorganization of the original group who had received the Fort Stanwix

[94] This agreement is in the Etting Collection, 1 *Ohio MSS.*, 49–50, Library of the Historical Society of Pennsylvania.

[95] *Ibid.*, at 82.

[96] George Morgan, born in 1743, had married the daughter of John Baynton; in 1765 he went to the Illinois country as the firm's representative in what was the pioneer large-scale trading effort beyond Fort Pitt. Savelle, *op. cit.*, 236–239. His later career as Indian agent and citizen was distinguished, typical of the group under whose direction a new nation was molded; some historians treat him unsympathetically.

grant,[97] at a meeting at Fort Pitt, September 21, 1776. From that date forward the Indiana Company acquired the group-consciousness and unification of management which, as will be seen, became increasingly marked in post-Revolutionary land enterprises.

At this meeting,[98] which occupied two days, there were present Callender, Trent, Morgan, Croghan, and five others. But the absentees included such large shareholders as the Whartons, William Franklin, and David Franks. Nevertheless, fourteen resolutions were passed setting up machinery for securing valid title and for merchandising the ceded area. William Trent, in a lengthy discussion, reiterated his belief in the validity of the cession without any later Crown approval, in accordance with that spring of eternal hope for the speculators of the day, the Camden-Yorke opinion. Croghan[99] had been the land officer; he was directed to procure from his former partner, Wharton, the original Fort Stanwix deeds as soon as possible, so that they could be recorded at Williamsburg. Four commissioners were appointed to supervise land sales, and Morgan was directed to design a seal.

[97] The holdings of the principal stockholders, or proprietors, in January, 1776, based on "par value" of one pound per share, were as follows:

William Trent	£ 7,147
Samuel Wharton	16,628
Baynton Estate	8,530
George Morgan	5,400
William Franklin	5,399
Robert Callender	8,651
David Franks	5,730
Joseph Simon	4,822

The total of all other interests at this time (about forty individuals were involved) was less than two thousand "shares." Originally Baynton, Wharton, and Morgan claimed 70 per cent. 6 *Calendar of Virginia State Papers*, 27.

[98] The minutes are in the Etting Collection, 2 *Ohio MSS.*, 9, Library of the Historical Society of Pennsylvania.

[99] Morgan was appointed to replace him.

Samuel Wharton later denied the validity of this meeting, on the ground that he had received no formal notice.[100]

The Fort Pitt meeting had named November[101] as the date for another meeting of the new body, at Carlisle. But this had to be postponed, because of the legal tangle in which Baynton, Wharton, and Morgan were involved. Their share of the grant would have to be turned over to trustees for the benefit of creditors, if the grant was found to be valid. Baynton was dead; Morgan and Thomas Wharton (as attorney for his brother) executed assignments of their shares, the proportion of the other "sufferers" was increased, and the way was apparently clear for selling off the grant under centralized direction. On January 19, 1777, the grant was formally assigned to three trustees[102] who would hold title to the property, while management would remain in the hands of elected officers. On the next day, rough articles of agreement[103] were adopted. Apparently these were later supplemented by by-laws,[104] for in 1779 William Trent described the company as having 88,867 "shares" with one vote for each 300 held, but with a maximum of ten votes for one shareholder; no transfers would be valid unless entered on the company's books, the purchaser agreeing "to abide by all rules and regulations."[105]

[100] Etting Collection, 2 *Ohio MSS.*, 17.

[101] Savelle incorrectly states January, 1776. *Op. cit.*, 65.

[102] Owen Jones, Richard Bache, and Isaac Wharton.

[103] These articles are legalistic in the extreme; they are in the *Indiana Deed Book*, Library of the Historical Society of Pennsylvania.

[104] In accordance with a clause in the agreement providing for "rules, orders and regulations" by majority vote.

[105] In a letter accompanying the deed of his shares to William Grayson of Virginia, out of which ultimately resulted the suit of *Grayson* v. *Virginia; cf.* Savelle, *op. cit.*, 109–110, and 3 Dallas (U.S.) 320. In describing the title, the deed referred to the meeting of January 20, 1776: "They did erect and form themselves into one Joint Company of Proprietors of the Tract of Country aforesaid called 'Indiana.' " This phrase is one more bit of testimony in support of the thesis advanced here—that men creating such an organization as this thought of it as a unitary body and a practical, though not a legal, corporate entity.

Twenty-two individuals signed these articles. At a later meeting, on March 20, in Philadelphia, Joseph Galloway was named president and Thomas Wharton vice-president. Morgan had been made land office secretary[106] and proceeded to advertise the land for sale in the *Pennsylvania Packet*.[107]

This active revival of a dormant claim aroused Virginia's land-minded patriots to a defense of her boundaries, led by George Mason.[108] After more than two years of testimony and discussion, the Indiana claim was invalidated by the same resolution of the House of Delegates which voided the Henderson and the Illinois-Wabash purchases, in June, 1779. Trent and Morgan immediately took their plea before the Continental Congress, in September, 1779.[109] From this time forward, the contest centered in the Continental Congress; other claimants followed their lead, and the whole question of confirmation became bound up with the historically important controversy over western land cessions.[110] At a meeting of the company on May 8, 1783, the chief

[106] Writing to Trent of a later meeting (1778) Morgan said: "Our constitution requires two months' notice in the Philadelphia newspapers"; and one "can only be obtained by five of the proprietors making a written application to the President or Vice-President." He asked that Trent contribute his share of expenses, for which he would "have credit in the general account." Etting Collection, 1 *Ohio MSS.*, 28.

[107] Savelle, *op. cit.*, at 86, note 51.

[108] His possibly selfish motives have already been suggested.

[109] Trent's memorial is in the Etting Collection, 2 *Ohio MSS.*, 40.
Morgan had resigned his important post as Indian Commissioner at Fort Pitt to devote full attention to his share in the Indiana grant; assuming success for the American arms, its potential value would greatly increase. He became a citizen of New Jersey, and since Virginia refused to hear him as a private claimant, the New Jersey legislature instructed its delegates to ask for a hearing on the Indiana claim. Savelle, *op. cit.*, at 102.

[110] The Committee on Western Lands rejected, in November, 1781, the Virginia cession with its proviso that her title to land east and south of the Ohio be guaranteed. But the battle was a losing one; the final acceptance by Congress early in 1784 of Virginia's land included the retention of the "guaranteed title" to land east of the Ohio. Immediately afterward, New Jersey permitted Morgan as its official agent to ask Congress for a special court to hear its claim under Article IX of the Articles of Confederation. This came to naught; finally in 1791 Morgan appealed directly to the Vir-

business was the approval of legal expense accounts.[111] Trent's
account of £369 was met by authorizing him to sell one voter's
share (300 real shares) for his compensation. A fee of £9 to
James Wilson was included in Trent's total; but the latter had
already been given 300 shares (one vote) in 1781 for legal services,[112] and he remained its counsel at least up to the time that
Grayson v. *Virginia* was filed. No compensation or redress was
ever secured, and the company shared the fate of the Illinois-
Wabash body.

THE GRAND OHIO COMPANY, OR VANDALIA[113]

As has just been indicated, Samuel Wharton and William
Trent went to England in January, 1769, to carry out the mission
of securing confirmation of the "suffering traders" grant, or Indiana Company. Their expenses had been underwritten. Within

ginia Assembly, in vain. The next summer, probably at Morgan's instiga-
tion, William Grayson (who had purchased shares from Trent) brought
on behalf of himself and the other shareholders his suit, which, after being held in suspense for six years, was finally thrown out of court by the
ratification of the Eleventh Amendment. Damages sought in the action
were $233,124, an amount apparently computed arbitrarily by Morgan
(6 *Calendar of Virginia State Papers,* 33); $5,000 was specifically stated as
his own out-of-pocket expense.

[111] The minutes are in the Etting Collection, 2 *Ohio MSS.,* 64.

[112] Thomas Paine was also given 300 shares, as "public relations counsel."

[113] Politically, this was the most important enterprise concerned with
the new western territory acquired in 1763, although as a land merchandising project it is of slighter consequence. A discussion of its genesis and
career occupies fully one-fourth of Alvord's detailed study of the maze of
English colonial policy in this period—*Mississippi Valley in British Politics.* With the help of original English records he has reconstructed the
story of the effort to acquire a huge new colony. The summary here is
shortened because of the general accessibility of Alvord's work. A shorter
but excellent summary is by Abernethy, *Western Lands,* ch. III; all important manuscript sources are there referred to and summarized.

The political struggle in England to have the grant approved brought
many controversial pamphlets in its train, typical of eighteenth century
politics. Several of these are in the John Carter Brown Library and have
been consulted there. Alvord and Abernethy summarize the information
and arguments which they contain. Wharton's *Statement of the Petitioners* (1771) and *Facts & Observations* (1775) contain the essential facts.

six months, instead of pushing the Indiana grant to a conclusion, Wharton had embarked on a much grander project, and gave evidence of being adept in the intrigue necessary to secure any favors from the court oligarchy in London. He was undoubtedly influenced by the troubles which his brother and partners were then facing in Philadelphia, from which the only salvation seemed to be a master stroke of this kind.

In the spring of 1769 the project was no more than a duplicate of the Mississippi Company—a group organized to purchase about two and a half million acres. But the land was to be within Virginia territory, part of that ceded by the Six Nations at Fort Stanwix. Another important difference was that Wharton had quickly interested a number of the Grenville court faction as members, in order to grease the way for approval of a petition. At this time he was still keeping alive the separate grant to the traders, and probably hoped to secure both.

When this relatively modest petition came before Lord Hillsborough at the Board of Trade in June, 1769, he suggested that the most feasible step would be to purchase a tract large enough to warrant a new colony. This suggestion was attractive. But it meant a much heavier expense, more political "pull" to see it through in the face of probable opposition from Virginia, and a widening of the circle of those interested. Nevertheless, in December, 1769, what is known as the Walpole scheme was gotten under way. Mergers with other groups then petitioning hopefully for land were made a part of the plan; the Indiana grant was to be included, as was the old Ohio Company. Seventy-two shares were created, 20,000,000 acres were to be asked for and a payment of £10,460 offered (the amount expended at Fort Stanwix), with quit-rents to begin after a term of twenty years. There was to be provided in each parish a "glebe" of 300 acres for the support of the Church of England. The new group also agreed to bear the cost of government for a new colony, to be established as a condition of the grant. Since a single share promised title to about 300,000 acres, it is easy to understand the enthu-siasm of Croghan and Wharton about the affair; to them it over-shadowed all previous land operations with which they had been connected. The determined political support for it, coming from the share-owners among the court hangers-on, set it far above other projects which struggled for years even to have a petition received and read. Historians recognize it as the climactic under-taking of the trans-Allegheny expansionists.

Just at the time when the Treasury was considering the en-larged project, in January, 1770, a petition from the Virginia House of Delegates was on its way asking that Virginia's juris-diction be extended over the same territory. Through the next three years there was constant opposition to the Vandalia grant by Virginia. Samuel Wharton continued to be active in refuting them, by letters to ministers and by pamphlets. Alvord concludes that, although there is no direct evidence, it was Virginia's oppo-sition which produced the fatal delays in securing final approval of the plan. In 1771 Hillsborough changed his attitude to one of opposition; it was necessary to force him out of office, and to substitute Dartmouth in August, 1772. In October, 1773, it was the two Crown law officers, Wedderburn and Thurlow, who refused to issue a final patent, despite a direct order to them to proceed. Typical English political intrigue probably also con-tributed to the difficulties of securing a final passage of the Great Seal for Vandalia.[114]

The changes and objections made by Wedderburn and Thur-low to the final set-up as presented to them in 1773 for formal issuance are of interest here. The colony as established was to be larger, for purposes of government, than the land asked for. The original terms were accepted, but the proprietors were to be burdened in addition with the payment of £2,600 yearly for the support of a government. The Crown would retain the right to

[114] The proposed colony was variously called Charlotta, Pittsylvania, Vandalia. 2 Alvord, *op. cit.*, 120.

sell the western part of the area, hoping thereby to build up a fund for American government and defense. The law officers objected, however, to making the grant to Walpole and associates as proprietors in joint tenancy, and substituted tenancy in common. The residual claim of the survivor and his heirs would have made under-grants impossible. The petitioners really preferred a title as tenants in common, and this suggested change was quickly accepted. This quarter-century was the period in English and American law when joint tenancy was being forced out of its old common law supremacy, due to its obvious unsuitability for group landholding or business enterprises.[115]

These delays extending over more than three years were fatal to Vandalia, for the year 1774 brought with it the period of reprisals against Massachusetts and the adoption as a governmental policy of the Quebec Bill as the method of governing the new West. Imperial control replaced the idea of erecting new and separate royal colonies, of which Vandalia was to have been one. The Grand Ohio scheme, far more pretentious than others of the period, became more certainly dead after 1774 than any of them.

THE DISMAL SWAMP ADVENTURERS[116]

Relatively informal organization marked a localized attempt to drain the Dismal Swamp region in southern Virginia and so

[115] Joint tenancy was assumed as ruling in all land grants, under common law doctrines. Its chief characteristic was that the entire tenancy upon the decease of any tenant remains to the survivors, and at length to the last survivor (Blackstone, 1 *Commentaries,* 184). Equity disliked survivorship rights, preferring the divisible and devisable rights of tenancy in common. Connecticut, in 1772, and Massachusetts, in 1785, made tenancy in common the assumed form in all joint grants, unless there was a clear intent otherwise. Joint tenancy was regarded as a survival of feudal aristocracy, and highly "undemocratic." But it is still the legal basis upon which joint trustees take title.

[116] The account is summarized largely from Chapter XXIV in Prussing, *The Estate of George Washington Deceased* (Boston, 1927). Prussing has examined the territory and some of the local county records. Other students of Washington's business affairs comment on it more briefly. Unless otherwise noted, the information here is taken from Prussing.

secure a new area of excellent plantation land. The method of authorizing the project, as well as its organization, finds a counterpart in the later grants of authority in the period 1770–1800 to waterworks companies, drainage districts, and roadbuilding enterprises in the colonies or states.

Formation of a group of "adventurers" to spend money reclaiming the Dismal Swamp undoubtedly grew out of discussions at Williamsburg concerning land projects during the winter sessions of the Virginia assembly. It was noted above that group land enterprises seem to have appeared first between 1745 and 1750; hence the political gossipers at the capital city after 1750 were familiar with the general methods of land speculation. Twelve men, many politically prominent, were authorized in a bill passed in January, 1764, "to enter upon, and have such a free passage, and make such canals, or causeways, through the lands of any person whatsoever adjacent to the said Dismal Swamp, as may be conducive to the more effectual draining thereof, without being subject to the action or suit of any such persons for the same." In the previous November, when the project was organized and the authorizing enactment introduced, the group had voted an initial fund of £600 to be raised by assessment. Whether all twelve contributed at the start is not certain. Also, it does not appear that there was any direct grant of underlying soil; this would presumably be patented to the group when the reclamation work was complete, since it had not been taken up by other private owners. Nor is there record of formal organization on the part of the Adventurers.

In 1764 some slaves were contributed and £300 was levied, and in 1766 a similar amount. Washington was made manager of the enterprise and seven trips to the region are recorded in his diaries, for which he charged expenses. These items, together with payments to surveyors and the hire of slave labor from nearby owners, made a substantial total charged to the company in Washington's ledger of this period. He, of course, paid his share of assessments. In December, 1766, some adjoining land was purchased from William Reddick, and in this deed the names of Nathaniel and William Nelson, Washington, and five others appear. In 1768 more adjoining land was purchased from the Norfleet family. In 1768 Washington ceased his active concern in the project, and turned it over to his favorite brother, John A. Washington. During this five-year period, two canals, known as the Washington Ditch and the Jericho, were built to connect with rivers, on which lumber could be floated. Some house shingles seem to have been made and sold. Apparently also the plantation was begun at that time.

After the long interval of war activities, Washington called a meeting[117] of the group in May, 1785, at Richmond. This followed the making of a definite grant of about 40,000 acres to Nelson and his associates by the Virginia legislature, thus carrying out the implied promise of the old enactment in 1764. Although the state records are lost, Prussing discovered in the Norfolk and Nansemond County records the necessary deed from the devisees of William Nelson (in whose name the state grant was made) to their associates. Here the first full list of the twelve original proprietors (not all of whom were still alive) is found. But the shares given to the heirs of this group were two twenty-firsts to each, indicating that one and a half shares had been defaulted, apparently for the familiar reason of non-payment of assessments. Washington received one share. There is no record of any dividend or distribution of earnings in this whole period. From 1785 on the property was profitably managed by a resident agent.

In 1792 and 1793, Washington was making efforts to dispose of large portions of his property, perhaps to take advantage of

---

[117] He had previously (March 31, 1784) written to Hugh Williamson that he knew "as little of the affairs and present management of the Swamp Company (though a member of it) as you do" and had heard nothing of it for nine years. Sparks, 12 *Life and Writings of George Washington* (Boston, 1837), 267.

the boom prices then prevailing as the result of four years of business revival. To Governor "Light-Horse Harry" Lee he offered his Dismal Swamp interest for £5,000 Virginia currency. The final sale price was £4,000, or $20,000. In a memorandum at this time he described his interest as two twenty-first parts of 40,000 acres plus a share in the separate plantation, its Negroes, and a sum of money on hand. From this time until 1799, Lee tried valiantly to make the necessary payments. Several letters indicate he was a loser by the bankruptcy of Robert Morris[118] and by the failure of James Wilson to meet an obligation. Lee had paid out approximately $5,000 at the time of Washington's death, but in 1809 he released the executors from his claim, so that dividends could be received and the share resold.

At the time of the original sale to Lee, Washington wrote as follows: "To the Members of the Dismal Swamp Land Company. Gentlemen: Having disposed of my share and all interest in the Dismal Swamp Company to Henry Lee, Esq., I request that he may henceforth be considered as being standing in my place. He is not only to receive the profits which may hereafter arise from that concern but if anything is due thereto he is entitled to my share thereof and in like manner to pay all unsatisfied demands upon me on this acct. and to come." There was evidently no restriction on such a transfer of interest by a member.

In 1814 the Virginia legislature incorporated the company but named the members as "proprietors" and specified that the shares should be regarded as real and not personal property. In 1825, when the affairs of the estate were being finally closed, Washington's one share in the incorporated company was sold at auction in Alexandria to a dummy buyer for $12,100, who by deed (recorded in Alexandria) immediately reconveyed it to Bushrod Washington, one of the executors, for the same price.

[118] This is corroborated by Morris' *Account* of 1800, printed privately for his creditors.

The records of the executors from 1810 to 1825, show that $18,815 had been collected in dividends, or about $1,220 per year, and the share was regarded as one of the most profitable of Washington's investments. The price can thus be considered a fair one, since the share had been capitalized by the familiar modern 10 per cent rule.

In 1877, there was a new act of incorporation making the shares personal property, under which the then fifty-three proprietors conveyed their interests to the new corporation in exchange for shares of stock. In 1899, the property was sold to the John L. Roper Company, and by it later to the Camp Manufacturing Company, which concern now holds it as a timber reserve. Lumbering operations were carried on throughout the century, but the land was never well enough drained to become arable, as had been the original intent in 1763.

LESSER LAND PROJECTS

The foregoing descriptions include the important pre-Revolutionary land enterprises concerning which information in much detail is available. But since what is being attempted is synthesis based on many types of enterprise over a half-century, it is desirable to include here briefer descriptions of a few other projects that have found their way into historical records. In these cases information is more scanty and consequently less satisfactory. But enough can usually be ascertained to bring out one or two characteristics of especial interest in this study.

Loose usage of the term "company" is illustrated by its application to a group of eight investors or lenders in Burlington, New Jersey, who in 1768 loaned George Croghan £3,000 so that he could patent his Otsego Tract in New York state.[119] The loan was obtained through the intermediation of Governor William Temple Franklin of New Jersey. To him Croghan gave a mortgage on the patent, and included as further security his house

[119] *Cf.* Volwiler, *George Croghan*, 282, 329–332.

and eighteen acres of land in Philadelphia together with 40,000 additional acres adjacent to his new patent. Governor Franklin then assigned the mortgage to the Burlington group and added his own personal bond. The "company" were thus acting only as bankers, but it is probable that they had been associated in other land transactions in a joint capacity. Included in the group were Richard Wells as the owner of three "shares" (a total of £900) and seven others of the town as owners of single shares (£300). Among the latter was Richard Smith, apparently the father of the young adventurer who in 1769 made his celebrated visit to the Otsego Lake district.[120] There is no direct mention of the loan in his book, but the family interest in the area is referred to frequently.

Franklin's bond was worded as a separate obligation to each of "eight persons in ten shares, usually called the Burlington Company."[121] In 1772 Governor Franklin bought out the interests of Wells and two of the others in the mortgage; he claimed later that he believed this transfer made him a "member" of the company and therefore entitled to share in its assets. This demonstrates an extremely interesting *group* attitude toward a mere collection of joint lenders on mortgage. Since Franklin was a Tory, he fled the country during the Revolution and did not attempt to settle this affair until after 1783. Meanwhile Croghan's affairs had become involved in bankruptcy proceedings; he died in 1781. The shares of the other five lenders had in the intervening decade been sold (probably very cheaply, since the Cooper family never revealed the price) to William Cooper and Andrew Craig, the latter a dummy who immediately reassigned to Cooper. Cooper, the founder of Cooperstown and father of

[120] His diary of the trip up the Hudson and down the Susquehanna and Delaware is well known to historians—*A Tour of Four Great Rivers*, written in 1769 (edited by F. W. Halsey, New York, 1906).

[121] A copy is in the *Vanderpoel MSS., William Franklin Papers*, Box I, New York Public Library. Aaron Vanderpoel was Franklin's administrator.

James Fenimore Cooper, thus became the sole claimant on the mortgage and on the Franklin bond. In the winter of 1785–1786 he arranged a hasty and possibly illegal sheriff's sale to himself, for £2,700, of the land near Lake Otsego and Cooperstown that became in later years the princely estate made so famous by his son.[122] A representative of Franklin was prevented from bidding, but efforts to set aside the sale were vain—Franklin being an expatriate Tory. As late as 1813 the Franklin estate secured a legal opinion, from one Lawrence Williams of Philadelphia, on the question of Franklin's exact status in 1772; the conclusion was that as an obligor on the whole debt he was debarred from sharing in the later foreclosure action.[123]

Several instances can be cited of the device, apparently familiar at that time, of using dummy buyers to avoid the prohibition in the Colonies on purchases above a certain size. George Croghan used this method in securing New York lands. Aaron Vanderpoel purchased in 1826 at a tax sale 1,787 acres of land on the Susquehanna which was part of an original 1770 grant of 30,000 acres to "Thomas Wharton and others." The deed was recorded on February 26, 1770, in the names of thirty Philadelphians, in equal shares as tenants in common. Immediately afterwards other deeds were recorded reconveying the thirty parts to Wharton.[124] Similar instances of dummy transfers are frequently found in the New York land records in 1765–1790.

Famous in the history of Maine is the old Kennebec Company.[125] In 1629, the Council of Devon had granted to William Bradford and his associates the area later known as the Kennebec Purchase. In 1640 he turned it over to the freemen of Plymouth.

[122] An excellent account of the suspicious circumstances surrounding this sale is given by A. T. Volwiler in 4 *New York Historical Association Quarterly*, 35, in an article dealing with Croghan's career. A reply defending the Cooper family, written by James F. Cooper, appears in 12 *ibid.*, 390.

[123] *Vanderpoel MSS., Franklin Papers*, Box I.

[124] *Ibid.*

[125] Described in 2 *Maine Historical Society Collections*, 276 ff.

That colony regarded it only as a minor asset and made little or
no effort to develop it. For most of the period until 1661 it was
leased to fishermen or traders. In the latter year it was sold to
four individuals for £400; these four and their heirs held the
land for nearly one hundred years. In 1749 there was apparently
a revival of interest in the territory, for some new individuals
were admitted as part owners. In 1753 the general court of
Massachusetts passed the act giving to persons holding undivided land in common what amounted to corporate powers. This
law, as has been indicated above, was a definitive recognition of
the status of the proprietorship as a corporation in fact. Operating under this law, the proprietors formed the "Proprietors of
the Kennebec Purchase from the late Colony of New Plymouth."

Boundary disputes with adjoining claims were all settled by
1766. Regular meetings were apparently held by the proprietors
from the reorganization in 1749 until 1816. Progress in securing
settlers for the area was interrupted by the fact that many of the
proprietors were Tories, but about 1810 the land began to fill up
rapidly as the result of the adoption of a plan of granting free
alternate lots to actual settlers, with the usual requirements for
the building of homes within a stated period. The reserved lots
were to be divided among the proprietors, to be sold for cash as
the area filled up. In 1816 all the remaining lots were divided;
certain parts of the area which had not been surveyed into lots
were sold at auction in Boston.

The project illustrates the application of non-New England
methods to land so far removed from the centers of population
in Massachusetts as to require a different type of management.
In other words, the handling of this land resembled various
projects farther south which had used the proprietary governments as their model, more than it did the true early New England proprietorship. After 1750 a great many new towns in western Massachusetts, western Connecticut, and New Hampshire
were owned by absentee proprietors, though usually some of the

owners were actual settlers. In these cases the conduct of town affairs came more and more to resemble a quasi-business undertaking, such as the Kennebec Company clearly was.

Ethan Allen, pamphleteer, mob-leader,[126] military hero, and co-founder with his brother of the state of Vermont,[127] organized a land-selling enterprise with his brothers and cousin which deserves mention. It was known as the Onion River Company[128] and sold much of the land in a large area around Burlington. It would hardly have been more distinguished than many other groups which bought and sold land in the New Hampshire grants in opposition to New York were it not for the merchandising flavor which Allen's leadership added. Furthermore, Ethan and his brother Ira deliberately purchased the rights to land which they intended to resell. During 1773–1775, several meetings of the company were held in Hartford or in Salisbury, the home of the Allens.[129] It functioned much as other proprietorships in method, admitting as members those who bought shares from the Allens. During three years, 77,622 acres were bought and 16,793 were sold, leaving 60,829 acres belonging to the Allens, which in 1776 they valued at $297,408.50.[130] Several of Ethan Allen's famous pamphlets were inspired in large measure by his desire to break the potential jurisdiction of New York over his New Hampshire-granted lands; he charged to the Company the costs of printing and distributing them. He advertised several times in the *Connecticut Courant* under the title "Ethan Allen and Company." It has even been suggested that his eagerness to capture Ticonderoga arose in part from its nearness to the

[126] It is little realized that Allen was solicited by the later leaders of the Susquehannah Company to enter their employ, and by Daniel Shays to join his rebellion. Pell, *Ethan Allen* (Boston, 1929), 262.

[127] His biographer, Pell, terms Allen the "public relations counsel" of the new state. *Ibid.*, 57.

[128] The Onion is now the Winooski.

[129] Pell has found evidence of meetings on March 23, 1774, and another in March 1776; *ibid.*, 66, 74–75.

[130] *Ibid.*, 75.

Burlington area.[131] In 1783 the Allens and Thomas Chittenden still held much of the unsold area, but after ineffectual attempts to settle Tories in the area, Ira Allen in 1787 bought out his brother and controlled the ultimate sale of the district.

Turning to the opposite extremity of the frontier, we find John Sevier interested in a speculative venture at Muscle Shoals, or the Great Bend district of the Tennessee River. One biographer[132] of "Nolichucky Jack," first Governor of Tennessee, calls him a "frontier land gambler," but Sevier was simply one of the group of North Carolinians, headed by William Blount and Richard Caswell, who after 1777 sought to pre-empt by legal means the vast western claims of that state.[133] The self-interest of these men in preserving the validity of their claims has been recognized as the true foundation of the State of Franklin.[134] In this particular instance the small group interested turned tentatively to Spain for protection, and it has thus become a "crucial" phase of the story of Spanish intrigue in the Southwest.[135]

Associated with Sevier were William Blount, Richard Caswell, John Donelson, General Rutherford, and Joseph Martin— a dominant political sextet in North Carolina in 1783, when the plans were laid. William Blount[136] was the active head. It was

[131] *Ibid.,* 75.

[132] C. S. Driver, *John Sevier* (Chapel Hill, 1932).

[133] The early land "speculator" and the modern tax "evader" functioning on the hazy margins of indefinite legislation both invite censorious judgments. That a state or nation draws poor or ineffective laws does not, however, make those who take advantage of them law-breakers; it simply demonstrates the need for intelligent and foresighted legislation.

[134] The modern critical historiography exaggerates: "Historians have heretofore treated the Franklin movement as a serious rebellion—the cry of the West for freedom—in reality the movement was . . . a game played between two rival groups of land speculators." T. P. Abernethy, *From Frontier to Plantation in Tennessee,* 89.

[135] See A. P. Whitaker, "Muscle Shoals Speculation," 13 *Mississippi Valley Historical Review,* 365; also, by the same author, "Alexander McGillivray," 5 *North Carolina Historical Review,* 181, especially 196.

[136] Abernethy also treats Blount in the Beardian manner, as a "wicked" speculator; *op. cit.,* 51–53.

not known whether the Great Bend lay within the boundaries of Georgia, South Carolina, or North Carolina. After Donelson and Martin had made the purchase from the Cherokees, Blount successfully applied to the Georgia legislature to establish Houston County. Of the seven county commissioners who took office in 1784, three were members of the group whose prime interest was in purchasing the best land in the new county for themselves. Sevier was one, and helped to prepare the expedition down the river in the next year to lay out the boundaries of both the new county and the private purchase. Late in 1785, a land office was established and warrants were issued.[137] Sevier at first opposed the Franklin movement because he felt that the project would suffer thereunder but later reversed his position. In the following years, Georgia's vacillation over her land policy, the resistance of the Indians, failure to get satisfaction from overtures made to the Spanish, and the strong national policy in this area after 1790, all contributed to the indefinite postponement of the settlement. Like so many others of these settlement projects, the last heard of it was in a petition to Congress in 1818 by James Sevier, heir of Nolichucky Jack, and the heirs of the others in the group. They sought other land as compensation, unsuccessfully.[138]

[137] Driver, *op. cit.*, 70–73, and 71, note 32. This effort to establish a settlement is the subject of a letter to Donelson from Blount in the *Draper MSS.*, 1 XX 72. Referring to the group's efforts to secure official appointments from the Georgia legislature, he says, "you will see I have made use of Bledsoe's name although he had never signed the articles. My reasons for so doing were he was known to be an over-mountain man and of much influence." He felt the petition to the Georgia legislature was "best calculated to suit the temper of the general Assembly and to answer the purposes of the Company that I could invent." That there were articles of association, and that the members thought of their project as a company, is thus apparent; but a copy of the articles is not known to exist.

[138] Supporting affidavits to this petition are cited by Driver, *op. cit.*, 71, note 32.

V

POST-REVOLUTIONARY LAND COMPANIES

CERTAIN influences tended to restrict the number of new group efforts for land acquisition and sale after 1783. Plentiful territory had been made available near the old settlements. Vermont had been organized and freed from inter-colony bickering; the Mohawk Valley was protected; additional parts of Maine and New Hampshire had been found attractive; in the South, the highland region of North Carolina had become familiar, as well as the sparsely settled region of northern Georgia and the area now included in West Virginia. Much Tory land had been seized and redistributed in the seaboard states. The years 1783 and 1784 produced a series of land acts in the various states making individual land settlement extremely easy. Especially in New York and North Carolina the terms of these acts reflected the agrarian or radical character of the legislatures. Favorable terms granted to small settlers in territory easily reached made people correspondingly less interested in new areas farther west. This condition also made such enterprises as the Holland Land Company and the Eastern Land Associates somewhat premature; real demand from settlers for these lands in western New York and in Maine did not arise until after 1800. It must also be recognized that the radical tone of the legislatures in many cases produced emotional hostility to large speculative purchases or grants.

But in spite of seemingly adverse conditions, projects for large-scale land merchandising were astonishingly numerous, particularly after 1789. In selecting post-Revolutionary companies for presentation here, the same plan has been followed as in the preceding chapters. Only those concerning which there is definite original data relating to internal structure and sufficient descriptive or historical narrative to determine the attitude of the leaders concerned, have been used. In the group as a whole will be found clear evidence of the growth of the corporate concept, with less and less evidence of older partnership forms. Some of the projects were, on the other hand, quite clearly of the joint adventure or syndicate species, strikingly suggestive of such organizations today.[1] More will be said of this differentiation in type in the next chapter.

THE OHIO COMPANY[2]

Unquestionably entitled to first place in any discussion of land companies possessing a corporate character in this period is the Ohio Company. Led by a group of outstanding Revolutionary officers, and marked by a truly corporate management of its million acres of land for a decade or more, it was an important influence in translating the spirit of the Ordinance of 1787 into an actual settlement in Ohio. Southeastern Ohio owes as much to this company as does the northeastern part to the settlers of the Western Reserve.

As early as 1783 a group of Revolutionary officers at Newburgh, New York, discussed the idea of grouping land bounties in the West in one tract for settlement. The Newburgh Petition resulted. Rufus Putnam, experienced surveyor, emerged as the leader who kept the project alive in the next three years. He corresponded with Washington and considered the merits of re-

---

[1] The erroneous view that both the joint adventure and the syndicate are nineteenth century concepts has been often reiterated by legal writers. For a typical example, cf. *Corpus Juris,* article "Joint Adventure." Unquestionably they were used in sixteenth century German practice and in Holland in the seventeenth century, almost exactly in their modern forms.

[2] Under the editorship of A. B. Hulbert, *Records of the Ohio Company* have been printed—though not in full—in two volumes of the *Marietta Historical Commission Collections* (Marietta, 1917). The introduction sketches the whole history of the plan, with comment on its importance in Ohio history. The company receives mention in all standard histories of the 1785–1795 period. The best and least prejudiced account of William Duer's connection with it is Davis, "William Duer, Entrepreneur," 1 *Essays,* 111.

gions other than Ohio; at one time it was thought best to purchase from Massachusetts land in Maine. Of the men who became active leaders in the company, nearly all were members of the Cincinnati, and a smaller number were also members of that wandering Masonic group, the American Union lodge, that was established in Roxbury during the siege of Boston, with power to move as its members moved. These personal bonds between the members of the group undoubtedly contributed to the solidarity and continuous interest which characterized the ten years of the company's active administration of its lands.

Generals Tupper and Putnam were both surveyors; in 1785 they visited Ohio and Maine, respectively. In January of 1786 they met in Putnam's home in Rutland, Massachusetts, and evolved a general "call" to a meeting in Boston to carry out the original Newburgh plan. Those interested were to meet in various towns and elect delegates to the Boston meeting in March. On the third day of the meeting, March 3, articles of association were drawn up by a committee and approved the next day.

The articles need to be repeated in full.[3] They represent the best example to be found in the fifty-year period under review of a blend between a New England proprietorship and a true corporate enterprise. This blending is further illustrated by the later career of the company. In actual operation it came to be almost an exact replica of a modern joint stock association. The articles are also of especial interest because no one of the framing committee seems to have had legal training, so that their effort reflects the understanding of intelligent men of the period as to the requirements of such a compact, rather than any strained legalistic framework.[4]

Zealous students might easily point to apparent analogies in the framework of the company—its lack of a single executive

[3] In Appendix D.
[4] Such as the agreement in the case of Transylvania, which is given in Appendix B.

was comparable to the structure of the Confederation, its idea of divisions under agents suggests the old chamber form of the Dutch East India Company. Actually the contemplated association reflected the practical experience of its Massachusetts authors with the proprietorship, supplemented by their political experience in electing or acting as political representatives in townships or counties. They added to these ingredients an uncertain amount of acquaintance with business bodies—and a fund of innate good sense.

The wording of the twelfth article indicates plainly that the group felt Congress possessed the power to incorporate the body, a point on which there was wide division of opinion in 1781–1785. There was a strong and generally held belief that Congress would have supreme power over the new Northwest Territory. Sovereignty would carry with it the right to bestow charters. The Land Law of 1785 had already been passed, and the company's first proposal to take up land was framed in accordance with its terms. Under these conditions laymen would naturally conclude that Congress could grant them incorporation, since their activities would be centered in Federal territory.

Two years later, on March 7, 1788, at a meeting of the company's directors, it was "Resolved, that they apply to Congress for an Act of Incorporation agreeable to the 12th Article of Association." The editor of the company's records states that nowhere else is found any trace of such an application, or of any reasons why it was dropped. The carefully kept diaries of Manasseh Cutler, who was most active in these early years, do not mention the matter, but he did state in private correspondence that in Congress the status of the company had been mildly challenged as an unincorporated body.[5] At this time, the new government was on its way (Massachusetts, a "crucial" state, had ratified early in

[5] W. P. & J. P. Cutler, *Life and Journals of Manasseh Cutler* (Cincinnati, 1888).

Material in the John May Papers (in the library of the Western Re-

February), and the vote may well have been passed in anticipation of the adoption of the 1787 Constitution. It can be conjectured that later in the year the directors were informed that the power of the new Congress to grant incorporation had been discussed in the Convention and eliminated from the list of specific delegated powers. In consequence no action would have been taken. A more probable guess is that the whole matter of incorporation was regarded as of minor importance, and was simply forgotten or neglected, once the purchase of the land had been negotiated. Incorporation was not highly prized in the business world until after 1800 or even 1820.

Subscribers were to be represented in groups by agents who would exercise voting power and elect the managing body of five directors. This unique plan was apparently intended to overcome the geographical difficulties of managing land in far-off Ohio. But the actual functioning of the structure set up in the articles was different in important respects than was first contemplated. Of the 817 shares which were finally paid up, less than one-third were held by actual emigrants to the acquired

serve Historical Society) relating to the company is included in Tract No. 97, published in the *Annual Report of the Society* (1917), 64 *ff.* John May, a Boston merchant, owned four shares and in 1788 was the agent for a total of 35. He was at Marietta in the winter of 1788–1789. Among his papers is a statement made by Cutler in 1788 regarding the dual purchase. Citing the obstacles encountered in getting consent from Congress to sell land to the company alone, he recounts that "Mr. Holton (a member of Congress) called upon me to produce evidence of our being a Company. I put into his hands our articles of Association, which he read in Congress. But it was still objected that we were a self-created body, and not legally incorporated, and therefore Congress could not know us as such." *Ibid.,* 130. Duer's intervention (he was then a member of the Board of Treasury) smoothed the path of Cutler, and made unnecessary further efforts to secure incorporation or to please members of Congress.

In the John Carter Brown Library, Providence, is a four-page pamphlet reprint of the proceedings of a company meeting of March 5–6, 1788, with a handwritten list of Rhode Island subscribers added. There is also a form of transfer of a right or share—a small slip of paper about two by six inches in size containing a simple form with blank spaces for names of transferer and transferee.

territory. Proxy voting, specifically provided for, became an established part of the operation, and at most meetings from 1790 to 1797 eight or ten men held all the proxies. Thus agents' meetings were simply enlarged directors' meetings, or rather meetings of a few men (including most of the directors themselves) exercising rather detailed supervision over the acts of the directors. Such a large percentage of absenteeism was hardly foreseen. The result is suggestive of conditions surrounding the voting power of stockholders in modern corporations.

To historians the detailed story of the 1787 transaction with the old Board of Treasury whereby the company obtained its land has been of great interest. How William Duer persuaded Cutler to make a much larger application for land than he originally intended—5,000,000 acres instead of 1,500,000—of which the major part was for the secret benefit of a typical Duer group of speculators, the mythical "Scioto Associates," is a familiar tale to students of this period in our history.[6] Of specific interest here, however, is the exact character of this Scioto group, so far as it can be determined. Being created solely as a means of securing easy control over 3,500,000 acres which Duer intended to resell in Europe before the specified installment payments came due, it had little need for formal organization. The formally managed Ohio Company was to have the other 1,500,000 for its several hundred New England members. In return for Cutler's acquiescence to the coupling of the two diverse enterprises, Duer agreed to advance the $143,000 needed for a down payment.

The history of the dual purchase requires some further space here, because it illustrates well the activities of men who typically used in their speculative transactions the modern business

[6] The two best accounts are by T. T. Belote, "Scioto Speculation and the French Settlement at Gallipolis," 3 *University of Cincinnati Studies,* Series II (1907), 43; and by E. C. Dawes, "Scioto Purchase in 1787," 22 *Magazine of American History,* 470. A. B. Hulbert's "Methods and Operations of the Scioto Group," 1 *Mississippi Valley Historical Review,* 4, discusses the "morals" of the projectors.

syndicate,[7] distinguished from the joint adventure by its concentration of nearly complete authority in the hands of a manager.

Immediately after the deal was closed, Cutler and Sargent, the nominal buyers, deeded to the Ohio Company its share and to Duer a one-half interest in the remaining Scioto area. A little later these three agreed to set up the latter speculation in thirty shares, of which Duer would control thirteen, Cutler and Sargent thirteen, and four would be sold "for the general good." This was to facilitate reassignment; Rufus Putnam, Generals Tupper and Parsons, Joel Barlow, Richard Platt, and Royal Flint all received shares from one or the other of the principals. The first three received their shares from Cutler and Sargent, so that nearly all the prominent leaders of the Ohio Company were thus mixed up in the Scioto deal—the supposed shadiness of which has bothered patriotic Ohio historians[8] considerably! Quite obviously, these able men saw nothing reprehensible in a plan to encourage land purchases by French or English emigrants, albeit modern hypercritical historians seem anxious to condemn them. Joel Barlow, the poet, received his share because he was chosen in 1788 to go to France to resell the lands to prospective French *émigrés*. His trip was a fiasco. He first transferred one of the four "free" shares to an English adventurer, Playfair, who proceeded to misappropriate the funds of the *Compagnie du Scioto* which they formed in October, 1789, to handle the sale of the land.[9]

[7] American courts did not recognize the syndicate as a distinct business device until late in the nineteenth century; *infra,* Chapter VI, note 14.

[8] In particular, A. B. Hulbert. *Cf.* his "Methods of the Scioto Group," *op. cit.* Since Duer and his associate Osgood were both federal officials, linking the two purchases to give them an option on a huge tract of land with no down payment seems "immoral" to the Ohio historian. The fact of their loss and the unwillingness of any one else to buy are sufficient refutation of this judgment.

[9] This French *Compagnie du Scioto* was similar to "Castorland" (*infra,* p. 209). It was formed by a registered "act of formation" before a city official in Paris. There were to be 8,000 transferable shares of 1,000 livres each. Playfair and a French merchant were given full power to manage the sales of land (which Barlow deeded to the *Compagnie* by his power of attor-

Barlow, before he quit his task, sent over the boatload of settlers whose career at the first Gallipolis settlement is so familiar in Ohio history.

The arrival of these unfortunate French settlers in the spring of 1789 caused a change to be made in the Scioto set-up. Duer had as yet no title to land upon which he could place them, yet a smooth and happy reception was deemed essential to future sales in France. Just at this time the Ohio Company directors were worrying about their course of action in dealing with 148 of their 1,000 shares that, by a check-up in May, 1789, were found to be delinquent in payments and had been forfeited. The solution suggested was excellent: Duer would buy the delinquent shares and so secure immediately the equivalent amount of land in the Ohio Company's area, where surveyors and settlers had already arrived. Duer intended to pay for them with the proceeds of drafts on Barlow; the drafts were later defaulted because the latter had none of the money which had been collected. The Ohio Company was pleased to have a ready sale for its shares. Subscriptions had been slow in coming in, and the loss of the 148 shares was serious. At the price to the government of one dollar per acre, which had been agreed upon (to be paid in certificates, not in specie) a subscription to the full 1,000 shares was necessary in order to secure the 1,000,000 acres contemplated; the other 500,000 acres would be secured if and as 500 more shares could be disposed of. By 1789 only the first payment of $500,000 had been made, and one-seventh of this amount had been received in the form of military bounty warrants. Facing the necessity of closing up subscriptions, the directors empowered Cutler and Putnam to dispose of the 148 shares as they saw fit.

The Scioto syndicate members were chary of entering directly

ney), from which the proceeds would be divided, two-thirds to pay the purchase price and one-third for improvements (three-fourths and one-fourth when sales were made to non-shareholders). The organization only lasted three months, because in January, 1790, Playfair disappeared with the proceeds of the sales which had been made from a Paris office.

into such a bargain, if Duer was to be their managing director.[10] It was finally decided that three trustees, Duer, Flint, and Craigie, would take title to the shares and assume the obligation of payment. They were appointed at a meeting on April 20, 1790, and entered into a formal agreement (apparently drawn up by counsel) to buy the shares on April 23.[11] In the trust agreement, the duties of the trustees were specified: to see that the contract with the United States was executed; to see that remittances reached "superintendent" Duer and that they were applied to the purchase of land. The trustees were also eventually to distribute any surplus to the participants. Craigie related later that on the night of April 20 he took particular pains to ascertain whether or not he would be under any personal liability if he acted as a trustee.[12] He was reassured on this point;[13] apparently Duer had frequently used the trustee device in his no-down-payment contracts in the past, in order more easily to escape from them if they proved unattractive. Unfortunately there is no record of the presence of any lawyer at this meeting or of the group's seeking legal advice; but Duer's close friendship with Alexander Hamilton in the years 1785–1789 and later is well known.

[10] In a note on a letter sent to France at this time, Duer signed himself "Superintendent of the affairs of the Scioto Company." 2 *Duer Papers*, No. 68, New York Historical Society Library. Craigie in correspondence said that Duer had the full management of the affair. He wrote to Thomas Porter on June 18, 1790: "The power of drawing on France is with him [Duer] as well as the whole management of the business, and you must not consider me as responsible for any engagements." Further on he declared that he did not have "sufficient control of the funds" to want to make himself personally liable. 2 *Craigie MSS.*, American Antiquarian Society Library (no paging).

[11] A notarial copy of the agreement is in 2 *Duer Papers*, No. 59.

[12] Letter in 2 *Craigie MSS.*

[13] In 2 *Craigie MSS.*, there is a letter from Flint to Putnam in which the former said that the Scioto contract did not "lay us trustees under any personal obligations. This was your opinion"; but he wished that Putnam would engineer an agreement with the Ohio Company not to try to enforce the Scioto contract. Putnam was a Scioto proprietor, and as such might be liable on its contracts. On June 30, 1792, the Scioto trustees did receive a general release from Tallmadge, treasurer of the Ohio Company.

Even before Duer's bankruptcy in 1792,[14] this transaction led to serious criticism of the dominant group in the Ohio Company. A "minority stockholders' committee" was formed late in 1790 and demanded a review of the actions of Putnam and Cutler. The two men, however, were vindicated in full. Previously Putnam had brought before the agents a proposal to hold directors liable (in accordance with the tenth article) only for those votes in which they were recorded on the affirmative side. This was rejected by the voting agents as too great a departure from the articles. But they then proceeded to resolve that in future "we the Agents will, and in Justice ought to make a due discrimination" between directors voting for or against any action that might later be questioned. From then on directors noted any dissenting vote in the margin of the minute book. A year earlier, in November, 1789, a motion had been lost at an agents' meeting whereby an agent could demand at any time a special report from the directors on the state of the "Funds." But it was decided instead to have quarterly reports presented to the agents.[15]

The whole problem of handling the shares of delinquent subscribers was a bothersome one for the company directors. No special method of enforcing payment had been set forth in the articles. The attitude of the law at this time was distinctly unfriendly to suits against a delinquent, because of the impossibility of one partner suing another at common law. Shares in some of the companies of the period were specifically pledged

[14] Davis, 1 *Essays,* 295.

[15] This is an extremely interesting example of a modern practice; no early corporate charters require more than an annual report, and many in New York around 1800 called for triennial reports only. In Massachusetts, many early charters made no requirement as to reports, or, as in the case of banks, required them triennially. Dodd, *Statutory Regulation of Business Corporations in Massachusetts,* in *Harvard Legal Essays* (Cambridge, 1934), 87, 89. In Dutch practice in the eighteenth century, the annual report was an exception. Earlier still, the original charter of the Dutch East India Company required a report only at the end of ten years.

in advance as security to insure the payment of future assessments. In agreeing to articles of association, subscribers in such cases automatically gave permission for the forfeiture of their shares at any time.

Earlier, when the directors were discussing their course of action with regard to delinquent shares in 1788, Rufus Putnam wrote to director Cutler:[16] "I never had an idea that the money paid by any subscriber should be forfeited, but that every agent would have a deed for the aggregate quantity of lands he paid for, and that he should arrange the matter among his subscribers in such manner as he thought proper." However, this point of view was apparently not adopted, because when Putnam and Cutler, acting as agents, sold the 148 shares to the Scioto group in May of 1789, the sale of the shares was absolute and was not prorated according to the amounts paid in on them, as Putnam seemed to desire. The board directed them: "In case any share subscribed is not paid to the Treasurer they are empowered to dispose of such shares to the best advantage, and account with the Board." Later on, in 1796, the directors carried out forfeiture sales of specific lots for which full payment had not been made, since at that time the shares had received the major allotments of land.

Donation tracts (free rights of land upon certain prescribed conditions) were used in order to attract non-member settlers, and much of the directors' time was used in regulating them. One hundred acres for each share were allocated for this purpose in addition to extra lands awarded to members who complied with the specified conditions. Several tracts originally granted were forfeited because of "neglect of military duty."[17] In 1790 groups of forty shareholders were permitted to draw their allotted lands as one block of 4,000 acres and divide it as

---

[16] Cutler, *Life and Journals,* 146.

[17] A condition which recalls the use of this same device by the Susquehannah Company.

they saw fit. There was also systematic encouragement of mills, blacksmith shops, etc., by free grants.[18]

Scattered throughout the records[19] of the agents' meetings are votes or resolutions that, taken together, form a rough set of by-laws. In December, 1788, for example, it was voted that grants of donation land must be referred to the agents for approval. They were to be made to proprietors and non-proprietors. In 1789 it was decided that the books of the company would be open at all times to agents and directors, and that copies would be made for all others upon payment of a notary fee. In May, 1789, it was decided that the acts of two directors would be valid, except in overriding a previous vote where more than two had been present; this was decided by the directors themselves, in order to permit an "East" and a "West" group. In November, 1789, exact instructions were given the secretary in recording transfers of stock: he must make a mark against the name of the original holder, together with a note showing on what page the transfer had been recorded.

After the bankruptcies of Duer and Treasurer Platt in 1792, the finances of the company were in a "deranged state."[20] Put-

[18] Interesting comment on conditions in Marietta in the early Spring of 1790 is contained in Thomas Wallcott's Journal, printed in 17 *Proceedings of the Massachusetts Historical Society,* 1st Series, 174. It was apparently overlooked by the editor of the *Records.* The presence of "unemployed poor" in the town only one year after its founding, with fertile land freely available on all sides, is startling evidence that unemployment is not a by-product of industrialism.

[19] 2 *Records,* 52, 106, 134, 154.

[20] The events of 1791–1792 preceding their spectacular failures in the Spring of 1792 are described by Davis, 1 *Essays,* 174–212, as the first Wall Street boom and panic.

In the John May Papers (Library of the Western Reserve Historical Society) is a statement made by Platt as treasurer to the directors explaining his embarrassment. He detailed the causes as follows: (1) A loss of $75,000 in 1790–1791 caused by the rise in price of United States certificates which he had agreed to deliver to the Treasury before he had actually purchased them. (2) A loss of $45,000 from "European speculations," in one of which involving total commitments of $300,000 he had lost $25,000 as one of three participants; two of his personal "speculations" had lost

nam successfully secured from Congress a final act deeding enough land to make up the original 1,000,000 acres, but at a much reduced price. This deed ran to Putnam, Cutler, Richard Oliver, and Griffin Greene "in fee simple, in trust for the persons composing the Ohio Company, according to their several rights and interests, as tenants in common." To remedy the great scarcity of cash among the settlers, the directors voted to loan $2,000 from the treasury where it would do the most good. In 1790 they had also ingeniously voted to pay the surveyors who were employed in six-month bills, which would be receivable for debts owed to the company by settlers or members within two months—an example of "scrip" issuance to speed up debt collection.

By 1795 the directors were anxious to clean up the project. They began to sell all company-owned property (forts and defences largely) at public auction, set up an elaborate system to complete the surveys that were a compulsory feature of the government's grants, and voted to give the treasurer 4 per cent on all monies that had come into his hands since taking office (1792) in full discharge of any claim for fees or salary. At the time a "final dividend" was ordered (1796) an independent committee

$20,000. (3) As United States certificates came in from the members, he sold them "at my own hazard," hoping for a decline in their price; obviously these were short sales although Platt did not use the term. (4) His loans and advances to Duer, also in bankruptcy, were $40,000. (5) He had sold other Treasury obligations short; the loss was not detailed. (6) Miscellaneous uncollectible debts were $25,000. (7) The failure of Leonard Bleecker and Benjamin Luxar would mean a $50,000 loss to him as a participant in syndicates with them. (8) Miscellaneous short sales, or "delivery of U. S. stock on a rising market over two years," caused a $50,000 loss. (9) "Minor losses" would amount to $16,250. He placed the grand total of his operating losses as a security speculator at $402,450. He obviously tried to maximize them in order to stress his inability to repay funds of the Ohio Company in his care. Commingling of private funds with those of enterprises or public bodies was common business and political practice in the eighteenth century, and Platt's defalcation involved no separate criminal liability other than commitment to debtors' prison pending a settlement with his creditors.

of five was appointed, of which Alexander Hamilton was a member, as "a committee in behalf of the Ohio Company (any two of whom shall be competent to execute the business) who are hereby vested with full power to examine, audit, and finally settle all the Treasurer's accounts." Detailed instructions were added for this audit. This seems to indicate that Hamilton had had a previous advisory connection with the company.

As a result of the audit the treasurer was directed to petition Congress for settlement of some forged loan office certificates that had been given by Platt in 1792 in partial settlement of his accounts as treasurer, while in bankruptcy. Nothing was done, and the certificates ultimately caused the prolongation of the life of the company to 1870—being the only property of the company not divided up as land or cash. After 1830 one Nahum Ward bought up all the shares of the company that he could trace[21] and attempted to revive the claim. In 1870 the Supreme Court (on an appeal from the Court of Claims) finally rejected it, upholding the original 1792 decision of the Treasury that they had been forged in Georgia. This ended the career of the company, but no formal vote of dissolution was ever recorded, except perhaps by Mr. Ward in privacy.

THE YAZOO COMPANIES[22]

Because their activities became a public scandal of the first magnitude in the first decade after the adoption of the Constitution, the Yazoo Companies have always been well known. They have served as the favorite example of early corruption of

---

[21] Thomas Wallcott (*supra,* note 18) sold his share, at least his remaining equitable interest after long-continued tax defaults, to Ward in 1835 for $100.

[22] C. H. Haskins, *Yazoo Land Companies* (New York, 1891), is the best known historical account. Senator Beveridge devotes fifty-six pages to the episode in order to show the background of Marshall's opinion in *Fletcher* v. *Peck* (3 *Life of John Marshall* [Boston, 1919], 546–602). Beveridge drew heavily upon the picturesque account of A. H. Chappell, *Miscellanies of Georgia* (Atlanta, 1874), 74–135, which was taken largely

legislatures, and of the outburst of "wild" speculation during Washington's administration.

A situation arose in Georgia immediately after the end of the Revolution strikingly similar to that in New York. A large area of land lying directly west of the present state of Georgia had been acquired, reaching to the Mississippi River and containing almost no white settlers. Georgia claimed it as within the boundaries of her original charter. The Federal Government claimed title and jurisdiction on the ground that it had been secured directly and *de novo* from England by the terms of peace. After 1789 Washington's cabinet especially desired control because it was anxious to maintain peace with the Indians. The succeeding controversy was similar to those in the North.

Georgia was a small, poor state, and its leaders were far less able men than those of New York, Connecticut, or Virginia. The attractiveness of a sale of this land increased after 1784 as the state's financial troubles multiplied. One or two applications were made to purchase parts of the territory and the state itself tried to encourage direct settlement, but no plan succeeded until the offer of the South Carolina Yazoo Company. This group was headed by a notorious promoter named Walsh who had changed his name to Thomas Washington. The company requested a grant of land in November, 1789, and in December the legislature passed an act granting to them more than 10,000,000 acres, to be paid for in debt certificates over a period of two years.

Three other groups which had petitioned for similar allotments were included in the terms of the same act. They were

from contemporary newspaper accounts. Beveridge calls the whole episode the "greatest financial scandal in American history" (vol. 3, 174). Sakolski, in his *Great American Land Bubble* (New York, 1932), has a good summary (chapter VI). The principal original sources, other than newspapers, upon which all these students drew are the Congressional records in the series of *American State Papers, Public Lands*. The latter volumes have been examined by the present author; they yielded much of the specific information concerning the form of the companies which is not included in any of the historical accounts.

called respectively the Virginia,[23] the Tennessee, and the Georgia Yazoo Companies. The total area granted exceeded 25,000,000 acres and included practically all of the present states of Alabama and Mississippi. The total price was only $200,000 (less than one cent per acre); and that was payable in certificates. It is evident that the groups securing these grants had been hastily formed and had no well-developed plans for exploiting the territory. The South Carolina Company, leader of the group, immediately sent out James O'Fallon to secure settlers; he established contacts with James Wilkinson and John Sevier, two prominent leaders of the western colonists. Later he carried on negotiations with Mero, the Spanish governor in Louisiana, and his relations with the latter form a well-known part of the story of Spanish intrigue in the Southwest during these years.[24]

Some recently published letters illustrate the methods and beliefs of the promoters of this group.[25] Alexander Moultrie, who was a director of the South Carolina Yazoo Company, is the author of one, written in January, 1790, at Charleston, to Benjamin Farrar, a wealthy planter who had just removed to the new Natchez district. In this letter Moultrie described the grant of 8,750,000 acres to his company as lying just south of the area

[23] Patrick Henry was prominent in this company; cf. W. W. Henry, 2 *Patrick Henry* (New York, 1891), 510–512. There is no clear evidence that he soon "withdrew" as Beveridge seems to think; *op. cit.,* 553.

[24] Haskins, *op. cit.,* 6–17; *supra,* p. 131, note 135, and J. C. Parish, "Intrigues of Doctor James O'Fallon," 17 *Mississippi Valley Historical Review,* 230.

James O'Fallon, Irish-born brother-in-law of George Rogers Clark, had been an army surgeon in the latter part of the Revolution. *Draper MSS.,* V 72. Detailed instructions given him by "Director" Moultrie, under date of March 9, 1790, contained fifteen articles covering all the problems which he was expected to solve, from encouraging immigration to securing the good-will of the Indians. *Ibid.,* V 73. In April, O'Fallon wrote to Sevier: "I am one of the 20 proprietors of that Company, and their agent general, by commission, with power to appoint Deputy Agents all over this whole Western Territory of the Union." *Ibid.,* 5 VV 23.

[25] "The South Carolina Yazoo Company," 16 *Mississippi Valley Historical Review,* 383, edited by A. P. Whitaker.

granted to the Virginia group, which was headed by Patrick Henry. A grant had been made to Moultrie and three others "in behalf of ourselves and the other original associates." The company was divided into twenty shares, each one represented by an ostensible holder who alone had the right to attend meetings and to vote. Any holder of these original shares might sell out to others in part, or sell the complete share. If an outright sale of the whole share were made, the new owner would be unable to vote until he had been approved by the company. Each such transfer, either for the whole or for part of a share, was to be made on the books of the company.

It was planned to set aside the eastern half of the grant to be leased for a period of seven years. It would then be sold; the tenants then occupying the land would receive a discount of $6 per acre plus the cost of improvements on whatever selling price might be fixed. Each tenant in making purchases would be limited to 100 acres for each person eighteen years old in his family. The western half of the tract was to be sold only in 640 acre tracts. The original proprietors were permitted to buy anywhere in the tract, and were to be debited on the books for the purchase price. Later sales to outsiders would be credited to each account *pro rata* and thus offset the debits. Owners of sub-shares, if recorded on the books, were also to have this privilege. The original promoters intended to raise a loan (optimistically!) on the security of the portion of the tract that was to be leased. Moultrie's own share in the project was 500,000 acres, of which he offered 5,000 or 10,000 acres to Farrar at a price to be determined by negotiation.

In a letter about the same time to Alexander McGillivray, Moultrie offered to reserve for him more than one-half of his total allotment, or 295,000 acres.[26] In this letter he predicted that each of the three big companies would eventually become a

[26] *Ibid.*, 391.

separate state in the Union. Later records show that Moultrie was probably writing both these letters simply because he was seriously in need of cash.

The later Yazoo Companies had no connection with these first attempts, but the knowledge of them, and the low price secured from Georgia, undoubtedly kept speculative interest alive in the intervening five years.

Within a few months of the sale in 1789 to the original four companies, Washington's cabinet had discussed the effects of the transaction, and a proclamation was issued in August warning purchasers of the lands from interfering with treaty rights of the Indians or making any efforts to eject the latter from the territory. In the autumn of 1790, steps were taken to arrest O'Fallon and to prevent any colonization. The final blow to the hopes of the four groups was delivered by a resolution of the Georgia legislature, by which the state treasurer was instructed to receive payments due to the state only in specie.[27] This was in effect a repudiation of the original contract.[28] Added to the difficulty of interesting outsiders in the project, this new obstacle convinced the various leaders that consummation of the purchase was impossible. It is interesting to note that Patrick Henry, as the leader of the Virginia group, had accumulated a large amount of the Georgia certificates with which payment was originally to have been made; when Hamilton's funding scheme was adopted he secured a large profit from his holdings—a fact which perhaps helps to explain his support of Hamilton politically in his last years.

The failure of the four groups to carry out their bargain did not at all shut the door to future sales as far as Georgia was concerned. The Virginia group tried several times in later years to force completion of the sale. In 1794, for instance, Robert Morris

[27] 1 *American State Papers, Public Lands,* 257.

[28] This group suffered in their attempts to obtain redress because in the public mind they were associated with the 1795 purchasers.

and Wade Hampton offered to help finance a new purchase,[29] but no results were achieved. In the case of the Tennessee group, Zachariah Cox made unsuccessful efforts to establish a settlement around Natchez.[30] Meanwhile outsiders who had not been concerned in the first deal became interested in making an entirely new transaction.

Finally, in 1794 an offer by four new companies of $500,000 for an area similar to that sold in 1789 was approved by the legislature. Governor Mathews vetoed the bill, but after slight changes were made he signed a similar act in January, 1795. Well over 30,000,000 acres were included in this second sale.[31] These four new groups were called the Upper Mississippi, the Tennessee, the Georgia Mississippi, and the Georgia Companies. They received approximately three, four, eleven, and seventeen million acres. Thus the last-named group received about one-half the total grant and furnished one-half the total payment of $500,000. One-fifth of this price—$100,000—was paid down; the balance was to be paid before November 1, 1795, secured by a mortgage. All payments were to be made in specie.

By the terms of the sale, 2,000,000 acres of the 30,000,000 were to be reserved for settlement by citizens of Georgia who would be entitled to membership in any of the four companies and also would be beneficiaries of the low initial price. The state specifically did *not* guarantee title to the land against any other claimants, including the Indian tribes whose rights had been recognized by the Federal Government. Each company was to handle the Indian claims itself, *providing* approval was received from Washington—a difficult condition. A final term in the sale was the requirement that actual settlement should begin within five years after final title had been secured.[32] It was a good trade for

---

[29] 1 *Am. St. Pap., Pub. Lands*, 139.   [30] *Ibid.*, 142.

[31] The stated amount varies; actual surveys in later years showed 35,-000,000 as about the actual amount.

[32] The act is reprinted in full in 1 *Am. St. Pap., Pub. Lands*, 152.

a poor state which desperately needed ready cash—a sale of land, to which its title was defective on two grounds, for half a million in specie.

Among those interested in one or more of the four bidding companies were individuals celebrated in the land history of the period. James Greenleaf, associate of Morris, was a leading purchaser of the largest area in the group—that of the Georgia Company. James Wilson, Wade Hampton, Andrew Craigie, Oliver Phelps, John Sevier, and William Blount were among those holding shares in one or more of the companies. Greenleaf helped to engineer an immediate resale in Boston of the entire Georgia Mississippi Company's purchase, as well as 4,000,000 acres in the Georgia Company's grant, at a price of $1,375,000. The original purchase price was about $215,000.[33] This sale brought into the subsequent controversy one group of Boston speculators who later organized an entirely new company under the name of the New England Mississippi Land Company. The various shares of this Boston purchase became known as "Mississippi scrip," and for a few months there was widespread speculation in them. In this case, as in the earlier instance, few of the men concerned seemed to realize the difficulties of really acquiring title to the land in the face of the Federal Government's attitude.

The variation in form among the several groups originally concerned in the purchase when they proceeded to organize themselves has escaped the comment of historians, who have otherwise placed great emphasis upon the transaction. The Georgia Company was formed, just prior to the final legislative grant, by articles of agreement dated January 1, 1795.[34] The preamble included the phrase, "Whereas, the aforesaid persons did form themselves into a company, known and distinguished by the name of the Georgia Company." Following a description of the

[33] *Ibid.,* 149.   [34] *Ibid.,* 140.

land the agreement went on to state that the members "are hereby equally entitled to all the lands . . . share and share alike, as tenants in common, and not as joint tenants, and all expenses . . . shall be borne equally and the profits or produce of any sale shall be divided share and share alike." There were ten shares in this agreement, which resembles quite closely such a pre-Revolutionary plan as Croghan's Illinois Company. Of the ten shares Wade Hampton, famous South Carolinian, held three and James Gunn, leading Georgia politician and then United States Senator, held two. These shares were called in the agreement "original shares," and each had one vote.

In a postscript to the agreement dated January 10, 1795,[35] there was a list of participants to whom sub-shares (taken, *pro rata,* from the original shares) were to be granted. There were two groups, one consisting of contributors of cash and the other of political leaders who were backing the act. The reason for the second group was naïvely stated as follows: "We found it necessary to distribute to a variety of citizens of this state certain sub-shares in order that the benefit of the purchase . . . should be as generally diffused as possible."[36] Of the first group, James Wilson was the most important, contributing $25,000 out of a total subscribed of $55,000. The form of the sub-shares was given in this postscript also. A sub-share was described as containing so many acres; there was a provision for issuing a negotiable certificate as soon as payments were completed.[37]

James Greenleaf[38] purchased from the Georgia Company on August 22, 1795, a large portion of its purchase, excepting only the part reserved for Georgia citizens[39]—a total of 13,500,000

[35] *Ibid.,* 141.   [36] *Ibid.,* 140.

[37] *Ibid.,* 142; the clause in the sub-share was: "We do further certify that, so soon as the mortgage shall be satisfied, the said holder shall, upon returning this certificate . . . receive a certificate of a negotiable nature."

[38] For a sketch of Greenleaf's career, *cf.* note 66, *infra.*

[39] 2 *Am. St. Pap., Pub. Lands,* 882; Greenleaf's deposition.

acres. Of this huge amount, he resold immediately (August 24) 1,000,000 acres to James Wilson[40] and another million to Zachariah Cox, promoter of the Tennessee group. Greenleaf sold about 9,000,000 acres of the remainder in blocks to Boston and New York buyers (some of whom were also included in the New England Mississippi Company), the largest, consisting of 2,800,000 acres, to Nathaniel Prime. This sale included the area later involved in the suit of *Fletcher* v. *Peck*.[41]

The 2,500,000 acres which he retained for himself were, in 1796, put in the so-called Simpson or "381" trust, which he was forced to establish, along with many other assets, for the benefit of his creditors. Henry Pratt and the other trustees proceeded naïvely to appoint Greenleaf their attorney in petitioning for relief from Congress after 1800. Greenleaf mentioned in one of these petitions[42] that he acted in all these transactions under the advice of "able counsel"—naming Alexander Hamilton and his own brother-in-law, William Tilghman.

In addition to these sales of land, there were numerous transfers of Georgia Company shares; in effect a share became simply a claim on future installment payments by the land purchasers, to the extent that cash was not paid down. Hampton and Gunn sold five of the ten Georgia Company shares to Hugh Rose of Philadelphia, who resold a half interest in them to one Valentine Jones in England.[43] There were probably other transfers also, but historical record is lacking.

Two other leaders in the deal, Zachariah Cox and Matthias Maher, headed the Tennessee Company. They divided their pur-

[40] Wilson immediately resold to Harry Lee and one Elie Williams; the latter in 1814 appeared as the owner (in behalf of others) in petitions to a Congressional committee. *Ibid.*, 884.

[41] 6 Cranch 87.

[42] 2 *Am. St. Pap., Pub. Lands,* 884. In this period, as will be discussed below, Greenleaf was attempting to realize on his interests in the North American Land Company, in association with the same group of Philadelphians.

[43] 1 *Am. St. Pap., Pub. Lands,* 139.

chase into 420 equal shares, of which they jointly retained about three hundred. In their articles of agreement, the form of a share was stated as: "We hereby certify that .... or his assigns, is entitled to the 1/420th part of the said territory, provided the sum of 1/420th of the purchase money be paid before August 1st, next, when a deed of conveyance will be issued, in lieu of the certificate." A failure to make payment would make the certificate null and void. Cox and Maher were the only two signers of this agreement, which resembled an agreement of proprietors with prospective purchasers.[44]

The Georgia Mississippi Company divided its purchase into 1,600 equal shares, but, as was pointed out above, the whole tract was immediately resold to men who became trustees for the New England Mississippi Company, with the exception of the 620,000 acres reserved for Georgia citizens.

The last of the group, the Upper Mississippi Company, had only twelve equal shares. This was the unit organized at the last minute by one Scott, who was supposedly on the ground as the agent of the old 1789 Virginia Company. Convinced that he could make no headway for the old company, he had interested Wade Hampton in participating in the new sale; Hampton, as pointed out above, was also associated at the time with Gunn, the leader in engineering the entire deal in the Georgia legislature. Hampton later testified that he believed Scott was still acting for the old Virginia Company, and that the latter had told him that he could exchange his old Virginia certificate, which he had purchased from David Ross the previous October, for shares in the new group. Scott hastened to sell out his interest within ten days for $10,000 and seems to have disappeared.

---

[44] In 1814, one E. Jackson, as "surviving trustee" of the Tennessee Company (he was one of an original body of three who held the legal title) deposed that only 302 of the 420 shares remained outstanding. "It is conjectured that most of the residue of the 118 shares were relinquished to the State of Georgia." 2 *ibid.*, 882. For Cox's later activities, *cf.* 6 *ibid.*, 174–177.

In later testimony, Hampton stated that when he bought his Virginia shares, just prior to the new sale, he was told to execute a power of attorney for someone who could sign the articles and who could also vote by proxy for him at meetings. When this was done, Scott wrote that "I shall take care to have you recognized as a partner, and your share entered on the books."[45] This procedure throws light on the methods used for conducting business in such a relatively small group, which preserved its existence for six years and was to be a petitioner before Congress for more than a decade later.[46]

The spectacular repudiation of the whole sale in February, 1796, because of the alleged bribery of members of the granting legislature, is a notorious incident in American history.[47] With considerable mock formality, the two houses of the legislature, in response to an apparent public resentment, paraded in front of the State House and publicly burned a copy of the original act of

[45] 1 *ibid.*, 138.

[46] In 1803, many affidavits supporting the Virginia Company's claim, and emphasizing its lack of any connection with the 1795 deal, were presented to Congress by William Cowan, "agent for the Company," 1 *ibid.*, 172–178. This was at the time when a compromise offer of $10,000,000 to satisfy all claimants was being pressed, without success.

[47] Not all comment on this episode has been in the modern Beardian vein of praise for the repudiators and condemnation for the malevolent speculators. M. C. Klingelsmith, in an article on the whole Yazoo affair, "James Wilson and the So-called Yazoo Fraud," 56 *University of Pennsylvania Law Review*, 1 (January, 1908), points out that the obscurity and low character of the individuals who furnished affidavits of the previous winter's bribery in September–December, 1795, indicates that the campaign was stimulated by political hatred toward Gunn and others rather than by a sense of justice, and that the affidavits themselves may have been purchased. Governor Mathews, not accused of any connection with speculators, stigmatized the campaign for repudiation as due entirely to political hatreds. Historians also seem to overlook the fact that legislators commonly shared in purchases that they themselves approved during this period, without incurring charges of moral turpitude. This was particularly true in Massachusetts, where New York and Maine lands were then being sold. The fact that the state's title was doubtful, and it was difficult to induce any purchasers to come forward, seems also not to be realized. Political jealousy of the most selfish kind on the part of those left out of the deal seems to

the year previous. Technically, the sale was "void"; it was not "repudiated," in the language of the legislative resolution.[48] There was provision for a return of the down payment, which was hardly a remedy for those who had purchased in good faith. In the few weeks following this action, the original members of the purchasing groups who received early news of the event continued to sell their shares, so that when the action became generally known,[49] public resentment was great. Several suits were entered in the courts and within a year or two petitions began to appear in Congress asking for compensation. This last avenue of redress eventually became the only one for all those concerned in both the 1789 and the 1795 transactions, because within a few years Georgia had agreed to sell the whole territory to the United States for $1,250,000. Later, in 1800, Congress directed commissioners to investigate the claims of individuals to land in the area.

The relatively large group of individuals who felt themselves aggrieved by the two repudiations attempted to bolster their claims in Congress for some sort of compensation by publishing legal opinions in pamphlet form. The opinions were prepared in 1796 by the well-known Federalist politician, Robert Goodloe Harper, a brother-in-law of Alexander Hamilton, and by Hamilton himself, for submission to purchasers. A pamphlet[50] contain-

have helped the repudiation campaign on its way. Beveridge in his account naïvely accepted the estimate of most Georgia historians that there was a deliberate campaign of intimidation and bribery to secure passage of the bill, and that Senator Gunn especially was an evil character. B. A. Konkle, in his unpublished *Life* of Wilson, chapter 26, points out that judgment on the Yazoo sale has been one-sided in the extreme.

[48] The same sort of language, which hopes to circumvent probable unconstitutionality, has been witnessed in the preambles to modern national legislation. Marshall swept aside the distinction, and declared the state's action to be a clear impairment of a contract obligation. The repudiation statute is reprinted in 1 *Am. St. Pap., Pub. Lands,* 156.

[49] *Cf.* an affidavit by George Blake of Hartford that as late as August, 1795, the average individual there and in Boston had not heard of the campaign to repudiate. 2 *Am. St. Pap., Pub. Lands,* 885. Actual passage of the repudiation resolution was not known until March 6, 1796.

[50] A copy is in the New York Public Library; it has no title.

ing the opinions was published,[51] partly as an answer to several which upheld the repudiation.

A private suit growing out of the repudiation action has become well known as the leading constitutional case of *Fletcher v. Peck*.[52] Chief Justice Marshall's opinion is one of his best known arguments in behalf of the strict interpretation of the Constitution as against the power of the states, in this case based obviously on the obligation-of-contracts clause. The transfers out of which the suit arose included one from the original Georgia Company to Greenleaf, from Greenleaf to Nathaniel Prime, by

[51] In a short "advertisement" on the title page the opinion is stated to be "not merely a legal opinion, but such a statement as might enable persons to understand the case, and judge for themselves." Harper first disposed of the contention that the lands belonged to the United States and not to Georgia by virtue of the 1783 Treaty. He pointed out that "everyone is presumed to know his own rights" and since the Federal Government had not protested against the sale in 1789 (except so far as it disturbed Indian relations), they could not validly object to the 1795 sale. This summary, prepared in the manner of a legal brief, formed by far the largest section of the opinion, apparently reflecting the uncertainty of the purchasers concerning the treaty's effect on their position.

Arguing that the United States courts as well as Congress should uphold the purchase, Harper made this interesting statement: "Our courts make no difficulty of declaring legislative acts void, even those of the Union, where they are contrary to the constitution." Written in 1796, it foreshadowed Marshall's later decisions, and is also interesting as an early avowal of Federalist doctrine concerning the power of the judiciary. He then concluded his argument by pointing out that the state of Georgia was as much bound by its agreement to sell the lands as would be any individual. The 1796 act of the Georgia legislature, therefore, could have "no legal effect."

For this part of his statement he referred for corroboration to a short opinion by Alexander Hamilton, reprinted as an appendix to the pamphlet. This had been written somewhat earlier than Harper's own lengthier brief, on March 25, 1796, as a private opinion rendered to Boston clients who had pooled their purchases in the New England Mississippi Company. Hamilton devoted his opinion to the effect of the obligation-of-contracts clause as forbidding any repeal of such a land sale by a state. He closed by certifying as his opinion the validity of the claims of the purchasers.

[52] 6 Cranch 87. Beveridge discusses the arguments and participants, 3 *Life of Marshall*, 583–593.

him to Oliver Phelps, and by him to Peck, who in turn sold in 1803 to Fletcher. The latter sale, according to Beveridge, was made simply to form the basis of the suit.

After this decision of Marshall's in 1810, most members of Congress recognized that compensation would have to be paid to the purchasers. In the preceding ten or twelve years the so-called Yazoo Question had come up in every session, and a small "anti-Yazoo" bloc, led by John Randolph, had organized and successfully prevented any payments. Many continued their opposition when Randolph was no longer in the House. However, in 1814 Congress finally passed an act authorizing payment of about $4,700,000 to the shareholders of the four companies. The allocation of part of this payment to the organization of sub-purchasers, the New England Mississippi Company, gave rise to litigation.[53]

The case of *Gilman* v. *Brown*[54] arose because the final payment of indemnity to the shareholders in the New England Mississippi Company had to be divided equitably by commissioners among contending claimants. It was noted above that, about a month before the repeal acts of Georgia were passed, this latter group purchased a tract of 11,000,000 acres from Greenleaf. One Wetmore had organized a syndicate in Boston to make the purchase and subsequently helped to organize this company.

The articles of association were scrutinized by the Massachusetts Supreme Court, and reviewed again by the Federal Supreme Court when the case was appealed.[55] They set up the most interesting example of a land merchandising body in the whole Yazoo group, one that has apparently been little known. On

[53] Compensation awarded was: Upper Mississippi Company, $350,000; Tennessee Company, $600,000; Georgia Mississippi Company, $1,550,000; and Georgia Company, $2,250,000. The New England Company received all but $95,000 of the third award. 6 *Am. St. Pap., Pub. Lands,* 959.

[54] 14 Mass. 123.

[55] As *Brown* v. *Gilman,* 4 Wheaton 255; the opinion was by Marshall.

February 13, 1796, the Georgia Mississippi Company executed a deed of conveyance to three agents, Messrs. Wetmore, Jarvis, and Hull, to be held in trust for other purchasers. The deed was placed in escrow with George Minot, pending the first payment of two cents an acre; an absolute deed was to be given after that payment. Soon after the execution of the purchase agreement, but before the delivery of the final deed, these three agents organized a group of purchasers in an association and executed articles of agreement. The first step in the organization was a deed in trust to John Peck (he of the *Fletcher* v. *Peck* suit), by the same agents, of 3,400,000 acres originally in the Georgia Company purchase. Peck redeeded, in exchange for shares in the new company, to new trustees—Jarvis, Hull, and Newman (eliminating Wetmore). A week later, twenty other Bostonians deeded over 7,000,000 additional acres to the same trustees, consisting of land in the original Georgia Mississippi Company sale. This was done in order to consolidate forces to resist the repudiation, which had just then become known. John Apthorp, William Scollay, James Sullivan, and Elias Haskett Derby were in this group,[56] all of them well-known business leaders. Sullivan was then the leader of the Boston bar.

The first article of the agreement[57] specified the name as "The New England Mississippi Land Company." The second article named Jarvis, Newman, and Hull as trustees to hold title to the property. In the third article it was required that these three should execute deeds to the original purchasing members of the association in proportion to their shareholdings, but that they should hold these deeds until each member signed the articles and had in turn executed a deed of trust to a new group of trustees in which Newman was to be replaced by William Howe, Jarvis and Hull serving in the same capacity as they had for the original purchase. In later articles it was specified that the busi-

[56] 1 *Am. St. Pap., Pub. Lands,* 220–221.
[57] *Brown* v. *Gilman, op. cit.,* 281 *ff.*

ness of the association should be managed by a board of directors with full power to sell or otherwise dispose of all or any part of the property and to pay out the proceeds to the shareholders. This was the only reference to the absorbing duty of the directors to secure some sort of validation of title or compensation. It was further specified that the trustees were to issue a negotiable certificate to each shareholder (or "proprietor," as they were called in the articles), to be recorded on the books and to serve as "complete evidence to each of his rights in the said purchase." However, it was provided that transfer could be accomplished by *simple endorsement* and the transferee would be able to vote as a member of the association. In this respect the articles differed sharply from most of those drawn up in this period. Marshall stressed this negotiability and the centralization of control of the company's affairs, when he examined the articles twenty-two years later.

The eleventh article divided the purchase into 2,226 shares. The twelfth described the form of the certificate, and the thirteenth provided that although no certificate would technically be issued for less than one share, the company would provide fractional shares upon request. A final article provided that the directors should promptly make payment of all proceeds of a sale to the holders of certificates, as a dividend.

Wetmore had given notes to James Greenleaf for $85,000 at the time of the original purchase, endorsed by one Mrs. Waldo. He defaulted on these notes, but $40,000 had later been paid in full by the endorser. He had received about one-tenth of the certificates issued by the company and had sold them to Mrs. Gilman and others. The commissioners awarding the 1814 Congressional indemnity tried to deduct from the amount to be paid to the various stockholders in the association the amount of Wetmore's unpaid notes. Mrs. Gilman and others were upheld by the Supreme Court in their contention that the whole fund was to be divided equally among the ultimate purchasers of the land, no matter through whom their title was derived. The ruling of the commissioners was thus reversed,[58] and after a quarter-century of petitions and litigation, the last of the ill-fated companies dropped from sight.

THE NORTH AMERICAN LAND COMPANY

The career of Robert Morris as Superintendent of Finance in 1781–1783 has been properly glorified as one of the great contributions to the Revolution. Actually his administration was under constant criticism, both during and after his tenancy of office. In the Jacksonian period his memory was so far forgotten that a biography[59] purported to be written solely to aid in dispelling the widespread ignorance of Morris' service. His unfortunate career as a land speculator and his subsequent confinement in debtors' prison helped to dim his reputation.

Morris' devotion to land projects after 1789 was probably in large part the result of success in his first important "deal"—the resale of land in central New York to the Pulteney Associates[60] at a handsome profit, almost before he himself had taken title. He seemed ever after convinced that he could not fail, and that all of his plans could be carried out; in this belief he was no more mistaken than countless other speculators before and since. His initial participation in land schemes is more remote; there is record that in 1780, for instance, he was the owner of a share in

---

[58] The Georgia Yazoo Company appeared in litigation elsewhere. In a South Carolina case (*Blake* v. *Jones,* 1 Bailey 136) in 1830, inheritance of part of the 1814 indemnity was in dispute. Speaking of one of the original shares, or certificates of interest, in that company the court said: "Such an instrument as that described could not have operated as a legal conveyance. If the Company was incorporated, the seal is wanting; if not, the members of the Company were joint tenants, and the President could not convey. . . . The certificate could have been nothing more than an equitable agreement." The certificate was not produced in court. The judge was uncertain of the nature of the Georgia Yazoo Company, but obviously hostile to any quality of transferability in its shares.

[59] David Gould, *Life of Robert Morris* (Boston, 1834).

[60] *Infra,* p. 203.

the United Illinois & Wabash Companies,[61] of which James Wilson was then the leader. But this was largely a political speculation, similar in its appeal to the shares in bankrupt estates, or shares in claims upon such estates, which were a favorite medium for speculation in the 1780's. By 1789 the adoption of the new government created a widespread interest in land among American merchants, on the theory that a stable government would stimulate a new flow of immigration from Europe. Morris was doing no more than following the trend when he began to center all his attention on land. He simply participated on a larger scale than any other individual of the time, benefiting particularly in his earlier ventures from the high reputation which he enjoyed in Amsterdam and Paris.

Although much of Morris' correspondence was recovered in France after a mysterious disappearance and finally acquired by Congress,[62] there is a great gap in it from 1784 to 1797[63] that makes it difficult to determine the exact basis upon which he conducted his operations. In the great New York trades he apparently made agreements on his own responsibility, but gave out "interests" in his purchases to others in the manner of modern private syndicate operations; in effect they were an underwriting agreement to protect him if resale were not possible. In other cases, notably in Washington city lots, he operated on the basis of a joint adventure, mostly with Greenleaf and Nicholson. He arranged personally for agents in European cities, and paid them commissions for sales. William Franklin was especially helpful in London.

Trouble came after 1793, with the ebb in speculative enthu-

[61] W. G. Sumner, 2 *Financier and Finances of the American Revolution* (New York, 1891), 251.

[62] *Cf.* the introduction to Oberholtzer, *Life of Robert Morris* (New York, 1903).

[63] The *Dreer Collection,* in the library of the Historical Society of Pennsylvania, consisting of scattered letters and documents pertaining to political leaders of all periods, has been useful for what follows here, in addition to standard sources.

siasm which followed the panic year of 1792. Morris and his partners then resorted to a scheme that is still employed—formation of companies of which shares could be sold to the public or given to their creditors in satisfaction of debts. The most noteworthy of these ventures was the North American Land Company.

This company has been frequently described because it was the most prominent of the many schemes in which Morris was concerned—the "largest land trust ever known in America."[64] Because of the wide publicity which it received, and the long litigation which followed its practical failure, considerable specific information is available.

The North American Land Company had a distinctly different purpose than most of the companies so far described here. The set-up recalls the familiar device in modern finance of a company formed to "take over" bank loans or other debts. It was to acquire scattered blocks of land which Morris, Nicholson[65] and Greenleaf[66] held and desired to use for satisfaction of

[64] Sakolski, *American Land Bubble*, 38.

[65] John Nicholson had been Receiver General of Pennsylvania during the Revolution, with dictatorial power to enforce tax payments. On charges of dishonesty, he was impeached in 1789, but was not convicted. *Cf.* the article in *Cyclopedia of American Biography* (Scribners); more than 700 pages in *Pennsylvania State Trials* (Hogan edition, 1794) are necessary to include all the testimony in these impeachment proceedings.

[66] James Greenleaf was an extraordinary character. He has been badly served by biographers; a biography in the modern manner of historical students could be made extraordinarily stimulating. In November, 1901, A. C. Clark read a sketch of Greenleaf's career before the Columbia Historical Society, without giving (in the manner of his time) a single source reference for his material. "James Greenleaf," 5 *Proceedings of the Columbia Historical Society*, 212.

Greenleaf was born in 1765, in Boston, the twelfth of fifteen children. His father was sheriff of Suffolk County in 1776; his sisters made prominent marriages. In 1781 the family removed to New Bedford, whence in 1788 he went to Philadelphia and to New York later in the year, where he formed Watson & Greenleaf as an importing firm. Almost immediately Greenleaf left for Holland to interest Dutch capital in the purchase of United States securities. From January 31, 1789, until August, 1793, he

their creditors. Six million acres were to be turned over to the company at a flat valuation of fifty cents an acre. There were thus 30,000 shares of stock of $100 par value. "Titles to these estates are vested in trustees as joint tenants in trust to convey the same to purchasers conformably to the articles of agreement hereto annexed; the monies arising from the sales are for the use and account of the holders of shares." In the prospectus this introductory statement is followed by "Articles of Agreement, indented and made this twentieth day of February, 1795 . . ."[67] by and between Morris, Greenleaf, and Nicholson on the one part and "those who shall become purchasers . . . of shares."[68]

was in Amsterdam, working in close association with Daniel Crommelin & Sons. Twelve separate "negotiations" were organized under his direction, involving the pledge of nearly two million of government bonds and $160,000 in Bank of United States stock; Dutch certificates were issued against these pledges. He married a baroness; he deserted her as well as their two children when he returned to America.

In September, 1793, he was in Washington to witness the laying of the Capitol cornerstone. By December he had entered the famous syndicate of Morris, Nicholson and himself, organized to purchase lots in the new city. In 1794 he was in Holland attempting to sell these lots under the same form used by the Dutch bankers for selling United States securities. This was a failure, and despite the large sales to Thomas Law, the nabob merchant prince who came to live there (Law bought lots at $297.50 which had cost the syndicate $80), Greenleaf defaulted. He finally quarreled violently with Nicholson in 1797, with Morris acting as mediator. For this episode, cf. Sakolski, *American Land Bubble*, 57–68. Earlier, in 1795 he was in partnership with Tobias Lear (Washington's secretary) in several enterprises. Nathan Appleton and Judge Cranch were at various times his representatives in Washington. The year 1795 also marked his association with the Yazoo purchasers.

By his second marriage he became the brother-in-law of Chief Justice Tilghman and Henry W. Livingston. His father-in-law, William Allen, had been Chief Justice of Pennsylvania; the latter owned the site of Allentown, and Greenleaf helped to promote the sale of city lots around 1810. He lived, much of the time in Allentown, until 1842. Relations with the North American Land Company occupied his later years.

[67] Copies are available in several libraries; one in the library of the Historical Society of Pennsylvania has been used here.

[68] The wording in this well-known prospectus and in the articles is almost exactly similar to that found in many small agreements made in this period by James Wilson, who had been trained in Scotland as a lawyer be-

The first article stated the name, the second provided that every owner of at least one share shall become a "member of the Company," such membership to cease when he sold. The capital stock—or assets—was to consist of 6,000,000 acres of land, for which legal title would rest in the trustees; Messrs. Willing, Nixon, and Barclay of Philadelphia were named as the permanent trustees. The fourth article provided that suits should be brought in the name of a board of managers, to quiet titles; upon actual settlement, the board would direct the trustees to convey title. There were to be "thirty thousand shares or *actions* of two hundred acres each"[69]—so that each share would be one-thirty thousandth part of the described capital stock or the money resulting from its sale. The board of managers (Article VI) was to be elected annually on December 30; proxies were permitted and the form of a proxy was given. The board was to consist of a president and four others (chosen from the stockholders) of whom three would constitute a quorum (Article VII); they were to meet regularly once a week. Article VIII named the first board, to hold office until the first election: Morris, Nicholson, John Ball, Thomas Fitzsimmons, and John Vaughan. The board was to hire and pay employees, make sales of land (Article IX), and have custody of money received (Article X). Contracts of sale for land were to be made in the names of members of the board, or their survivors or survivor and his heirs (Article XIII).

The death of a trustee would require a new deed in joint tenancy to a new third trustee, to be selected by the board of managers (Article XII). The trustees would issue deeds only by re-

---

fore he emigrated, with buyers of land on shares. Many of them are to be found in 9 *Wilson MSS.,* library of the Historical Society of Pennsylvania. To be noted is the frank exposition of one of the inherent characteristics of a modern corporate charter—a contract between the incorporators and those who buy shares in the future.

[69] The use of the word "action" clearly suggests Dutch or French influence, further testimony to Morris' familiarity with business practice in those countries.

quest of the president, and upon satisfactory evidence that
money or security had been received. In Article XV, however,
the board was specifically empowered to make sales on contract
with no title passing. The secretary's office was described in several articles. He was to keep books in a permanent office where
records would be open at all times, and was to present a yearly
account; an annual report of sales was to be printed and mailed
to each shareholder. Shares were to be freely transferable on the
secretary's books, but all such transfers had to be made in the
presence of the holder or his specific attorney.

Article XXII optimistically provided that a dividend was to be
declared annually, to include all income from sales, except that
a "contingent fund" of not more than $4,000 could be accumu-
lated at the will of the managers. Extras could be paid at other
times. A most important provision was in Article XXIII, namely
that the "Big Three" who established the company agreed to
guarantee at least 6 per cent dividends annually on the $100 par
value shares. To secure this guaranty each was to put in escrow
3,000 shares of his stock; their advances under the guaranty were
to be repaid out of future sales of land by the board. The pledged
shares were to be sold after a stated time, if the guaranty were
defaulted. This was unmistakably a feature copied from Dutch
practice of the period.

On sales of land, a commission of two and one-half per cent
was to be paid to the president and the managers, divided into
five equal shares. Bonds of $20,000 were required from the five
board members and the elected secretary.

The company was to exist definitely for fifteen years or until
all lands were sold and money collected "and as much longer as
may be necessary to close and settle their concerns and make a
final dividend." A dissolution meeting of shareholders would
determine by majority vote the best course of action to wind up
affairs. Amendments to the articles were to be presented at one
annual meeting, laid over a year, and then passed only by a two-

thirds vote. At the end was a schedule of the lands being assigned, certified by three witnesses, and recorded in the public
records of Pennsylvania.

No more complete corporate mechanism is encountered in this
whole period, nor one more obviously similar to present-day
bodies.[70] But only 22,365 shares were ever issued, since only
4,479,317 acres of land were turned over to the trustees. For the
first two years, the 6 per cent guaranty was paid—probably to the
"Big Three" themselves largely, for they used only 8,447 of the
shares they received to pay off creditors. To make the whole proposal more attractive to such creditors was obviously the reason
why the extraordinary guaranty clause was inserted. Each posted
2,485 shares as security for the guaranty.

On May 28, 1796, Greenleaf sold to Morris and Nicholson his
entire one-third interest in the company's original distribution
of shares. He received $1,500,000 payable in one, two, three, and
four-year notes. The shares involved were not to be transferred
until full payment had been made. In the agreement Morris and

[70] The summary history of the company in the next following para-
graphs is taken from a pamphlet in the *Vanderpoel MSS., Frankin Papers,*
Box 1, New York Public Library, or from Sumner, 2 *Financier and Finances,* 251 ff.
Even a prospectus strikingly suggestive of modern mining or oil enterprises forms a part of the written record of this truly modern corporate
enterprise. Under the title of "Observations on the North American Land
Company," Morris published in 1796 in London a collection of material
relating to the enterprise calculated to stimulate sales. He began with an
introduction describing the free life of America and the chances for making money in land. Following the articles of the company he gave a schedule of the land it owned: 647,000 acres in Pennsylvania, 832,000 acres in
Virginia, 717,000 in North Carolina, 957,000 in South Carolina, 2,314,796
in Georgia, and 431,000 in Kentucky. A brief description of each state's
topography, climate, and possibilities was added. He finished with a suc-
cinct outline of the procedure in purchasing, and final exhortations to act
—bolstered by a reference to his own profits on the sale to Lord Pulteney in
1791. As appendices, there were letters from Pulteney, Citizen Faucher,
and Robert Goodloe Harper commenting favorably on American lands in
general. A copy of this very interesting document is in the John Carter
Brown Library, Providence.

Nicholson undertook to indemnify Greenleaf against the operation of the 6 per cent clause. This was an extraordinary contract, considering the bankrupt condition of both Morris and Nicholson in the summer of 1796. The first payment was probably cared for by transfer of lots in the new city of Washington.

Immediately after this transfer, Greenleaf executed for the benefit of creditors the trust already referred to—the "381" trust —including in it all his claims against Morris and Nicholson for payments on the serial notes. A few years later, when Morris and Nicholson had defaulted, Greenleaf proceeded to transfer his equitable claim to his 6,119 shares to Henry Pratt and others as trustees for the benefit of his creditors. But later he rebought 541 shares in the open market and became secretary of the company. Morris died in May, 1806; Nicholson had perished in prison some years before.

Because the company continued to exist for over seventy-five years by reason of litigation in the courts, it duplicates even more faithfully a true corporate career. Sweeping amendments to the articles were proposed by Pratt and others at the 1805 meeting. These were printed under the direction of Secretary Greenleaf.[71] After referring to the twenty-eighth article in a "whereas" clause, the proposals went on to state that "it being found on an experience of ten years, that the business of the North American Land Company cannot be conducted in the manner marked out in the articles of agreement and association," the following amendments ought to be passed: (a) That all managerial powers be placed in the hands of John Ashley, John Vaughan, Robert Porter, Henry Pratt, and John Miller, or a majority of them, or a majority of their survivors. They were to have full power to sell the land and full discretion "in all possible cases." (b) Willing, Nixon, and Barclay, the trustees, "shall have power and are hereby ordered" to transfer titles, both to the land and to forfeited

[71] A copy of this rare pamphlet is in the New York Public Library.

shares of stock, to the new managers, themselves being saved harmless. (c) The pledged shares of stock were to be held for the benefit of the remaining stockholders in lieu of arrearages of interest, to be shared among them *pro rata*. (d) After all property had been sold, the managers were to call a meeting and divide the proceeds, but no limit to the life of the company was set. (e) Anything "repugnant to or incompatible with" the 1795 agreement was "forever rescinded and annulled." In a crude form, what was being proposed was a reorganization of the modern type, with the concomitant features of what amounted to a perpetual voting trust.

Just before these amendments were to be voted on at the 1806[72] meeting, the Pratt group ordered sold at auction the pledged shares of Morris and Nicholson, at seven cents each, supposedly to satisfy the guaranty. But the group themselves bought the 7,445 shares, through a dummy, and proceeded to vote them at the meeting in favor of the amendments! Greenleaf secured on his 541 shares part of the dividends that were later paid from this 1806 sale. In the later litigation it was successfully claimed that this was illegal because he was still bound by his original guaranty at the time. Pratt died in 1838, and in 1843 a court action determined that the 6,119 shares assigned to him must revert to the original "381" trust. In defending later actions aimed at preventing these 6,119 shares from also sharing in any distribution, because they were tainted with Greenleaf's guaranty also, the "381" trustees pointed out that the articles in the guaranty clause bound the heirs and executors of the "Big Three," but *not* their assigns. The "381" trust had become the largest beneficiary of the fund that was gradually accumulating from sales of land up to 1865.

About 7,235 other shares in the hands of heirs of original creditors of the "Big Three" also participated in the many court

---

[72] An 1864 pamphlet dealing with the company, of which a copy is in the *Vanderpoel MSS.*, Box 1, New York Public Library, confuses the date.

battles over the fund that then amounted (net) to a little over
$50,000. Although in an earlier action, the Morris and Nicholson
estates had been barred[73] from their approximate 40 per cent
interest (based on the shares which they had never sold or
pledged), in this fund by reason of the 6 per cent guaranty clause,
the Pennsylvania Supreme Court in 1869[74] finally permitted
them to participate on the ground that the 1806 sale was fraudulent, since it was made to secure voting control and not to pay
the defaulted dividends as provided in the original articles. Since
the adoption of the 1806 amendments had obviously been postponed until after the death of both Morris and Nicholson, neither
had had an opportunity to interpose objections. Furthermore,
the Court interpreted the 1806 amendments as releasing all
claims for arrearages under the guaranty clause, as well as the
guaranty itself for the two remaining years (to complete the
fifteen-year life of the company).[75]

THE ASYLUM COMPANY

Of the other companies in which Morris or Nicholson was interested,[76] one may be selected for brief treatment as typical. The
Asylum Company drew its title from the intention of its promoters to provide a new home for Royalist *émigrés,* the same
potential customers whom Duer, Constable, and others hoped to
secure at this time (1792–1794).

The project originated in the efforts of Talon and de Noailles
to buy 200,000 acres on the Susquehanna as a refuge for San Do-

[73] In 1862, 7 *Wright's Reports,* 27.

[74] 10 P. F. *Smith's Reports,* 247.

[75] About $30,000 was distributed under court orders after 1870, over
half of which went to Morris' and Nicholson's heirs. *Vanderpoel MSS.,*
Box 1.

[76] For the Pennsylvania Property Company, *cf.* Sumner, 2 *Financier
and Finances,* 305. Its articles are in the library of the Historical Society
of Pennsylvania. The Population Company was another project on the
same lines; *cf.* Evans, *Holland Land Company,* 110 *ff.,* and Van Winter,
2 *Amsterdam en de Opbow van Amerika* ('s Gravenhage, 1933), 252–254.

mingo planters. They bought land from Morris and Nicholson directly, but were unable to meet the payments. The latter agreed to rescind, and on April 22, 1794, drew up articles for the Asylum Company,[77] which was to merchandise a much larger tract of one million acres for which they had Pennsylvania state warrants. The two Frenchmen were given shares entitling them to 6,000 acres each. The agreement was between Morris and Nicholson on behalf of future associates. Since it preceded the formation of the North American Land Company by less than a year, in form the two pacts resembled each other closely. The name and description of the property were the first two articles. The "shares or actions" were to represent 200 acres each, or 5,000 in all. Each share had one vote, with no restrictions, in the election of a president and four other members of a board of managers, who were to hire a land agent (Talon received this post) and other officers, and to make surveys and additional purchases (Articles IV and VII). The legal title was to be vested in the president, who was to execute a deed of trust in favor of the shareholders, to be deposited in escrow in the Bank of the United States; he was to execute all deeds (Articles IX and XI). But the board of managers was to execute contracts of sale at a minimum price of $2.00 an acre, and to determine the condition of sale and the time of passing title in each case (Articles X and XII). The president was to call meetings, but either two board members or twenty shareholders could do so; notices were to be mailed, and the meetings were to be held at the company's office in Philadelphia (Articles XIII and XVII). Minutes and accounts were to be kept and an annual report rendered to shareholders, in addition to a semi-annual statement of land sales printed and

[77] A copy of the articles is in the library of the Historical Society of Pennsylvania. The Duc de la Rochefoucald-Liancourt described the undertaking as it was in 1795, in 7 *Travels* (London, 1799), 157–177. He mistakenly states that it had been established fifteen years when he made his visit. The location of the settlement is passed by tourists today at a point on the Sullivan Trail, in Bradford County, Pennsylvania.

mailed to each holder (Articles XVI and XX). The certificates of stock were to be freely transferable at the secretary's office by signature in the transfer book (Article XVIII). Dividends were to be paid by vote of the board of managers (Article XIX). The company's life was set at fifteen years, after which an auction sale, advertised for six months, would be held to dispose of remaining property, and a distribution to the shareholders made sixty days thereafter (Articles XX and XXI).

The following February, 1795, in order to stimulate sales of shares, Nicholson and Morris added a guaranty of 6 per cent interest on each $500 share, and permission to the board of managers to borrow in order to carry this out. It was also promised that the board would buy back shares at $500 after three years. Immediately after this Nicholson bought out Morris' interest, and in April, 1795, the articles were still further amended. Nicholson continued the guaranty idea by agreeing to pledge 1,667, or one-third of the total shares, as had been done in the North American Company.[78] Provision was made for amendments, to be prepared at one annual meeting and accepted by a two-thirds vote a year later. Title was vested in two trustees, Jared Ingersoll and Matthew Clarkson, with a third to be added. Provision was made for friendly title suits against the trustees, for paying dividends in Europe, and for exchanging original shares for a new form. Thus amended, the articles were to be binding only on purchasers or holders by exchange for *new* shares, but those who did hold new shares were definitely bound by the new articles "as fully as if such owner had actually signed and sealed these presents," and his rights as a member would cease immediately upon sale of his share. Non-exchanging old shareholders would thus have claims to assets, but practically no control.

These articles included nearly every typical clause of actual

[78] The ideas of guaranty and pledge thus seem to have been adopted late in 1794, since they were not in the original Asylum Company articles.

corporate charters of the period. Just as truly as for the North American Land Company, the resulting organization and operation, if it had ever flourished, would have been indistinguishable from those of a chartered corporation. Yet in neither case was a formal charter sought or thought to be necessary. In both cases financial difficulties of the sponsors prevented the shares from ever being issued up to the intended total, and no real land merchandising was accomplished. But the conception which these two promoters had of the sort of organization they wanted stands out unmistakably in the articles—they were to be business entities, functioning under centralized managerial control for the benefit of scattered, non-partner stockholders whose control was to be general and to whom impersonal reports were to be made. Unfortunately, only the plan and intention and little actual operation testify to these aims.

After two years of inactivity, Nicholson wrote to the board of managers asking that at least 3,250 shares be formally issued, so that he could pledge his 1,667 shares and so that the shares could be used to clear titles on disputed parts of the land.[79] Nothing happened, Nicholson soon died, and in 1801 a new company was formed with 2,000 shares, of which little is known. In 1819 its remaining property was offered for sale.[80]

THE EASTERN LAND ASSOCIATES

In 1791, William Duer headed, with Henry Knox, a project for purchasing lands in Maine owned by the state of Massachusetts. This project must be included here not because of any resemblance to corporate enterprise, but because in form and intent it resembled with surprising fidelity a modern security or real estate syndicate operation.[81]

[79] The letter, dated November 5, 1798, is in the library of the Historical Society of Pennsylvania.

[80] Cf. 2 Sumner, op. cit., 263.

[81] That the syndicate form was not confined to unsettled land is demonstrated by such an important operation as the Mount Vernon Proprie-

Henry Knox's wife had inherited an undivided fifth of the Waldo patent in Maine, a tract of nearly 170,000 acres near Thomaston, on which, after resigning as Secretary of War in Washington's cabinet, he built his homestead. In 1790 he and Duer were close friends—too close, perhaps, in view of the fact that Duer was a contractor of supplies to the Army[82]—as a result of their long service together in the Revolutionary cause. Knox probably suggested to Duer that they jointly purchase an additional quantity of the Maine land which the state of Massachusetts was preparing to sell; successful disposal of its lands in New York to Phelps, Gorham, and Morris had engendered a desire to reduce the state debt further by other sales. Duer was interested because he was still enthusiastic at this time (early 1791) over the chances for immediate resale to French *émigrés*. Quite logically he and many others expected emigration from France to grow in volume as the Revolution progressed.

William Constable was interested in the same objective, and after a private agreement with him, Duer and Constable met Knox at Princeton on June 2, 1791, and signed a formal contract which resembles roughly an agreement between two modern private banking firms for the purchase of a new issue of securities.[83] These "Principles of Agreement" stated that Knox and Duer were to be jointly and equally interested in a land purchase

tors in Boston, headed by Harrison Grey Otis; Morison, 1 *Life of Harrison Grey Otis* (Boston, 1913), 42–44. In 1795 Otis secured an agreement with J. S. Copley's agents to sell the latter's property on the southwestern slope of Beacon Hill for $18,450. A syndicate was formed, in which Otis held a three-tenths interest, Jonathan Mason three-tenths, Joseph Woodward two-tenths and Charles Apthorp two-tenths. The latter sold his interest in 1796 or 1797 to Benjamin Joy. Under Otis' management the area (including Louisburg Square) was sold for high-class building lots, at a substantial profit. Copley unsuccessfully attempted to repudiate the action of his agent, who had acted under a power of attorney.

[82] *Cf.* Davis, 1 *Essays*, 265.

[83] This agreement is reprinted in Appendix E. Many other letters relating to the projects are in volumes 28, 29, and 32 of the *Knox MSS.*, Massachusetts Historical Society Library.

of from one to four million acres at a maximum price of twelve cents an acre. Each party could "associate in their respective proportions" other parties, subject to the "exclusive direction" of the entire project in the two principals' hands. Thus others admitted would be in the status of modern syndicate members, not partners or stockholders. An exception was made for Constable, who was given an option to come in as a third "director"; but in that case Knox was given a veto power in all decisions. Henry Jackson and Royal Flint were appointed agents to negotiate the purchase and to admit others to "subordinate interests" in the purchase. Such buyers were to be forced to offer their shares first to the two directors before selling, and to sell to the directors at 300 per cent profit any time within three years at the latter's option. These "subordinate interests" were thus subjected to more restriction than the potential sharers whom Duer and Knox themselves would admit into the undertaking; presumably members of the Massachusetts legislature were to be "subordinate interests" after the agents started negotiations.

The agents were given definite instructions in the agreement (Article VI) as to the terms of purchase, but some latitude was of course to be allowed them. Tax exemption and rights to mortgage freely and to sell to aliens were necessary terms which the state must grant, in view of difficulties elsewhere when these powers were forbidden; for example, in the case of Lord Pulteney's purchase from Morris. After the purchase was complete, the "Principles of Agreement" were to be drawn into "Legal Terms." Finally, Knox agreed to exchange land from the Waldo patent for tracts within the purchase to give access to the sea; obviously the project was framed to buy land at a low price because it lacked seacoast. Since both Knox's and Duer's identities as purchasers were to be kept strictly secret, the legislators would not see through the scheme by which the back lands would be given value in the eyes of settlers.

Just a month later, Jackson, with some help from Flint, closed a contract[84] with the state for 2,000,000 acres, at ten cents an acre ($200,000), payable in specie within eight years. None of the installments were to fall due until after surveys were completed the next summer. Duer began immediately to negotiate with some of the disappointed Scioto *émigrés*. But when Duer's bankruptcy came in April of 1792, Jackson became worried over the first payment of $25,000 due on August 8 as well as the $5,000 due on a third purchase which he had made after the first contract. After a hectic five months (Duer was in debtors' prison), the whole contract was assigned to William Bingham of Philadelphia for $50,000; he assumed the $200,000 obligation and $111,250 more for the additional purchase which had been made.[85] No other of the fallen Duer's enterprises was salvaged so successfully. Knox was disappointed at the abrupt termination of the plan, but enthusiasm over emigration was then beginning to wane in all quarters. The Bingham family retained large portions of the tract, and shared in the tremendous profits from Maine land sales a quarter-century later.

THE CONNECTICUT LAND COMPANY

Second only in importance to the Susquehannah Company in the fifty-year history of the state of Connecticut's western land claims is the Connecticut Land Company, or the "Reserve Company." Its career was of especial importance in the development of northeastern Ohio. The term Western Reserve, ubiquitous in the Cleveland area, evidences this lasting influence.

Connecticut's claim to western territory lay, as was indicated above,[86] in her well-known charter of 1662 by which she received a notably liberal grant of power and territory from Charles II. A belt of land between 41° N and 42° 2′ N, extending to the South Sea, comprised the granted area. The ill fate of this claim as it conflicted with Pennsylvania made the state's leaders doubly

---

[84] 28 *Knox MSS.*, 157–158.   [85] Davis, *op. cit.*, 321–325.
[86] *Supra,* p. 83.

anxious to preserve the western end of the original grant. The special fate of the claim to the three-mile strip between 42° N, the fixed northern boundary of Pennsylvania, and 42° 2′ N, the claimed northern boundary of the greater Connecticut—the "Gore," now part of New York's southern tier of counties—will be discussed below. The disposition of the much larger and more important territory west of Pennsylvania's western boundary is to be considered here.

In September, 1786, the state of Connecticut, as an aftermath of the discussions in the Congress of the Confederation which began in 1777, agreed to limit her claim on the west by a meridian to be run one hundred twenty miles west of Pennsylvania's line.[87] The resulting "reserve" which she retained by this deed of release was thus one hundred twenty miles wide and bounded south and north by the parallels of 41° and 42° 2′, respectively. It was much less liberal a cession to the old Confederation than had been made by any other state. There was no distinction made in the original act of release between title to the land which the state retained and political jurisdiction over it. Immediately after the passage of the act the assembly directed that the land included in the retained area be surveyed into townships six miles square, and provided that 500 acres in each such township should be set aside for schools and another 500 acres for the "support of the gospel." An extra 240 acres would be given to the first ministers settling in the area. Sales were to be made by a committee, and a minimum price was set, to be the "equivalent" of fifty cents an acre.

The surveys were not completed, but one sale of 24,000 acres was made to General Samuel H. Parsons of Middletown. His purchase was in the "Salt Spring Tract" in present Trumbull County. Parsons made sales to numerous settlers, whose legal status in the thirteen years before the United States secured juris-

[87] Cf. H. B. Adams, *Maryland's Influence Upon Land Cessions to the United States* (Baltimore, 1885), *passim*.

diction was a matter of complete uncertainty. They probably considered themselves residents and citizens of Connecticut, and there is evidence that they refused to pay taxes to agents of the Northwest Territory on this ground (though it may as well have been due to a general dislike of taxation).

In 1792 the "Fire Lands" were disposed of, in the western end of the Reserve. In May, 1793, a new effort was made to get rid of the eastern portion. The enabling act passed at this time provided that all money received should be placed in a perpetual fund, the interest from which should be devoted to the support of the ecclesiastical societies of the state and for the support of ministers and of schools for training ministers. This act became involved in the next election campaign; it was unpopular as obviously inspired by the clerical aristocracy of the state, and was repealed in 1794.[88]

Finally, in May of 1795, a committee of the assembly, composed of one member from each county and headed by one Treadwell, was appointed as the agent of the state to receive bids and make a prompt sale. Proceeds were now to go into a perpetual common school fund. All during the summer there was great excitement in the towns over the speculative possibilities in buying land, and an unknown number of buying groups were formed, of which at least four made formal offers. Early in September the committee sold the area to thirty-five persons on five years' credit, at a price of $1,200,000.[89] This price was substantially above the minimum of $1,000,000 set by the assembly when the committee was appointed. In true modern fashion, the final sale was made to an association that was essentially a combination of the various competing groups,[90] which had agreed among themselves to make this price their maximum.

[88] This summary of events leading up to the final sale is derived from B. A. Hinsdale, *The Old Northwest* (New York, 1888), 370 *ff*.

[89] Tract No. 96, Western Reserve Historical Society, included in 1916 *Annual Report*.

[90] The list of subscribers and the sums contributed by each can be found

The purchasers individually executed bonds to the state for the purchase price, plus interest of 6 per cent, and in turn received deeds naming them as tenants in common of shares in the area according to the price they agreed to pay. Immediately after these transfers by deed from the state, the individuals concerned formed the Connecticut Land Company. The agreement between these purchasers is rather generally accessible,[91] but its chief provisions may be summarized here. It resulted in the formation of a truly corporate undertaking.

In the first article, the members named themselves the Connecticut Land Company. The next article set forth the method by which the deeds from the state should be handed over to a committee as evidence of membership, to be held until each member executed a proper deed in trust, running to three trustees (John Caldwell, Jonathan Brace, and John Morgan, the survivors or last survivor or his heirs). These trust deeds specified that the land represented by each share should be held in trust for as long as necessary to carry out the program of the association. The trustees gave a joint bond to the state to further secure payment.

The third article dealt with the management of the trust property for the benefit of the shareholders. It provided that seven men should be appointed by the company at a regular meeting to act as directors, their duties to be as follows: to extinguish the Indian title, to lay out and subdivide 16,000 acre town-

in Charles Whittlesey, *Early History of Cleveland* (Cleveland, 1867), 163–164. Nine men in the group had been or still were stockholders in the Ohio Company. Tract No. 97, published in the 1917 *Annual Report* of the Western Reserve Historical Society, 70.

[91] In pamphlet form: *Articles of Association of the Connecticut Land Company*. The original articles and a minute book covering the years 1795–1797 are in the Litchfield (Connecticut) Historical Society. Photostatic copies of both are in the Connecticut State Library and have been used here. At an early meeting it was ordered that four hundred copies of the articles be printed for distribution, and these pamphlets are now to be found in many libraries.

ships, to select the first area to be settled and to subdivide the area into small lots which would be sold only to actual settlers, and, in addition, to select and lay out other towns as needed within two years; and, finally, to divide up all remaining land among the shareholders by a method to be decided upon later at a regular meeting.

A file book was to be kept by the directors, a clerk was to be appointed to keep the books, the directors were to "settle accounts" with the shareholders once a year. No power to declare dividends was vested in the directors; all distributions would be by vote at a regular meeting only. The trustees in whom the land title was vested were directed to furnish certificates to all the proprietors as evidenced by the full list of persons receiving the original deeds.[92] This section was apparently inserted in recognition of the fact that many of the listed purchasers were themselves representing sub-partnerships. Transfers of the certificates of interest, after they had been issued to deed-holders, were to be made on the books of the association only. The title of no assignee would be recognized unless properly recorded. The foregoing provisions were in the fourth, fifth, and sixth articles.

In the next three articles the voting power of shareholders was described. It was one vote for one share, then one vote for every two shares up to forty. Above forty shares it was one vote for each five shares held. On the specific question, however, of deciding upon the final division of the land, every share would have one vote, and of course would receive an equal share in the land. It was provided that a first tax or assessment on each share of $10 for expenses should be paid before October 6, 1795. The form of certificate to be issued by the trustees was described in detail as follows:[93]

[92] Thirty-five bonds were executed to secure payment, but 57 names appeared in the original deeds. Whittlesey, *op. cit.,* 164.

[93] It was included in the articles (Article IX). The form of transfer to be used was added in the minute book (p. 11): "Know all men . . . that

This certifies that Mr. —— is entitled to the trust and benefit of one million two hundred thousandths of the Connecticut Western Reserve, so called, as held by Messrs. Caldwell, Brace and Morgan, trustees in a deed of trust dated September 5, 1795, to hold said proportion or share for the said holder according to terms in the trust and in certain articles of agreement . . . which said share is transferable by assignment before two witnesses and before a Justice of the Peace or a notary, to be recorded on the books of the association.

The first annual meeting was scheduled in the tenth article for October 6, 1795, and thereafter regularly on the Monday before the second Thursday of October each year. Special meetings could be called by the trustees, but they were to be advertised three weeks in advance in a Hartford paper and must be held in Hartford.

The remaining four articles included some extremely interesting provisions. The eleventh article provided that one-third in value of the shares could request a drawing by lot of the property into three equal parts. This group could then secure separation of one of these parts from the trusteeship by suitable deeds from the trustees.[94] In the twelfth article the directors were specially given power to sell the interest in each certificate, or to dispose of enough land in the reserve to pay any assessment or taxes which might be overdue. Delinquency in payment was permitted for a period of fifty days, or for one hundred twenty days in the case of a non-resident of Connecticut.

In case of death of a trustee, the shareholders could appoint a successor at the next regular meeting. The two other trustees

I . . . . do hereby sell, assign and transfer to the said . . . . the trust and benefit of . . . . twelve hundred thousandths of the Connecticut Western Reserve, so called, being the share or proportion to which I am entitled according to the terms of the annexed certificate . . . to have and to hold . . . according to the terms, conditions, covenants and exceptions in the deed of trust and articles of agreement referred to in said certificate."

[94] This provision was obviously inserted at the insistence of the group who formed the Erie Company, to be described below, p. 184.

were required to execute a new deed to the new trustee. In the last article, directors were declared to be subject to the control of the shareholders by a vote of at least three-fourths in interest of the shareholders. This clause presumably meant that actions of the directors could be overruled by the indicated majority. In one instance to be described, a stockholders' committee was appointed, which might presumably have vetoed certain acts of the directors.

Among the individuals concerned in the purchase were several prominent citizens of the state, and members of the aristocratic legislature.[95] The largest subscriber was Oliver Phelps, the co-purchaser of the great area in New York seven years previously. Phelps subscribed $168,000 directly and, in association with Gideon Granger, another $80,000. Henry Champion II subscribed $85,675; Pierpont Edwards, $60,000; Ephraim Root, $40,000. The original seven directors included Phelps and Champion as well as Moses Cleaveland, who was later appointed chief surveyor.

It was indicated above that during the summer of 1795 other groups were securing subscriptions in order to make competing bids for the property. The most prominent group was headed by the same John Livingston who had gained notoriety in connection with the lease of Indian lands in New York in 1787. The compromise agreement with Livingston, under which he agreed not to compete further with the Phelps-Granger group, provided that another association would be organized to receive the excess acreage in the purchase over and above 3,000,000 acres. Interests in this nebulous area were, of course, a pure speculation, and the participants were never formally organized. In April, 1796, the whole claim of this so-called "Excess Company"[96] was sold for

[95] Whittlesey, *op. cit.,* 164.
[96] Described in Tract No. 91, Western Reserve Historical Society (1915), 175. The agreement by Livingston and the terms of the sale to Hull are reprinted in the minute book, 20–23. Formal confirmation of the Livingston agreement by all shareholders is found on 24–27.

$50,000 to William Hull of Newton, Massachusetts (of Yazoo fame). By the survey completed in the summer of 1796, it was discovered that the purchase actually included much less than 3,000,000 acres, so that the Hull claim automatically became worthless. Hull apparently had others associated with him, in modern syndicate fashion.

Growing out of the purchase was another interesting organization of which little has been said in historical accounts. This was called the Erie Company,[97] and was composed of twelve leading members of the Connecticut Land Company group. It was apparently formed to exploit a compact area in the grant with greater facility and consequently with greater profit than would be possible under the aegis of the larger and clumsier company. An interesting extract from the brief articles of agreement runs as follows: "Whereas we, the subscribers, are severally interested in the Connecticut reserve, we do agree that we will unite our stock for the above purposes, and that two persons of our number shall draw the quantity of land which may fall to our several shares together, in one undivided and common stock, to be and remain in the hands of such persons, to be managed for the best good of all concerned, and the said persons so appointed shall be constituted trustees and agents to dispose of the lands agreeably to articles which shall be entered into." Several meetings of this Erie Company were held at Norwich, Connecticut,[98] and it remained in existence until 1812. Most of the land which it acquired was divided among the twelve members, no land being sold to outsiders as was apparently the original intention.

[97] *Ibid.*

[98] A notice of one early meeting appears in the February 4, 1801, issue of the *Connecticut Gazette* (New London), to receive returns of land surveys and "To adopt regulations necessary to make a complete division of their property in the Connecticut Reserve." Moses Cleaveland, Daniel Coit, and Joseph Perkins were named as "trustees and agents" in this announcement. The file of the *Gazette* in the library of the Buffalo Historical Society was consulted by the present author.

The story of the visit of Cleaveland's surveying party to the site of the present city has been often told.[99] The party returned in the fall of 1796 with fairly complete data regarding the character of the territory. The great interest of the directors in securing equality in the assignments of land is evidenced by the frequent resurveys and discussions in the following ten years. At the time the original party returned, a meeting of the directors was called at which the problem of settling jurisdiction over the territory overshadowed the problem of alloting land. Was Connecticut or the Congress to establish political machinery? This primary problem was not finally settled until an act of Congress was passed in May of 1800. In the intervening three years, the company was in an uncertain position, unable to promise any governmental stability and doubtful of its right to give adequate land titles to purchasers.

A meeting of the shareholders immediately following the surveying trip (in January, 1797) voted to appoint a committee of inquiry into the acts of the directors. Dissatisfaction centered largely about failure to prepare for sale a suitable area along the shore of Lake Erie, which would have provided some cash income to defray further surveying expenses. Late in February this committee reported, in effect suggesting to the stockholders what would be in modern terminology a complete "whitewash" for the directors.[100]

At this same meeting a "Committee of Partition" was appointed. The method of dividing up the territory was established by vote. It was as follows: Six townships just east of the Cuyahoga townships in the same area were to be surveyed into one hundred lots each to be sold for the benefit of the company as a whole, while a total of four hundred additional lots were to be allotted to members of the association. The balance of the land was to be

[99] *Cf.* Whittlesey, *op. cit.,* 171–234.
[100] The vote for an inquiry is recorded on page 57 of the minute book. The "whitewash" report is on 59–60.

left in townships and drawn at later dates as might be directed. It is probable that some other groups similar to the Erie Company, mentioned above, were formed to unite the drawings of individual members. There were three later "drafts" or drawings of additional land, one in 1798, another in 1802, and another in 1807, all assigned to members. The sale of the six townships to outsiders was delayed until after 1800 by the lack of proper government for the district. The state consistently refused to provide even a temporary government, pending the passage of the 1800 act by which the Northwest Territory government assumed control.

During this period, assessments were regularly levied on the shares, usually for $5 or $10. This money was used simply to cover operating expenses. The payments to the state on the bonds that had been executed by both the individual members and by the trustees in behalf of the whole body were badly in arrears until after 1801. The delay in assigning land together with the inability of the company to sell land to outsiders were the legitimate reasons for this delay in payments. Even as late as 1809 the school fund[101] into which payments were being made still had outstanding claims against the members of the company.

The deeds executed by the trustees[102] were examined critically by the courts in a case arising in 1816 between one Huntington and Edwards—the Pierpont Edwards of the original group.[103] By an act passed in 1801, the legislature authorized cancellation

---

[101] Tract No. 96, *op. cit.* For over 120 years the fund was constantly administered by the state and the income used to pay the expenses of county schools. After 1910 it did not provide more than 8 per cent of the total school expenses, and in the middle of the last century it was regarded as a detriment rather than a help, because towns and counties tended to limit their educational budgets to the amounts received from the fund. *Cf.* B. A. Hinsdale, *The Old Northwest* (New York, 1888), 383.

[102] It is interesting to note that the three original trustees survived as late as 1836, and in later years their names appeared constantly in land transfers in northwestern Ohio.

[103] *Huntington* v. *Edwards,* 1 Conn. 564.

of two years' interest on the bonds executed by the purchasers in 1795. Huntington had bought $9,000 worth of the shares in the purchase, or about one-sixth of Edwards' original subscription. This sale occurred in July, 1797, and thus included part of the period for which interest was being remitted. Huntington sued for recovery of his equitable share in the refund of interest, but the court decided that the deeds executed by the trustees vested any benefit in the original group of purchasers, and that transfers of the certificates of interest related only to the specific proportions of the land to which the certificate gave beneficial title. They stressed the fact also, that, by these "trust and benefit" deeds, full legal title lay in the three trustees, who were responsible only to the original group.

THE FIRE LANDS

Another and slightly earlier distribution of land in the Western Reserve was made in entirely different manner.[104] Even before final settlement of Connecticut's claim to the Reserve, the legislature of that state had voted (in 1792) to assign land to a group of sufferers in the Revolution. These sufferers were inhabitants of eight townships in Fairfield County, where frequent British invasions had resulted in the destruction of a great deal of property. The validity of the claims had been reviewed in detail by a committee of the Connecticut legislature several years before. In 1796 these people were included in a peculiar act

---

[104] The best description is that by Helen M. Carpenter, "Origin and Location of the Fire Lands," 44 *Ohio State Archaeological and Historical Quarterly*, 163 (1935). Hinsdale, *op. cit.*, discusses it briefly, 369–370. Carpenter found records of this early organization only in issues of the *Connecticut Gazette*. By the terms of the statute, the groups from each of the eight towns where "sufferers" resided were to meet annually to elect officers and agents to represent them at the general meeting. At the only general meeting, at Hartford in May, 1797, the agents levied a tax of one cent on the pound (as they were empowered to do by the act), but only $120 was secured, and some interests were sold because of tax default. Losses were computed in pounds because of confusion in Revolutionary currency standards.

of incorporation which constituted them, "the proprietors of the half million acres lying south of Lake Erie." This Connecticut act was apparently designed solely to facilitate the division of the land among the individuals concerned and was more nearly analogous to the incorporation of a town proprietorship than to a business corporation. The only records of the activity of this body are in the newspapers of the period, and, moreover, there seems to have been nothing done for a decade after the first annual meeting in 1797. Surveys were not completed until after 1800, and in April, 1803, the Ohio legislature repeated the incorporation[105] of the individuals concerned under the same name but with the phrase "Called Sufferers' Land" added; under this latter act the division of the territory was conducted. Nine directors were named in the act,[106] who were given power to meet outside Ohio (presumably in Connecticut) and to supervise the drawing of shares.[107]

The land was surveyed into 120 equal tracts, each being one-fourth of a township or about 4,000 acres. The total area, as finally surveyed, included 496,590 acres. The Indian title to the area was purchased by treaty at Fort Industry early in 1806, for $28,617; this amount was raised by the first assessment of twenty-five cents on the pound (a curious mixture of currency stand-

---

[105] 1 *Ohio Acts,* 106.

[106] The act is in *Acts and Laws of Connecticut* (1805 edition), at 451. A copy, separately bound, is in the New York Public Library.

[107] The first nine were named in the act, of whom five could call the first meeting; their successors were to be chosen every two years. A clerk and treasurer were to be appointed, and the clerk's records "shall in all cases be received and allowed as evidence" (a striking similarity to the New England proprietorship). There was to be an annual meeting at which the directors were required to report, and the books of the corporation were to be open for inspection at any time. The directors inherited the powers of the agents under the Connecticut act. The Record Book is now in the Recorder's office of Huron County in Norwalk, Ohio. Carpenter, *op. cit.,* summarizes from it the important actions of the directors up to the annual meeting of 1811, when it was resolved that the meeting "be adjourned without day [*sic*] and never to be holden again." A balance of $2,600 in the treasury was spent on roads.

ards!) levied in 1804. There were 1,870 "sufferers" concerned, whose allowed losses had exceeded £161,000. This group was arbitrarily divided into 120 "classifications," so that each had claim to £1344 7s. in compensation. The land tracts were matched up, by lot, with the groups of claimants who had been classified. The resulting division of the land was carefully registered, and remains the original source of land titles in the area because the state gave no other formal deed than the act authorizing such a division to be made. Title abstracts in Huron and Erie Counties all originally began with a formal recitation of the act, the classification, and the drawings.

The actual drawing was not carried out until November, 1808, in New Haven. Each of the 120 groups so created then decided separately within itself what to do with the land received: sell it *en bloc,* divide it up by agreement, or seek court approval for a partition that would be binding on possible dissenters (by the familiar legal procedure for dividing a tract held by tenants in common).

It has been alleged that this body of individuals was the only incorporated land company in the period. An examination of the machinery by which this half-million-acre tract was divided shows that the acts in connection were practically enabling acts to give public effect to the transfer of land in place of a series of small deeds.[108] In the case of the 1796 enactment, there was also

[108] Davis (in 2 *Essays,* 289) refers to this body as "the one incorporated land company," but this description seems presumptive, since neither the Ohio nor the Connecticut act gave any powers of merchandising or other business operations but rather, as will be pointed out below, endowed the body with limited functions. Article I of the 1803 Ohio enactment stated that unnamed individuals, *i.e.,* those mentioned in the 1796 Connecticut statute, were "ordained and constituted a body politic and corporate, in fact and in name, by the name of the Proprietors of the Half Million Acres Lying South of Lake Erie, called Sufferers' Lands." It was to have perpetual succession, could sue and be sued, could plea and be impleaded. But there was no mention of a corporate seal or of a corporate office, both of which essentials are stipulated in the contemporary act incorporating the subscribers to the Miami Exporting Company (1 *Acts of the State of Ohio,*

provision in the act for the collection of taxes, obviously an expedient to bridge the gap before there would be a political government in the area. No need for incorporation for *business* reasons existed. As embodied in a "public act," the division of land needed no further proof in court in suits over titles than citation of the act, a fact indicative of its primary purpose.

Careful interpretation of the 1803 act of Ohio regarding this land is to be found, as in other similar instances, in court litigation which arose in 1825 in the Federal district courts in Ohio, and in 1830 came before the United States Supreme Court.[109] One Jonathan Douglas had become a proprietor under the 1792 allotment in Connecticut, and had died in 1800 vested with the legal title to 2,400 acres of land on which taxes were in arrears. In 1808 by a properly advertised tax sale, the property had been conveyed to one Perkins who conveyed it to Beaty; at the time of the sale four of Douglas' heirs, who were entitled to 1,200 acres of his holdings, were minors. They brought suit for ejectment, alleging that not only had the taxes in question been improperly levied but that as minors they possessed the right of redemption under the Ohio law. The District Court ruled in their favor.

Justice McLean analyzed the powers of the nine directors under the 1803 act. Principally they were empowered (1) to extinguish the Indian title, (2) to survey the land, and (3) at a suitable time to order a partition in the manner described above. In the same Article II of the act they were given power to levy a tax or taxes for these purposes "and all other necessary expenses." They were empowered to sell land through the collectors if such levies remained unpaid. The status of minor owners was not

ch. 33). The Connecticut act of 1796 had provided for a seal but did not establish a corporate office. The body was structurally almost an exact copy of the proprietorship, which since 1718 had enjoyed quasi-corporate privileges in Connecticut. But no one has presumed to call the proprietorship a full-fledged legal corporation, albeit it was such in the business sense.

[109] *Beaty* v. *The Lessee of Knowler,* 4 Peters 152.

mentioned. In Article X, a general clause, the directors were permitted to do what "shall to them appear necessary and proper to be done" for the "well ordering and interest of said owners and proprietors," not contrary to the laws of Ohio. Article XI directed that any surplus money should be used for roads, while Article XII named the act as "public."

In 1806 a land tax was levied by the new state of Ohio. A perpetual lien was created against all land for the amount of the tax; a special clause permitted minors to redeem land sold for taxes within one year after the expiration of their minority. On May 5, 1808, the directors of the company, meeting in New Haven, voted a tax of two cents on each pound of value (or losses originally computed) to pay the state's tax in a lump sum. This was prior to any final drawings of land (although Justice McLean and counsel both expressed ignorance on this point). Failure to pay this tax had occasioned the sale of Douglas' land; it was conducted by the company's own collector, not by state officials.

McLean, in upholding the ruling in the court below, felt that the directors had exceeded their powers. The state had not looked particularly to the group as a whole for payment; it had provided its own office in Warren, within the area, and paid its own collectors (while the expense of collection by the company was an extra expense to the "sufferers"). Moreover, the state was more favorable in its treatment of minors. Justice McLean felt that "the power to impose a tax . . . is a high prerogative and should never be exercised where the right is doubtful"; further, "it clearly appears that the incorporation was designed . . . to accomplish *specific* objects," and therefore "a tax to the State is not a necessary expense of the Company." Article X, he felt, was only intended to give the "exercise of a discretion, within the scope of the authority conferred."[110] Justice McLean added that otherwise the directors "would dispose of the land and vest the proceeds in

[110] The Justice did not trouble to discuss how the sharers (living in Connecticut) of a large tract of land as yet not allotted could practicably

any manner which they might suppose would advance the interest of the proprietors," a consequence which he believed absurd. The possession of such discretion would seem to be essential if the body were to be a corporation in the *business* sense. The implications of this decision are therefore such as to substantiate the conclusion reached herein that if the word company is to possess a functional significance, there had not been created by the two acts a business organization, but a public body with specific powers similar to modern port authorities or public park trustees.

THE GORE LAND COMPANY[111]

Beginning in May of 1792, Connecticut was engaged for three years in attempting to build a new state house. The assembly had appointed a five-man committee to raise money from citizens; the state had agreed to pay about $5,000 into the fund if the city,

pay their own taxes levied in Ohio on specific plots. Clearly expediency and convenience were on the side of the directors. The decision shows, however, that the act was regarded as a specific empowering of directors to do certain things, rather than as the creation of a business corporation. It shows also the influence of the doctrine of *ultra vires,* particularly in some of the phrases used by McLean in condemning the act of the directors. The counsel for Douglas' heirs referred to the leading case of *Head* v. *Providence Insurance Co.,* 2 Cranch 167, to uphold his position. The same counsel raised one other interesting point: because no names were mentioned in either of the acts, he claimed that Douglas never assented to the terms of the 1803 act, and that in the absence of any overt consent he was not bound by the acts of the directors. This further attack was dismissed by the court; if it had been accepted, the act would have become even more of a hybrid piece of legislation than it was.

[111] A. C. Bates' account in "The Connecticut Gore Land Company," 1898 *American Historical Association Reports,* 139, summarizes the important sources of information.

The later fate of the project is reviewed in a pamphlet, *Enquiry Concerning the Grant of the Legislature of Connecticut to Ward and Halsey,* published in behalf of Thomas Bull in 1829; this and a copy of the articles of agreement are in the Connecticut State Library. An earlier pamphlet (Hartford, 1799) gives a detailed defense of Connecticut's claim, and reprints early charter grants in full. A copy is in the New York State Library, Albany.

township, and county of Hartford would do likewise. Prominent citizens of Hartford paid in substantial amounts and this first sum was easily raised. But $10,000 was not enough to build a complete structure, so in May of 1793 the same committee applied for a lottery privilege, which was readily granted. The lottery dragged along for two years before enough tickets had been sold to warrant a drawing, and the final margin of profit to the committee was much less than 10 per cent.

In the meantime, Colonel Jeremiah Halsey and General Andrew Ward had proposed that if the state would deed them the narrow strip of land on the southern border of New York known as "the Gore," they would undertake to sell it abroad and return to the state one-half the proceeds. This strip of land, by later surveys, was discovered to be two and one-half miles wide and about two hundred and twenty miles long. As indicated previously, it was included in Connecticut's claims to western land because of the faulty adjustment of the boundary between New York and Pennsylvania. The northern boundary of Pennsylvania was 42° latitude, while the southern boundary of Massachusetts, extended westward, was 42° 2'. New York, uncertain of her western claims until the 1786 treaty with Massachusetts, never claimed the area formally until 1791, when in an act establishing Tioga County, the Pennsylvania boundary was named as the state's southern limit. Halsey and Ward's first offer was made in May of 1794 and was rejected by the committee, but in the following October a renewed offer was accepted in modified form.

The summer of 1794 was just the period when the unfinished state house and the unsuccessful lottery were topics of political conversation. A new committee, appointed in the winter of 1794-1795, was therefore able to secure from the same two men a revised offer to finish the state house in lieu of a cash payment. A bill was finally passed offering to deed over the Gore in return for completion of the state house by May 1, 1797. A bond of

$40,000 guaranteeing completion at that date was to be required; it would also serve as an indemnity bond to the state for any claims arising out of the construction. The existing fund of cash on hand for the building was to be turned over to the purchasers, but they were prohibited from operating any lotteries in the future.

Halsey purchased Ward's interest, and immediately organized an association to be called "The Connecticut Gore Land Company"; it was never incorporated. Shares were divided according to contributions. One John Bishop had originally held five-twelfths of the total capital and the other shares were at first in the form of twelfths. But in April, 1796, the title to the property was turned over to trustees, and ninety-six "scrip shares" or certificates of interest were issued. In the first year two assessments of $7 and $5 were levied on the shares, and during 1797 the ninety-six shares were split up on a four-for-one basis.

New York vigorously denied Connecticut's claim to this area, and in 1797 passed an act which declared it to be treason to aid or encourage the transfer of title or settlement in the district, directed the militia to destroy settlements, and made settlers under Connecticut title guilty of a "high misdemeanor." This law was vigorously enforced against a small group of settlers who had purchased from or were tenants of the company. In one case, several buildings and homes were deliberately burned as directed by the statute. The company immediately brought a test suit in a Federal Court,[112] questioning the validity of the New York law. The land specifically in question was situated in the present town of Lindley, Steuben County.

Just at this time the speculative value of the shares reached a peak, and an offer of $300,000 was made for the area as a whole. This offer was refused because the proprietors stated that they believed their claims to be worth at least $600,000. When the test

[112] A summary of the subsequent litigation is included in *Fowler* v. *Lindley* and *Fowler* v. *Miller*, 3 Dallas 411 (1799).

cases first came up for argument the defendant, Miller, failed to appear and $1,000 damages was awarded the plaintiffs. Since he had only five days to reach Hartford after receiving a summons, Miller's plea for rehearing was granted. It became apparent that New York intended to seek delay by questioning the jurisdiction of the Federal Court in Connecticut. Judge Cushing, although granting delay until the following April, indicated that he believed the land lay within the boundaries of Connecticut, and that a jury chosen in Hartford would be competent to try the case. In April there was a postponement.

In September, 1797, counsel for the state of New York secured another postponement on the grounds that the deputy marshal who had secured the papers in the case was prejudiced, being the owner of shares in the company.

After several other postponements, an application for an injunction to force a change in jurisdiction to another circuit was rejected by the Supreme Court in September, 1799.[113] During these years New York employed Alexander Hamilton and Theophilus Parsons as special counsel, while the company was represented by James Sullivan of Boston; the two states also participated through their Attorneys General. As delays accumulated, confidence in the enterprise waned. An assessment of $12 levied in 1797 was paid promptly, but one in March, 1800, was defaulted by most of the holders and many shares were forfeited and sold.

In October, 1799, Connecticut had appointed commissioners to treat with New York on the long-familiar offer—that jurisdiction would be given up provided that private claims to the Gore were recognized. New York had consistently refused to appoint commissioners or pay any attention to the claims, but in the winter of 1799–1800 chances that she would do so seemed brighter.

But meanwhile some political jockeying in Congress brought the debacle. Connecticut's representatives in Congress agreed, in

[113] *Ibid.*

order to secure a valid claim to the Western Reserve from the
Federal Government, to renounce jurisdiction and claims to title
to all other lands either to the United States or to the "several
states who may be concerned." This, of course, included renun-
ciation of all claims to the Gore in favor of New York. Political
pressure from the Connecticut Land Company was greater, and
of course the territory involved was larger, so the Gore Company
was sacrificed.

The actual expenditures by this ill-fated association had been
about $45,000, roughly half of it spent on the state house and
half for legal expenses. The acquisition cost to the "ruined"
shareholders had been about $300,000. Nearly all of them had
been purchasers in 1796, at the height of the excitement over the
fertile strip of territory. The shares gradually dropped to a price
of $70, as compared with a peak value of $1,000 in 1796. For the
shares outstanding in 1800, the low price represented about two-
thirds of the actual expenditure, for which it was hoped the state
would remunerate the shareholders. After several petitions, another $6 per share assessment was levied in 1803 to finance the
lobby efforts before legislative committees. Finally, $40,000 was
appropriated by the legislature and paid in annual installments
to the remaining shareholders during 1805–1808. These payments
(about $10 per share) constituted only a fraction of the money
cost of the shares to most holders, and as late as 1829 one Thomas
Bull petitioned for more redress from the state, but with no
results.[114]

[114] There is a statement in an 1802 pamphlet, *Rise Progress and Effect
of the Claim of the Proprietors of the Connecticut Gore, Stated and Considered,* that $50,000 had been spent for legal costs. A copy is in the Colum-
bia University Library.

In the pamphlet defending shareholder Bull's petition for assistance,
cited in note 111, *supra,* his total investment up to 1805 is shown as $36,-
317.47, presumably including all assessments. He originally held one-
eighth of all the shares, and had acquired three-tenths by 1805. This confirms the estimate of nearly $300,000 as the total "cost" to shareholders.
Bull and Woodbridge, who were among the five agents of the stockholders

WESTERN NEW YORK COMPANIES

The purchases and sales of land in the western third of New York state after 1787 illustrate the rapidity with which the frontier was pushed westward after the coming of peace. But these transactions do not offer as valuable examples of business or legal organization as have been found elsewhere. In most cases there were informal syndicates, and no articles of agreement survive to give any detailed information. There were, however, three organizations involved directly or indirectly with the speculative trading in New York land which will be commented upon separately—the New York–Genesee Land Company, the Pulteney Associates, and the Holland Land Company.

The story of the disposition of the area ceded by New York to Massachusetts in the treaty of 1786 has been often told.[115] Oliver Phelps was an experienced speculator, having been connected with the commissary department of the Revolutionary Army. He had become associated with Nathaniel Gorham of Charlestown, Massachusetts, solely because they were both attempting, in 1786, to purchase the Massachusetts cession at a low price, and decided to join forces in order to check competitive bidding. Phelps had promised shares in his purchase to various Connecticut friends, but ultimately these shares were relatively small. These participants appear in the records only as owners in several

at the time of the 1805 appropriation by the legislature, had been a dissenting minority to the acceptance of that sum. They believed that they had thus not been bound by the deed of release and conveyance given to the state, and had preserved their right to further compensation.

[115] For example, Turner, *Pioneer History of the Phelps and Gorham Purchase* (Rochester, 1851), the original treatment; Sakolski has a chapter devoted largely to it in his *Great American Land Bubble;* most standard histories give the essential facts. The relations of Phelps with Gorham, and with Connecticut friends, were strikingly parallel to those of J. C. Symmes with Elias Boudinot and other Jerseymen in his ill-managed Miami purchase (1788). Symmes' dominance made it a one-man project despite participation of others as proprietors in "reserved" land; it is therefore not discussed here. See B. W. Bond, ed., *Correspondence of John Cleves Symmes* (New York, 1926), 1–26.

partition deeds around 1800, affecting lands north of Canandaigua. Since the early resale to Morris (1790) was profitable, these six or eight participants (including the two Elys of Westfield, Jeremiah Wadsworth, and Gideon King) probably received cash. It is also known that there were informal meetings of the group at Phelps' home in 1788 and 1789, just as members of a modern speculative syndicate meet to discuss plans. At such a meeting in January, 1789, several small shares in the purchase were retired, and the group became much smaller.

One of the chief obstacles faced in the winter of 1787–1788 by Phelps and Gorham in securing the Indian title to lands they had purchased from Massachusetts was the nine-hundred-ninety-nine-year lease which had been secured from the Seneca Nation by a group known as the New York–Genesee Land Company. The career of this speculative project needs some comment, although the information concerning it is scanty.

The New York–Genesee Land Company

This company was formed in Hudson, New York, in the autumn of 1787. Apparently between eighty and ninety individuals took shares, although no written record survives.[116] John Livingston was a leader, but in the negotiations with the Indians Dr. Caleb Benton, well known in the Indian trade, was most active. Other "members" were merchants or fur and skin dealers of Hudson.

The Constitution of New York (Article 37) forbade all purchases of land directly from the Indians, except by the state itself or under its direct sanction. To circumvent this, Benton in November of 1787 procured from Cayuga and Seneca chiefs a nine-hundred-ninety-nine-year lease of territory which included the

---

[116] Turner, in his *Pioneer History*, 106–109, gives a good account of it, but specific facts are chiefly accessible in a pamphlet published in 1811 at the expense of the Holland Land Company entitled *Refutation of the Claim of John Livingston*. A copy is in the Columbia University Library.

Phelps and Gorham purchase. In January a similar lease was procured from the Oneidas for the same long term covering territory just west of the Military Tract. The rentals were to be $2,000 Spanish for the first area and $1,000 for the second, the latter payment to increase to $1,500 in the second ten years. The news of these transactions spread quickly, and Governor Clinton immediately acted to nullify their effect. They were obviously efforts to circumvent his plans for a treaty with the Indians that would result in a formal cession to the state of all the area which had not been ceded to Massachusetts.

A legislative committee appointed in January, 1788, reported in February that the leases were in reality purchases in direct violation of the Constitution. In approving the committee's report, the legislature resolved that force ought to be used to prevent Livingston and his associates from entering their lands, ordered a public proclamation stating the attitude of the government, rejected the petition of the company for confirmation, and finally appointed commissioners to assist the governor in the coming treaty.

Immediately after these resolutions were passed, Livingston and Benton offered to divide with the state the area they had secured, if and after a definitive purchase from the Indians had been negotiated at their expense under state supervision. This proposal was rejected by the Senate, which in turn asked Livingston to surrender his leases so that they might be displayed to convince the Indians of the validity of a sale to the state. In conclusion the Senate in its resolution made a suggestion of compensation in the phrase, "they ought to depend on the justice of the public for expenses and such other allowances as to the legislature shall appear proper and equitable." The leases were delivered to the treaty commissioners, not by Livingston who was apparently disgruntled, but by Bryan and Birdsall, two of the other leading members of the company. The display of the leases was of material help in securing an agreement to the treaty which Clinton concluded in the next winter.[117]

Phelps and Gorham were concerned about the leases because they covered their purchase from Massachusetts. Phelps visited Livingston in Hudson early in the winter of 1787–1788 and made a trade with him, apparently on the basis that he would give Livingston a share in his purchase in return for a cancellation of the leases. However, Phelps in letters at this same time indicated his belief that the leases would be declared invalid. But he obviously felt that Livingston and Benton would be of material assistance in dealing with the Indians. In July, 1788, Livingston accompanied Phelps to a meeting at Buffalo Creek at which they discussed a sale of land with the Senecas. At this same time they met John Butler who headed what has been called the Canadian branch of the New York–Genesee Land Company. It is known that at this meeting Phelps promised fifteen one-hundred-twentieths of the coming purchase to Butler and his associates who in later litigation under this promise were known as the Niagara-Genesee Land Company. Benjamin Barton was a member of this group, all of the others being residents of Upper Canada.

The New York legislature and Phelps were both forgetful of their promises to Livingston as soon as the Indian purchases were completed in 1789. Phelps apparently ignored his promise, and the legislature was unwilling to grant any compensation for the surrender of the original leases. However, in April, 1790, ten square miles were awarded to the group in a bill which was rejected by the Council of Revision. In 1792 Birdsall petitioned for reenactment; he cited the importance of the preliminary negotiations with the Indians in counteracting British influence. In 1793 a bill was finally passed directing the land office to issue patents totaling ten square miles to all persons who were concerned in the leases. The list of names of the participants appears

[117] This course of events is fully described by Turner, *op. cit.*, 117–119.

in this bill and includes three Livingstons, Robert Troup, Jacob Henry Wendell, James Dean, and two Van Rensselaers.[118] Ten of the members were holders of half shares. The surveying of the ten-mile tract was to be at the expense of the beneficiaries. No method of actually allotting land was specified, so the matter was delayed until 1797. At that time another bill ordered the holding of a lottery to award specific lots, under which John Livingston received about 850 acres as his share.

During 1809 rumors spread among settlers on the Holland Land Company territory that the whole Livingston lease would be held valid by the courts and that this would impair the title to all the land in the Holland Company's New York purchase. To combat this rumor the company published a pamphlet[119] rehearsing the history of the New York–Genesee Land Company in careful detail. Appended to this pamphlet were four interesting opinions of leading lawyers, apparently solicited and paid for by the Holland Land Company. Robert Harison, Thomas Addis Emmet, Abraham Van Vechten of Albany, and Jonas Platt of Whitestown were apparently considered the leading legal authorities in New York state. They all agreed that the leases were in reality purchases and that Livingston and other associates had lost all claim by surrendering their leases and also by accepting compensation. They declared in conclusion that settlers need not fear ejectment actions.

Robert Morris also came into conflict with Livingston at the time he was purchasing from Massachusetts the western two-thirds of its area, after Phelps and Gorham had given up their chances to buy it in 1789. In a letter written to Thomas Russell

[118] Writing in February, 1788, to Stephen Van Rensselaer, General Schuyler regretted the connection of General Robert Van Rensselaer with the affair: "The whole business is pernicious to us as a family, and not less to the interest of our party." The connection of young Federalists with Livingston and Benton gave Clinton a "talking point." Cf. Spaulding, New York in the Critical Period (New York, 1932), 17.

[119] Refutation of the Claim of John Livingston.

of Boston asking him to endorse any notes which Morris' agent, Ogden, might make, he said: "you may depend that if I get it I will make a greater fortune out of it in a short time than any other person can now believe."[120] On the same day (January 20, 1791) writing to Ogden he said: "I am informed that Mr. John Livingston of New York associated a company for which he will appear at Boston as the agent to make this purchase. I am likewise informed that another company of New Yorkers have associated for the same purpose and that Dr. Craigie has gone forward as their agent. . . . Mr. Livingston you know better than I do and I trust that you can manage him. Dr. Craigie is quick, sly, sensible and penetrating. He will try to discover your business and conceal his own."

Further on in the same letter Morris said: "Mr. Gorham will probably have a reluctance to sign these agreements [a three-cornered agreement which Morris had tentatively worked out with Phelps and Gorham] because he had inadvertently given a writing to Mr. John Livingston purporting that he, upon certain conditions, would not oppose this Livingston in his pursuit of the Preemption Right." From a later letter it appears that Phelps and Gorham were unwilling to go ahead without including certain others in the purchase. In writing to them Morris said at this time: "I would not for my part choose to increase the number of persons to be concerned in the purchase for it will be affected with great hazard and I will be sufficiently rewarded by holding a large share or have nothing to do with it."[121] Morris' method in making such purchases is illustrated by a postscript to a letter written to Samuel Ogden in Boston by which Morris admitted Ogden's brother to a one-sixtieth share in the proposed purchase simply by an informal phrase.[122]

A number of Livingston's original associates were involved in

---

[120] Letter in the *O'Rielly Collection,* library of the New York Historical Society.

[121] *Ibid.*   [122] *Ibid.*

the agitation at Canandaigua in the spring of 1793 to set up a separate state government and secede from New York. A circular was proposed and sent to leading settlers, but at an exciting meeting the whole idea was condemned. This incident in Ontario County history has been neglected by historians who have recorded the various movements to establish new states after the Revolution.

The Pulteney Associates[123]

Of the area paid for by Phelps and Gorham in 1788, for which they also cleared the Indian title, about 1,300,000 acres out of the total 2,000,000 were resold in 1790 to Robert Morris. This was independent of the latter's purchase, in the next winter, of the 4,000,000 acres in extreme western New York that Phelps and Gorham had been unable to purchase in 1789 because of the rise in the price of Massachusetts debt certificates. This latter was the area sold to the Dutch through Cazenove and Morris' son, to become celebrated as the Holland Land Company holdings.

Morris had scarcely purchased the first tract of about 1,300,000 acres in 1790 when his friend and agent in London, William Temple Franklin, resold it to Sir William Pulteney at a profit.[124] It has already been pointed out that this quick turnover of a large piece of land probably encouraged Morris to the recklessness which marked his enterprises later in the decade. Associated with Pulteney were William Hornby, who held a two-twelfths interest, and Patrick Colquhoun,[125] with a one-twelfth interest. The latter was a well-known public figure in Scotland and later in

[123] Paul D. Evans has sketched the history of this purchase in an article, "The Pulteney Purchase," 3 *New York State Historical Association Quarterly*, 131.

[124] Of probably $50,000, at the most. The profit was much over-estimated at the time; varying exchange rates and discounts make an exact calculation impossible.

[125] Colquhoun's career is outlined in material relating to this purchase, in the *Pulteney MSS.*, Ontario County Historical Society (Canandaigua, New York).

London for nearly half a century, famous for his sponsorship and direction of philanthropic societies. He conducted all the negotiations with Franklin at first without revealing his principals, and even the final agreement[126] was made in the name of Colquhoun, "acting for himself and in behalf of certain other persons, who have formed an association . . . and have empowered the said Colquhoun to enter into this agreement." This agreement for sale was signed in London March 17, 1791. It includes some provisions that are strikingly suggestive of twentieth century transactions involving industrial or mining properties that have uncertain potential value.

Four articles specified the area—supposedly 1,000,000 acres, but really by a survey 1,300,000—and the price to be paid—£75,000. Payment was to be made in full by January 1, 1797, with any advance payments reduced by a 5 per cent annual discount. Morris was to complete a survey at his own expense, any deductions made necessary because of occupancy by squatters were to be credited to the purchasers, and any "overplus" shown by the survey within the boundaries was to go to them also. In 1814, just before his death, Colquhoun asked[127] the Johnstone executors (then holders of Pulteney's title) to deed him 53,460 acres as a reward for his efforts in getting this "excess clause" inserted, by which 1,314,569 acres were actually secured. In the course of this request Colquhoun stated that his one-twelfth participation was in the nature of a commission[128] since he had put in no cash. At this same time (1814) he was apparently receiving payment to liquidate his interest, as from that time only the Pulteney and Hornby heirs appear as owners.

The fifth article specified that both Morris and Franklin were to receive one-fifteenth of the net profit of the enterprise in return

---

[126] A copy is among the *Pulteney MSS.*

[127] A copy of his written request is in the *Pulteney MSS.*

[128] About the same percentage is commonly an intermediary's commission in modern Wall Street transactions.

for their efforts to colonize the land speedily, "without being considered in any respect as partners in the Association"—a profit-sharing arrangement again suggestive of modern contracts of this sort. The tenth article specified that Franklin was to act as the selling agent for the association, at 10 per cent commission for cash sales, 7 per cent for those made on credit; he was to be allowed 600 guineas per year as expenses on a drawing account basis.

The remaining articles dealt with the method of making payments, the protection of the buyers as aliens (until 1798 New York did not permit them to take title), and gave the buyers one year to refuse the tract after an inspection. A bond of £50,000 on both sides was agreed to, guaranteeing the carrying out of the agreement.

The historian[129] who has surveyed this enterprise estimates that by 1840 it about "broke even," although it is impossible to make an exact estimate. Up to 1810 it was very unprofitable. The story of Charles Williamson's and Robert Troup's[130] agencies are familiar in Steuben County history. After 1815, when the title was held in trust, there was considerable resentment among the local purchasers who were tied up with a long series of payments, but no such outbursts occurred as marked the later history of the Holland Company. The heirs of Pulteney were true absentee owners; for seventy-five years apparently none of them ever visited the district from which they were receiving continuous revenue.

The Holland Land Company

From the standpoint of pure historical interest, the five enterprises which are ordinarily grouped under this inclusive title

[129] Evans, *op. cit.*

[130] The *Robert Troup MSS.*, in the New York Public Library, include much interesting material on his career as a speculator in soldiers' bounty lands in the Military Tract. He became a well-known political figure.

occupy first place among all the projects here considered, with the possible exception of the Ohio Company. Their story as written by an outstanding student of this period in American history is the most penetrating account of a land undertaking yet written.[131] But the actual structure of these units is of lesser interest here, simply because they were formed entirely under Dutch law. Together with Castorland, they illustrate the method in civil law countries at the end of the eighteenth century of working with unincorporated associations. Because acquaintance with their internal structure at a critical period may have affected the thinking of American business leaders, some description of them must be included here.

Theophile Cazenove came to New York in 1790 as the representative of the Dutch firms of Stadnitski, Van Staphorst, Van Eeghen, and Ten Cate and Vollenhoven. The first two were the more prominent, Stadnitski having begun speculation in American federal and state securities at least as early as 1786[132] and the Van Staphorsts soon after. Presumably by the summer of 1789 their profits had been extremely large because of the certainty of acceptance of Hamilton's funding plans. Cazenove proceeded leisurely to discover equally good opportunities in the purchase of other American bonds, stocks, or land as he saw fit. By the summer of 1791, the purpose of his travels and inquiries had become known to all the leading speculators of the day. He had made heavy purchases of state debt obligations and of United States Bank stock for his principals.[133] He also bought shares in most of the pioneer canal companies then being promoted—the Potomac Company, Inland Lock Navigation, James River, and others. In 1791 the same group sent over Gerrit Boon and Jan Lincklaen[134] to make a special study of maple sugar lands; Caze-

[131] Paul D. Evans, *Holland Land Company.*
[132] *Ibid.,* 3.   [133] *Ibid.,* 7, 8.
[134] For an interesting account of young Lincklaen's travels in 1791–1792, *cf.* Helen Lincklaen Fairchild, *Journals of Jan Lincklaen* (New York, 1897).

nove was to cooperate with them in any purchases they might recommend.[135] By the summer of 1792, Stadnitski was ready to go ahead with land purchases on a large scale, stimulated by Cazenove's reports; he had interested also the firm of W. & J. Willink, co-sponsor of the first Dutch loan to the United States.[136]

This long period of preparation led to confusion in the purchase. Almost simultaneously Cazenove bought 1,500,000 acres from Robert Morris, and young Morris, as agent for his father, sold to Stadnitski in Holland another million acres. Both tracts were in the area which Morris had purchased from Massachusetts a year and a half previously after the failure of Phelps and Gorham to complete their contract. Stadnitski had gone ahead to make a deal with young Morris because he felt that the appetite of the investing Dutch was ready. His *negotie* based on the million acres was announced in a glowing prospectus late in December, 1792, and the books were opened for subscriptions on January 1, 1793. The details of this offering are of interest in showing methods of the day in dealing with the general public.[137]

The firm of Stadnitski was to be director of the enterprise, subject to the direction and control of five commissioners chosen from the partners of the other houses that had sent Cazenove to America. The commissioners were in effect the active partners, subscribers were to be limited partners, and the director (itself a

[135] The famed Cazenovia settlement in central New York grew out of their efforts—a purchase of about 64,000 acres. The present town of the same name is rich in evidence of this early effort (1792–1797) to establish the production of maple sugar on the basis of large-scale factory production.

[136] Evans, *Holland Land Company*, 20.

[137] Professor Paul Evans has kindly made available to the author his detailed notes on the pamphlet or prospectus which Stadnitski issued at this time. They provide a greater wealth of detail than he saw fit to include in his *Holland Land Company*, pp. 28–29. The extensive "sales talk" with which Stadnitski prefaced the actual description of the *negotie* would be of particular interest to the Securities and Exchange Commission of today.

partnership in this case) was the agent of the commissioners. This prevalent Dutch structure was a considerable modification of the idea of limited partnership. Title was to be held jointly by the commissioners and Pieter Stadnitski.

In case of death or resignation of a commissioner, the remaining four were empowered to choose another; the managerial group was thus self-perpetuating. In fact the only power granted to purchasers of shares was the privilege of "consulting" at the end of five years as to the wisdom of accepting a potential large offer for all remaining land or of continuing the project for its maximum expected duration of twenty years. The only report required was one at the end of this five-year period. Otherwise the commissioners were to be in full charge of the enterprise, supervising the work of the Stadnitski firm. On the other hand, shares were made especially attractive by the deposit of £1,200,000 to secure the payment of interest at five per cent to the directing firm, and the annual payments to shareholders. Commissioners received no other compensation, but the Stadnitski firm received an initial fee of one per cent of the principal and one-half per cent of the annual interest payment.

Shares were for fl. 1,000 each, issued either to bearer or in a registered name, signed by the directors and countersigned by a public notary. The right was reserved to return the full purchase price and cancel the shares at any time, in order to provide for the contingency that the commissioners might not be able to secure adequate titles as aliens.

The offering was so successful that another similar *negotie* was undertaken in June of 1793, with a capital of fl. 3,450,000 secured upon 1,000,000 acres of Cazenove's purchase. The guaranteed interest was five and one-half per cent instead of five per cent. Still remaining were 1,300,000 acres, held in private account by the six firms interested. After the purchases in Pennsylvania from James Wilson in 1793, the total withheld from public sale rose to 2,800,000 acres. This amount was turned over to the *true* Holland Land Company, formally organized early in 1796 by a similar private contract registered before a notary. There were 896 shares, and six commissioners (one from each firm) with plenary powers of management. The director, who received 20 per cent on all net revenue, was Van Eeghen, well known to students of early western New York history.[138] The last of the five organizations that are known collectively as the Holland Land Company (though only the company of 1796 truly deserves this title) was the small Cazenovia settlement of 64,000 acres where Lincklaen and Boon tried their sugar experiment. In form this smallest *negotie,* formed in 1794, closely resembled the others.[139]

The later history of the five enterprises need not be recounted. Shares in the two public offerings were quoted more or less continuously in Amsterdam. Professor Evans concludes that despite the long delays in winding up the various projects, and the losses sustained in Pennsylvania, "the original investment was retrieved with interest of five to six per cent."[140] By modern standards this seems low, but compared with the two or three per cent available at the time on Dutch Government securities it was quite satisfactory.

"CASTORLAND"[141]

This project has become well known as an enterprise growing out of the sale of northern New York lands to Alexander Macomb in 1791. Macomb made a ridiculously low bid for the Adirondack area offered by the legislature, and a typical modern

---

[138] *Cf.* Evans, *op. cit.,* 34–35.

[139] Information supplied by Professor Evans.

[140] Evans, *op. cit.,* 435.

[141] This description is taken largely from F. B. Hough, *History of Lewis County, New York* (Albany, 1860). The area sold was in this county. The later fate of the few settlements in the area is discussed by A. M. Ralph, "The Chassanis or Castorland Settlement," 10 *New York State Historical Association Quarterly Journal,* 333. For the original purchase from New York state by Macomb and Constable, *cf.* Davis, 1 *Essays,* 279–280.

"investigation" was demanded in the legislature about three years later.

There seems to be no evidence that Macomb formed any organization to handle his project, but it is certain that William Constable was interested as a partner, and it is probable that informal shares in the tract were given out to his friends by the purchaser. Eventually Constable came into control of much of the area, and parts of it remained in his family's possession for nearly one hundred years.

Macomb and Constable followed the usual plan of the speculators of the period in immediately attempting a quick resale abroad. In August, 1792, Constable was successful in disposing of 630,000 acres in the tract to one Peter Chassanis of Paris. The latter was acting as agent for an association of French emigrants, and it was to be held in trust by him pending final payment. The resulting association is also worthy of description here as another foreign-born effort to carry through a settlement project in this country. The company furnishes an extraordinarily good example of the French unincorporated *société* of the time.

Acting as trustee, Chassanis immediately issued a prospectus that declared that a meeting would be held promptly to elect *commissaries,* of whom three would reside in Paris and three in New York. Certificates to represent one hundred acres each were to be issued at a price of approximately $152, or a total of 6,000 shares for the whole tract. This preliminary announcement was to be supplemented by rules adopted at the first meeting.

Such a meeting was not held until June, 1793, just prior to the climax of the Reign of Terror. Only 1,808 certificates were represented, so it was decided, in drawing up the agreement, to provide for only 2,000 shares. Constable agreed to withdraw the balance of the tract. He confirmed title to this amount, as of April, 1793, and received a total payment of about £2,500 in English currency. The agreement that was adopted at this June meeting, following Constable's assent, represents the conception of this

French group as to the business mechanism needed to carry out a program of colonization.

The first section of the agreement[142] (the sections are called "titles") provided a rehearsal of the history of the transaction as conducted by Chassanis. The second section declared all purchasers to be proprietors in common, under the title of "The Company of New York." They were further described by the phrase, "dormant partners." The name "Castorland" was adopted at a later time. The third section was typically French in setting forth the high aims of the association, referring in particular to the relief the project offered for the harassed members of the French upper classes at that particular moment. Other parts of this section divided up the territory into two parts, one to be held in common for the benefit of all and a smaller section to be divided up into shares. The next section described the shares in more detail and provided that each one should be issued in two parts, one for a specific divided share of land and the other for a share in the undivided land. Holders of temporary receipts were to exchange them promptly for these shares. The holders of shares in the undivided land (holders of *coupon indivis*) were declared to be true members of the association, whereas the holders of the divided shares, which could be sold separately, received no privileges except that of compelling a transfer of their shares on the books of the association.

The government of the group was to be in the hands of a director and four commissaries, who must own either ten full shares or twenty of the divided shares. They would automatically lose office if they sold their shares. The director was to be a permanent officer, except that he might be deposed by a two-thirds vote at a special meeting. The other commissaries were to be elected every three years by a majority vote. The director had personal charge of records and correspondence, called meetings of shareholders, kept the transfer books, exercised a deciding vote

[142] The agreement is reprinted *verbatim* in Hough, *op. cit.,* 37 *ff.*

in meetings of the four commissaries; he paid out money when orders were countersigned by two of the latter. The commissaries also were charged with watching the general operation of the company, with ordering the directors' accounts, signing shares, and preparing the order of business for meetings. They received fees for attending monthly meetings and were given complete executive powers as a body, acting with the director, with the exception that they were not permitted to borrow money.

In order to manage the association's land in New York, two American sub-directors or agents were to be selected by the assembly of shareholders to carry on administrative work and make surveys of the land. Other duties might be assigned to these resident agents by the five Parisian directors. They were required to give bonds and were allotted $600 a year for their expenses. Their appointment was to be indefinite, and if they disagreed at any time they were to select an arbitrator among the American shareholders.

General meetings of the holders of undivided shares were to be held three times a year or by special call of the director. One thousand shares was to be a quorum, and voting power was to be exercised as follows: one vote up to five shares, each additional ten shares up to forty-five an extra vote, with five votes the maximum permitted at any time to any individual holder.

A preliminary survey of property was to be carried out under the direction of Constable (to which he agreed in his deed) and was to include the laying out of roads and the location of a city in a central part of the territory. The 100,000 acres of the land to be divided up among the shareholders was to be laid out in strips intermixed with the area held in common. The division of the 100,000 acres and of the two thousand city lots was to be made in the order of numbers of the shares (determined by lot). A shareholder was not to receive a city lot unless he promised to build a house.

At the end of seven years and again after fourteen years, there was to be a mandatory vote on dissolution. If a majority did not vote in favor at either of these times, the life of the association would extend to a maximum of twenty-one years; six months before this time the regular assembly of shareholders would be required to adopt some definite plans for liquidation.

A final section of the agreement provided for securing legal approval of the purchase from the United States minister and for the adoption of amendments by a two-thirds vote at any regular meeting. The original prospectus under which preliminary certificates had been sold was declared to be "only a simple record," as a result of the adoption of this formal agreement. A seal was to be provided for the acts of directors, and copies of the agreement were to be signed in triplicate and kept on file.

This ambitious project never went beyond the embryonic stage. Events in France in 1793–1794 prevented many of the shareholders from taking an active interest. There was insufficient money to pay for a proper survey of the land and absolutely no progress was made in selling to outsiders any of the undivided land. It was inaccessible, and much less desirable than Pennsylvania or Ohio lands. It was these sales that were expected to provide money for the expense of the group in transporting themselves to America. In following years, various meetings of shareholders authorized borrowing money to complete the survey, and by 1814 a debt of 360,000 livres had been accumulated. This was the date of automatic liquidation of the association by the terms of the original agreement. At a public sale held in Paris, Swiss creditors who had advanced the loans bid in the property at a nominal figure and appointed Herman LeRoy as a sort of liquidating agent. From him many of the titles in this area are now derived, through sales made slowly and intermittently in the following two decades. Much of this district was of course not settled at all until after 1850, and much of it is today included in New York state parks.

Twelve years after the property had thus passed into the hands of creditors, the American Consul (Barnett) in Paris wrote to lawyer Vanderpoel of New York asking him to sell the lands represented by two certificates in the "Castor Land Company." He described the company briefly and referred to its "Act of Incorporation" of June 8, 1793. It has been seen that this same error of attributing incorporation to land bodies has frequently been made by historical commentators on other land companies a century later. Attached to the certificates in the letter to Vanderpoel was a "bulletin" assigning fifty acres to one Le Febre, referring to "deliberations" (a drawing of lots) and setting forth that "the title of property shall be delivered to him conformably to those deliberations." Barnett had been given the two certificates by a lawyer handling an estate, and obviously neither of them knew anything about the status of "Castorland" in 1826. Vanderpoel, better informed probably, did nothing about the matter.[143]

[143] This correspondence is in the *Vanderpoel MSS., William Frankin Papers,* Box 1, New York Public Library.

VI

CORPORATIONS VERSUS ASSOCIATIONS:
THE BUSINESS COMMUNITY'S ATTITUDE

NO ONE of the enterprises described in the two preceding chapters possessed a charter. Yet they are typical of the activity of business men during the entire half-century; land speculation was an absorbing side-enterprise with the many, and a chief occupation for the few. To all with the necessary capital and connection, it was the avenue to potential riches. Why then was the aid of a charter not thought to be necessary?

The answer is clearly one which has at previous points been stressed.[1] A charter was needed only for some exclusive privilege which included the right to govern an area (for example, the proprietary colonies) or the right to engage in a business otherwise closed to private enterprise for reasons of public policy (as banking, turnpike roads). Occasionally the limitation of liability was needed in order to attract capital (as in insurance). But in the merchandising of land none of these particular considerations intruded. Purely private organization there held the field, and experimentation in form and operation, unhampered by legislative restriction, was the rule.

As a result, what was being created, step by step, was the clearly defined business association, supplanting in many directions the partnership of previous centuries. In England the typical joint stock "business company" was given final form in this same period, ready to form the model for the modern registered company, or corporation. With the flexible English deed of settlement becoming equivalent to a charter, the functional character-

---

[1] *Supra,* pp. 65–69. The impression gained by many students from a reading of Davis' *Essays,* the standard work dealing with early American business, is unfortunately erroneous, *viz.,* that all important enterprises in the period 1765–1800 were chartered corporations.

istics of the association becoming almost exactly those of the corporation and its business usefulness even greater, the individually-chartered corporation was relegated to the business curio shelf by the middle of the nineteenth century. In the United States the smoothly operating associations were ready for "adoption" by our legislatures in the general incorporation laws, acquiring thereby the few legal privileges of corporations which they had not as yet appropriated. They became the true progenitors of the modern business corporation. In two following chapters the legislative attitude and the attitude of the courts toward this process of absorption or displacement will be examined in some detail. Here it is necessary first to assay the emerging association from a functional standpoint, as it was exemplified in the most important area of business activity in which it appeared.[2]

There is ample evidence that after 1800 the business association came into more frequent use, as did also the chartered corporation. But before that date, and particularly in the decade 1785–1795, the land enterprises which have been described stand out as the most important and absorbing activity that called for organization of a more advanced type than the simple partnership. It seems demonstrably true that all the various stages of complexity in modern business organization beyond the partnership had counterparts among these speculative projects.

Before beginning our assay, it is well to glance back at certain specific forces which influenced the form of land enterprises. In Chapter II it was pointed out that the existing example of proprietary grants affected the plans of certain speculators. In the case of Transylvania, Henderson's assumption that he could secure a proprietary grant seems astonishingly naïve in the light of our knowledge of the Whig oligarchy as it functioned after 1760. The backers of Vandalia had the necessary influence in high

[2] DuBois, *The English Business Company after the Bubble Act,* deals with this period in England. Particularly after 1765 the development of the unincorporated business company there was rapid.

places, but such complete governmental power as they desired in the new colony aroused opposition in more than one direction— enough to block the scheme. In both instances the plan revolved around a formal grant or charter, so that the internal operations or relationships of the self-styled "proprietors" are of little value for the analysis to be made here.

The situation was quite different so far as those companies which were based on the New England proprietorship model were concerned. The point was stressed in Chapter II above that the proprietorship grew up without sanction by the general court in both Massachusetts and Connecticut, only to be later recognized and bolstered up by statutes. It gradually assumed more and more formality and power, by the initiative of those whose welfare it concerned; the role of statutes was a purely passive one. Thus the leaders who formed the Susquehannah and Ohio Companies, the Military Adventurers, and the Onion River Company, quite obviously could regard the familiar proprietorship as a flexible model to be turned to their own particular needs. They would reason thus: "It is our inherent right to set up a functioning body according to our needs; if any sanction by the state is necessary later, it will be forthcoming as readily as have various statutes placing behind proprietorship activities the force of law." It was exactly this reasoning which brought into being the full-fledged private association and eventually the modern corporation freely organized under permissive statutes.[3]

With the exception of the two enterprises which were clearly modeled on Continental law and practice,[4] the projectors of other land companies drew upon their general knowledge of business practice. There is danger of imputing to them or to the lawyers who advised them a conscious effort to create organizations which would be generic models. There is clear evidence in

[3] Cf. supra, pp. 5–6.
[4] "Castorland" and the Holland Land Company (the latter really five separate enterprises).

the Ohio Company of mere experimentation, a trial and error attitude, in the first three years. There was just as obviously, on the other hand, imitation of European examples known to individuals who were concerned in specific plans. Thus quite obviously Morris and Nicholson in setting up their North American Land Company borrowed from Stadnitski's Dutch "negotiations," used to dispose of western New York land. The close similarity between charters of the period and the actual practice of private associations will be commented upon at a later point. One did not imitate the other; rather, chartered and unchartered bodies were progressing slowly, as do mountain climbers roped together. All or any of such a group may contribute the suggestion which changes slightly or measurably the exact course of a long journey.

Among these land companies, then, what did result from this mixture of experimentation and imitation over a half-century? To attempt an answer to this question we ought first to examine and classify roughly the score or more which have been described. Of especial interest are those which can be dubbed true business associations or, in the English phrase, joint stock associations. The simpler types which can with difficulty be distinguished from ordinary partnerships need concern us chiefly only as illustrative of early steps away from the basic partnership model. These latter may be considered first.

A substantial number in this group may be termed joint adventures. Such were, quite clearly, those projects formed solely to obtain a grant of land, with no plans laid for its later merchandising. The best examples of this prior to 1775 were the Illinois Company,[5] of which George Croghan was the leader, and the original Indiana Company[6] as it existed from 1768 to 1774. In the later period the groups associated with Phelps and Gorham and with Alexander Macomb in purchases of New

[5] *Supra,* p. 111.
[6] *Supra,* p. 113.

York state land, the Erie Company group associated with the Connecticut Land Company, and the Eastern Land Associates of Knox and Duer, were more nearly what ought properly to be regarded as joint adventures. The line of demarcation between these groups and the more formal and continuous association is, of course, shadowy. Thus, in the case of the Mississippi Company,[7] there was the formal structure illustrative of the association, while the abortive nature of the project hardly entitles it to inclusion in that group.

The joint adventure, as such, is of little interest here, because it has existed in the English-speaking business world almost since the beginning of commercial relations. The members of the early regulated companies, for example, participated habitually in such joint undertakings. It was common among members of the Merchant Adventurers.[8] Overseas trade in all countries has been a favorite field. Typically, joint adventurers possess common property as tenants in common, make decisions by majority rule, act through agents, and liquidate both capital and profits at the conclusion of a specific enterprise. The joint adventure clearly was an accepted mode of procedure peculiarly adapted to speculative land efforts where slow retail distribution was not contemplated. It has been used continuously in modern business in enterprises ranging from mining exploration to the management of race horses. It has been typically distinguished from the partnership (*a*) by its temporary and specific character or purpose, (*b*) by the delegation of substantial authority to a representative or agent, with a corresponding lack of power in the members to bind the group, and (*c*) by the limitation of liability

[7] *Supra,* p. 102.

[8] Lipson, 2 *Economic History of England,* 227: "Actually groups of partners . . . were formed, so that within the framework of the regulated company there existed a series of embryonic joint stocks." The privateering expeditions under Elizabeth in 1565–1581 were typical joint adventures. One of Frobisher's voyages had a charter, but his others and Drake's did not; there was no apparent difference in their conduct. Scott, 1 *Joint Stock Companies,* 74–75.

of the members to their contributions.[9] Between themselves, members of an adventure are to be treated as partners.

Secondly, it is apparent from several examples that land operations were on occasion conducted in a strikingly analogous manner to modern security or real estate syndicates.[10] A syndicate is not a true joint adventure. Only in very recent years have courts come to deal with the pure syndicate; legislatures never have. This is all the more surprising when it is realized that in essentials it existed in the business community prior to 1800. It was stressed above[11] that William Duer, in the Scioto transaction, possessed the full discretion which is a distinguishing characteristic of the modern syndicate. In the Mount Vernon Proprietors,[12]

[9] Kent recognized this only as affecting the sea-venture, in which liability *in solido* for group debts had long been eliminated, even in Roman Law. This difference from common law doctrine must have been known to New England enterprisers. 3 *Commentaries* (12th edition), 35.

[10] One of the most ubiquitous types of syndicate encountered since 1870 in American business life is the speculative stock "pool." Yet it is almost completely absent from court records because litigation involving such groups never reaches the point of judicial decision. W. E. Hickernell, *What Makes Stock Prices* (New York, 1932) at 129, describes the typical pool agreement: (1) A fixed subscription is made involving *pro rata* profits or losses. (2) A definite term of existence is set, typically three or six months, subject to extension if a majority or agreed proportion of the members so vote. (3) The syndicate is expressly declared *not* to be a partnership in any sense; liability of the members is clearly restricted to the *cost* of the shares or bonds subscribed for. (4) Complete discretion and freedom is expressly granted to the pool manager in buying, selling, or borrowing on the pool property—and his acts are made expressly binding on the members.

The object of such pools is to purchase securities in the open market, to be resold at a profit (it may be applied to similar "bulling" of mineral claims, land, patents, royalty contracts, or rights to the American use of foreign processes or methods of manufacture, etc.). In the mechanism of investment banking, the syndicate form is used in distributing securities. The same characteristics are present. The degree of liability varies as between the underwriting and selling syndicates. The "joint account" to support the market for a security previously sold is also typically in syndicate form.

[11] P. 141.   [12] *Supra,* Chapter V, note 81.

Harrison Grey Otis apparently occupied the same position.[13] In analyzing the relationships consequent upon the formation of such a group, the courts in several modern cases[14] have come to describe the members of the group as *cestuis* and the syndicate manager as a trustee.[15] They have reached this conclusion on reasoning closely analogous to that in the leading cases defining the legal relationships inherent in the Massachusetts Trust.[16]

The syndicate and the joint adventure are both formed for a

[13] As apparently did Samuel Wharton in representing the "Sufferers of 1763" in London, 1768–1773. *Supra*, pp. 119–120.

[14] *Jones* v. *Gould*, 209 New York 419; *Byrnes* v. *Chase National Bank*, 232 N.Y.S. 230; *Gates* v. *Megargel*, 266 Fed. 811. But the best judicial summary of the nature of a syndicate is that by Rugg, C. J., in *Minot* v. *Burroughs*, 223 Mass. 595 (1916). The Massachusetts Chief Justice there said, at 602: "A syndicate in this connection means an association of persons with a community of interests in the fund raised for the purpose of carrying on the particular undertaking. The members share the profits and bear the losses in proportion to their respective interests. This syndicate was simply an association of those who furnished money to make the purchase with an agreement that the managers shall have full control of the venture and divide the proceeds or assets among the members in proportion to their interests. So far as concerned each other, their relation and rights were analogous to those of co-partners. . . . Indeed it is expressly provided that . . . the subscribers shall not be partners. . . . Whether, as between themselves, they were simply beneficiaries under a trust or quasi-partners, is not involved here. . . . Owners in fee, so far as concerned the direction of the enterprise and the means to be used could have no larger an authority than was conferred upon the managers." And further, at 605: "So long as the syndicate managers do not exceed their powers under the agreement, the syndicate receipt-holders cannot break through its terms. They are bound inexorably by the conduct of the managers within the ambit of that agreement."

[15] A note on "Relationship of Syndicate Managers and Members," 8 *Harvard Business Review*, 88, examines the nature of a syndicate. It is there pointed out that "the term syndicate does not have a definite legal meaning" (p. 88). The balance of business and legal opinion inclines toward regarding it as a trusteeship, because unlimited power for the manager is positively essential (p. 93). But because of its temporary and specific nature "a syndicate may be assumed to be somewhere between a joint adventure and a trusteeship" (p. 94).

[16] *William* v. *Town of Milton*, 215 Mass. 1, best delineates these relationships as distinct from those in a partnership.

single specific purpose; they are of relatively short duration and narrow in scope. But the joint adventure is to be clearly distinguished from the syndicate on this ground: that the members have some regular and continuing control over the actions of their selected officers or agents, albeit such a representative may possess considerable power and be able to bind the members in contracts. The syndicate, on the other hand, presumes a complete and largely irrevocable power in the hands of a manager.

From the standpoint of business utility and practical effectiveness, both the syndicate and the joint adventure possess that characteristic which becomes fundamental in the modern business association, and, ultimately, in the modern corporation. That is the quality of "side-issue"—the facility offered to participants whose chief or time-absorbing business interest is elsewhere. The importance of this characteristic has been previously stressed.[17] But the continuous association possesses this same quality in a more important sense than do these temporary organizations. It sets up a *permanent* structure to conduct enterprise on this postulate of a "side-issue." The examples of the more permanent and structurally developed associations found among the land companies therefore become of major interest. The proposition that, as functioning business enterprises, they clearly foreshadowed the modern corporation may receive some detailed support at this point from a survey of the group which has been described in the two preceding chapters.

Such support can be easily marshaled from the material at hand. Furthermore, it must be stressed that the discoverable characteristics were solely the creation of business men. In dealing with individual charter grants of past centuries, we inevitably encounter a mixture of legislative vagaries and real business requirements. The apparent needs of public policy which result in peculiar charter clauses may be nothing more than the result of concessions to "watchdog" legislators. They may not mark in

[17] *Supra,* Chapter I, note 2.

any sense significant forward steps in the evolution of today's ubiquitous business corporation.[18] In contrast, the private company is the end-result of a single force—the wants of a business group. It will be seen that, in the most advanced cases, what men were building was in functional effectiveness the equivalent of the corporation. Furthermore, the specific features which facilitated smooth operation in some cases preceded in time the introduction of those features in corporate charters. The conclusion seems inescapable that the association, as exemplified in land enterprises and elsewhere at this same period, contributed to the late eighteenth century and early nineteenth century corporation important portions of its organic structure.

The major tests by which, under modern conditions, the comparative business value of partnership, joint stock association, business trust, and chartered corporation may be judged, have been frequently set forth.[19] They can be made to serve here in judging the advances made by the land groups in re-fashioning the simple partnership into the equivalent of the modern corporation.

Formation

Facility in initial organization is of value to a business group seeking a form to adopt. Little or no sacrifice was entailed on this score by the promoters of the more formal associations that have been examined. The advice of counsel was necessary, but in the establishment of important partnerships this had long been customary. The framework could be erected and the relationships of potential associates between themselves and to their managers or trustees defined. All who purchased shares were

[18] Dodd, *Statutory Regulation of Business Corporations in Massachusetts,* 68, points out the complex forces affecting charters; one force was the "legislature's opinion as to what is socially wise or politically expedient to give them [the incorporators]."

[19] *Cf.* C. S. Tippetts and S. Livermore, *Business Organization and Control* (New York, 1932), 38–64.

presumed to be bound by the articles, with as little formality in assent as that undergone by a partner signing a simple partnership agreement.

The modern corporation offers similar facility, albeit many charters granted by American states do not adequately define the future relationships of the stock purchasers who are bound thereby.[20] But certainly the old chartered corporation stood in sharp contrast on this score to the freely planned, freely organized private company. Political jockeying and bargains, long delays, elaborate petitions and hearings before legislative committees were necessary in England and later in the American states during the period when charters were granted by the Crown or by special act.[21] It cannot be over-emphasized that the ease of incorporating, swiftly and cheaply, enjoyed by the business man today stems not from these older chartered bodies but from the practice made familiar by voluntary associations.

Formal articles of agreement were used quite generally in this whole group. Undoubtedly the 1748 Ohio Company had such articles, which probably were destroyed with its other papers.[22] In 1753 such articles were drawn up for the Susquehannah Company, in that instance simply imitating the time-honored custom of New England settlers in making a formal compact following upon (or in some cases, prior to) a grant of land from the legislature. From this time forward stress was always laid upon a written agreement. Most frequently the agreement was drawn up subsequently to the securing of land, as in the case of the Yazoo Companies, the Connecticut Land Company, and the later companies which Robert Morris and Nicholson set up to receive their properties. There were, however, situa-

[20] *Cf.* Berle, *Cases on Corporation Finance* (St. Paul, 1930), 4.

[21] Unless, of course, the project was close to the heart of the sovereign or, in later days, to the collective heart (or pocketbook) of a ruling oligarchy. *Cf.* the instance of the Lake Superior copper mine charter, *supra,* Chapter III, note 46.

[22] *Supra,* Chapter IV, note 1.

tions in which an association was formed in the expectation that a grant would be received by the group as a unit; the later Ohio Company is an illustration.

As the various agreements are examined chronologically, the growth of the conception that a true business unit or company was being formed is strikingly apparent. Any such feeling is clearly absent in the Mississippi Company, where separate deeds for any land secured were to be made out to the individual members. There are strong traces of the group concept in the Transylvania agreement and in the long-drawn-out history of the Dismal Swamp project. It is unquestionably strongly present in the Ohio Company and in the Connecticut Land Company. These latter companies were active, aggressively functioning bodies; members and officers thought of their creation as the "company" for a considerable period, in the manner of modern shareholders and officers. Of course the doctrines of English law made the members of such a group tenants in common of their acquired real estate, just as English partnership law required each partner to share the group's real estate as a tenant in common, no matter how close-knit the partnership might be in other respects.[23] In opposition to this hewing-to-the-line, the idea of using trustees to hold title to land emerged early and became familiar in England;[24] the desire to act as a single unit is the motivating aim behind this device.

Before 1775, actual operation of the projected company was in many of the instances dependent upon the acquisition or confirmation of a land grant.[25] To this extent it could be claimed that they thereby lacked the quality of freedom in self-creation

[23] The persistence of both English and American courts in treating these groups as partnerships will be discussed below.

[24] *Cf.* Maitland's emphasis on this development, *supra,* Chapter II, note 4.

[25] Appearance of a carefully worded, specific "purpose clause" is to be noted in both the Susquehannah and the 1787 Ohio Companies. It is interesting to speculate on the action and possible remedies open to shareholders

which is fundamental to the business company. But there was no prescription of form, mode of operation, or internal structure attached to these grants.[26] A much closer analogy exists with the group of enterprises which appeared during the 1693–1696 boom in England; these were possessors of Crown-granted patent privileges but independent of sovereign sanction in their internal affairs.[27] They organized and offered shares to the public[28] indistinguishably from the numerous chartered bodies which were a by-product of that early boom period, so suggestive in many of its aspects of later similar periods.[29]

A clear limitation on maximum capital or membership is overwhelmingly present, suggesting a characteristic of the nineteenth century corporation which has, in the twentieth century, disappeared. In the case of the second Ohio Company there was

if that clause had been violated by the "standing committee" or the directors. In other articles which are available, such clauses do not appear. But, on the other hand, there is no record that managements wandered far from the purpose implicit in the undertaking. From a social standpoint, these bodies were better behaved than were corporations twenty-five and fifty years later; the doctrine of *ultra vires* had then to be summoned into existence.

[26] As typified in the 1748 Ohio grant, and in the Vandalia grant as it was approved by the Lords of Trade and Privy Council (though never finally passed). The Dismal Swamp Company secured a permit similar to those granted at a later period to canal and turnpike companies. But there was no charter, as there was in the latter projects.

[27] *Cf.* Scott, 1 *Joint Stock Companies,* 326 *ff.*

[28] The fact that in many instances these companies issued pamphlets, statements, or advertisements soliciting purchasers of shares allies them in the business sense with corporations, and breaks down their kinship with the joint adventure, which in the business sense has always remained strictly a *private* affair. It may of course be argued that this difference is not clear, and that all the projects here examined were essentially temporary in that they envisaged a specific task of land merchandising, and no more. Modern mining is similar, yet no one claims that mining corporations are not *truly corporate* in character. When they do remain private in character, then they clearly may be joint adventures.

[29] Thus in 1792–1797, land company shares (especially those in the Yazoo group) were offered simultaneously with stocks in newly chartered banks or canal companies. The buying public made no discrimination between them.

a specific requirement that any increase of capital would have to be approved by a formal vote; this is implicit in the history of other units. It suggests that the later typical limitation on size of corporations may have originated in the desire of the promoters to limit their brother participants, and not, as is commonly stated, to the fear of corporate size in general as an axiom of public policy. Thus, although the subscribers may not have chosen to pay for their shares all at once, they knew the approximate maximum. Flexibility of size in a quite different sense was, however, provided in the case of the Illinois-Wabash and the Georgia Yazoo articles; "bonus" shares could be distributed or sold where they would do the most good!

The Organization of Ownership

More and more formality appears in the structure of these bodies as they are examined chronologically. The informality characteristic of partnership or joint adventure disappears; increasingly formal prescription of meetings, reports, voting power, and the status of shareholders in relation to management either effectively duplicates the structure of chartered corporations then in operation or foreshadows some improvement in organization eventually adopted by the nineteenth century corporation. A great deal of inconsistency in details reflects experimentation; the groups interested were not certain of what the best mode of operation should be. They were living in an era of experimentation with larger-scale business operations. They did not have the century of experience possessed by English business men and lawyers to draw upon. Growing realization after 1790 that a quick turnover of capital could not be expected may well have led to more permanence of organization.

The principle of "one vote to one share"[30] is general among

[30] The controversy over the exact status of a shareholder runs through the history of English chartered companies for nearly two hundred years. Because of the influence of gilds and regulated companies such as the Mer-

these bodies, far more so than in early bank charters or public utility charters (canals and turnpikes). Research[31] may well bring out the fact that the prevalence of scaled-down voting power in charters was due to the general prejudice against corporations that was deep seated in the minds of the fervent believers in liberty and equality.[32] Such a restriction supposedly would weaken the power of those most able to turn them into agencies of evil. Business men as such perhaps had only a mild prejudice against the modern form of voting power,[33] but the

chant Adventurers, the idea that a shareholder in a company was primarily a *member* rather than the owner of a fractional part of the assets and earning power had a strong foothold until late in the seventeenth century (1 Scott, *op. cit.,* 156). According to this principle, everyone present at a meeting could have one vote regardless of his capital investment. There could also be subscribers to capital who were not voting members. Capital put in by a single member often grew disproportionately large. On the other hand, as such companies as the East India Company grew older, constant pressure was exerted to regulate voting power according to the amount a member had at stake. In these private associations for land ownership, the same conflict appears. Its influence was noted in the very early case of the Land and Silver Banks in Massachusetts in 1740 (*supra,* p. 60) where in the "democratic" Land Bank the scaled-down principle was used, while in the "aristocratic" Silver Bank the modern direct ratio was specified. The final emergence of the modern idea of one vote per share was late in coming, as compared to other characteristics of the modern corporation.

[31] Davis devotes only brief space to this problem in his *Essays* (Vol. 2, 323–324) and does not attempt to analyze the origin or strength of the rival conceptions. Dodd comments on it in several places, *Statutory Regulation,* 65–132. Certainly in the case of the first Bank of the United States, fear of dominance by foreign stockholders affected voting rules; this was true in English insurance and trading companies of the mid-eighteenth century, when Dutch holdings became very large. 1 Scott, *op. cit.,* 286.

[32] *Supra,* p. 67, and note 73.

[33] Hamilton, in writing the final draft of the articles for the Bank of New York in 1784, increased the ratio of voting power granted to large stockholders from the first draft. He believed in some scaling down of votes for higher holdings, however; *e.g.,* in the first Bank of the United States, and in the "Society for Establishing Useful Manufactures," or S.U.M. *Cf.* H. W. Domett, *History of Bank of New York* (published by the Bank, New York, 1888), 10.

prevalent political prejudice against large individual holdings would find some reflection among them, of course. The power of larger holders of bank stock to divert lending to themselves by their control over the election of directors was another specific cause for scaling down that applied only to banks. Certainly within fifty years the practice died away, and the modern principle is that found in the land companies. Another modern practice that was long forbidden by the common law,[34] proxy voting, was permitted by special provision in many of the agreements. The earliest example is the Illinois-Wabash agreement of 1774. Apparently it was not permissible in any other of the pre-1775 bodies, but it was an indispensable cog in the functioning of the later Ohio Company. Specific permission for the use of proxies at corporation meetings did not become common until well after 1800.[35]

Most important from a business standpoint, free transferability of shares or interests (in the case of agreements which were very near the partnership model) was an outstanding feature of practically every agreement studied. The only certain exception was the Mississippi Company, where a prior offer to the company or to existing members had to be made before a share could be sold. But this is in the practical sense a perfunctory barrier, and may well have existed in such groups as the first Ohio Company and the Dismal Swamp Adventurers, where the actual agreements are lacking. Furthermore, in several instances there was an exact mode set up for effecting the obviously ex-

[34] *Cf.* Angell and Ames, *Private Corporations* (Boston, 1846 edition), 95.

[35] The special practice found in many of these companies of permitting a sale of sub-shares while the original owner retained his vote had its appeal to speculators. This has disappeared in modern corporations. It reaches back to the old conception that a group of privileged persons made up a "company," and that late comers must take a figurative back seat in control, albeit they might share in profits.

pected sales and purchases. Thus the meeting of agents of the later Ohio Company, acting in effect as a stockholders' body would act today, established detailed rules for handling transfers.[36] In the New England Mississippi Company, there was a provision permitting free transfer of shares by simple endorsement, apparently without any entry on the books of the company. This is the ultimate in free transfer of shares. But almost exactly the modern procedure is found in the Illinois-Wabash agreement and in that of the Connecticut Land Company: a direct sale, but only recognizable when and as it was recorded on a transfer book and if attested by a notary (two witnesses were specifically required in the latter case, whereas one is needed at present). The North American Land Company and the Asylum Company both prescribed this method. In some of the earlier cases, there was a survival of the legal conception that a share in a concern owning land was itself real estate, transferable only by deed;[37] thus George Mason so treated his share in the first Ohio Company in his will, and George Washington apparently transferred his Dismal Swamp share by a deed.

Because the modern American corporation in the past generation has almost universally issued fully paid shares, there is a tendency to forget the fact that periodical assessments have been typical in both England and America[38] for three hundred years. In the twentieth century most English corporations still use this method of raising their capital, rather than calling for the whole

[36] The delegation of authority from shareholders to agents, and by them to directors, was simply an ingenious solution of the geographic difficulty in securing adequate participation by shareholders in the company's affairs; it does not represent any general attitude of the period, or a desire to imitate political government in business organization.

[37] The stubborn persistence of this legal archaism until well into the nineteenth century is familiar.

[38] Cf. Dodd, op. cit., 94, for the survival of the unlimited assessment idea in the carefully framed general incorporation law of 1830 in Massachusetts.

planned amount at the beginning of the enterprise. The American practice of a frequent issue of new shares, which are offered to existing shareholders on particularly favorable terms, is in effect a substitute for the assessment.

Many of the land companies used the assessment method for current expenses as well as for expansion of capital. There are no instances, however, of any maximum limit being placed upon the amount of these expense calls, as had begun to appear by this time in England.[39] But in spite of the fact that the practice of setting a maximum or par value on shares did not become a typical practice until the early nineteenth century, it was an important feature of the later Ohio Company, the North American Land Company, and the Asylum Company. In quite a few of the companies described here, assessments could only be levied by shareholders meeting as a group, which would place a check upon the issue of any excessive number of calls. Another check was the fact that few extraordinary expenses were encountered. An exception to this general situation is seen in the Connecticut Gore Land Company, where an extraordinary legal complication necessitated heavy expenditure, with resulting frequent levies on the members, many of whom defaulted.

Of course it must be recognized that a land company presented a situation considerably different from that of a manufacturing or trading enterprise. There was no current income, either for the reason that all the land was eventually to be divided among the shareholders (as in the case of the Fire Lands), or for the reason that sales in the earlier years were naturally small or at very low prices. There would be much more reason for retaining the conception of a share as simply a proportional claim on assets, subject to a similar burden of any expenses that might be incurred. In manufacturing enterprises par value of shares emerged early, because a certain amount of capital was to

[39] Holdsworth, 8 *H.E.L.*, 205.

be invested which would yield enough revenue almost immediately to cover operating expenses.

There is no clear demarcation in these companies between the idea that dividends were to be paid out of capital and the idea that current earnings should provide such payments. The sale of capital assets would provide earnings. It has been clearly shown by Scott that in the first twenty-five years of its existence the East India Company retained the notion that each period's capital (three years became the typical operating period) should be divided up—a "dividend"—and then re-subscribed to a new venture by the stockholders, should they so desire.[40] The same authority points out that dividends were frequently paid out of capital by enterprises formed either with or without charter.[41] The legal rule that dividends must not be paid out of capital, as a means of protecting creditors, did not emerge until the nineteenth century.[42] Obviously in the case of land companies such a rule would be meaningless, just as it is today in the case of corporations exploiting land or natural resources. Dividends were thus quite generally thought of as a share in the distribution of previously acquired assets, earned or purchased.

In getting enterprises under way, it is essential to assure the enforcement of promises to subscribe to the capital fund, or to pay later assessments. As soon as business enterprise is established on a basis of attracting capital from men whose primary activity continues to be centered elsewhere, this difficulty appears. It was a pressing problem to those land groups which had trouble in immediately consummating their plans. The modern American corporation has succeeded in eliminating this handicap by the device of full-paid shares.

In the Susquehannah Company there was provision for the

---

[40] 1 Scott, *op. cit.*, 280–281.   [41] *Ibid.*, 153–154.

[42] The charter of the Massachusetts Fire Insurance Company in 1795 provided that any losses of capital should be restored before dividends could be paid. Dodd, *op. cit.*, 82. In Pennsylvania the charter of the Farm-

forfeit and sale at auction of delinquent shares. In the Illinois-Wabash articles (pioneer exemplar of so many modern practices) there was a clause pledging such member's share or claim as security for later payments as demanded; failure to pay automatically forfeited the share. But there is a real distinction between an outright forfeit and a sale at auction[43]—in the latter case the holder might conceivably fare so well as to receive a cash return. Thus in the Ohio Company there was a difference of opinion as to which penalty should be applied. In the Connecticut Land Company the directors were given power to sell delinquent shares in order to pay assessments; the presumption was that any surplus would be transferred to the original owner. The phrase "sink a share in the Company" occurs in the records of the 1748 Ohio Company and the Dismal Swamp Adventurers; this apparently meant outright forfeit, thereby reducing the net number of outstanding shares or claims on the assets.[44]

Typical of the whole group is provision for definitely scheduled meetings, often by public notice, which is so characteristic of corporate enterprise. The provision that impersonal public notices must be given, or meetings scheduled in advance, marks a definite break away from the partnership concept. The articles of the Illinois-Wabash Company specified that four regular meetings should be held each year. The Mississippi Company, the later Ohio Company, the North American Land Company, and the Connecticut Land Company all provided for an annual meeting. In other early cases the "standing committee" was

ers and Mechanics Bank had a similar prohibitory clause against the impairment of capital. Pennsylvania *Laws,* 1808, Ch. 33 (1808 ed., p. 43). In New York, the United Insurance Company (headed by Nicholas Low) had such a clause in 1798. 4 N.Y. *Statutes* (1885 edition) 192.

[43] Davis calls attention to the confusion between the two in early charters. 2 *Essays,* 321. The legislative and judicial attitudes on these separable penalties will be examined below.

[44] The effect of such forfeits on the arithmetical divisions of assets is seen also in the later history of the Principio Company. *Supra,* Chapter III, page 55.

empowered to call meetings as needed (for example, the Susquehannah Company and the Military Adventurers). Another indication of departure from partnership methods was the requirement that meetings be advertised in newspapers for certain periods; later this was exactly the procedure of the majority of chartered turnpike, toll bridge, and canal companies. The 1748 Ohio Company, the Dismal Swamp Adventurers, and a number of others provided for such public notification, usually coupled with power in an executive or a standing committee to issue the call.

Regular reports to a body of shareholders who otherwise may be ill informed about the affairs of their company is a final feature of organization which distinguishes the corporate body from the private partnership. Here again the land companies duplicated corporate practice. Quarterly reports were required in the Illinois-Wabash and the later Ohio Companies, while annual statements from directors or standing committees were required elsewhere. A report was to be printed and mailed to each stockholder in the North American Land Company—the true modern practice. Participants in these enterprises were better served than the stockholders in such early corporations as the Bank of New York and the Bank of Albany, where only triennial reports were specified.[45] Davis, in characterizing charters before 1800, states that "reports . . . to the stockholders were sometimes specified."[46] It must be admitted, however, that after 1800 the requirements of annual reports became more general among chartered companies, *following* rather than *preceding* the practice of these unincorporated groups.

Delegation of Authority

Fundamentally requisite to the success of the corporate unit is the ability and power to concentrate authority in the hands of

[45] 3 N.Y. *Statutes* (1885 edition) 237, 364.
[46] 2 *Essays*, 323.

a few. This change comes early in the process of molding an organization that will be superior to the partnership. The joint adventure has this characteristic, while the syndicate is distinguished by the almost complete concentration of power which it permits. The earliest chartered corporations obviously possessed it. It is therefore of less importance here to stress the fact that such concentration of authority was almost universal in the land groups, ranging from the crude device of appointing agents possessing power of attorney to the modern device of electing directors or officers with full authority.[47]

One allied business problem was the question of an incentive for effort on the part of these nearly independent officers. The danger of laziness, chicanery, or incompetence on the part of managers was, at the end of the eighteenth century, an argument against any and all chartered bodies or large associations.[48] The evidence available on this point is mixed. Certainly the leaders of the 1748 Ohio Company, the Military Adventurers, and the Mississippi Company did little to further the interests of their groups; General Lyman (perhaps excusably) had a particularly poor record as leader. But the number of aggressive, hard-working leaders is much greater: in the Susquehannah, the Grand Ohio, the Indiana, the Illinois-Wabash, the Transylvania, the later Ohio, the Connecticut Land, and the Connecticut Gore Companies, they were certainly present. The North American Land Company and the Asylum Company were crippled at the start in securing leadership by their close connection with Morris' and Nicholson's misfortunes.

The modern large business unit (whether or not incorporated) has been criticized as ineffective and even dangerous because it discourages the small investor from active participation or interest. A good deal of this criticism rests on a misconception of the

[47] The most interesting variation in the group examined here was "Castorland," where the managing director was to hold office *permanently*.

[48] A doctrine fostered by Adam Smith and other early economic writers.

true purpose of a corporation and the function of stockholders; democracy may well be an alien conception in the business corporation. Such apathy was clearly present in these early associations —and it must be accepted as emphasizing still further their corporate nature! George Mason's remarks on the difficulty of securing a quorum for a meeting of the relatively small Ohio Company are illuminating.[49] Washington lost track of Dismal Swamp affairs, and only a handful of men were interested in the later careers of the Susquehannah, the Illinois-Wabash, and the Connecticut Gore Companies. The Ohio Company was an exception to prove the rule; over a period of nearly a decade there was active, continuous interest on the part of a substantial group of agents and members. In 1791 there was even a stockholders' investigation of the acts of its directors and officers, a mode of discipline that is all too little employed in the twentieth century.

Risk

The limitation of liability is of course a primary aim of modern business groups in choosing the chartered form. But, curiously, it seemed of little importance in the eighteenth century except in cases where risk was unusually great, as in banking (because of the issue of notes to an amount greater than the paid-in capital) and, obviously, in insurance.[50] The quest for charters to authorize canal, bridge, turnpike, and water projects was due primarily to the need for a grant of semi-public authority. Considerations of public policy affected, therefore, the question of liability as much or more than business policy. Not until after the War of 1812 was there any widespread demand among business classes for limited liability.

[49] *Supra,* Chapter IV, note 14.

[50] DuBois, *The English Business Company after the Bubble Act* (New York, 1938), pp. 93–94, confirms this slight emphasis placed on the liability factor prior to 1785. Davis' remark that it was a "principal object" of incorporation applies only to banks and insurance companies. 2 *Essays,* 317.

Attraction of Capital

To make certain that new capital may be continuously secured is another prominent function of the modern corporation. It is correspondingly important to stress the success with which a majority of these land companies secured the amounts which they solicited from the investing public of the day. Their needs were not large by modern standards, but neither were the corporations of the period. Banks in several cases had large capital funds, but the monopoly character of banking and the rapid growth of business gave them a particular advantage.[51] Otherwise chartered and unchartered bodies were on an equal footing in this regard.

Duration

Uninterrupted life is a final objective that is of business importance. Here the association ranked ahead of the corporation, for the existence of many land groups was prolonged beyond the five, ten, or twenty-year periods to which corporations were increasingly limited after 1795.[52] The Ohio Company and the North American Land Company remained entities for over seventy-five years. The New England Mississippi Company and the even less formal Yazoo Companies received indemnity nearly twenty years after their formation. Groups were active on behalf of the Military Adventurers and the Indiana and Illinois-Wabash Companies nearly twenty-five years after their organization. The considerations of public policy which affected the relative status of association and corporation in this respect will be considered in the next chapter.[53]

[51] Davis points out that the majority of chartered concerns before 1800 raised less than $50,000 and that the only bodies with more than $500,000 were banks and insurance companies. 2 *ibid.*, 291.

[52] The Connecticut Land Company articles provided that its land should be held in trust "as long as necessary"; only legal obstacles in the way of a perpetual trust could limit its term of existence.

[53] More might be said of the relative possibility for amendments to the

STRENGTH OF THE ASSOCIATION PRINCIPLE

An evaluation of the association need not rest alone on the evidence which has been summarized. But it was pointed out in Chapter I that land speculation presented the first arena wherein could be tried out the notions concerning organization which men were evolving. They wished to go outside the pale of strict partnership, yet saw no need for securing the special sanction of a charter. Elsewhere a similar necessity did not arise so urgently. In shipping, private banking, and the private underwriting of insurance, diligent search could undoubtedly uncover some few illustrations prior to 1800 of the same type of companies which merchandised land. Lack of space here prevents any thorough marshaling of the diverse evidence which exists.[54] One or two specific examples will suffice to indicate that in entirely distinct fields the same developments were occurring.[55]

From W. R. Bagnall's study of the textile industry[56] it is possible to assemble numerous examples of the method of organization used in the cotton and woolen undertakings from 1780 to 1810. Bagnall quotes or refers to a large number of original documents, permitting a broader view of the attitude of business men

articles during the life of an enterprise. The material, however, is too scanty for any generalizations. The controversy over the 1806 changes in the North American Land Company, which amounted to reorganization, is practically the only illustrative case. The same company's provision for a year's delay in voting on amendments was also unique. No corporation charter of the period included anything similar to it.

[54] Public written evidence of charters is obviously more likely to have been preserved; researchers, furthermore, have hitherto mistakenly considered corporate activity to be the whole story of progress.

[55] DuBois, *op. cit.*, 230 *ff.*, has found that in England mining and insurance furnished fertile fields for experimentation with the unincorporated company in this same 1750–1800 period; without the special opportunity of land speculation the same familiarity with this form of organization was reached by 1820 or 1825 in England as in the United States. Hunt presents evidence that in the 1824 "boom" nearly one thousand unincorporated companies offered shares to the public. *Development of the Business Corporation in England,* 45–48.

[56] *Textile Industries of the United States* (Boston, 1893).

in these pioneer industries than would be possible from any analysis of documents relating to a single enterprise, as has been done in several instances.[57]

First, in approximately fifty cases where Bagnall refers to articles of partnership and to transfers of interest, there is overwhelming evidence that even the smallest groups in this industry regarded their interests as freely transferable.[58] The mode of transfer was usually by formal deed, inasmuch as the real property involved (land and mill buildings) was regarded as the principal value inherent in a share. Although transfers were made most frequently to one or another of the small groups which organized and directed the mills, there apparently were no severe restrictions on the persons who might be permitted to purchase shares.[59]

Secondly, Bagnall's cases demonstrate that there was delegation of authority within the group, with elections of single managers or small boards of directors. In very few instances in this industry was there any incorporation until after 1810. The exceptions to this rule have been frequently studied and described as though they were the most important enterprises of the period.[60] The incorporated companies were decidedly *not* the leaders in the early period of textile experimentation, as Bagnall's record amply demonstrates.

[57] For example, S. M. Ames, "A Virginia Business Man," 3 *Journal of Economic and Business History,* 407.

[58] The Coventry Manufacturing Company (Bagnall, *op. cit.,* 406–409) is the best example. Although its form was that of a partnership, it clearly evidences kinship with the land company type of association. It was specified that there should always be sixteen shares ("The concern shall always be holden in sixteenths," Article V), and the term of life was set at ten years. In 1809, these shares had a book value of $3,832.50 each. Later the number of shares was increased to twenty-six; in 1865 a charter was granted to a successor company with 1,800 shares. This cotton company was extremely profitable, and had a continuous existence of sixty years as an unincorporated association.

[59] Bagnall, *op. cit.,* 217–219, 453, 546–550, 564, 589.

[60] For example, Ware, *Early New England Cotton Manufacture* (Boston, 1925), *passim.*

In the next chapter incidental mention will be made of numerous banking groups organized *without* charters that flourished in nearly all the seaboard states until the end of the War of 1812. Although mining was of much less importance in America than it was in England in this period, a number of examples in this traditionally fertile field for group enterprise can be discovered. The record of one project for the exploitation of the first known anthracite coal deposits in eastern Pennsylvania in 1791–1792, the Lehigh Coal Mine Company, may be briefly mentioned. It has survived to the present day through an incorporated successor company.

Michael Hillegas, first treasurer of the United States, was the leader in its organization. Forty shares of $200 each were subscribed by a small group, of which ten shares were given to one Jacob Weiss, owner of the land.[61] The shares were to be paid for in three installments of $50, $50, and $100. The failure of a subscriber to pay the installments promptly would cause a forfeiture and sale by auction to outside parties of the shares involved. The members of the group were to choose a president, eight managers, and a treasurer. Each shareholder would be entitled to one vote, irrespective of the number of shares he held. A bond was to be required from the treasurer, and ordinary rules and by-laws were to be passed. All records of the company were to be open to inspection at any time. The president and managers

---

[61] The articles are contained in a crude prospectus, reprinted in "First Coal Mining Company of the Lehigh Region," 39 *Pennsylvania Magazine of History and Biography,* 170–175.

Each $200 subscribed as the original price of thirty shares, or $6,000, was to be paid to Weiss, in addition to the stock he received. By the articles, he was required to issue to each subscriber a certificate of "stock" or interest as soon as $50 had been paid, which carried with it the prescribed voting power. Upon completion of the last payment, he was to issue a deed to the several subscribers for their share in the property. In case the property did not come up to his representations, the articles specifically provided that there should be a return of the money collected. Actual mining was undertaken, but was pursued only intermittently until after the War of 1812.

were to have full power and authority over the property and could draw on the treasurer for expenditures. For operating capital, the articles specified that a contribution of $10 per share could be levied, but that any further assessment must be voted on at an annual meeting. This levy was in addition to the original subscription, which was for the capital investment.[62] Here was a complete business mechanism, established without the aid of any state-granted charter.

It may be noted finally that in situations where the limited partnership came to be used in the next century, such as private banking and large-scale merchandising, the simple partnership was also undergoing change. For example, late in 1801 Alexander Hamilton proposed to Oliver Wolcott, his protégé and successor as Secretary of the Treasury, a plan for the latter's entry into private business.[63] The Oliver Wolcott Company would be organized with a total capital of $100,000, in shares of $100 each. One-tenth of each subscription would be paid in immediately, and, to encourage payment of the balance, 7 per cent would be paid on payments above the required one-tenth, prior to other distribution of earnings (suggestive of preferred stock). Wolcott and two others would "form a board of direction," but Wolcott alone would have the power of contracting. He would receive a salary of $1,500 and an equal share in profits according to his subscription. Hamilton suggested that the firm act as (a) an agency for land and stock sales (brokerage); (b) a factor in

[62] In 1817 another unincorporated association known as the Lehigh Coal Company, succeeded the original body. Since canal properties were also acquired at that time, it was found desirable to secure a charter in order to obtain rights of eminent domain—again a *legal* and not a *business* reason for seeking a charter. The charter, granted in a special act of 1822 by the Pennsylvania legislature, created the Lehigh Coal and Navigation Company. The bonds of this company, nearly 115 years of age, are now listed on the New York Stock Exchange and its stock on the Philadelphia Stock Exchange. The directors, by the terms of the charter, are still known as "managers."

[63] Alexander Hamilton, 7 *Works* (2nd Lodge edition, New York, 1904), 603–604.

sales of commodities; (c) a purchaser and seller in the auctions which were then growing in prominence in New York business life; and (d) a lender on endorsed paper to responsible merchants (private banking). He added that he "should be willing to become a partner for from $5,000 to $10,000." The suggested character of the firm is a tribute to Hamilton as a creative lawyer.[64]

But even without reference to these enterprises in other fields, the conclusion cannot be escaped after detailed inquiry into the structure of the land companies that here was evolving no simple process of tacking on to the partnership whimsical variations. Needing a form of organization suitable for specific purposes, business leaders were moved to create it and to disregard entirely the legal doctrine that nothing between a partnership and a chartered body could exist.

[64] The fruition of Hamilton's suggestion appears in the *Wolcott MSS.*, library of the Connecticut Historical Society, Vol. 53, no paging. Articles of agreement were dated February 3, 1803, but Hamilton was not included. James Watson, Moses Rogers, Archibald Gracie, and W. W. Woolsey each contributed $15,000, and each would receive 7 per cent interest. Wolcott was to put in a corresponding amount "at convenience"; his salary was set at $3,000. He possessed full powers of management, and was to render an annual report, although the other four were to "help and advise" him, and the books were to be open to them at any time. The activities of the firm followed Hamilton's suggestions closely. One member could withdraw at the end of four, six, or eight years, or a majority could vote to dissolve at any time. Obviously partnership influence was still strong, but in important respects the agreement suggests the later limited partnership or small joint stock association.

In 1805 Wolcott rendered an annual report, the tone of which is much more suggestive of a report by a president to his stockholders than of one partner to others. The project had not been and, according to later references, was not later successful. *Ibid.*

VII

CORPORATIONS VERSUS ASSOCIATIONS:
LEGISLATIVE VAGARIES

THE history of corporations in England for six centuries pro-
vides countless examples of the jealousy of the sovereign
state toward the assumption of a corporate status by bodies of
its subjects, and a reluctance to grant such a status without de-
liberation.[1] The state, to which the structure of feudalism was of
great fiscal importance, feared the organized and deathless religious bodies which could undermine its foundations. Unincorporated craft gilds were forced to pay the costs of a charter at the
behest of Crown advisors anxious to subordinate them to an or-
derly city government in London and elsewhere,[2] and even
where bodies possessed charters the sovereign, into modern times,
was fearful of the power that was consequent upon such grants.[3]

But in the case of commercial bodies an opposed influence intermittently appeared to combat this natural political jealousy.
Participation in the great commercial struggle with Holland and
France made the corporation-haters pause. Every weapon that
could be used in the duels with these two great opponents must
be welcomed. The East India Company was to be regarded as
such a prop, albeit it was the object of interminable Parliamentary attacks and the subject of violent pamphlets and lawsuits.[4]
Patriotic desire to promote commerce and flay the enemy clashed
with and overrode inborn jealousy of monopoly and so perpetu-
ated economic power.

Thus, because of long-continued warfare during the seventeenth century, the commercial corporation happened to achieve

[1] *Cf.* Holdsworth, 3 *H.E.L.*, 475–479.   [2] *Cf. supra*, pp. 15–16.
[3] *City of London Case*, 8 State Trials 1039.
[4] These opposed points of view are strikingly presented in the arguments of counsel in *East India Company* v. *Sandys*, 10 State Trials 371.

relatively high favor. But it became too popular, and in the period 1689–1720 private groups took advantage of that popularity to abuse charter privileges and to act as corporations, without legal sanction. Retribution came in the form of the Bubble Act and a long period when Parliament was wary of granting charters except for relatively specialized undertakings (for example, the canal companies after 1750). The effect of the Bubble Act was far greater than that of most similar "reforms."[5] But the business class came to realize that no great loss had been sustained; charters, though necessary for certain undertakings where some special privilege was involved, were a needless luxury. In England, and after 1750 in this country, a perfect substitute was being molded. Legislative jealousy was being circumvented.

The newly independent American States thus inherited a curious composite of attitudes toward the chartered corporation. From a political standpoint, corporations were to be feared as potential rivals of the state in the exercise of sovereign power. Local government units as well as commercial organizations have ever since felt the weight of this suspicion.[6] But in so far as they reflected the commercial aggressiveness of an independent and ambitious population, legislatures wished to foster business corporations in the interest of national strength. Charters received consideration on that ground, if on no other. Where the state and the business leaders of the moment both recognized advantages in the possession of a charter, corporate charters were readily forthcoming. Turnpike construction best illustrates this agreement of the interested groups on a common solution.

But, as in England after the Bubble Act, many groups who might have been expected to seek charters often failed to do so.

[5] *Cf. supra,* p. 62.

[6] Antagonism between great cities and their parent state governments, and our attitude toward railroads and more recently toward public utilities, are phases of this long-continued fear.

Of the post-Revolution land companies, as has already been stressed, none asked for a charter; the effective substitutes described in the preceding chapters could be set up instead. It is obvious that the advantages of legal incorporation seemed far less clear to the eighteenth century business man than economic historians have hitherto supposed. The state thus was permitted to turn its head aside and avoid the question: to grant or not to grant? Furthermore, to permit freedom for the business entrepreneur to establish his own group organization fitted in with the growing philosophy of freedom in enterprise, so recently bolstered in popularity by a successful revolution.

Conflict over Banking Privileges

All might have proceeded smoothly if both parties to the optional charter contract had seen eye to eye in all instances. Public utilities would have been chartered, and purely private undertakings would have avoided asking for charters and established private associations instead. But a serious conflict arose in respect to the assumption of banking privileges by such private groups. The issue of paper money and the provision of deposit banking facilities increased rapidly in importance after 1785.

From the Colonial period and from England came the attitude that such privileges belonged solely to the state to delegate only if it saw fit to do so, and only by special sanction could they be exercised by non-chartered groups. Consequently banking charters were regarded as a great privilege, to be awarded only with discrimination. Strong groups in legislatures before 1800 opposed all banking grants.[7] A later compromise with this opposition was the common practice of either permitting the state to own a substantial portion of the stock or paying into the state

[7] *Cf.* Starnes, *Sixty Years of Branch Banking in Virginia* (New York, 1931), 38–92; Davis, 2 *Essays*, 34–108, sets forth the facts regarding charters granted prior to 1800.

treasury an outright bonus, in recognition of the charter's value.[8] The long tradition of central government control over currency as an earmark of sovereignty made the states particularly jealous of letting banking corporations assume powers that were not carefully restricted. Charters were to be given only after inquiry, and were given in the spirit of delegating a sovereign power to a special group in the community. This was the medieval conception of the charter, derived from the Church's attitude toward its creatures, and from the English Crown's long struggle to maintain itself as the fount of all exceptional jurisdictional rights. It is the attitude which we have revived in the twentieth century with respect to banks, insurance companies, small loan companies—where the public interest is supposedly the primary basis for the restricted number of charter grants, not the wishes of the group making application. It is important here to appraise the strength of this attitude in 1800–1825, when the doctrine of free incorporation as the right of everyone was gaining ground so rapidly.

Legislators' fear of private associations in the field of banking has never been satisfactorily described, nor has it been recognized as prevalent long before Jackson's time and before any general acts authorizing bank incorporations appeared.[9] The type of business leader described in modern slang as the "insider" of course accepted the state's jealous attitude toward bank charters as in his own best interest. Free entry into shipping, importing, and land speculation he welcomed. But he was glad to have one field fenced off in such a manner that profitable privileges (and banking prior to 1830 was surely a high-profit enterprise)

[8] For example, the Merchants Bank (1805) and the Bank of America (1812) charters both provided for contributions to the New York school fund. Similar requirements were imposed in Massachusetts.

[9] The anti-monopoly attitude toward bank privileges has been almost universally linked with Andrew Jackson's reign by historians and economists. Thus D. R. Dewey in his "State Banking before the Civil War," 9 *National Monetary Commission Studies,* devotes only a few pages (143–151) to the earlier manifestations of this sentiment.

once secured could be exercised to the exclusion of others. Not so the average business man. As early as 1784 the attitude erroneously identified by historians as Jacksonian was clearly existent: entry into the banking field should be as free to all as entry into retail trade; restriction by the state as a supposed protection of its sovereignty simply led to dangerous monopolies.[10]

Massachusetts was the first state to set banking apart as a spe-

[10] A short delineation of these two opposed points of view, which has been entirely neglected by banking historians, is to be found in an exchange of arguments between James Wilson and Gouverneur Morris on one side, and Messrs. Myers, Fisher, Ingersoll, and Bradford on the other, before a committee of the Pennsylvania legislature early in 1784.

An application for a charter establishing a Bank of Pennsylvania was before the legislature; Wilson and Morris as counsel for the Bank of North America were opposing the grant. Wilson argued in answer to the charge of monopoly that there was "only so much capital to be used, why distribute it" between two banks and so reduce its usefulness. His notes on the arguments of his opponents are of great interest here. They argued that monopoly was dangerous, and that Congress was not bound to leave the Bank of North America as the only bank, nor was Pennsylvania. Bradford argued that two banks would be friendly since "the State of Banks like that of Nature is a State of Peace" (an obvious result of Rousseau-Montesquieu influence). Fisher, a prominent lawyer, attacked the Bank of North America as not having enough reserves to care for all borrowers, and as the "Father of usurious contracts." He argued that two banks would lower interest rates because of competition, as had been the case in Edinburgh. Sergeant, the last opponent to be heard by the committee, argued that the right to secure a charter when demanded is an inherent right of the citizens of Pennsylvania. This last—apparently considered the most telling argument—is extremely important as upholding the "popular" point of view stressed herein.

Wilson replied that the petitioners were simply seeking to share the monopoly they dubbed odious, and that in any case the Bank of North America was under the supervision of the Superintendent of Finance. He then said that the new group "may try the Experiment *without a charter*" if they chose (italics added). He then stressed the value of having only one large bank in maintaining national credit abroad.

This exchange of opinion took place a year and a half before the repeal of the Bank of North America charter—and nearly fifty years before Jackson's message on the charter of the Second Bank (1832); the legislature passed the competing charter in spite of Morris' and Wilson's efforts. Wilson's notes on this hearing are in 2 *Wilson MSS.*, 92–95, library of the Historical Society of Pennsylvania.

cial business to be entered only with sovereign approval. In 1799 she forbade any inhabitant to join any unchartered association formed for banking purposes.[11] The notes of any such group were made void, and any citizen possessing such notes could recover up to $1,000 on an action of debt, of which one-half would go to the state. In the succeeding decade, New Hampshire, Rhode Island, New York, Pennsylvania, Maryland, and Virginia took similar action of greater or less severity.[12] The circumstances of the legislation in New York, Pennsylvania, and Virginia deserve some further comment.

The political warfare between parties in New York after 1798 had as one of its many phases the 1804 restriction act.[13] The success of Burr and his associates in 1799 in securing the banking clause in the perpetual charter of the Manhattan Company had aroused the ambitions of a group of Federalist leaders in New York to establish a third bank. The clamor for charters had disappeared after the panic days of March, 1792,[14] but seemed to reappear under the stimulus of this jealousy. A plan for the Merchants Bank was the result, put forward in 1803. Alexander Hamilton was retained as counsel, and obviously set out to draft articles for the new organization which would permit it to operate for a considerable period before a charter was received. He inserted a notable clause designed to limit the liability of the stockholders for the bank's obligations (primarily its notes) during this expected interim.[15] Whether or not he was in advance of

---

[11] *Mass. Acts*, 1799, Ch. 2.   [12] *Cf*. Dewey, *op. cit.*, 143–148.

[13] The surrounding circumstances are set forth in Fox, *Decline of Aristocracy in the Politics of New York* (New York, 1919), 61–70.

[14] The grandiose plans of January, 1792, for a "Million Bank," *i.e.,* with $1,000,000 capital, are suggestive of the 1929 peak of speculation; they came to naught, but in the various states more bank charters dated from the winter of 1791–1792 than from any other year prior to 1800. *Cf.* Davis, 1 *Essays*, 283, and vol. 2, 333.

[15] The preamble to the articles (reprinted in Philip G. Hubert, *Merchants National Bank, 1803–1903* [New York, 1903], 3–8, and in Hamilton, 7 *Works* [2nd Lodge edition, New York, 1904]), which were drawn up by Hamilton, included the following descriptive phrase: "We the sub-

the received common law on this point will be examined below. Certainly from a practical angle he was simply repeating more elaborately his own procedure in the Bank of New York situation twenty years before.[16] To have done so argues that he be-

scribers have formed a company or limited partnership." In the first article the capital was stated as $1,250,000 to be divided into 50,000 shares. Two hundred and fifty thousand dollars was to be paid at once, the balance to be called up on fifteen days' notice. In the second article it was stated that the bank would have sixteen directors, of whom one would be elected president by the group as a whole. The first directors were named in the articles, with provision for annual elections thereafter. To make loans, approval of five members of the board would be required. All of them must be stockholders. Proxies were to be permitted in voting, and the stockholders could exercise the privilege of cumulative voting for candidates for the board of directors.

Seven more articles provided the typical framework of a corporate structure of this period. There was one exception in the tenth article, which provided that every retiring shareholder "shall *ipso facto* cease to be a member of this company" and that each incoming shareholder would by the same token automatically become a member. This was necessary to avoid the implication that stockholders might be treated as partners, subject to some procedure of approval before they could acquire their full rights.

In the eleventh article is found the very important clause that distinguishes this project from almost all others of the period: "It is hereby expressly and explicitly declared to be the object and intention of the persons who associate under the style or title of the Merchants Bank, that the joint stock or property of the said company (exclusive of dividends) shall alone be responsible for the debts and engagements of the said company. And it is further declared that no person, who shall or may deal with this company . . . shall on any pretense whatever have recourse against the separate property of any present or future member of this company . . . and all suits to be brought against this company shall be brought against the president for the time being." In further detail it was provided that any judgments recovered against the president would be paid by the company out of the joint stock or capital. In Article 14, it was provided that the foregoing Article 11 should be printed in full in all customers' bank books and that no contract entered into by the bank would be valid unless this article were printed in full as part of the contract. Any contract inadvertently issued without the clause was expressly voided. Depositors and creditors were thus thoroughly "on notice" as to the limited liability of shareholders.

[16] As soon as the monopoly of the Bank of North America in New York state had expired in 1783 with the ending of war, it was proposed to issue notes through a similar bank, based on land security. In March of 1784, Hamilton had written to his brother-in-law, John Church, opposing

lieved such clauses could and would be effective in actual suits by creditors.

The restriction act was originally aimed specifically at the

the idea. *Cf.* H. W. Domett, *History of Bank of New York,* 8. Just previous to this time a group of merchants had held one or two meetings for the purpose of establishing a specie bank and had written some preliminary articles of agreement. Hamilton was asked in April to write the final draft of the articles, at a time when an effort to secure a charter was being planned.

The articles provided for capital of $500,000 in shares of $500 each and a board of thirteen directors elected annually, who must be stockholders (Domett, *op. cit.,* 11–15). In the provisions for voting power, it was specified that holders of more than ten shares would have no additional votes, but Hamilton altered the clause to permit an additional vote for each five shares in excess of this amount. Other provisions were typical of corporate organization in this period. Somewhat exceptional were the strict penalties against directors, who could be removed on the grounds of fraud, expelled from the company, and lose their shares by forfeiture. Proxy voting was permitted.

Article XVI provided that "No stockholder shall be accountable to any individual or to the public for money lodging in the bank for a greater sum than the amount of his stock." In the next month, May, 1784, anonymous subscribers wrote that Article XVI "presupposes the granting of a charter; for, without it this article could not take effect, should the subscription money be at present paid in. The stockholders become . . . bankers, and every man is liable" (Domett, *op. cit.,* 18). It is well known that the bank started business in spite of this attitude, and for nearly eight years operated as an association, apparently under the advice of Hamilton. Hamilton's influence was responsible for the selection of Jeremiah Wadsworth as the first president. In June, 1785, Hamilton wrote to Wadsworth urging him to accept the office, remarking that "there is a much better prospect of a Charter with the present Legislature than there has been with any former one"—a bad prophecy. *Wadsworth MSS.,* Connecticut Historical Society, unclassified.

In the 1789 petition to the legislature, the primary reason cited for the need of a charter was that many men had refused to become stockholders so long as the bank stood on "the footing of a private company, in which each member is supposed to be personally responsible for all the engagements entered into" (Domett, *op. cit.,* 32). When the charter was granted in April of 1791, subscriptions immediately increased, and by August the capital had grown to $900,000 from the previous figure of $318,250. A large amount of new notes were issued during the summer and fall of 1791. Although there was no clear limitation of liability in the case of this first bank, its leaders thought of it in other respects as a normal business unit able to function effectively while awaiting legislative approval. They

Merchants Bank.[17] In the charter which was finally granted to the bank in 1806, the preamble included the phrase "to save them from the operation of the Act to restrain unincorporated banking associations."[18] Between the passage of the act and the final grant of a charter, the legislature received many protests from those who felt the blanket provisions of the act would interfere with the ordinary issue of short-term obligations in trade among importers and others. It was made clear by the legislature that individual merchants or small partnerships could continue to issue notes of definite maturity as they had been doing.[19] Such issues, in reality for currency purposes, continued to be common until the detailed prohibition of 1818 which said that "no person, association of persons, or body corporate, except such bodies corporate as are expressly authorized by law" should receive deposits or put notes of any kind into circulation.[20] Violations continued to reflect the business attitude that banking should be left open to private groups and may well have discouraged the legislators from continuing to restrict banking privileges to a few select corporations. But an even more potent cause of the ultimate repeal in 1837 of the restraining act was the serious mismanagement of many of the "expressly authorized" banking corporations. In that year the field was thrown open to unincorporated bodies who could meet certain uniform requirements.

Pennsylvania in 1808 prohibited banks chartered in other states from entering the banking field. In the same year an act made all members of unincorporated banking associations specifically liable for debts. In 1810 she went further and passed a

simply used caution in increasing their liabilities by note issues in the interval. Allan Nevins' more recent *History of the Bank of New York* (New York, 1934) does not add to Domett's treatment on the above points.

[17] N.Y. *Acts,* 1804, Ch. CXVII. One clause exempted the Merchants Bank by name for one year, and allowed the same period for any other "association, institution or company" to liquidate its affairs.

[18] N.Y. *Acts,* 1805, Ch. XLIII.

[19] *Cf.* references to these protests in *Warner* v. *Beers,* 23 Wendell 103.

[20] *Cf.* Dewey, *op. cit.,* p. 144.

restriction act aimed at voluntary associations, prohibiting them from issuing notes or receiving deposits.[21] Because this act was so generally violated, particularly in the first two war years, and because there was an acute scarcity of currency which would be heightened if such groups were forced to recall their note issues, the legislature in 1814 tacitly recognized its error by passing a general law providing for inspection and supervision of all bodies issuing circulating notes, whether or not they were chartered. In effect this was the principle adopted in New York twenty-three years later.

Virginia had the same difficulty in enforcing her 1805 law making it unlawful to receive or pass a note of any unchartered bank. This had been passed primarily to protect the monopoly of the Bank of Virginia, established in 1804. After 1811 numerous small unchartered banks grew up, especially in the western part of the state, in technical violation of this law. In 1816 thirteen were known to exist, and a more stringent law was passed declaring them to be illegal and setting August 31, 1818, as the date when they must finally liquidate.[22]

The effort of leading legislatures to exclude free enterprise in one important direction was thus astutely resisted.[23] Banking before 1832 was certainly not the exclusive privilege of a Bank

[21] This legislation is best reviewed in *Myers* v. *Irwin,* 2 S. & R. 368 (1816). *Cf.* also *infra,* Chapter VIII. Dewey's summary in his *State Banking* is incomplete.

[22] For discussion of this episode, *cf.* Starnes, *Sixty Years of Branch Banking in Virginia, op. cit.,* pp. 35, 39, 59. One of the group became involved in litigation (*U.S.* v. *Saline Bank of Virginia,* 1 Peters 100), so that provisions of its articles of agreement survive. The fourth article of association was quoted as follows (*ibid.,* at 102): "No stockholder shall be answerable in his person, or individual property, for any contract of the said company, or for any losses, deficiencies, or defalcations of the capital stock of said company; but the whole of said capital stock . . . and nothing more, shall be answerable for the legal and equitable demands against the said company."

[23] The historical thread of business men's resistance to the grant of exclusive privileges by charter is a beautifully complete and continuous one, only ending with the triumph of the general-incorporation principle. The

of the United States and the tight little group of state-chartered banks; there were guerrilla attacks from unincorporated bodies long before Jackson rose to slay the dragon of privilege. So it was elsewhere: insurance charters did not bring a cessation of private underwritings, nor did textile company charters encompass some of the strongest pioneers in that manufacture. Legislatures trod carefully elsewhere than in banking. Either they kept hands off and permitted the unincorporated group to function unchecked, or they granted charters in special fields freely enough so that the element of monopoly was lacking.[24]

Chartered Corporations circa 1800

Although it is important to deny that corporations were the chief force in business development in this period,[25] it is none the less necessary to examine the legislative conception of a corporate body, in the decades just prior to and after 1800. What privileges were offered in the cases where charters were available? Could a corporation claim, as a business instrument, any clear advantages? Or must it confess to serious handicaps in the eyes of those business men who had the choice of seeking a charter or proceeding as the land companies had done? Except in banking, and in the fields where the public utility principle was

rise of unincorporated gilds (*supra*, p. 15), the arguments of Pollexfen and Treby in *East India Company* v. *Sandys* (10 State Trials 371), and the arguments of President Bradish of the New York Senate in 1839 (*infra*, p. 293) are all component strands in different centuries.

Nathan Appleton, prominent representative of New England industry in Congress and elsewhere, wrote in 1831: "The business of banking should be open to as free a competition as *any other branch* of commercial business [italics added]; there should be nothing like monopoly, or exclusiveness about it. . . . A monopoly of banking is the most dangerous of monopolies." *Examination of the Banking System of Massachusetts* (Boston, 1831), 43–44.

[24] The turnpike charters, prolific in all states, illustrate this solution. In addition, the regulation of charges and profits, which was also prescribed in canal charters, further offset the monopoly element present in the banking grants.

[25] *Supra*, p. 61.

emerging, the choice was perfectly unhampered. *Laissez faire* was the rule.[26] What the association afforded has already been summarized. There remains to be surveyed in some detail the competing corporation as it was legislatively conceived toward the end of the eighteenth century and in the first quarter of the nineteenth.

Obviously the bases upon which business men, then as now, judged the two alternatives overlap any specifically legal criteria.[27] For example, freedom from a constant threat of unwanted dissolution is highly important in a business sense. How fundamental free transferability becomes has been frequently adverted to in this study. So also with concentration of power. Town meeting democracy, or the give-and-take of partners' meetings, are hardly suited to a large-scale enterprise whose participants have many other interests and have invested partly *because* they can be free from day-to-day responsibility. Lastly, curtailment of liability is attractive to the "side-issue" investor, but it was of less importance in this early period than it is today. Status before the courts would have received the least consideration, but the particular problem of suits by the organization against one of its members was of very real business importance.[28]

An estimate of the corporation's attractiveness at this period must rest first upon a detailed survey of a typical charter of the period. Unquestionably entitled to first place among the early charters that are available is the one granted *in duo* by the legis-

[26] Actual expense of hearings and attorneys to appear before a legislative committee may seem to have been relatively small by modern standards; but there was the ever-present danger that the charter, if of especial importance, could only be snared if bribery were employed. The Yazoo case and the 1812 Bank of America scandal in New York are familiar examples.

[27] The qualities distinguished as attractive in the business sense were: ease of formation; effective internal organization; easy delegation of authority; limitation of liability; ability to attract capital; and uninterrupted existence, or perpetuity.

[28] Because of the necessity of enforcing subscriptions to delinquent capital stock.

latures of Maryland and Virginia to the Potomac Company, in 1784. It was earlier than any other important instrument; it was sought by a large and representative body of business men, headed by George Washington; it involved collaboration by two legislatures; and it was the culmination of long agitation for a project of great significance to the young nation.[29]

There were twenty-one articles in the charter, which by current standards was prolix. Six of the articles, however, dealt with the public utility aspects of the enterprise—granting the right of eminent domain, the imposition of tolls, and agreements regarding the potential water power. The first article was simply a "whereas" declaration of need and purpose. The twentieth provided that each state should subscribe to fifty shares, and the twenty-first voided all existing statutes which might be in conflict. The twelve remaining articles dealt with actual organization, in extraordinary detail.

An elaborate procedure of securing subscriptions was outlined, with rules for dealing with over- or under-subscription. Getting under way was, in other words, much more complicated than if the project had been in the hands of a private association. Voting power was one vote per share up to ten shares, then a vote for each additional five shares owned. Proxy voting was permitted, and shares were freely transferable but only by deed and subsequent registry on the transfer books. Four directors and a president were to be elected for three-year terms, but they were removable for cause at any annual meeting. They were to take an oath of loyalty, and were given definite, prescribed powers, broad enough to insure freedom of action. Calls for

[29] A canal which would eliminate the falls and rapids in the Potomac had long been recognized as the most feasible way of opening free communication with the Ohio country. It was projected as early as 1762; at a meeting in Frederick, Maryland, in May of that year, a "number of prominent gentlemen were elected managers." Rowland, 1 *Life of George Mason*, 189. Washington was interested as early as 1770. The history of the enterprise is best described by C. Bacon-Foster, *Potomac Route to the West* (Washington, 1912); the charter is there reprinted as an appendix.

additional payments on the shares were to be made by the directors, and were to be advertised for one month in the Virginia and Maryland gazettes. One month's delinquency would lead to sale at auction of the share, to be followed—and this was of great importance—by an action of debt if the auction's results were inadequate. The total capital could be increased by a specified majority vote of the shareholders; for one month after the books were opened, old owners would have preference in purchasing. But there was no limitation of price on such new shares. Some were sold above par.

On the score of an effective internal set-up, the Potomac Company stands high—equal to or better than any of the land companies which have been examined. But, curiously, Article IX provided that the land and works were to be vested in the shareholders as "tenants in common, in proportion to their respective shares; and the same shall be deemed real estate." Title lay not in the corporation, but in the individual shareholders. Legally, therefore, the company lacked an important corporate characteristic. Furthermore, nothing was said of the company's status in suits. It did possess, on the other hand, perpetuity and limited liability, and it was successful (at least in its early years) in attracting capital.

The historian of the pre-1800 business corporation has made a detailed study of another equally important pioneer corporation, the Society for Establishing Useful Manufactures, of Hamilton and Duer.[30] Here again was a carefully established mechanism. The same elaborate provisions for organization were present. Powers of the thirteen directors were especially detailed, and were *in toto* very broad in scope. The only important omission was any provision for enforcement of subscription either by forfeiture or suit; a special supplementary act had to be secured to

[30] The Society for Establishing Useful Manufactures is treated at length by Davis, 2 *Essays,* 349–522. The details of the charter are discussed exhaustively at pp. 379–387.

remedy this defect.[31] The total capital of "S.U.M.," moreover, was set at $1,000,000 with $100,000 paid in—far larger than the general run of corporations or associations, excepting only the banks. Here again capital was successfully attracted.

Most other charters of the period were much briefer than these two famous examples.[32] The tendency more and more was to leave the details to be set forth in the by-laws of the corporation. The manufacturing societies, which were patriotically established in various cities after 1789, represent the briefer type of charter. Thus, the proposed charter of the Baltimore Manufacturing Society in 1789 had only twelve articles, yet all the essentials of corporate activity were covered, including provision for forfeiture of delinquent shares and for voluntary dissolution by a three-fourths vote at the third or any succeeding meeting. The actual charter was never secured.[33] After 1790, this brief form became typical for all except the public utility group of chartered projects.

As the corporation *circa* 1800, represented fairly accurately by the foregoing examples, is examined in the light of these specific tests,[34] the impression cannot be gainsaid that it was an attractive business mechanism. Alert to discover the means by which their ends could be achieved without the support of a charter, business pioneers were quick to imitate corporate advantages so far

[31] N.J. *Session Laws*, 1792, 804.

[32] The author has examined all charters granted by the New York legislature up to 1814; all those in Connecticut from 1800 to 1830; all in Pennsylvania up to 1805; and all in South Carolina up to 1812. Professor Dodd has made available a summary of his painstaking examination of all those granted by Massachusetts from 1800 to 1830. *Statutory Regulation*, 70–80. Thus a fair cross-section of legislative practice forms the basis of the conclusions stated.

In a technical legal sense, legislatures "passed statutes of incorporation" and did not "grant charters." The word charter throughout this chapter is therefore a popular and convenient usage, and not legally accurate.

[33] The proposed charter is reprinted in "Constitution of the Baltimore Manufacturing Society," 5 *American Museum* 591.

[34] Davis summarizes its characteristics as of 1800; detailed study of the changes which came after that time awaits the work of other investigators.

as they legally could do so. How well they succeeded has been indicated in the preceding chapters. Nevertheless, the task of creating a business mechanism that could be compared favorably with corporations was not easy, for by elaborate and thoughtfully drawn charters legislatures were establishing business bodies of enviable efficacy. The patriotic urge to build up the new country led political leaders to accede to every wish of enthusiastic promoters.[35] Legislators themselves, up to 1800, were in many cases directly concerned or were personally close to the small, active business community in each of the seaboard states. Thus the race for favor (if the situation can be dramatized) between the corporation and its rival seemed likely to be won by the state-created body.

Crippling the Corporation

But, after 1800 or 1805, the situation took on an obverse aspect. After the turn of the century, corporation primacy was threatened by the growing tendency on the part of legislators to impose disabilities on the corporation, even while they continued to grant those particular legal advantages which set it apart from the association. That there was, in the generation 1795–1825, such a distinct legislative trend has been little realized by modern students of corporate development. On the one hand we have come to believe that the legislative history of corporations has been wholly a story of relaxation in requirements and more and more privileges for those incorporating; on the other hand we have felt that business development after 1785 was entirely in the hands of the corporation and therefore was facilitated by the increasing power and flexibility which it was acquiring. Both these beliefs are incorrect. The implications of this peculiar period have been neglected.[36]

[35] No single enterprise illustrates this better than "S.U.M."

[36] Professor Dodd has perceived the importance of the period 1800–1825 in producing restrictions on chartered bodies rather than increased favors for them, but his conclusions are based only on the record in Massachusetts.

That the leading legislatures should have embarked on this restrictive policy after 1800 seems to have been due fundamentally to a recurrence of familiar eighteenth century fear of the corporation's monopoly position. The "monster of special privilege" was brought out of the political storeyard to frighten voter and legislator. The rise of the Jeffersonian party was a contributing influence. More and more, legislators were permitted to insert crippling clauses into charters, many of them just prior to final passage on the floor of the assemblies. The corporation began to lose its attractiveness.

As a result of this shift in legislative attitude, a number of weakening inroads were made on what, until 1790 or 1795, had been thought to be the ideal corporate makeup. The most serious of these was the rise of the doctrine that corporate charters could be repealed or altered at the will of the legislative body that had granted them. First appearing in Pennsylvania in 1779, when the charter of the College of Philadelphia was summarily altered,[37] the controversy over this serious invasion of the privilege of perpetuity came to a head in that state. The circumstances surrounding the repeal and the later re-grant of the Bank of North America's charter have been too frequently discussed to warrant review here.[38] Legislators were quick to circumvent the obligation-of-contracts clause of the new Constitution by inserting in corporate charters the direct proviso permitting repeal or alteration at any time that has become familiar in modern incorporation laws. The first instance of this was in Connecticut, in the

---

[37] 10 Pennsylvania *Statutes-at-Large,* 23–30.

[38] James Wilson was the leading protagonist among lawyers of the sanctity of charters as contracts, and deserves the credit which Webster has received for the basic defense of this privilege. His arguments before the legislature are summarized in 3 *Works,* 565–577. Such legislative light-headedness was regarded by the framers of the Constitution as simply one among other examples of interference with private contracts; the obligation-of-contracts clause was the result. Rufus King and Wilson apparently both proposed it, though extant records of the Convention do not disclose the real authorship.

charter of January, 1789, incorporating certain Mansfield silk manufacturers.[39] Many succeeding Connecticut charters included a similar clause. Advance reservation of the right to amend or repeal a charter thus antedated by a generation the doctrine of the Dartmouth College case.

The limitation of corporate life was a second attack, of somewhat lesser importance. Certainly perpetuity was regarded as a *sine qua non* of the common law corporation,[40] at least as late as 1765. To achieve freedom from an uncertain demise was, in the case of municipalities, religious bodies, and gilds, a primary reason for charter-seeking. But disregard of English tradition brought about a steady reduction in the term of existence granted by the terms of post-1790 charters.[41] Certainly from the standpoint of relative corporate advantages, this trend was trimming away from a charter a sizeable fraction of its appraised value in the business community. Another slice disappeared when new corporations were required to make some contribution to tax or school funds, or were forced to permit the state to become a stockholder *gratis*.[42] Specific reports or examinations of corporate affairs by state officials or state bodies were still another superfi-

[39] 2 *Connecticut MS. Archives*, "Industry," 237.

[40] Holdsworth, 8 *H.E.L.*, 202, especially note 2; Blackstone, 1 *Commentaries*, 475; Kent, 2 *Commentaries* (12th edition), 303, where he places perpetuity as one primary quality of a corporation, but recognizes the statutory inroads upon it.

[41] The Bank of North America had been chartered for the period of the war only, in the various supporting state statutes passed in 1781–1782. The United Insurance Company charter, granted by New York in March, 1798, was limited to ten years. 4 N.Y. *Statutes* (1885 edition), 192. A ten-year term for insurance companies became common. Twenty- to thirty-year terms appeared in bridge and turnpike charters in some states, side by side with perpetual grants in others, indicating a definite legislative determination to turn away from the prevailing custom. In Massachusetts the Union Bank charter of 1792 provided for ten years of life only, and this was copied in nearly all subsequent bank creations. Thus, the imposition of similar limitations (to as little as five years) in manufacturing charters had a surplus of precedent.

[42] Thus in the Manhattan Company charter of 1799, New York City was permitted to buy 2,000 shares. This common provision degenerated

cially minor handicap which was nevertheless resented by business men and their lawyers. Direct limitation of profits or tolls of course appeared at this same time in turnpike and canal charters, but it must be remembered that the compensating privileges for these semi-public enterprises were usually substantial. Nevertheless, because of other legislative "nibbling" (for example, limitations on capital and on annual income) the private association was constantly gaining in favor.

This restrictive attitude of legislatures is nowhere better illustrated than in the 1811 act of New York,[43] so often referred to as ushering in the era of general incorporation laws.[44] Properly interpreted, this act did not quite possess such a pioneer status. It was passed as a rather inept attempt to encourage groups with small capital in the field of manufacture. The date of its passage is also suggestive of the close connection it had with national Republican policies.[45] The act limited capital of each unit formed to $100,000, and the period for securing charters to five years. These were certainly unattractive features. The directors were termed "trustees" throughout the act, possibly indicating a specialized position for them in the minds of the legislators—as semi-public guardians of the to-be-encouraged expansion of manufacture. There was a clause imposing a proportional liability upon any stockholder who had received a distribution of assets upon dissolution. Since existence was limited to twenty years, this was equivalent in practice to the ordinary liability of

in the next decade to clauses allowing states to receive free shares, *e.g.,* in the Merchants Bank charter of 1805. Of course by the middle of the nineteenth century, comparative freedom from taxation became a leading business reason for choosing the joint stock association or Massachusetts Trust form of organization. *Cf.* the court's remarks in *Hibbs* v. *Brown,* 190 N.Y. 167.

[43] 3 N.Y. *Statutes* (1863 edition), 726. The date was March 22, 1811.

[44] *Cf.* A. A. Berle and G. C. Means, "Corporations," 4 *Encyclopedia of Social Sciences,* 412, and many other writers.

[45] Supporters of Jefferson's embargo and the succeeding hostile policy of Madison toward England naturally regarded domestic manufacture as a desirable weapon to decrease English prominence in our importing trade.

partners or shareholders in an association; debts, even though incurred during a company's existence, could hardly be evaded or
compromised before the corporate character of the enterprise
was automatically destroyed. There was a clause making the
shares personal estate, and another permitting transfer of shares
to be carried out as each company might require in its by-laws.
Of the considerable number of projects receiving charters under
this act, few lasted beyond 1815. During the next twenty years
it had only a slight effect upon the attitude of business men
toward charters; they continued to choose the association form
in preference, just as manufacturers did in the other states.[46]

This act certainly did not grant unquestionable freedom from
liability to the corporators who might make use of it. And it was
against the major advantage of limited liability (indubitably
a foremost attribute of the sovereign-sanctioned corporation for
nearly four centuries) that legislative meddling was directed in
other states as well as New York. It is clear that the eighteenth
century business man prized this advantage far less than we have
thought.[47] Nevertheless after 1800 it was to be more and more
desired; and as lawyers and courts frowned on efforts to secure
this advantage by other means,[48] a charter granting it became
correspondingly more valuable.

[46] No less than six supplementary acts were passed in 1815–1822, either
extending the time limit for securing charters or clarifying the meaning of
the 1811 act, in a futile effort to encourage manufacturing companies. *Cf.*
N.Y. *Statutes* (1863 edition), 729–732. The limited partnership statute of
1822 was a truer reflection of business sentiment, and no further general
acts were passed until 1848. In a special act of the same 1811 session
(April) the Montgomery Manufacturing Society (textiles) was given a
perpetual charter, limited liability, and the right to sue delinquent shareholders (rather than auctioning shares)—a more attractive charter than
that provided in the "general" act. *Laws* of N.Y. (1811), 308. For judicial
interpretation of the act, *cf. Briggs* v. *Penniman,* 8 *Cowen* 387 (1826).

[47] DuBois found numerous comments and correspondence in English
records of 1720–1780 indicating that liability was a minor consideration in
organizing business companies. *English Business Company,* 93, 223.

[48] DuBois points out that English law opposed any limitation by agreement; but there were exceptions in stannary law, in Ireland by a statute of

In modern discussions of the theoretical structure of corporations, attention has been concentrated upon this question of liability.[49] Only a few vestiges of this unfavorable legislative attitude toward limited liability between 1800 and 1830 have remained[50] as indications of the uncertain status of this favorite modern attribute of corporateness.[51] But neither legislatures nor

1781, and in Scottish practice until the late eighteenth century. *Ibid.*, 223–226, and notes 71, 74, and 78.

[49] *Cf.* Radin's emphasis upon liability in his analysis of the theoretical implications of incorporation, "Endless Problem of Corporate Personality," 32 *C.L.R.* 643, at 653–655.

[50] The constitution of California, imposing proportional liability, has been a notable modern example. *Cf.* H. W. Ballantine, *Private Corporations* (Chicago, 1927), 699. Legislative attitudes toward bank stockholders' liability is another exception. But compare the recent change in California's attitude, and the removal of double liability for national as well as many state-chartered banks.

[51] The modern point of view was summarized by Justice Finch in 1892 in the case of *People ex rel. Winchester* v. *Coleman,* 133 N.Y. 279. That case brought to issue the question of whether the act of 1849 recognizing joint stock associations had made a valid distinction between them and corporations. A tax on "monied or stock corporations" had been assessed against an association by state officials. The decision declared the tax to be improperly imposed, because the taxing act referred specifically to corporations. It was obviously necessary to show *why* the court regarded an association as still distinct from a chartered corporation.

Justice Finch conceded that "almost the full measure of corporate attributes has, by legislative enactment, been bestowed upon joint stock associations, until the difference, if there be one, is obscure, illusive and difficult to see and describe." Recognizing frankly that limited liability, one of the primary points of difference under the common law, had been eliminated by various legislative acts in the early part of the century, he nevertheless claimed that "the creation of the corporation merges and drowns the liability of its creditors. The creation of the stock company leaves unharmed and unchanged the liability of the association." Where there has been any legislation designed to impose liability upon stockholders, he pointed out, it has either been true that "their liability arises after the usual remedies against the corporation have been exhausted"; if not, destruction of the common law limitation on liability requires on the part of the legislature "an affirmative imposition of new personal liability." Exactly the opposite is true of the association, for its formation destroys none of the liability of the members by its collective debts. He shows finally that specific enactment is necessary to change that relationship or the method of enforcing it (as, for example, through a representative officer).

courts in this period under review felt that, by common law principles, limited liability was sacrosanct.[52] No thorough examination of this surprising retrogression has apparently ever been made.[53] Some effort to fill in this surprising gap in the history of the American corporation is important not only for the thesis advanced here—that unchartered associations in the quarter century after 1800 crept up to a position of equality with corporations—but for a clearer understanding of corporate evolution in this country. No such period appeared in England; the process there was rather one of endowing private associations gradually with the attributes of corporations. In short, the leveling-off between the two forms was there a *positive* procedure, while here it tended to be *negative* in character. In three of the four major industrial states before 1825, the attack on the liability principle appeared in greater or less degree. In other states that did not participate, corporations tended to be almost entirely of a public utility character, with a sprinkling of banks and insurance companies.

There were in Massachusetts, first of all, a group of early charters which specifically imposed full liability upon the share-

[52] Frequently overlooked is the most striking evidence of this attitude. In Massachusetts, as well as in other New England states, the inhabitants of townships and cities were early made liable for any debts of the corporate body which could not be satisfied from the public treasury. This doctrine was exactly opposed to the common law rule, which had been first developed with regard to the incorporated boroughs as far back as 1400. For the later common law attitude, *cf. Edmunds* v. *Brown and Tillard,* 1 Lev. 237 (1668). Tampering with this ancient common law principle in the sphere of township organization, where the doctrine was much more firmly entrenched, would naturally lead to a similar attitude toward private corporations.

[53] Williston, writing in 1888 ("History of the Law of Business Corporations before 1800," 2 *H.L.R.,* 105, 149), did not go beyond 1800; Dodd, *op. cit.,* has treated Massachusetts' meddling with the liability principle as a minor feature of the 1800–1830 period. The topic is discussed by the present author in "Unlimited Liability in Early American Corporations," 43 *Journal of Political Economy,* 674, from which much of the discussion here is taken.

holders.[54] Such charters were granted to the following companies: Proprietors of the Locks and Canals on the Connecticut River (1792), Proprietors of the Boston Water Works (1795), Massachusetts Mutual Fire Insurance Company (1798), Ossapee Mining Company (1801), Danvers and Beverly Iron Works Company (1803), Amesbury Nail Factory Company (1805). These charters were sprinkled through a period of years when others were being granted with no variation in the common law principle. In the case of insurance companies, if the president or directors knowingly wrote policies after the capital stocks had been impaired by losses, charters provided that their property would be held liable in actions by the policyholders.

The first general Massachusetts statute imposing liability was passed in 1808. By its terms executions could, after fourteen days, be levied on "members" of any corporation if the latter failed to show sufficient property to satisfy the judgment. This, of course, was a different sort of liability than that imposed by the charters mentioned above, since it was a remedy applicable only *after* ordinary recourse against the corporate treasury had failed.[55] On February 24, 1818, this statute was amended to provide that the members liable were those who held their shares at the time the debt was incurred, not at the time action was brought.[56] In 1821 it was further amended to provide that "every person who shall become a member of any manufacturing corporation, shall be liable for all debts contracted during the time of his continuing a member." This statute during its life (it was finally repealed in 1829) applied only to manufacturing corporations. Banking

[54] In speaking of these charters Justice Field in 1884 said that they had been framed by the legislature "apparently following the analogy of inhabitants of towns." *Child* v. *Brown and Fairhaven Iron Works*, 137 Mass. 516. The summary of Massachusetts legislation in the text follows that of Justice Field in this case. Of value also is Chapter XVII in Angell and Ames, *Private Corporations* (1846 edition).

[55] For Chief Justice Parker's interpretation of this statute, *cf. Leland* v. *March*, 16 Mass. 389, and *Marcy* v. *Clark*, 17 Mass. 334.

[56] This was the point of controversy in the cases just named.

and insurance companies were governed by the provisions in their charters. Turnpike companies were exempt from this imposition of liability.

The unpopularity of the law, especially after the change in 1821, led to its modification in 1827. Creditors were forced to bring suit, against the corporation and also against any individual stockholders, within one year after a debt was in default. The principle of contribution from brother stockholders was introduced to protect an individual singled out for suit. Trustees and holders of stock pledged as collateral were exempt from liability, and thus from creditors' suits. This led to a wholesale evasion of the law in the next three years by placing stock in the hands of trustees, or pledging it as collateral.[57] The repealing act of 1829, which was really an act of the modern type, simply provided for the filing of a certificate stating the amount of fully paid-in stock. Maine, in 1823, had already abandoned the unlimited liability principle, soon after her establishment as an independent state.

The situation concerning corporate liability in Connecticut during this period was even more interesting, because the experimentation was largely conducted by inserting varying clauses in successive charters.[58] A charter granted in 1813 to the Andros Manufacturing Company[59] illustrates the early attitude of the legislature. In case of a judgment brought against the corporation where execution was defaulted, a levy could be made after thirty days upon the private property and bodies of the members.

[57] Angell and Ames, *op. cit.,* 548–549.

[58] Angell and Ames (*op. cit.,* 548) summarizing legislation on this point, curiously omitted mention of the various experiments tried by the Connecticut legislature in imposing liability on stockholders, and implied that Massachusetts was the only state which made efforts along this line. Apparently no detailed study of Connecticut's "wobbling" has been made; for this reason the discussion in the text has been amplified.

[59] *Resolves and Private Laws of Connecticut, 1781–1836* (2 vols., Hartford, 1837), 723. Unless otherwise noted, the course of events in Connecticut as described here is summarized from the statutes therein.

A typical phrase of this kind in charters of 1813, 1814, and 1815 was that members "shall be responsible in their private capacity, provided said corporation shall become insolvent, or its property cannot be found."[60] Thus their liability remained secondary to that of the corporation itself, but no specific time limit was mentioned. There was no uniformity among the charters of these three years as to whether liability should be determined as of the date when debts were contracted or the date when judgment was defaulted. This led to exactly the same difficulty of interpretation as occurred in Massachusetts.

The inconsistency of the Connecticut legislature in imposing these liability provisions upon various corporations led to a statute of 1817 declaring that in the future no members of manufacturing corporations should be liable for debts. The inconsistency had been startling in some cases. In May of 1814, for example, the Groton Manufacturing Company had been incorporated with a clause imposing liability upon "those who were stockholders at the time of contracting such debts." In October, 1814, the Hartford Manufacturing Company was incorporated; in its charter liability was imposed with no particular qualifying phrase. This had also been the case in the charter of the Middletown Manufacturing Company. The 1817 act required, as an alternative, that, if they chose, corporations could certify to a proper county official the amount of their capital stock. If this were done annually, so that creditors could be kept up to date, no liability would be imposed.

But the legislature seemed unwilling to be bound by its own actions. In the next few years some new charters were granted that imposed capital liability in the former manner. This was true of the Hartford Brewing Company in 1821. Where the privilege of certifying an amount of stock was granted, the typical phrase was "the company shall be bound to keep the said

[60] Phraseology is almost never exactly the same, reflecting a lack of expert draftsmanship.

amount of capital stock subject to the demand of creditors, unless the stock shall be reduced by a vote of said company, in
which case public notice shall be given." The notice was to be by
newspaper publication in the proper county.

This procedure seems to have been unsatisfactory to the legislators, for by 1826 there had begun to be a liability imposed on
officers or directors who permitted the reduction of capital. In
the charter of the Connecticut Carpet Manufacturing Company
of 1827, directors causing or allowing a reduction of capital
"shall be liable as traders in common, jointly and severally, for
any debts incurred at the time of or subsequent to the reduction
of capital." Obviously this involved the old English attitude
toward corporate capital as a "joint stock" or fund, assumed to
exist intact for the benefit of creditors. Although modern accounting knowledge shows it to be an archaic notion, its influence has by no means disappeared from present-day legislation.

Still further change in the legislative attitude came as late as
1833 in the Chelsea Manufacturing Company's charter. The liability formerly applying only to directors or officers (there had
been no consistency in assigning liability to one or both) was
extended to include stockholders "consenting thereto or causing
the same to be done." In 1834 the Connecticut Soap Manufacturing Company charter had a slightly different phrase; liability
was to be imposed after a reduction of capital, but only upon the
stockholders who had received the distribution. Apparently the
event aimed at was a deliberate vote to return part of the capital
to stockholders when profits were seen to be declining.[61]

Enough has been said to show quite clearly that seekers for a
charter in Connecticut at this period could have no certainty of
the exact attitude of the legislature. Small wonder that the early
textile industry of the state was in the hands of unincorporated
associations, and that, at least until 1825, chartered textile corpo-

[61] The modern stockholder in large corporations would certainly benefit
if this practice were more common in the twentieth century.

rations were exceptions and in many cases were headed by those who wished to use chicanery in twisting charter privileges to defraud creditors.

The unusual 1786 statute of New York,[62] creating proportional liability for a specific group, has almost been forgotten. By its terms a group of leading business men, including Samuel Ogden and William Constable, received a grant of proportional liability; each member of the group was to be responsible only for his share of the potential debts, measured by his contribution to the "whole stock." The statute further provided that the articles of agreement must be filed in the office of the Clerk of New York County, and that every person joining the association must sign the articles and indicate the size of his contribution. No one who failed to sign could benefit from the limitation of liability. The grant was limited to a term of seven years. Although it was thus the first state to tamper by statute with the liability principle, New York did much less experimentation than its two New England neighbors in varying the common law rule of limited liability. Nevertheless, as was indicated above, in its 1811 act, their lead was being followed. Specific clauses were also occasionally inserted in earlier charters,[63] making some changes in the principle of liability.

In March, 1797, the first American exception to the rule of

[62] 2 N.Y. *Statutes* (1885 edition), 295. The group were to be known as "The Associated Manufacturing Iron Company of the City and County of New York." The proportional liability was granted "any law, usage or custom to the contrary notwithstanding."

[63] In March, 1791, in the charter for the President, Directors and Company of the Bank of New York (3 N.Y. *Statutes* [1885 edition], 237), it was provided that the debts (*i.e.*, the notes) of the bank should not exceed three times its capital stock. The directors were to be liable for any excess beyond this limitation, excepting those who were absent or cast a dissenting vote when the debt was authorized. This same clause was repeated in the charter of the Bank of Albany (*ibid.*, 364) in 1792, and in that of the Bank of Columbia (*ibid.*, 429) in 1793. In the United Insurance and Mutual Insurance Company charters of 1798, double liability was imposed on those who might be stockholders at the end of the specified ten years of

limited liability is found in the charter of the Hamilton Manu-facturing Society,[64] which was later known as the Albany Glass Works. One clause provided that nothing in the charter should be construed "to exonerate the members of the said corporation from any debts which may hereafter be incurred by the direc-tors"; on the contrary every member "shall of his individual capacity be liable to be prosecuted for any debt due from the said corporation to any person whomsoever." The charter further di-rected that the directors were to publish annually in newspapers a list of the stockholders and that a similar list must be filed with the Albany County Clerk, so that creditors could know whom to sue.[65]

A generation later New York again joined in the game of crippling the corporation, when by the limited partnership act of 1822 she moved to endow bodies of business men with the right to achieve a limitation of liability. This act was enacted partly to offset the two-thirds rule for charter passage imposed by the 1821 Constitution, and partly as a result of the increasing familiarity of New York business men and lawyers with Louisi-ana law, the Code Napoleon, and the practice of the Dutch and French business communities. In effect it was a partial legal recognition of the association principle.[66]

This trend toward hamstringing the corporate body after 1800

existence. Such clauses, later common in bank and insurance charters, were then rare. In Massachusetts very similar clauses were used, beginning with the Union Bank in 1792. *Cf.* Dodd, *op. cit.,* 79, 83.

[64] 4 N.Y. *Statutes* (1885 edition), 95.

[65] In a charter of 1806 to the Rensselaer Glass Factory, there was no im-position of any liability upon the stockholders as had been the case in the Glass Works charter nine years before. In the many turnpike charters there was no effort to change the common law rule. This was true also of the Niagara Canal Company, chartered in 1788 (4 N.Y. *Statutes,* 269), and the various charters for the early Mohawk Valley canal companies.

[66] The scheme proposed to Oliver Wolcott by Alexander Hamilton in 1801 is prophetic of the limited partnership. *Supra,* 241. Professor S. E. Howard, in "The Limited Partnership," 7 *Journal of Business,* 296, analyzes the spread of limited partnership laws to other states. From his study of legislative records, he stresses two reasons for the imitation of

is deserving of far more attention than it has yet received, for undoubtedly dissatisfaction with the vacillation of the legislatures in Massachusetts and Connecticut was a potent force in bringing about the general acts governing incorporation, which in effect took the unincorporated association under the wing of the state. As it affected business men, the whole situation in 1825 or 1830 could have been summarized in some such manner as the following: "By private articles of agreement we can effect a working organization which is the equal of the corporation except in so far as it suffers certain legal disabilities. The most important of these, unlimited liability, is being taken away or interfered with in recent charters. We would like to use a generalized corporate form, especially since we are more and more in need of limitation of liability. Cease depriving corporations of that essential quality. If you continue to weaken corporations, we shall be forced to use exclusively the private association as it has been perfected by land company promoters and many others in the past generation. Better to gather these enterprises under the aegis of the State than to let them exist, in so large a degree as in the past forty years, beyond the cognizance of the State."

The ultimate answer to this challenge of the business community was the general act. How far this interim of confusion and uncertainty felt by business groups as the result of legislative vagaries extended into the thinking of lawyers and judges will be examined in the following chapter. Strengthened in business esteem during this period, the joint stock association as first used by the land companies had meantime reached full stature and was ready to serve as the model for the generalized incorporation that we know today.

New York's step: first, the need for a readily available form of "collective enterprise organization"; second, the legislative "fear of economic domination by business corporations." Kent pointed out the influence of French law and the Civil Code of Louisiana upon the New York enactment. 3 *Commentaries* (12th edition), 35–36.

VIII

CORPORATIONS VERSUS ASSOCIATIONS:
JUDICIAL INERTIA

HOW did the courts regard the actively functioning associations which by 1800 had assumed a clearly defined form and were serving business men so satisfactorily? Institutions developed out of economic need have ever had to face a gauntlet of legislative and judicial disapproval.[1] So it was with the unincorporated association here under examination. It was universally refused recognition by the courts. Legislatures simply ignored it, but courts in many instances actively opposed it. They maintained a stubborn opposition in spite of the fact that there was a clear differentiation in form from either partnership or corporation, exhibited by such an important group of business undertakings as the land enterprises. The most advanced of these land companies had created almost exactly what we know now as the business corporation. The widespread adoption of this form, following the pioneering by the land merchandisers, stimulated the demand for free incorporation under general acts. In England, where the same form appeared after 1750, its effect was even greater; there the business association was the direct antecedent of the modern registered company, which during the course of the nineteenth century completely displaced the old chartered bodies in business usage. Yet in the face of this development, courts in both America and England continued their opposition.[2]

To obtain perspective on the juristic attitude to be explored in

---

[1] John R. Commons, among American economic thinkers, has been intensely concerned with this conflict. *Cf.* especially his *Legal Foundations of Capitalism* (New York, 1924).

[2] English legal history is replete with comparable conflicts between social or economic practice and the dogma of the law. See, for example, in regard to bills of exchange and promissory notes, Holdsworth, 8 *H.E.L.*, ch. 4, especially 172–177.

this chapter, it is necessary first to summarize the modern estimate of the joint stock association. This can be found succinctly
expressed by Judge Hiscock of the New York Court of Appeals
in the leading case of *Hibbs* v. *Brown*.[3] Judge Hiscock there
pointed out that by statute, as well as by court decisions, the association has been recognized as distinct from the corporation, and
has been regulated (and, of course, taxed!). He traced the process by which the joint stock association had achieved an independent position in the eyes of the courts. This ultimate result
has obscured the real effect upon corporate character of these
early associations, a character existent entirely beyond the judicial pale. They really were the root of our modern business
bodies, adopted and made respectable by the general acts of
1830–1875. Sporadic reappearance of the same independent spirit
in the business world, to avoid unfair taxation or discrimination
against corporations, brought with it more modern examples of
the association principle. These, coming before a more enlight-
ened judiciary in 1850–1900, were accorded recognition as independent types of business organization. Since 1900 they have become insignificant in number, as the true promise of the general
acts—free right of association as a *private* privilege—has been
widely fulfilled.

But during the years 1785–1830 business men and their counsel were faced with the obstacle that between partnerships on one
side and chartered bodies on the other, no form of organization had judicial approval.[4] As one way out, they occasionally attempted to secure for an unauthorized body the status of a corporation simply by implication. The Pennsylvania legislation di-

[3] 190 N.Y. 167 (1907). The case concerned the negotiability of bonds
issued on the general credit of the Adams Express Company, a joint stock
association. The court was divided on the issue, and Hiscock's excellent
analysis of the character of a joint stock association was only incidental in
his opinion.

[4] The persistence of this attitude in England was adverted to above,
pp. 5–6.

rected against unincorporated banks has been briefly reviewed.[5] This legislation came before the Pennsylvania Supreme Court for review in *Myers* v. *Irwin*.[6] The Farmers' Bank of Lancaster had been formed just before the 1810 act, and continued to operate. When its right to carry on banking was challenged in this case, counsel contended that the 1808 act had *impliedly* incorporated the bank, and that it was therefore exempt from the 1810 act. But Chief Justice Tilghman said in reply that "nothing was farther from the intent of the legislature than to incorporate this or any other company." Yeates, concurring, said "the act speaks of no incorporation, nor confers any powers or privileges on such societies, but attaches a personal liability on the individual members, never known in the case of corporations"![7]

Just the opposite of this attitude finally appeared a generation later among the Supreme Court Justices of New York who had occasion to rule upon the real nature of the associations formed under the 1838 Free Banking Act. They there declared such groups to have been incorporated by implication on the ground that the "sanction of sovereignty" had been in effect conferred.[8] Such was the primary test of corporate existence, as Coke and later Blackstone had laid it down.[9]

How the courts further maintained the rigid classification of all business organization into the two simple categories, and how they resisted attempts by legislators or business men to weaken or defy that separation, may best be understood by examining in order their attitude on the several points of distinction between partnerships and corporations which have been generally ac-

---

[5] *Supra*, p. 251.   [6] 2 S. & R. 368 (1816).

[7] How far wrong Justice Yeates was in his belief that liability for corporate shareholders was always limited is obvious in the light of legislation and charter grants in New York, Massachusetts, and Connecticut from 1797 until 1830.

[8] *Thomas* v. *Dakin*, 22 Wendell 9.

[9] *Case of Sutton's Hospital*, 10 Coke 32; *cf.* also Blackstone, 1 *Commentaries*, 472.

cepted as determinative.[10] Coupled with this analysis, and equally important for the point of view taken here, will be a survey of the restrictions or handicaps which the courts imposed upon corporations, thereby strengthening the association's value to business men. Lastly, it must be noted that associations could slip past this judicial opposition and achieve corporate advantages.

The tendency in American charters after 1790 to limit corporate existence brought to the fore the inconveniences of dissolution. Partnership obligations on the occasion of involuntary dissolution must be discharged before assets are distributed; in sharp distinction, the common law had regarded corporate dissolution as extinguishing all obligations *instanter*.[11] Finally turning away from this illogical doctrine—but not until well into the nineteenth century—the courts came to declare that assets in case of dissolution should be treated as a trust fund for the protection of creditors, at least for a term of years.[12] The legislators took a hand in enforcing such a liability on corporations by statutes. If it is assumed that members of an association would always have been so liable for their debts, the effect of this change in the common law was simply to place chartered corporations more nearly in the position of associations.

The mode of taking title to property is the second basic difference between partnerships and corporations. Partners are tenants in common of real property (though not all tenants in common are partners). A corporation under common law prin-

[10] These have been surveyed in detail by Warren in his *Corporate Advantages Without Incorporation*, pp. 17–29.

[11] Blackstone, 1 *Commentaries*, 484; a few states adopted this principle before 1860; *cf.* H. W. Ballantine, *Private Corporations*, 800, note 92.

[12] The general doctrine came to be that, although actions at law were impossible, equity would enforce claims against stockholders of a dissolved corporation as tenants in common of the divided property. *Cf. Curran* v. *Arkansas*, 15 Howard (U.S.) 304. Confusion among lawyers on this point is evident as late as 1834 in the arguments of counsel in *Mumma* v. *Potomac Company*, 8 Peters 281.

ciples had as one of its chief distinguishing characteristics the ability to take title as a legal personality. The courts without a second thought always upheld this basic difference. How then did the association receive permission from the law to place itself *pro tanto* on the same plane with the corporation?

To have trustees take title and make transfers has become familiar in modern American law as the method by which this is accomplished.[13] The trustees may either be outsiders not in any way connected with the association, or they may be active officers who occupy a position as trustees in addition to other duties. It was, of course, an extension of the latter device during the nineteenth century which became the distinctive Massachusetts business trust. The trust principle was so firmly imbedded in English and American law that the courts obviously could not frown on its use to aid the business association.[14] How frequently trustees were used to facilitate property acquisition, especially after 1785, has been noted in a preceding chapter. Land companies necessarily experimented with this device to avoid clumsy title deeds, long before American courts had occasion to pass on any cases where the validity of a transfer by trustees was involved. As a matter of fact, all cases cited by the authorities as upholding the principle are modern.[15]

The ability to place concentrated power in the hands of a selected managerial group has been regarded as one of the greatest advantages of the modern corporation. It is not such a clear point of advantage over ordinary partnerships, however, since from

[13] Professor E. M. Dodd, in "Dogma and Practice in the Law of Associations," 42 *H.L.R.*, 977, summarizes this doctrine: "There is no doubt, however, that tangible property may be held in trust for a partnership either by a stranger or by a member of the partnership . . . or by an agent . . . not a member of it. If so, all legal rights of action arising out of the ownership . . . would be vested in the agent-trustee." The North American Land Company, the Asylum Company, and the Connecticut Land Company were perfect illustrations of this device.

[14] Maitland, 3 *Collected Papers* (Cambridge, 1896), 304, 321.

[15] *Cf.* Warren, *Corporate Advantages,* 338, note 23.

very early times articles of agreement among ordinary partners provided for some delegation and limitation of authority. By creating a managerial group the association was simply extending further an established partnership practice. In practically all the land companies the delegation of power within an association was accepted as an essential part of its mechanism with as little question as was the validity of rule by a majority vote at meetings of shareholders. So slowly did the courts on both sides of the Atlantic accept this fact that as late as 1849 Lord Campbell could discuss the question as though he were laying down a new rule of law: "A distinction must be made between a member of a common mercantile partnership and a shareholder in a joint stock company. . . . It is known that the power of carrying on the business of the company, and of drawing, accepting, and endorsing bills of exchange, is vested exclusively in the directors. This shows that, although a joint stock company is a partnership, it is a partnership of a different description. . . . All who have dealings with a joint stock company know that the authority to manage the business is conferred upon the directors, and that a shareholder, as such, has no power to contract for the company. For this purpose, it is wholly immaterial whether the company is incorporated or unincorporated."[16] In actual business practice there had been no real difference for a century before the learned lord spoke.

A fourth difference relates to the position of the two forms of organization in legal actions by or against strangers. This is a difference much more concerned with status before the courts than with effectiveness in business operations. Two methods have become familiar in modern times for bringing the association into substantial parity with the corporation. One is to have important contracts made by trustees, the other is to permit one or more officers to stand in court as the representative of all the other shareholders. The first method was never seriously resisted

[16] In *Burnes* v. *Fennell,* 2 H. L. Cases, 497.

by the courts, again because of the sanctity of the trust principle. It was effectively used by the Connecticut Land Company, the North American Land Company, the Scioto associates, and several other land companies which have been reviewed.

Designation of a representative officer to appear in suits has been resisted strongly by the common law courts.[17] As a general rule, such representatives will not be accepted except (*a*) where specific statutory authority has been granted, or (*b*) where a prior agreement to use such a representative has been made by the contending parties. So far as the joint stock association is concerned, it has depended for help upon the first of these supports. Thus, in England beginning in 1801, private acts were regularly passed permitting a designated officer to appear in court. About one hundred such acts were passed between 1801 and 1844.[18] In each case a clause was inserted specifically stating that the act was not to be deemed to create a corporation. This type of act was not imitated by American legislators until well over a generation later.

Alexander Hamilton was, therefore, again in advance of his time when he inserted an article in the agreement constituting the Merchants' Bank[19] in 1803, providing that all suits which might be brought against the company should be brought against the "president for the time being." Under the law as it stood at that time in England (and, less certainly, in America) this clause would have been ineffective. But commentators have overlooked the fact that Hamilton placed this clause in Article

[17] The leading cases are summarized effectively by Warren, *op. cit.,* 343–347.

[18] See H. A. Shannon, "The Coming of General Limited Liability," Economic History Supplement to *Economic Journal,* 267 (January, 1931). Shannon mistakenly looked upon these acts as beginning the evolution of the joint stock association into the modern English corporation. He says of the acts that "they broke the bundle of corporate rights." This is scarcely true except as it refers to legal rights; in a business sense the break had already occurred.

[19] For a description of the articles, see Chapter VII, note 15.

XI of the agreement, the same article which provided for the limitation of liability. It was intended that Article XI *in toto* would be inserted in every passbook and as a clause in every note discounted by the bank and every contract entered into. Thus there would have existed the sort of advance agreement between potential contending parties which the English courts later expressed willingness to accept in the leading case of *Radenhurst* v. *Bates*.[20] If Hamilton really intended that this clause was to be made a part of every single agreement or contract of the bank, it is testimony to his grasp of the confusion in the law on the point (as yet undecided in any American case) and a refutation of the statement that he was attempting the impossible.[21]

The fifth test to distinguish between corporation and partnership is the status of members when suits arise among themselves. As affecting the partnership of Anglo-American law, the logical rule that a partner cannot sue his partners collectively has been a most troublesome doctrine. Advocates of the entity theory of the partnership have used the difficulties arising because of this situation to argue against the aggregate theory.[22] Here again the difference, so far as the association was concerned, was a legal rather than a business difficulty and the question of shareholders' status in suing their brother members was an academic one.

Where the early association (and the corporation as well) desired specific legal help was in securing redress against delinquent subscribers to the capital stock.[23] Could the shares be forfeited, and a suit maintained against the delinquent as an additional remedy? It seems to have been little realized that the an-

[20] 3 Bing. 463. The case is not a strong one, since it relates to suits against members of a loose association, but has been accepted as a valid precedent.

[21] As Warren seems to believe, *op. cit.,* 347; for the conflict in English and Scottish law, *cf. supra,* p. 262, note 48.

[22] Dodd summarizes the problem, "Dogma and Practice in the Law of Associations," 42 *H.L.R.,* 977, at 997.

[23] Compare here the inclusion of the right to sue delinquent members as early as 1740, in the Land Bank of Massachusetts. *Supra,* page 60.

swer was "no" for the corporation as well as for the association, at least in Massachusetts and Connecticut before 1820.

In the case of the *Andover and Medford Turnpike Corporation*,[24] decided in 1809, the Supreme Court of Massachusetts ruled that a chartered corporation could have no recourse against a subscriber except to auction off his shares. In the general statute of 1809 in Massachusetts (containing standard provisions for future charters of manufacturing corporations), there was a provision to the effect that sale by auction should be the only remedy against delinquent subscribers. That a joint stock association was then, and had been for half a century, on a parity with chartered corporations in this respect was clearly recognized by the Supreme Court of Massachusetts in an 1817 case[25] in the following words: "It is true that a private company of merchants, not incorporated, have their remedy against one of their company who does not furnish his agreed share . . . but all the rights and duties of such an association are by the common law." Strictly interpreted, this statement placed the association in a more advantageous position than was enjoyed until 1828 by Massachusetts corporations.

In a contemporary Connecticut case,[26] any inherent power to assess stockholders was denied to a manufacturing company chartered in 1815. The directors had felt it necessary to apply to the legislature for authority of this sort in 1816. Chief Justice Swift denied the validity of both the application to the legislature and the assessments which were made (following a joint resolution authorizing them). He pointed out that only by vote of the stockholders could this power be secured. This attitude in the Supreme Courts of two prominent states shows that the universality of any doctrine that corporations may enforce assess-

[24] 6 Mass. 40, at 43: "Very clearly a corporation has not power, as incident to it at common law, to assess for its own use a sum of money on the corporators, and compel them, by action at law, to the payment of it."

[25] *Franklin Glass Company* v. *Thomas White*, 14 Mass. 285.

[26] *Marlborough Manufacturing Company* v. *Smith*, 2 Conn. 579 (1818).

ments on stockholders at law, often said to have originated in the 1671 case of *Salmon* v. *The Hambrough Company*,[27] has been largely the creation of historical hindsight. Corporations and associations were clearly at the same disadvantage in this respect, in the two states which were leaders in shaping the law of corporations before 1825.

In England, in the leading case of *Venning* v. *Lockie*,[28] Lord Ellenborough upheld the right of a partnership to have a special remedy at law against one of its members who had promised to subscribe capital, thus avoiding the complicated equity action which would otherwise be necessary.[29] He said: "A specific promised arrangement, though in respect to a part of the common fund . . . makes it the subject of an action at law." It cannot be said, however, that this doctrine was accepted in England prior to 1825. As has been noted previously, most of the early associations used the remedy of a sale at auction, quite often specifically provided for in advance by the articles of agreement. The situation in the Ohio Company[30] is of particular interest in showing the early attitude on this question.[31]

[27] 1 Chancery Cases 204 (1671). It is frequently overlooked that the levies ordered in this case against members of the Merchant Adventurers were ordered by Parliament as a *special* relief for Dr. Salmon, unobtainable in either the law or equity courts and not therefore sanctioned by the common law. Holdsworth's comment on this is misleading; 8 *H.E.L.* 209, and note 4.

[28] 13 East 7.

[29] Similar to the jurisdiction of equity in cases of dispute among partners over a disposition of assets.

[30] *Supra*, p. 142.

[31] Curiously, the case of *Townsend* v. *Goewey*, 19 Wendell 242, seems to be regarded as a leading American authority on this point, although decided as late as 1838. In that case, seven trustees of a joint stock association's property (the Albany Exchange Company) had brought suit to collect delinquent payments from certain subscribers. A ground of defense was that the trustees, being also members of the association, were in partnership with the subscribers. Justice Cowen, however, upheld the action as the sort of express contract among partners which justified an action at law, following the doctrine of Lord Ellenborough. Justice Cowen cited no precedents among American cases for his decision.

The statutes passed in England permitting a specified officer to represent the members of an association in suits have been mentioned. Prior to 1825, these statutes were effective only in suits by or against strangers. But in 6 *George IV*, c. 42, a clause was inserted permitting such representation in suits brought by or against persons "whether a member of the company or not"; this became the model for many other such enabling statutes up to 1844.[32] The 1838 act of New York included such permission, but it apparently was not copied elsewhere until after the 1849 act of New York. Today, such statutes extending this corporate privilege to modern associations are quite general in the various states.[33]

The final and indubitably the most important modern distinction between the corporation and its rivals—liability—came before the courts from two entirely separate causes. Some cases arose out of the earnest efforts of active associations, already in possession of so many powers conceived of as belonging only to the corporation, to garner this last and increasingly coveted privilege. In another series of cases in Massachusetts and Connecticut the legislative vacillation described in the preceding chapter came before the courts for interpretation. What various judges said under such circumstances reflected their estimate of the importance of liability and their belief as to whether it ought to be inseparably associated with incorporated bodies.

The modern rule that, by express stipulation made in advance, an unincorporated association may limit the liability of its members to an agreed extent was laid down, *obiter,* in an early Pennsylvania decision.[34] One of the same sort of unincorporated banks that flourished in other states as well as Pennsylvania had issued circulating notes payable on demand "out of their joint

---

[32] The tangle in legal theory brought about by such permissive acts, especially among judges adhering to the belief that all associations must be treated as partnerships, is summarized by Warren, *op. cit.,* 409–412.

[33] *Ibid.,* 543.   [34] *Hess* v. *Werts,* 4 S. & R. 356.

funds, according to their articles of association." The 1808 statute, under review earlier in the same court,[35] had been repealed. All notes issued by such associations were still illegal,[36] but this did not affect the rights of any holders of them against the issuing bodies.[37] The plaintiff sought to recover from the private property of the members. In determining whether the clause printed on the face of the notes could save the members harmless, Gibson, J., said, after laying down the general rules of unlimited liability: "But I see no reason to doubt but they may limit their responsibility, by an explicit stipulation, *made with the party* with whom they contract, and clearly understood by him at the time. But this is a stipulation, so unreasonable on the part of the partnership, and affording such facility to the commission of fraud, that unless it appear unequivocally plain, from the terms of the contract, I will never suppose it to have been in the view of the parties. . . . The defendants attempted, if they designed this clause for individual exoneration, to secure to themselves the substantial benefit of a corporate character, in a business forbidden by law to all but corporate bodies. They have, therefore, no claim to an indulgent construction. . . . ."

Story, writing two decades later, affirmed the rule which Gibson had mentioned but had not been willing to invoke. Since that time express and explicit agreements limiting liability on the part of members of associations have been upheld by the courts, though reluctantly in many jurisdictions.[38] In England, conditional sanction to such agreements is found in an 1833 decision by Lord Brougham, Chancellor.[39]

Much more illuminating judicial comments on the importance of limited liability as the corporate hallmark are to be

[35] *Myers* v. *Irwin,* 2 S. & R. 368.

[36] By a statute of March, 1814, just a month after the formation of the Farmers' and Mechanics' Bank, of which the defendant, Werts, was a member.

[37] By a statute of March, 1817. [38] *Cf.* Warren, *op. cit.,* 367.

[39] *Walburn* v. *Ingilby,* 1 M. & K. 61.

found in cases involving interpretation of particular charters whereby that privilege had been denied. There were two early cases in the Connecticut Supreme Court involving such charters. In the first,[40] Chief Justice Hosmer ruled that, "while the members of the company enjoy all the privileges of a corporation, their creditors possess the rights . . . furnished by law against an ordinary copartnership. . . . They are answerable precisely as if there had been no incorporation"—that is, for debts incurred when they were members. But in another suit brought by the Middletown Bank against a stockholder in a manufacturing company in that town (the Middletown Manufacturing Company)[41] the court again had occasion to pass on a similar charter that failed to specify under what exact condition liability arose. Of the five members then comprising the court, Chief Justice Hosmer and another argued that the liability should have been determined when the debt was originally contracted with the bank, as in the former case. But the majority of the court favored the opposite view, on the ground that the liability was entirely secondary in a corporate body, and that to adopt the view of Hosmer would be to treat the members simply as co-partners. Both groups were obviously hostile to the activity of the legislature in imposing any liability upon the corporate shareholders.[42] Hosmer pointed out sarcastically that there were no cases from

[40] *Southmayd* v. *Russ,* 3 Conn. 52.

[41] *Middletown Bank* v. *Magill,* 5 Conn. 28, at 70.

[42] The doctrine referred to above as prevailing in Massachusetts, that citizens in an incorporated town or city are liable for its defaulted debts, also prevailed in Connecticut. In holding citizens of Bridgeport liable for the city's debts, in *Beardsley* v. *Smith,* 16 Conn. 367 (1837), the court limited the doctrine to what were called public or quasi-public corporations; in *Jewett* v. *The Thames Bank,* 16 Conn. 511, decided in the same year, members of a religious association formed under a general statute permitting their organization were not liable for its debts. The court pointed out that they were essentially a private corporation. The unfriendly attitude of the courts toward the liability clauses which have been discussed may thus have been based in part on the feeling that the legislature had violated a distinction between public and private corporations.

England bearing on the point: "none at all bearing upon the question can be found. No such being as the one under consideration ever existed there. This is a creature of our own manufacture." Justice Chapman of the majority, similarly critical, said: "was it the intention of the legislature that a man should be in jeopardy all his lifetime if he should purchase a single share in the stock of this company?" In his decision he accordingly narrowed down the possible effect of the liability clause.[43]

The attitude of the Connecticut court toward liability changed, however. A few years later, in *Deming* v. *Bull*,[44] the court had to pass upon the liability clause in the charter of the Hartford Brewing Company (chartered in 1821). The clause read: "that for debts which may, at any time, be due from said company, the stockholders shall be responsible in their private capacity, provided said corporation shall become insolvent, or the property

---

[43] The arguments of counsel in this case provide interesting support for the thesis recurrently stressed throughout this study, that at this time no important distinction was felt to exist between associations and corporations. Counsel for the plaintiff bank obviously desired to show that the manufacturing company was essentially an association, wherein there would naturally be liability on the part of the members. He said in part: "It is true, that the charter has so modified this association, that it has not exactly the same characteristics as a general trading company at common law; but it has not deprived the company, collectively or individually, of any one power which is essential to a co-partnership, although it has conferred some privileges—perpetual succession, the right to sue collectively, to hold real estate as personal estate, and so forth. . . . It has been said that each member has the power to bind the group [in a partnership], but this power may be prevented by special stipulation . . . so also a member, by transferring his stock, may here introduce a new partner. The same might be true in any other case, if so stipulated." Further on he declared that, since this group could freely dissolve by surrendering their charter, they were in that additional respect in the status of a partnership. The opposing counsel less convincingly argued that they were "a different sort of body" than a partnership and should therefore be treated less harshly than would be members in an ordinary partnership. But neither this counsel nor the court were willing to call the body a real corporation. It is obvious that the legal mind in this tangle was shocked by legislative tampering with the Blackstonian conception of a chartered corporation.

[44] 10 Conn. 409.

and estate cannot be found, and not otherwise." The defendant, Bull, owned sixty-two of the one thousand shares and had been sued for the total debt claimed by the plaintiff against the corporation. The Supreme Court unanimously decided that the liability was equivalent to the common law obligation of joint debtors or co-partners. Since the defendant was a stockholder both when the debt was incurred and when judgment was defaulted, the issue in *Middletown Bank* v. *Magill* above did not arise. But the court's comments implied that, in that case, they would have agreed with the minority doctrine rather than the majority. The defendant attempted to limit his liability to a *pro rata* basis, that is, six and two-tenths per cent of the total, but the court rejected this plea. The language of the decision indicates clearly that the court regarded the stockholders as partners.

On the other hand, in interpreting a charter of 1832, the same court decided in *Ward* v. *Griswoldville Manufacturing Company*[45] that unpaid balances on stock subscriptions could not be collected after a corporation had entered bankruptcy. The unpaid amount had been figured as part of the total capital stock, but the certification of capital in Wethersfield had specified that the total stock should not be "below $5,000." The amount actually paid in had been well above this certified minimum and the court declared that the stockholders were not subject to any further liability, either for their unpaid subscriptions or otherwise. This construction obviously favored the deliberate understatement of capital in the filed certificates.

The unfriendly attitude of the Massachusetts courts is reflected in the opinion of Chief Justice Shaw in *Gray* v. *Coffin*.[46] "To create any individual liability of members for the debt of a corporation . . . is a wide departure from established rules of law founded in consideration of public policy. . . . It is therefore to be construed strictly. . . ." But judicial coldness was perhaps less important in that state than the protests of the business

---

[45] 16 Conn. 593.   [46] 9 Cushing 192, at 199.

community in bringing about a reversal of the tendency to impose liability on corporate shareholders. As yet we know little of similar dissatisfaction among Connecticut manufacturers and bankers, but it seems certain that the shifting legislative attitude on charter provisions must have been in substantial degree traceable to this influence.

Chief Justice Parker of Massachusetts was less sympathetic with stockholders suffering under the imposition of liability for corporate debts. In two cases[47] he interpreted strictly the law involving members of a corporation upon whom execution had been levied for unsatisfied debts of the corporation. In one of them[48] he dealt harshly with one Marcy, who had transferred his shares to a dummy in an effort to defeat the 1808 statute. His action was "fraudulent and void."[49] The reporter of this case, Benjamin Rand, was so incensed by the Chief Justice's logic that he appended four hostile notes to the text of the decision. In one he said: "This is a most extraordinary decision. The question was, whether Marcy was a member of the corporation at the time of the levy. He had a right, undoubtedly, to divest himself of his membership at any time. It did not depend on the consideration received, or his purpose in doing it. No one had a right to question the intent with which it was done."[50] Rand more nearly expressed the temper of business men after 1820 than did the Chief Justice's opinion.

In New York, the famous group of cases arising out of the Free Banking Act of 1838 provide us not only with a discussion of liability but also with a remarkably complete cross-section of judicial thinking on the problem here reviewed.[51] Clearly,

[47] *Leland* v. *Marsh,* 16 Mass. 389 (1820), and *Marcy* v. *Clark,* 17 Mass. 329 (1821).

[48] *Marcy* v. *Clark.*

[49] To justify this, he said (*ibid.,* at 335): "Those who become inhabitants of towns after liability for debt is incurred, are in the same predicament."

[50] *Ibid.,* at 335, note 4.

[51] The cases referred to were a series in which the associations author-

lawyers arguing these cases, though not all the judges who decided them, had become cognizant of the right of joint stock associations to a "place in the sun" among distinct and legally recognized forms of organization.[52] Opposed to this nascent adjustment to the indisputable economic facts, Supreme Court Justices could still be found referring stubbornly in this group of

ized by the act either claimed a corporate status or were so treated by public taxing officials. In *Thomas* v. *Dakin* (22 Wendell 9), decided in 1839, the Supreme Court through Nelson, C. J., held that the associations were corporations. In this and the following cases the secondary question arose, of no interest here, as to whether the 1838 act had been passed by the necessary two-thirds constitutional majority, presuming the bodies to be corporations. In February–April, 1840, an almost identical case was argued before the Court of Errors—*Warner* v. *Beers,* 23 Wendell 103. The opinions there rendered presumably settled the issue by deciding that these bodies were not corporations. But in July, 1841, in deciding *People* v. *Assessors of Watertown,* 1 Hill 616, Justice Bronson refused to recognize the decision in *Warner* v. *Beers.* Nelson, C. J., acted similarly in 1842 in *Willoughby* v. *Comstock,* 3 Hill 389: "We have repeatedly held that associations organized under the banking law of 1838 are to be regarded as corporate bodies." *People* v. *Assessors of Niagara,* 4 Hill 20 (1843) and *Debow* v. *People,* 1 Denio 9 (1845) followed this lead also. Finally, in *Gifford* v. *Livingston,* 2 Denio 380 (1846), Chancellor Walworth overruled all these and reasserted the validity of the Senate's ruling in *Warner* v. *Beers.*

These cases were discussed in an article by Bray Hammond, "Free Banks and Corporations: The New York Free Banking Act of 1838," 44 *Journal of Political Economy,* 184 (1936). The author's primary concern is with the changing attitudes of New York toward banking privileges, part of the general trend in 1785–1835 described in Chapter VII, *supra.* Data and surrounding circumstances in each case are well summarized, but no attention is paid to the reasoning of Verplanck. The ensuing change in constitutional language permitting general acts is ascribed entirely to the conflict over the 1838 act, a view that can only be superficial in the light of the underlying economic pressure for free association in all fields. The author believes that "free banking is a direct heritage from Jacksonian democracy" (p. 184); the period 1812–1815 had seen as great a demand for it, in Pennsylvania and Virginia especially.

[52] Particularly S. A. Foot, in *Thomas* v. *Dakin, op. cit.,* at 33: "A joint stock company has a collective existence, and name." *Cf.* also W. Kent and D. B. Ogden, for the defendant in *Warner* v. *Beers, op. cit.;* the latter advanced one argument that is of extreme interest here. They declared that "Association of persons is a *common law right inherent in all persons, for every branch of business not prohibited by positive law*" (italics added).

decisions to Blackstone's division[53] of legal persons into two in-
flexible divisions—natural and artificial.[54] The legislature had
passed a law explicitly authorizing the voluntary formation of
banking associations, and had permitted them to assume many
of the powers of corporations as well as to enter the business of
banking, hitherto prohibited (by the 1804 act) to all except corporate bodies specifically chartered for the purpose. In so doing,
it was acting progressively and in response to arguments that
such permission would be democratic and would help to "slay the
dragon of privilege." Failures among the chartered banks and
pressure from the "Locofoco" group in the Democratic party
were immediate reasons for action.[55] Most important, it was
recognizing on the statute books a form of organization originated and desired by business men. But in spite of the logic of the
action the judicial mind hated to admit that there could be any
organization between the partnership and the chartered corporation.[56]

Senator Verplanck[57] delivered the most penetrating and best-

[53] I *Commentaries,* 123.

[54] Justice Cowen, in *Thomas* v. *Dakin, op. cit.,* at 90.

[55] Senator Verplanck, in his opinion discussed below, pointed out that
the 1804 act had been repealed for all those who would comply with certain
explicit conditions.

[56] An exception to this attitude was Chancellor Kent's opinion, written
in 1820, in *Livingston* v. *Lynch,* 4 Johnson's Chancery R. 573. "It appears
to me most clearly, that the association is not, in judgment of law, a partnership. . . . The evident character of the members of the company is that
of tenants-in-common, in which each has a distinct interest . . . and an
entire dominion over his own share of the property; but without any right
to bind . . . the other members." In discussing the status of Robert Ful-
ton and E. P. and R. L. Livingston under their famous 1814 agreement, he
said further: "they use the term 'partnership' in some popular, not in any
legal or technical sense." How exceptional was this view of Kent's is commented on by Justice Cowen in *Townsend* v. *Goewey,* 19 Wendell 424
(1837); he there claims that the line of authority contrary to Kent (*i.e.,*
that there could be nothing between a partnership and a corporation before the law) had been "unbroken by a single judicial opinion." Yet twelve
years later the New York legislature passed a law granting formal legal
status to the joint stock association.

[57] Gulian Verplanck is frequently referred to in Fox's *Decline of Aris-*

known opinion in the principal case of *Warner* v. *Beers*.[58] He supported the proposition, denied by the Supreme Court, that the 1838 associations were *not* corporate bodies, and in so doing supplied us with an extraordinarily complete survey of the tests which were then, as they are today, helpful in distinguishing the corporation from its rivals.

Verplanck first pointed out the fallacy of simply listing the Cokian or Blackstonian characteristics of a corporation, examining a legislative act to discover the presence of these attributes in any organization being authorized, and thereupon declaring such bodies to be corporations. This was essentially what the Supreme Court Justices had done in *Thomas* v. *Dakin*.[59] Exactly the same illogical method was used, thirty years later, by Justice Miller in his famous opinion in the *Liverpool Insurance Company* case.[60] The method was entirely foreign to the spirit of the common law in dealing with other legal concepts; the great common lawyers had always sought the spirit or intent behind a human act, a business contract, or a legislative enactment. In this case, the intent of the legislature had clearly been not to create corporations.[61]

Admitting that the creation of a legal personality is a facile test, Verplanck pointed out that the test is not so easy to apply as Justices Cowen and Bronson had seemed to believe.[62] With great pains, he pointed out what has been stressed here—that the attributes of legal personality had gradually been assumed, one

tocracy (New York, 1919), especially pp. 160–165, 274–281, 368–371. *Cf.* also the comments by W. C. Bryant in *N.Y. Historical Society Proceedings* (1879), 5.

[58] Occupying pp. 131–164 in 23 Wendell's Reports.

[59] 22 Wendell 9.   [60] 10 Wall 566.

[61] For the very practical reason, he might have added, that the law would have violated the Constitution if it had been interpreted to create corporations, lacking as it did a two-thirds majority; as a politically popular measure, it was essential to preserve it from these twin dangers by choosing the lesser.

[62] In *Thomas* v. *Dakin*, 22 Wendell 9, at 91.

by one, by the voluntary associations, a fact which the legislature was at last recognizing. Thus the phrase "legal personality" had become the only sure test. Methodically, the Senator assayed the various attributes that supposedly were characteristic of the "legal personality," so glibly talked of by the Supreme Court Justices. He intended to show that there were no infallible distinctions between corporations and associations. He unconsciously provided the best possible support for a quite different conclusion, contended for herein, namely that *the joint stock association as a business tool approximated in effectiveness the chartered corporation.*

In analyzing supposed distinctive corporate powers, Verplanck attempted to show that they were not at all "essential to a corporation." As regards the power to transfer shares freely, he referred to the Irish Bank Act[63] as evidence of statutory recognition by Parliament of the right of associations to exercise that privilege. He further cited English acts of 1838 giving banking partnerships the right to sue in a single name and permitting a member of one to bring suit against the collective body; acts similar to the first of these had been passed long before 1838,[64] but the Senator was apparently not cognizant of this fact. The use of a common name, he added, was hardly a distinctive characteristic of corporations; Lord Ellenborough had punctured that childish idea.[65] As practical examples of organizations which had functioned substantially as corporations, Verplanck cited the familiar cases of the Merchants Bank, the Merchants Exchange, and the Tontine Associations formed in Albany and New York.[66]

[63] 6 *Geo. IV*, c. 42.

[64] As early as 1800; *cf.* Shannon, *op. cit.,* at 274.

[65] In *Rex* v. *Webb,* 14 East 406, at 415. The Lord Chief Justice, in discussing the meaning of the term "presuming to act as a corporate body," pointed out that use of a common name was prevalent among partnerships, and had been for many decades.

[66] The last-named association had a managing board of directors,

Interestingly enough, neither Verplanck nor the other members of the Senate who delivered opinions devoted much time to the question of liability. Quite obviously, they considered it of minor importance. There were probably two reasons for this attitude. In the first place state legislatures had in numerous instances before and after 1800 altered the common law status of corporation stockholders by imposing upon them full or partial liability beyond their actual contributions. The specific nature of this legislation has been considered in the preceding chapter. Its effect was to reduce the corporations affected to the level of associations, so far as the liability of the investors was concerned. The other reason, stressed by Verplanck, was that in 1822 the legislature had moved to endow associations (or more exactly partnerships) with a measure of limited liability in the Limited Partnership Act. The Senator was also familiar with Hamilton's belief, as reflected in the articles of the Merchants Bank, that a limitation of liability could be legally attained by an association.

The other opinions delivered, by Chancellor Walworth and by Bradish, President of the Senate, were not as profound or sincere as Verplanck's. Votes to sustain Beers[67] were after all to be procured on a political basis; as lawyers, they probably agreed with the Supreme Court Justices rather than with Verplanck. They did not wish the act declared unconstitutional, for it was extremely popular politically, and new associations were constantly being formed. Bradish did, however, add one argument of in-

elected annually, a self-perpetuating board of trustees to hold title to real property and represent the association in legal actions, transferable shares, and no personal liability for debts—all provided for in its articles, drawn up in 1791 by Richard Harrison, well known at the time as a leader of the New York bar. It was projected to aid in the construction of the first Tammany Hall. Its constitution appears in the *New York Daily Advertiser* of September 17, 1791. Davis, 2 *Essays*, 285.

[67] In the lower courts, Beers as president of the North American Trust & Banking Company had sued on a note in his capacity as representative officer; Warner's demurrer, sustained below, had claimed that the suit should be brought as a corporation, and that, being a corporation, the 1838 act authorizing the company was unconstitutional.

terest here. He said:[68] "Shall we, in this land of free and equal government, become great sticklers for these corporate existences and carry the doctrine of their creation, by implication, still farther than has yet been known even under the monarchy of Great Britain, that country of *franchises* and *prerogative?* I trust not." Distrust of the corporation as a monopoly shows itself familiarly, in an opinion praising the freedom implicit in the nature of an association. Only eight years later, the principle of free incorporation for everyone on equal terms was to be recognized by statute in this same legislature, and nine years later joint stock associations were to be recognized as differing from chartered corporations or partnerships—a twin triumph for the principle of free association.

These cases cannot be left without reference to the stiff and dogmatic position of the Justices who, for five succeeding years, so persistently refused to bow to the logic of Verplanck's arguments. Justice Bronson, in one of the later cases,[69] stated that for a corporation to come into being, only "a grant of privileges from the sovereign power of the state" was necessary. He claimed further: "An association under our general laws for a village library, or to tan hides, possesses all the essential attributes of a corporation in its great perfection as the Bank of England, or the East India Company. Nor is it important in what mode this artificial being transacts its business. It is enough that it has a capacity to act in some form as a legal being." After discussing the diverse origins of the Bank of America (which possessed an old special charter of 1812) and the Bank of Commerce (formed under the 1838 law), he said: "I have yet to learn what corporate capacity the one wants that the other has." Finally, he attacked the methods of Senator Verplanck and other members of the Senate in reaching their decision in *Warner* v. *Beers,*[70] which he

---

[68] *Warner* v. *Beers,* at 180.

[69] *People* v. *The Assessors of Watertown,* 1 Hill 616, at 620.

[70] They had methodically examined the various tests or supposed points of difference.

was refusing to follow. "We must not examine the charter of these associations in detached parcels, and say that neither this power nor that makes a corporation. It is quite easy when the parts of a time-piece have been separated, to place the finger upon each wheel in succession and say, this is not a clock."[71] But the epitome of Bronson's mistaken attitude is expressed at a later point: "It may be true . . . that the legislature intended to make a legal being and give it all the essential attributes of a corporate body, and yet that [*sic*] it should not be a corporation. That, the legislature could not do. I do not refer to any *written* constitution. The constitution of things—the order of nature—forbids it."[72]

Thus in the face of a proven business utility for the conduct of enterprises existent more than a half-century previously, and of impending legislative recognition, a judge in a leading state could be found arguing that a private business association was forbidden by the law of nature! Quite to the contrary, nothing could be more expressive of "natural law" in the philosophical sense than the appearance of the full-fledged business company without a charter, meeting a need that had been recurrent for centuries in Anglo-American economic development. Men wanted and exercised what they conceived to be the inherent right to organize independently and freely, irrespective of the current temper of Crown or legislature. The partnership did not suffice, and in building their own private associations they left definitely behind the root ideas of the partnership.

[71] *Ibid.,* at 621.
[72] *Ibid.,* at 623.

IX

CONCLUSION

CHARTERS granted to separate enterprises by state legislatures, and in England by Parliament, have been regarded as the sole milestones marking the development of business enterprise prior to the general acts of 1830 and after. This is historically inaccurate; furthermore, this belief has led to a distorted interpretation of the legal and economic significance of the general acts of incorporation which have since become universal. The undercurrent of economic evolution was in the direction of free incorporation as a *right* of business bodies, not as a privilege to be granted or withheld. The coming of general incorporation privileges was thus not simply a result of dissatisfaction with the delay, whimsicality, and occasional corruptibility of legislatures in granting charters, or of a popular fear of monopoly, but was founded equally upon the business fact that private associations had grown in stature and business usefulness to a place of equality with (and even superiority over) chartered bodies. Legal recognition of these private agreements was necessary to secure a proper status before the courts, which characteristically blinded themselves to these developments of 1760–1830.

Historically, the shift to general incorporation has been regarded as a specific result of the fear that monopoly was being encouraged by the restriction of the privilege to the few. In so far as there was public argument or debate on this point, it seems to be true, for there are many pamphlets and speeches specifically urging the change on this ground alone.[1] The constitutional

---

[1] The antimonopoly spirit of the 1830's and the two succeeding decades has survived historically in the attention always paid to the Locofoco party in New York as well as to Jackson's second campaign and the platforms of the Democratic party in many states. Typical of the better pamphlet arguments it called forth is Theodore Sedgwick's *What Is a Mo-*

conventions of the succeeding two decades brought forth strong expressions of this point of view. *Contra,* it has been the purpose here to show that in the business sense, general incorporation was based upon a much more solid foundation than the purely political principle of opposition to monopoly. Just as social history has abandoned the mode of treating only political activity and has turned to the writings of leaders, to the newspapers, and to other extant records of social attitudes, so in business history there is much more to be examined than legislative acts or constitutional conventions.

The appearance of specific incorporation laws in the industrial states, beginning with that of Massachusetts in 1830, is important in tracing American corporation history, but it has been much over-stressed. Extending far back in Anglo-American business development was the tendency to organize spontaneously, independent of political sanctions, for any community-desired purpose. The gilds and boroughs of England show evidences of this fundamental attitude, while the new English colonies provide striking examples of it on this side of the Atlantic. As business enterprise grew and changed in character in such a way as to necessitate the joint management of capital contributions by many individuals, there reappeared in the eighteenth century this same fundamental point of view. Men did not seek specific license for going beyond the limits of the old-fashioned partnership, nor did they look exclusively to the numerically insignificant chartered corporation as a model of internal organization and management; they moved ahead along original lines, disregarding the fact that legislators were slow to endow them with

nopoly? (New York, 1835; a copy is in the New York Public Library). Sedgwick argued that special charter grants were fundamentally opposed to the conduct of free trade; he advocated general laws and in particular attacked the evils brought on in banking by closing that field to all except the few state-chartered banks. He discussed limited liability, and commented on the changes made in Massachusetts and Connecticut charters depriving corporations of that privilege.

legal privileges and legal status. They waited even less for the courts to catch up with the business facts of the situation.

The result was to be that these associations, first truly exemplified in this country by the land companies, possessed in the middle of the nineteenth century more of the spirit of the modern corporation than did the old chartered bodies that have been superficially accepted as the latter's progenitors. In America, unlike the situation in England, what is now called the joint stock association reappeared occasionally for another century to serve the business community as need demanded. In truth, however, the absorption into the present-day corporation of the association's principles destroyed most of its business value also; it has been little used for a half-century. In England the absorption— or merger—was complete. To understand this, and to possess some knowledge of the association's vigor, earliest demonstrated in the land companies whose internal structure and mode of operation have been examined here, is to gain a clearer understanding of the foundations upon which the present-day corporation rests.

It so happened that the nature of land merchandising required what we know today as corporate management and thus first called forth the organization and methods of the modern corporation. They thus became the proving-ground for the spontaneous sort of business organization which has become universal today. The methods and characteristics of partnership were in large measure abandoned, at least as the law had long described partnership. Business leaders went ahead freely with organization of these bodies and paid little or no attention to the rules of partnership as such. In so doing they were reasserting the centuries-old impulse to organize independently of governmental sanction. They experimented freely, drawing upon New England's experience in land management, upon the methods and organization of English chartered companies, and upon both French and Dutch business methods. They evolved bodies which in substance were counterparts of the modern business corporation. The business community was provided with a practical lesson in the principle of free association. When finally a legislative blessing was given to these bodies, there was not any radical change involved so far as the business community was concerned —rather a simple recognition of a state of affairs which had been familiar to business leaders for two generations.

APPENDIX A

ARTICLES OF ASSOCIATION OF THE
LOUISA COMPANY*

The undernamed Persons entered into an Agreement on the 27th August 1774 for the purchase of a large Territory or Tract of Land on the Western waters, from the Indian Tribes as follows—We Richard Henderson, John Williams, Thos. Hart, Nathaniel Hart, John Luttrell, & William Johnston Agree for ourselves and our heirs forever, to rent or purchase a certain Territory or Tract of Land lying, on the west side of the Mountains on the waters of the Mississippi River, from the Indian Tribes now in possession thereof, and do bind and oblige ourselves and our heirs each to furnish his Quota of Expenses necessary towards procuring a grant and settling the Country: —that we shall be equal sharers of the property, support each other with our lives and fortunes, and when Requisite will from time to time make and sign such rules and regulations as may be expedient for the security, safety and advantage of ourselves and posterity. In Testimony whereof we have hereunto set our hands at Hillsborough this 27th day of August 1774.

Witness

Jonathan Parker Juns
Alex^r Roxburgh
Lancelot Johnston
R. Harrison ⎫ present at
John Bacon ⎭ Col. Hart's signing

Richd Henderson
Jno. Williams
Thos. Hart
Nathl Hart
J. Luttrell
Wm. Johnston

* From the *Draper MSS.,* 1 CC 2, Wisconsin State Historical Society.

APPENDIX B

ARTICLES OF ASSOCIATION OF THE
TRANSYLVANIA COMPANY*

Sometime thereafter three other Copartners being admitted viz. James Hogg, David Hart, & Len'd Henly Bullock they assumed this name, Stile, or Title, of the Transylvania Company, and entered into a new agreement or Covenant as follows—

Be it known to all men by these presents that whereas we Richard Henderson, Thos. Hart, Nathl. Hart, William Johnston, James Hogg, John Luttrell, John Williams, David Hart & Len'd Henly Bullock, as copartners and Tenants in Common, by the Laws of England have purchased of the Cherokee Tribe of Indians, a certain Territory or Tract of Land lying on the Ohio River & waters thereof, including the Rivers Cumberland, Louisa etc. one Eighth part of which Tract or Territory of Land to the aforesaid Richard Henderson, his heirs and assigns, one Eighth part thereof to the aforesaid Thomas Hart his heirs and assigns, one Eighth part of which Tract or Territory of Land to the aforesaid Nathaniel Hart his heirs and assigns, one Eighth part thereof to the aforesaid William Johnston his heirs and assigns, one Eighth part to the aforesaid James Hogg his heirs and assigns, one Eighth part thereof to the aforesaid John Luttrell his heirs and assigns, one Eighth part thereof to the aforesaid John Williams his heirs and assigns, one Sixteenth part to the aforesaid David Hart his heirs and assigns, and one Sixteenth part to the aforesaid Leonard Henly Bullock his heirs and assigns, to be held and enjoyed by each and every of the aforesaid partners their heirs and assigns, Respectively, That is to say each man's particular part to their and each of their respective use & uses, and to no other Intent or purpose whatever, And be it further known, that if any or either of the aforesaid partners, should Give, Grant, Sell or Divise, or otherwise dispose of his particular part of the aforesaid Tract or Territory of Land to any or either of the said partners, or any other Person whatever, Such Donee, Grantee, or Divisee, shall by the rest of the Co-

* From the *Draper MSS.,* 1 CC 3, Wisconsin State Historical Society, *verbatim*, including obvious errors.

partners be considered as Tenants in Common with them and have all the Rights, Privileges and Immunities which the said Donor, Grantor, or Divisor could or might have had or enjoyed, from the benefit or advantage of the first purchase, made by him or them from the Indians above, Except that of sitting and voting as a proprietor & giving rules and Regulations for the Inhabitants etc. and also if any or either of the said partners, their or either of their assigns shall die & depart this life without having first giving, Granted, Sold, divised or otherwise disposed of his or their particular part of the aforesaid Lands lying on the Ohio River & the waters thereof, purchased of the Cherokee Indians as aforesaid, that then & in that case the part of such person or persons so dying without having first disposed of the same as aforesaid, shall remain to devolve upon the right Heir or Heirs of such Decendant or Decendants, & such heir or heirs, or such Decendant or Decendants, shall be considered as a Tenant or Tenants in Common, according to Laws of England, with the other Copartners in the aforesaid Lands & shall be entitled to have & receive all the rights, privileges, benefits, advantages & emoluments which his, her, or their Predecessor or Predecessors could or might have had were he, she or they, then living—

And also whereas the aforesaid Richard Henderson, Thomas Hart, Nathl Hart, William Johnston, James Hogg, John Luttrell, John Williams, David Hart, & Lend Henly Bullock Copartners & Tenants in Common in the aforesaid Lands purchased of the Cherokee Indians & lying on the Ohio River & the waters thereof, have purchased the same with an intent and Design to sell and dispose thereof, to such persons as are willing and chuse to become purchasers & to hold from under them the said Richard Henderson, Thomas Hart, Nathl Hart, William Johnston, James Hogg, John Luttrell, John Williams, David Hart, and Lend Henly Bullock, their heirs and assigns upon such terms & under such rules, Regulations and Restrictions as by them the said Copartners or their heirs of full age or a majority of them shall from time to time be adopted, and as in constructing, making & forming measures Rules and regulations to be observed and adhered to by the said Richard Henderson, Thomas Hart, Nathl Hart, William Johnston, James Hogg, John Luttrell, John Williams, David Hart, and Lend Henly Bullock, their heirs and assigns, purchasers and proprietors of aforesaid Lands, as well as on the part of all such persons or persons as shall chuse to purchase under them and become Inhabitants thereof. Some disputes may possibly arise among the first purchasers, proprietors as aforesaid in regard to letting out and disposing of said Lands or with respect to certain Customs, rules and regulations to be observed by all who are any ways concerned in selling or purchasing the same.—

Therefore we the above mentioned Richard Henderson, Thomas Hart, Nathl Hart, William Johnston, James Hogg, John Luttrell, John Williams, David Hart, and Lend Henly Bullock, first purchasers and proprietors as aforesaid do by these presents oblige ourselves and each of us, our & each of our heirs, Executors, Administrators, and assigns, to faithfully adhere, to fulfill, & keep and punctually abide by all such terms rules, and regulations, which by the said Richard Henderson, Thomas Hart, Nathl Hart, William Johnston, James Hogg, John Luttrell, John Williams, David Hart, and Lend Henly Bullock, or their heirs of the full age of twenty one years or a majority of them or their heirs of full age as aforesaid shall from time to time make and enter into as well as well [*sic*] for selling and disposing of the said Lands, as for Regulating and governing the Inhabitants thereof, always having regard to the Quantity as well as the Quality of the Proprietors who shall have votes in making and entering into such Rules and regulations, for the purpose aforesaid, that is to say, the votes to be given on all such occasions shall be only Eight, to wit, Richard Henderson or his heirs of the full age of twenty-one years one vote, Thos. Hart or his heirs of the full age as aforesaid, one vote, Nathl Hart or his heirs of the full age as aforesaid one vote, William Johnston or his heirs of the full age as aforesaid one vote, James Hogg or his heirs of the full age as aforesaid one vote, John Luttrell or his heirs of the full age as aforesaid one vote John Williams or his heirs of the full age as aforesaid one vote, David Hart & Lend Henly Bullock (making one Partner) or their heirs of the full age as aforesaid one vote, Except in case of an inequality of votes, then the said David Hart & Lend Henly Bullock or their heirs of full age as aforesaid to have two votes, but in no other case whatever, and all rules and regulations made and entered into respecting the premises by a majority of the said partners and proprietors aforesaid their votes being taken as aforesaid and all Lands sold and disposed of by them or a majority of them, or a majority of the survivors of them and the heirs

of the Decendants of full age as aforesaid, their votes being taken as
aforesaid, shall be good, binding upon the Minority of the said partners, them, their heirs and assigns forever. And likewise be it known
that we the said Richard Henderson, Thomas Hart, Nathl Hart, William Johnston, James Hogg, John Luttrell, John Williams, David
Hart, and Lend Henly Bullock, first purchasers as aforesaid, do by
these presents Covenant & agree, for us, our heirs etc. that if any or
either of us should Die without issue, or having heirs under the age
of twenty-one years that then & in that case, the survivor or survivors
or a majority of them (Respect being had to the method of voting as
aforesaid) may sell and dispose of the said lands with as full and
ample power, as the whole of the first purchasers or proprietors could
have done, had they have been then & there present always reserving
to & for the use of their heirs Executors administrators or assigns of
such decendant or Decendants there & each of their valuable part of
all the profits issuing from and arising out of the said lands by selling,
Leasing, letting, or in any manner disposing of the same and the and
the [sic] Rents & Quitrents arising therefrom such heirs, Executors,
Administrators & assigns always being answerable to the surviving
partners, proprietors as aforesaid for their and each of their proportionable part, for all such sums of money as shall be necessarily by
them the said partners laid out in supporting, maintaining and defending the said lands & premises & other incidental Expences.—
And further be it known altho we the aforesaid Richard Henderson,
Thomas Hart, Nathl Hart, William Johnston, James Hogg, John
Luttrell, John Williams, David Hart, and Lend Henly Bullock have
bargained & purchased of the said Cherokee Indians the aforesaid
Lands lying on the Ohio River and the waters thereof, still we have
not obtained a Grant for the same of the Chiefs of the said tribe of
Indians, but only bargained for the same and placing full confidence
in the said Indian Chiefs, that they will make to us the said purchasers
a sufficient Grant pursuant to the said agreement, we the said partners have bound ourselves our heirs etc. to be at equal expences agreeable to the proportionable part of each single individual, as aforesaid,
in purchasing the said Lands.—
Wherefore, we the said purchasers, bind ourselves our heirs etc. each
to the other, to pay & discharge his Quota as aforesaid and when
shuch [sic] Grant obtained that this Covenant or article of agreement

shall have Respect & Reference thereto, & that we & each of us shall & will be bound by the same as firmly as if the said Grant was now made, and if either of us purchasers as aforesaid, should die & depart this life after the signing and sealing these presents and before the Grant from the said Indians to us for the said Lands, shall be signed that the heirs of such person or persons so dying before the Grant from the said Indians for the Lands aforesaid shall be signed, shall be entitled to such part of the said Lands when a Grant shall be obtained for the same as his, her or their, predecessor would have been had he, she or they survived the obtaining the said Grant for the aforesaid Lands now purchased by us & to be Granted us by the said Indians as aforesaid. In consideration of which we the aforesaid Richard Henderson, Thomas Hart, Nathl Hart, William Johnston, James Hogg, John Luttrell, John Williams, David Hart, and Lend Henly Bullock do oblige ourselves and each of us Jointly & seperately, our and each of our heirs Executors Administrators & assigns Jointly and seperately to fulfill, perform, and keep this Covenant and article of Agreement, between and among us made by these presents, Ratifying and Confirming a Majority of us us [sic] or a majority of the Survivors of us, with the heirs of the Decendants of full age as aforesaid, shall Lawfully do in and about the Premises. In witness whereof, we have hereunto interchangeably set our hands & seals, this six day of January A. Dom. 1775—

To the aforesaid Covenant consisting of nine Pages the parties therein mentioned subscribed their names affixed their Seals and acknowledged the same according to the form required by the Laws of England.

In presence of
Lancelot Johnston
John Rice
David Johnson

Richard Henderson
Thos. Hart
Nathl Hart
Wm. Johnston
James Hogg
J. Luttrell
Jno. Williams
David Hart
Len. H. Bullock

APPENDIX C

EXTRACT FROM THE ARTICLES OF AGREEMENT OF THE ILLINOIS-WABASH LAND COMPANY*

The following articles are agreed to and established and it is directed that they be signed by the members of the said Companies entitled to a vote.

Whereas in and by a certain deed poll bearing date the 5th day of July in the year of Our Lord 1773 under the hands and seals of divers chiefs and sachems of the tribes of and effectually representing the different tribes of the Illinois Indians duly executed, they the said chiefs and sachems for the considerations in the same deed mentioned did grant sell alien release enfeoff and confirm unto William Murray and others in the same deed named (and who are since called and known by the name of the Illinois Company) and to their heirs and assigns, two several tracts pieces or parcels of land situate on the East Side of the River Mississippi in the Country of the Illinois and bounded and described as in the same deed . . . and known by the name of the Illinois Purchase or purchases.

And whereas by a certain other deed poll dated the eighteenth day of October 1775 duly executed under the hands and seals of divers chiefs and sachems fully representing the several tribes of the Piankashaw Indians they etc. did grant etc. unto Lewis Viviat and others in the said deed particularly named (and who are since called and known by the name of the Ouabache Company) and to their heirs and assigns two several tracts pieces or parcels of land . . . lying on both sides of the Ouabache River together with the hereditaments and appurtenances to the said several tracts of land respectively belonging (and . . . known by the name of the Ouabache purchases).

And whereas at a meeting of the grantees in the said above in part recited grants by themselves or their attorneys held at Philadelphia on the 13th day of March 1779 and distinguishing themselves by the

* Reprinted from *The Illinois-Wabash Land Company Manuscript,* edited by C. W. Alvord (privately printed, 1915, by Cyrus H. McCormick), but spelling has been modernized and capitalization of most nouns omitted in the interest of clarity.

name of the Illinois and Ouabache Companies it was proposed that the said two companies should be united on the terms in the minutes of the said Company then and therefore made and particularly expressed: and the same two companies were then and there resolved and declared accordingly to be and continue from thenceforth united, and that the lands should be in common between them. And whereas it is most expedient and for the better and easier management of the said companies interest in the said lands that a certain Constitution or Articles of Agreement should be formed and drawn up to be for the future governance and directions of and obligatory upon all and singular the members of the said United Companies their heirs successors and assigns respectively.

—Now therefore it is hereby resolved articled covenanted and consented to by the said United Companies—

First—That the said Companies or grantees shall from hence forth be called and known by the name of the

United Illinois and Ouabache Land Companies

Second—That the said United Companies shall have four stated meetings every year viz. on the last Mondays of the months of March, June, September and December and that till some other place be appointed by the Companies the said quarterly meetings shall be held in the City of Philadelphia provided nevertheless that on business of emergency the President and Council hereinafter named may call a special meeting at such time and place as they shall judge most convenient—and of all such meetings whether stated or special at least thirty days notice shall be given by the Secretary in one or more of the newspapers published in the States of Pennsylvania and Maryland where the said grantees or their attorneys principally reside.

Third—That the members of the said Company at all meetings stated or special may appear and vote either in person or by proxy or attorney duly constituted as is hereinafter mentioned.

Fourth—That as the said lands by an agreement of the Companies dated the 20th of August 1779 are to be divided in eighty-four shares part of which yet remains to be appropriated, the owners of a majority of appropriated shares appearing as aforesaid by themselves or attorneys shall constitute a quorum to do business and that the rules and laws made at any of the said four stated meetings and also the ordinances made at any special meeting for the execution of the said rules and laws shall be obligatory upon and duly observed by all and every of the grantees and members of the said United Companies.

Fifth—That each whole share in the said companies' land shall be entitled to four votes upon any question and that no representation less than that of one quarter of such share shall be entitled to a vote.

Sixth—That the letters of procuration or attorney of such members as shall appoint proxies or attornies to vote for them shall be certified by a Magistrate or Notary Public and registered in the Company's books by the Secretary.

Seventh—That the said United Companies when duly convened at their stated meetings as aforesaid shall have power to elect and appoint such officers with fit titles for such time and with such powers and salaries as to them shall seem expedient . . .

Eighth—That they shall have full power to appoint a President and a Council of four members who shall together be the owners of five full shares which said President and Council shall exercise such powers as the said Company shall from time to time vest in them . . .

Ninth—No future conveyance of a share or part of a share of the lands of the said Company shall be deemed valid unless it be attested before a Magistrate, or Notary Public and until such conveyance be recorded in the Company's book . . .

Tenth—All shares of the said Company's lands shall be deemed and taken as securities to oblige the due and full observance of the resolutions and regulations made or to be made by the said Company and to defray their proportion of such necessary expenses as have or may accrue and that unless payment of such expense be made by the owners thereof within the times to be limited by the said Company the said shares or such parts thereof as may be necessary shall be liable to sale in the manner the Company may hereafter direct.

Eleventh—That as by the agreement of the said Companies entered on their minutes of August 20th and November 8th, 1779 thirty of the said eighty-four shares were to be disposed of for the benefit of the forty-two original grantees of the said Illinois and Ouabache Companies their heirs and assigns, and ten more shares were reserved, also by the said original grantees to be disposed of or given in such manner as they might judge most for their interest (exclusive of two shares which by the said agreement is conceded to the Ouabache Company upon uniting their interest with the Illinois Company). Wherefore it is hereby agreed and finally resolved that such of the said shares as remain yet undisposed of or unappropriated shall (when disposed of or appropriated) be a bar against all claims of any of the members and the monies arising from such sales shall be for the sole and exclusive benefit of the said forty-two original grantees their heirs and assigns according to the bargains of sale or agreement which may be made for that purpose in pursuance of the resolutions of the said Companies entered in their minutes of August 20th and November 8th last past . . .

Twelfth—That all and singular the resolutions and regulations (not hereby altered) entered into and made by the said Companies before or since their union relative to their said lands shall be and are hereby ratified established and confirmed and the same shall have full operation according to their nature intent and meaning until the same may be altered or annulled by the said Company.

APPENDIX D

ARTICLES OF AGREEMENT OF THE
OHIO COMPANY*

Articles of agreement entered into by the Subscribers, for constituting an association, by the name of the Ohio Company.

The design of this association is to raise a fund in Continental Certificates, for the sole purpose, and to be appropriated to the entire use of purchasing Lands in the Western territory (belonging to the United States) for the benefit of the Company and to promote a settlement in that Country.

That the fund shall not exceed One Million of Dollars, in Continental Specie Certificates, exclusive of One years Interest due thereon (except as hereafter provided) and that each share or subscription shall consist of One thousand Dollars as aforesaid, and also ten Dollars in gold or silver, to be paid into the hands of such agents as the Subscribers may elect.

That whole fund of Certificates raised by this Association, except, One years Interest due thereon, mentioned under the first article, shall be apply'd to the purchase of Lands in some one of the proposed States, north westerly of the River Ohio, as soon as those lands are surveyed, and exposed for Sale by the Commissioners of Congress, according to the Ordinance of that Honourable Body, passed 20th May, 1785, or on any other plan that may be adopted by Congress not less advantageous to the Company. The One years interest shall be applied to the purpose of making a settlement in the Country, and assisting those who may be otherwise unable to remove themselves thither: The Gold and Silver is for defraying the expenses of those persons employed as Agents in purchasing the land and other contingent Charges that may arise in the prosecution of the business: The surplus (if any) to be appropriated as the One year's interest on the Certificates.

* Extract from the *Records of the Ohio Company*, vol. 1, pp. 6–11. Each paragraph after the first two constituted an article, but they were numbered only in the margin of the record book.

That there shall be five directors, a treasurer and Secretary, appointed in manner, and for the purposes, hereafter provided.

That the prosecution of the Company's designs may be the least expensive, and at the same time the Subscribers and agents as secure as possible; the proprietors of twenty shares shall constitute one grand division of the company; appoint their agent, and in case of vacancy by death, resignation, or otherways, shall fill it up as immediately as can be.

That the agent shall make himself accountable to each subscriber for certificates and monies received by duplicate receipts (one of which shall be lodged with the secretary) *that* the whole shall be appropriated according to those articles of association, and that the subscriber shall receive his just dividend as to quantity and quality of Lands purchased, as near as possibly may be, by lot drawn in person, or through proxy, and that deeds of conveyance shall be executed to individual subscribers, by the agents, similar to those he shall receive from the directors.

That no person shall be permitted to hold more than five shares in the companies funds, and no subscription for less than a full share will be admitted; but this is not meant to prevent those who cannot, or chuse not to adventure a full share from associating amongst themselves, and by one of their number subscribing the sum required.

That the directors shall have the sole disposal of the company's fund, for the purposes before mentioned: that they shall by themselves or such person or persons as they may think proper to intrust with the business, purchase lands for the benefit of the company, where, and in such way, either at publick or private sale, as they shall judge will be most advantageous to the company; they shall also direct the application of the one year's interest, and Gold and Silver mentioned in the first article, to the purposes mentioned under the 2nd article, in such way and manner as they shall think proper; for those purposes the directors shall draw on the treasurer from time to time, making themselves accountable for the application of the monies agreeably to this association.

That the agents being accountable to the Subscribers for their respective divisions shall appoint the directors, treasurer, and Secretary, and fill up all the vacancies that may happen in these offices respectively.

That the Agents shall pay all the certificates and monies received from subscribers into the hands of the Treasurer, who shall give bonds to the Agents, jointly and severally for the faithful discharge of his trust, and also, his receiving certificates, or monies from any particular agent, shall make himself accountable therefor, according to the condition of his bonds.

That the directors shall give bonds jointly and severally to each of the Agents, condition'd that the Certificates and monies they shall draw out of the Treasury shall be applied for the purposes stipulated in these articles, and that the lands purchased for the company, shall be divided among them within three months of the completion of the purchase, by lot, in such manner as the Agents or a majority of them shall agree, and that on such divisions being made, the directors shall execute deeds to the Agents respectively for the proportions which fall to their divisions, correspondent to those the directors may receive from the commissioners of Congress.

Provided also, that whereas a sufficient number of Subscribers may not appear to raise the fund to the sums proposed in the first Article, and thereby the number of divisions may not be compleated; it therefore agreed, that the agents of divisions of twenty shares each, shall after the 17th day of October next, proceed in the same manner as if the whole fund proposed had been raised.

Provided also, that whereas it will be for the common interest of the company to obtain an Ordinance of Incorporation from the honourable the Congress, or an act of Incorporation from some one of the States in the Union (for which the directors shall make application) it is therefore agreed, that in case such incorporation is obtained, the fund of the company (and consequently the shares and divisions thereof) may be extended to any sum, for which provision shall be made in said ordinance or act of incorporation; anything in this association to the contrary notwithstanding.

That all votes under this association may be given in person or by proxy, and in number justly proportionate to the stock holden, or interest represented.

APPENDIX E

EXTRACT FROM THE ARTICLES OF AGREEMENT OF THE EASTERN LAND ASSOCIATES*

Principles of Agreement between Henry Knox of the State of Massachusetts, but at present residing in the State of Pennsylvania, for himself and associates, and William Duer, of the City and State of New York for himself and associates, relative to the purchase of Lands belonging to the State of Massachusetts situated in the Province of Maine.

First. The Parties agree to be jointly and Equally interested in purchasing of the State of Massachusetts in one or more Tracts Situated in the Province of Maine a Quantity of Land not less than One Million or more than four million of Acres.

Second. In the Purchase above mentioned, it is Understood and Agreed that Henry Knox and William Duer may associate in their respective Proportions such parties, as they may think proper Subject to the General Regulations for Directing the Negotiating and future management of the above purchase as are pointed out in the fourth Article.

Third. The Price to be given for the Lands is not to Exceed twelve cents per Acre, although the Price in Contemplation of the Parties is at present no more than six; the periods of payment to be fixed at not less than five annual Installments; and as many more as can be obtained.

Fourth. It is understood and agreed that the said Henry Knox and William Duer are to have the Exclusive Direction of Matters relative to the Purchase of the Above Lands, or the Sale, Settlement, or Hypothecation of the same. Except Mr. William Constable of the City and State of New York shall at any Time within Six Months express in writing by a Letter directed to Henry Knox and William Duer his Consent to become a Director in the above Concern in which Case he is to be admitted—Provided nevertheless that in the Determi-

* Reprinted by permission from the *Knox MSS.* in Massachusetts Historical Society library, vol. 28; errors in spelling and punctuation corrected.

nation of all Measures relative to this Concern the Consent of Henry Knox shall be necessary.

Fifth. It is agreed that Henry Jackson of Boston in the State of Massachusetts and Royal Flint of the City and State of New York are to be the agents authorized to Negotiate and Conclude the Proposed Purchase, agreeably to such Instructions, as they may receive from the Directors; but in case the said Royal Flint should decline, or be unable to attend the Business, the said William Duer is to be at Liberty with the Approbation of Henry Knox to appoint another Gentleman to act in his Stead.

Sixth. The Agents appointed by the Directors are to be authorized to admit such Individuals as they may think proper into Subordinate Interests of the Purchase in Question, to an Extent not exceeding one Quarter Part of the same, subject however to the following Principles, viz:—

1). That the Subordinate Purchasers shall be subject to the Regulations established by the Directors.

2). That the Persons for whom the Agents act shall have a Right at any time within three years to purchase of them, or the persons acting under them their respective Proportions at a Price not exceeding three hundred per cent on the Rate of Purchase.

3). That if the Subordinate Parties interested in the Association should wish to sell, they shall in the first Instance make an offer in writing of their Respective Proportions, to the Principals for whom the Agents act, who shall have a right to accept of the same at any Time within thirty days from the Date of the Offer.

4). That the Principals shall always have a right to sell off to the Subordinate Purchasers their respective proportions of the Land purchased on Principles to be agreed on, between themselves and the Agents for negotiating the general Sale.

BIBLIOGRAPHY

References to standard collections or publications of historical societies, to periodical articles, to published court cases, and to collections of statutes or colonial laws have been omitted. Specific footnote references to these have been made. Included below, however, are the major sources used in this study both for specific references and for surrounding background.

Unpublished Manuscripts or Documents

American Antiquarian Society
    Craigie MSS.
Connecticut Historical Society
    Wadsworth MSS. Walcott MSS.
Connecticut State Library
    Connecticut MS. Archives. Susquehannah Company Documents
Litchfield (Conn.) Historical Society
    Connecticut Land Company MSS.
Massachusetts Historical Society
    Knox MSS.
New York Historical Society
    Duer MSS. O'Rielly Collection
New York Public Library
    Vanderpoel MSS. Schuyler MSS. Troup MSS.
Ontario County Historical Society (Canandaigua, N.Y.)
    Pulteney MSS.
Pennsylvania Historical Society
    Dreer Collection. Etting Collection, Ohio MSS. Wilson MSS.
Ridgway Library (Philadelphia)
    Gratz MSS.
Western Reserve Historical Society
    John May Papers
Wisconsin Historical Society
    Draper Collection

Secondary Sources: Legal

(Reports of court cases in England or America, state or colonial or town records, to which footnote references are made, are not included here.)

Angell, J. K., and Ames, S. Private Corporations. Boston, 1846 edition.
Baldwin, S. E. Private Corporations; III Essays in Anglo-American History. New York, 1898.

Berle, A. A., Jr. Cases on Corporation Finance. St. Paul, 1930.

Commons, J. R. Legal Foundations of Capitalism. New York, 1924.

Dodd, E. M. Statutory Regulation of Business Corporations in Massachusetts; in Harvard Legal Essays. Cambridge, 1934.

Gierke, Otto F. von. Natural Law and the Theory of Society (Barker Translation). Cambridge, England, 1934.

Gierke, Otto F. von. Political Theories of the Middle Age (Maitland Translation). Cambridge, England, 1900.

Holdsworth, W. S. History of English Law. London, 1903.

Kent, James. Commentaries (12th and 14th editions). Boston, 1873 and 1896.

Maitland, F. W. Collected Papers. Cambridge, England, 1911.

Maitland, F. W. Township and Borough. Cambridge, England, 1898.

Sullivan, James. History of Land Titles. Boston, 1801.

Warren, E. H. Corporate Advantages Without Incorporation. Chicago, 1929.

Wilson, James. Works. Philadelphia, 1804.

Secondary Sources: Historical

(Proceedings and publications of societies, public documents, pamphlets, or articles in journals, to which footnote references are made, are not included here.)

Abernethy, T. P. From Frontier to Plantation in Tennessee. New York, 1932.

Abernethy, T. P. Western Lands and the American Revolution. New York, 1937.

Adams, H. B. Maryland's Influence upon Land Cessions to the United States. Baltimore, 1885.

Adams, J. T. Founding of New England. Boston, 1921.

Adams, J. T. Revolutionary New England. Boston, 1923.

Akagi, R. H. Town Proprietors of the New England Colonies. Philadelphia, 1929.

Alvord, C. W. The Illinois Country, 1673–1818. Springfield, 1920.

Alvord, C. W., editor. The Illinois-Wabash Land Company Manuscript. Privately printed by Cyrus H. McCormick, Chicago, 1915.

Alvord, C. W. Mississippi Valley in British Politics. Cleveland, 1917.

Appleton, N. Examination of the Banking System of Massachusetts. Boston, 1831.

Bacon-Foster, C. Development of the Potomac Route to the West. Washington, 1912.

Bagnall, W. R. Textile Industries of the United States. Boston, 1893.

Barrett, W. (pseud.). The Old Merchants of New York City. New York, 1862.

Bates, A. C., editor. The Two Putnams. Hartford, 1931.

Beveridge, A. J. Life of John Marshall. Vol. 3. Boston, 1919.

Bond, B. W. Quit Rent System in the American Colonies. New Haven, 1919.

Bruce, V. Virginia Iron Manufacture. New York, 1930.

Byars, W. V., editor. Bernard and Michael Gratz, Merchants of Philadelphia, 1754–1798. Jefferson City, 1916.

Byrne, E. H. Genoese Shipping. Cambridge, 1930.

Cook, R. B. Washington's Western Lands. Strasburg, Va., 1930.

Cotterill, R. S. History of Pioneer Kentucky. Cincinnati, 1917.

Craig, N. B., editor. The Olden Time. Cincinnati, 1876.

Cutler, W. P. and J. P. Life and Journals of Manasseh Cutler. Cincinnati, 1888.

Darlington, W. M., editor. Journals of Christopher Gist. Pittsburgh, 1893.

Davis, J. S. Essays in the Earlier History of American Corporations. Cambridge, 1917.

Domett, H. W. History of the Bank of New York. Published by the Bank, New York, 1888.

Driver, C. S. John Sevier. Chapel Hill, 1932.

Egleston, M. Land System of the New England Colonies. Baltimore, 1908.

Evans, Paul D. Holland Land Company. Buffalo, 1924.

Fairchild, H. L. Journals of Jan Lincklaen. New York, 1897.

Fernow, Berthold. Ohio Valley in Colonial Days. Albany, 1890.

Fiske, John. Critical Period of American History. Boston, 1888.

Fox, D. R. Decline of Aristocracy in the Politics of New York. New York, 1919.

Gould, D. Life of Robert Morris. Boston, 1834.

Gross, Charles. Guild Merchant. Oxford, 1890.

Hall, James. Sketches of History, Life and Manners in the West. Philadelphia, 1835.

Halsey, F. W., editor. Tour of Four Great Rivers (Richard Smith's Journal). New York, 1906.

Haskins, C. H. Yazoo Land Companies. New York, 1891. American Historical Association Papers, V.

Henderson, A. Conquest of the Old Southwest. New York, 1920.

Henry, A. Travels and Adventures. New York, 1897.

Henry, W. W. Patrick Henry. New York, 1891.

Hildreth, S. P. Memoirs of the Pioneer Settlers of Ohio. Cincinnati, 1852.

Hinsdale, B. A. The Old Northwest. New York, 1888.

Hough, F. B. History of Lewis County (New York). Albany, 1860.

Hulbert, A. B., editor. Records of the Ohio Company. Marietta, 1917.

Hunt, B. C. Development of the Business Corporation in England, 1800–1867. Cambridge, Mass., 1936.

Lapsley, G. T. County Palatine. New York, 1900.

Lewis, G. R. The Stannaries. Cambridge, Mass., 1908.

Lewis, L. Bank of North America. Philadelphia, 1882.

Lipson, E. Economic History of England. London, 1920–1931.

MacLear, Anne. Early New England Towns. New York, 1908.

McKay, R. C. South Street. New York, 1934.

Mereness, N. D. Maryland as a Proprietary Province. New York, 1901.

Mershon, S. L. English Crown Grants. New York, 1918.

Morison, S. E. Life of Harrison Grey Otis. Boston, 1913.

Oberholtzer, E. P. Life of Robert Morris. New York, 1903.

Osgood, H. L. American Colonies in the Seventeenth Century. New York, 1904.

Osgood, H. L. American Colonies in the Eighteenth Century. New York, 1919.

Pell, John. Ethan Allen. Boston, 1929.

Pennypacker, S. W. Settlement of Germantown. Philadelphia, 1899.

Prussing, E. E. Estate of George Washington, Deceased. Boston, 1927.

Rice, F. P., editor. Records of the Proprietors of Worcester, Mass. Worcester, 1881.

Ritter, A. Philadelphia and Her Merchants. Philadelphia, 1860.

Rochefoucald-Liancourt, Duc de la. Travels through the United States of North America. London, 1799.

Rowland, K. M. Life of George Mason. New York, 1892.

Sakolski, A. M. Great American Land Bubble. New York, 1932.

Savelle, Max. George Morgan. New York, 1932.

Scharf, J. T., and Westcott, T. History of Philadelphia. Philadelphia, 1884.

Schlesinger, A. M. Colonial Merchants and the Revolution. New York, 1918.

Scott, W. R. The Constitution and Finance of English, Irish and Scottish Joint Stock Companies to 1720. Cambridge, England, 1910–1912.

Shepherd, W. R. Proprietary Government in Pennsylvania. New York, 1896.

Smith, W. H., editor. St. Clair Papers. Cincinnati, 1882.

Smith, W. R. South Carolina as a Royal Province. New York, 1903.

Sparks, J., editor. Life and Writings of George Washington. Boston, 1837.

Spaulding, E. W. New York in the Critical Period. New York, 1932.

Staples, W. R. Annals of Providence. Providence, 1843.

Starnes, G. T. Sixty Years of Branch Banking in Virginia. New York, 1931.

Starrett, L. S. General Henry Knox. Rockland, Me., 1902.

Strieder, J. Studien zur Geschichte Kapitalistischer Organisationsformen. Munich, 1925.

Sullivan, J., and Flick, A. C., editors. Papers of Sir William Johnson. Albany, 1921–1933.

Summers, L. P. History of Southwest Virginia. Richmond, 1903.

Sumner, W. G. Financier and Finances of the American Revolution. New York, 1891.

Turner, F. J. Frontier in American History. New York, 1920.

Turner, O. Pioneer History of the Phelps and Gorham Purchase. Rochester, 1851.

Unwin, G. Guilds and Companies of London. London, 1909.

Van Winter, E. Amsterdam en de Opbow van Amerika. 's Gravenhage, 1933.

Volwiler, A. T. George Croghan and the Westward Movement. Cleveland, 1926.

Ware, C. F. Early New England Cotton Manufacture. Boston, 1925.

Webb, Sydney and Beatrice. English Local Government. London, 1922.

Weber, Max. General Economic History (Knight translation). New York, 1927.

Whitaker, A. P. The Mississippi Question. New York, 1934.

Whittlesey, C. Early History of Cleveland. Cleveland, 1867.

Winsor, Justin. The Westward Movement. Boston, 1897.

Woodard, F. M. Town Proprietors in Vermont. New York, 1936.

Wright, C., and Fayle, C. E. History of Lloyd's. London, 1928.

INDEX

Abernethy, T. P., 7 n., 131 n.
Adams, Charles Francis, 19 n.
Adams, James Truslow, 20
Aggregate theory of partnership, 279
Akagi, R. H., 19 n., 27
Albany Congress, 86
Albany Glass Works, 270
Allen, Ethan, 130
Allen, Ira, 130
Alvord, C. W., 7 n., 102, 108, 119 n.,
    121
Anabaptists, xi
*Andover and Medford Turnpike Corpora-
    tion* case, 280
Andros Manufacturing Company, 266
Anglo-Saxon peoples, 12
"Anti-Yazoo" bloc, 159
Apathy, of stockholders, 236
Appleton, Nathan, 253 n.
Assessments on stockholders, 230, 232, 279
Association en participation, 70
Association principle, ix, 9, 12, 65, 273
    strength of, xix, 238, 296
Associations:
    articles of agreement, 224
    assessments, 230, 279
    attitude of organizers, 14, 227
    attraction of capital, 237
    comparative value, 222 ff.
    compared with corporations, 64, 254 ff.
    concentration of management, 276
    creation, 215, 223 ff.
    delegation of authority, 234
    great increase, 65
    in early textile industry, 238
    in 1807 Code, 72
    incentive to officers, 235
    land companies as, 74
    liability, 236, 282 ff.
    organization, 227 ff.
    payments of dividends, 232
    progenitors of corporation, 216, 273
    representative officers of, 278, 282
    right to form, 65, 245
    status before courts, 272 ff.

Associations *(cont.):*
    trustees, 276
    See also Voluntary associations
Asylum Company, 171 ff.

"Bachelors' rights," 29
Bagnall, W. R., 238, 239
Baltimore Manufacturing Society, 257
Bank of New York, 249, 269 n.
Bank of North America, 259
Banking privileges, conflict over, 245 ff.
Banks, Land and Silver, in Massachusetts,
    57 ff.
Barker, Ernest, 11 n.
Barlow, Joel, 139
Bates, A. C., 97 n.
Baynton, Wharton, and Morgan, 111, 113,
    114
Beatty v. *Lessee of Knowler,* 190
Benton, Dr. Caleb, 198 ff.
Berle, A. A., Jr., 22 n.
Beveridge, Albert J., 159
Bingham, William, 177
Blount, William, 131
Board of Treasury, 138
Boon, Gerrit, 206
Boone, Daniel, 90, 91
Borough:
    attack of Stuarts upon, 18
    corporate character of, 17-18
Boyd, Julian P., 82 n., 84, 90 n.
Bridges, Capt. Robert, 43
Bronson, Justice, 293
Brown v. *Gilman,* 159
Brownist theories, xi
Bruce, Virginia, 55 n.
Bubble Act:
    extension to colonies, xxii, 58, 66
    influence, 61 ff., 244
    interpretation of, 66
Bull, Thomas, 196
Burlington Company, 127
Business community:
    attitude toward gilds, 17